FIRST EPISTLE
OF
JOHN

FIRST EPISTLE
OF
JOHN

by
Robert S. Candlish

KREGEL PUBLICATIONS
Grand Rapids, Michigan 49501

First Epistle of John by Robert S. Candlish.
Published in 1979 by Kregel Publications, a
division of Kregel, Inc. All rights reserved.

Library of Congress Cataloging in Publication Data

Candlish, Robert Smith, 1806-1873.
   First Epistle of John.
   (Kregel Bible Study Classics)

   Reprint of the 3rd ed. published in 1877 by
A. and C. Black, Edinburgh, under title: *The
First Epistle of John* expounded in a series of
lectures:
   1. Bible. N.E. 1 John—Commentaries.
I. Title.
BS2805.C3   1979   227'.94'077   79-14801
ISBN 0-8254-2320-1

Printed in the United States of America

CONTENTS

BIOGRAPHICAL PREFACE

During the half-century beginning with the year 1830, Scotland saw a group of theological, ecclesiastical, and pulpit giants, the like of which were probably never before seen in that great country in any one period; and probably it would be recognized by all that nowhere in Scotland today is there even one man who can be equated with six or eight of the giants of that glorious period. First of all there was Thomas Chalmers, born in 1770 and ending his work about the time this period to which we refer begins; then that great theologian, William Cunningham, followed by David Cairns and Robert Rainy; bridging that day with the early part of our century, that brilliant preacher J. Oswald Dykes, the theologian and exegete Marcus Dods, and the peer of all Scotch preachers of the 19th century, the inimitable Alexander Whyte. In this group of great men, two stood out as pre-eminent, Thomas Chalmers and the author of this book, Robert Smith Candlish, and for the quarter-century following the death of Chalmers in 1847, no churchman in Scotland exercised such power as Robert Candlish.

Robert Smith Candlish — generally referred to as Robert S. Candlish — was born in Edinburgh in 1806, the son of a medical teacher who was one of the closest friends of Robert Burns. The boy was never sent to grammar school, but was trained at home so thoroughly that he was able to enter the University of Glasgow at the age of thirteen, and carried off nearly all the principal honors by the time of his graduation at seventeen years of age. At the close of the session of 1819-1820, his name appeared four times in the list of prizes. His biographer tells us:

He gained the second prize for original composition in Latin prose; the second for translation from English into Latan prose; the fifth for exemplary diligence; and the fifth prize in the Greek class for propriety of conduct, diligence, and eminent abilities displayed during the session. At the close of session 1820-1821 his name appears six times in the prize-lists. He gained the first prize for original Latin prose; the sole prize given for translation of Cicero 'De Amicitia'; the fourth prize in the senior Greek class; the fifth prize in the class Logic Juniores, the late Lord Ardmillan being the third on the same list; the first prize for the best specimen of recollection; and the second for excelling in the Blackstone examination. At the close of session 1821-1822 his name appears four times in the prize-lists, and during this session his name stands always first — in the class of Ethics Juniores; for superior excellence in Latin themes; for a vacation theme on the controversy between Nominalists and Realists; and for the best essay on the Roman Dictatorship. At the close of session 1822-1823 his name is found three times in the prize-lists — once for the best essay on Roman Censorship; once for the best essay on the poetical character of Aristophones as it is displayed in the conception and execution of the 'Clouds'; and his name is second in the prize-list of the Natural Philosophy class.

Strange to say, Candlish never graduated from the Divinity Hall, where he attended sessions from 1823 to 1826. Here he was noted for his purity of character. A colleague writing later said, "Not the most coarse and reckless of his comrades would have uttered in his ears a lewd or profane word."

After tutoring for a few years in England's famous boys' school, Eton, and serving as a minister in different parishes for about five years, Candlish in 1833 became the assistant at St. George's Church, Edinburgh, at that time the most influential congregation in the city. At once his great oratorical gifts, his constant insistence upon the close relationship of great theological truths to one's own personal religious experience and Christian life, and his capacity for executive work, led to his being recognized as the coming great churchman of Scotland at a time when a great man was needed — "the ruling spirit in the Free Church" from the time of

Chalmers' death in 1847, and probably for a few years before that.

As early as 1841 the College of New Jersey, now known as Princeton University, conferred upon him the degree of Doctor of Divinity. Many of my readers, I am sure, will be interested in a part of the letter which was addressed from New Jersey to Candlish at the time the degree was conferred:

> Whilst to you personally an entire stranger, I feel myself tolerably well acquainted with your character, and with the decided and noble part you take in the present controversy of *our* mother Church. Our whole Church is awake to the importance of your conflict, nor do I know of a minister, elder, or layman in the length and breadth of this land who does not entirely sympathize with you and the beloved brethren who are so ready to hazard all, that the Lord Jesus Christ may rule as King in His own Church, which He has purchased with His blood. You have the sympathies and the prayers of our whole American Zion, and were it desirable, you would have her contributions also to aid you in building churches, should you be disestablished. With one voice your Moderate Erastian party, led on by Dr. Cook, are condemned as the betrayers of Samson, and as delivering him over to the Philistines. If the unanimous approval of our whole church can cheer you to continue the conflict, let whatever consequences ensue, be assured that you and your brethren have it.
>
> Your many excellent pamphlets, and your many speeches made at different meetings, have been extensively read in this country. Many of your speeches have been reprinted in our religious papers, and many extracts from your pamphlets; so that your name is as familiar to us as if you resided among us, and were a pastor of one of our churches. Your speech at the meeting of 1200 ministers and elders at the West Church was republished here last week. You will not therefore wonder at our desire to honour one who is honouring himself in defending the purity of the Church of our fathers.

We must now look back briefly upon the great struggle in the Church of Scotland which is referred to in this communication. Candlish was rising to power when the issue of the relationship of the Scottish Church to the national government finally came to a head. For generations in Scotland it had been the custom for patrons, generally wealthy landowners, to present to the churches located on or near their properties ministers whom they wished to be installed as resident clergy. This system of patronage received its power from, and was vigorously supported by the civil courts and the national government. Many of the churches were experiencing a growing resentment against this order, insisting that churches be privileged to call, through the Presbytery, ministers of their own choosing and preference. It is not necessary in this preface to enter into the long, complicated debates that arose because of this issue. In these debates Candlish took the leading part, and after some years of fruitless endeavor to reach a compromise in May, 1843, the break was finally made and 420 ministers forsook the State Church of Scotland and established what came to be called the Free Church; 474 more signed the Deed of Demission and were joined by 97 theological students from the College of Edinburgh, and by a majority of the theological students at Aberdeen, in addition to about 200 parishoners in Scotland. Lord Cockburn in his Journal wrote:

> The Lord Provost of Edinburgh walked with them from St. Andrew's Church to Canonmills, where the Lord Provost of Glasgow and the Sheriff of Mid-Lothian joined them. And that extraordinary procession was dignified by about eight old Moderators, two Principals of Universities and four Theological Professors. It has often been said that Presbytery is not a religion for a gentleman; and it is certainly true that hitherto such of our gentlemen as have not been of our Church were nearly sure to be found among the Episcopalians. This is the first time that our gentry are not only not ashamed of Presbytery, but not ashamed of it with the additional vulgarity of unendowed Dissent . . . This is the most revolutionary event in modern history. Protestantism was our first Reformation; Presbytery our second; this erection of Presbytery freed from the State is our third.

The biographer of Dr. Candlish devotes chapter after chapter to this great conflict, and quotes thousands of words from the speeches of our author — great rolling sentences, language flashing with fire, coming up out of the depths of great convictions, moving and molding this vast body of sturdy churchmen, some of the noblest people that have ever lived on the island of Britain. He was the man for that hour, and with every passing day his greatness of mind and largeness of heart, his ability to think clearly through the most complicated problems and to unfold these issues with transparent sentences, were recognized by friend and foe alike. As Dr. Fleming has said in his *History of the Church of Scotland* 1843-1874, "For thirty years he stood at the helm and he never lost his hold. He combined the bold wisdom of a Moses with the fighting skill of a Joshua as he laid down the lines of their settlement in the free land of promise. The Free Church could not easily have worked out her destiny without him. Behind the ecclesiastical leaders one felt the spiritual power of a true minister of Christ, with a heart of tenderness as well as an intellect of razor-like keenness." In 1847 he was appointed to a professorship in New College, but declined. In 1862 he was elected principal of the same College, without a professorship, "the duties being chiefly honorary."

Candlish was made Moderator of the Assembly of the Free Church in 1861. Towards the end of his life, he recognized his increasing weakness, and was fully aware that his great church needed to call a younger man who would be able to carry its vast burdens. Therefore Candlish persuaded the congregation to extend an invitation to one whose sermons were soon to be recognized as the most remarkable that were ever preached in this pulpit, already famous for great sermons, Alexander Whyte, who was now (1870) but thirty-four years of age. Whyte later said of his predecessor:

> What a colleague Dr. Candlish was! How Dr. Candlish thought for me! How he planned for my comfort! How he spared me too much work! How he sent me off on frequent little holidays! And how we dined together and talked together, and how full of a high good humour and even rich fun he could be on occasion!

It is not often that men who take the leading place in great ecclesiastical crises are profound interpreters of the Word of God. Today we seem to have a scarcity of both, and particularly in our own country. We have church divisions, church quarrels, church union, and church machinery, but it has been a long time since we have seen in this country a truly great church leader, a man of massive intellect, oratorical powers, deep convictions and profound insight into contemporary ecclesiastical dangers and needs. As for profound exegetes in this country, they could almost be counted on the fingers of one hand. In Scotland, both were found in Candlish.

In the new revision of the British Museum Catalog (the volume carrying the name Candlish bears the date of 1940) Candlish is assigned five columns, possibly one hundred titles, by him and about him, the latter for the most part consisting of criticisms of some of his writings. Many of these titles were separate addresses delivered either during the great crisis leading to the Disruption, or addresses given at various institutions, frequently to theological students. He began publishing when he was thirty-five years of age in issuing his three-volume work, *Contributions Toward the Exposition of Genesis,* which in ten years required four editions. Some of these pages have never been surpassed for brilliance of exposition. My own opinion is that the greatest sermon, or lecture, or chapter, call it what you will, on that opening statement of the great faith chapter in the Epistle to the Hebrews, "By faith we understand that the worlds have been framed by the word of God," is to be found in the opening pages of this work by Candlish. (This was surprisingly confirmed to me when in looking at the British Museum Catalog I discovered that these particular pages were years ago reprinted in a then notable volume, *British Eloquence of the Nineteenth Century.*) This work was completely revised and reissued in two volumes in 1868. In 1845 he issued his volume on the atonement. Five years later appeared his then famous *Scripture Characters and Miscellanies.* In 1858 Candlish published that remarkable exposition of the fifteenth chapter of I Corinthians, *Life in a Risen Saviour;* in 1860 his now seldom-seen book, *The Two Great Commandments,* a work of over 350 pages, for the most part devoted to a careful exposition of the twelfth chapter of Romans; and in 1865 appeared the book which was in many circles very severely criticized, *The Fatherhood of God.* This work reached its fifth edition in 1870, appearing in two volumes, the second carrying a long reply to the severe criticism, in part justified, of Professor Thomas J. Crawford. It is not my purpose in this place to examine Candlish' conception of the fatherhood of God in relation to mankind — this belongs to the history of Scotch Theology. The following year appeared what is without doubt his greatest work, *The First Epistle of John Expounded in a Series of Lectures,* which must be recognized as the most remarkable volume of expositions of this Epistle that appeared in the whole of the nineteenth century. Since then two great works on John's Epistle have been published, one by Findlay and one by Robert Law, but there are chapters here in Candlish which have never been equalled by writers on the same passages, especially those on the "Passing Away of the World," "The Test of Antichrist," "The World's Murderous Hate," "Christian Faith Overcoming Antichristian Falsehood," "The Love of God," "The Three Witnesses," and that marvelous chapter which when read seems to bring one down into the darkness of the abyss, "The World Lying in the Wicked One."

Alexander Whyte himself has a paragraph on Candlish as an expositor which deserves place in this preface:

> He would set himself to unwind and unweave its texture, filament by filament, and fibre by fibre, with the most minute analysis and the most practised exegetical skill. And then how he would address himself to the reweaving of it all again, and that into a rich web of evangelical doctrine. After which he would, as it were, shape and fashion out of it so many gospel garments wherewith to clothe and adorn his listening and believing people, till you can have no idea what a favoured and what a delighted and what an evangelized congregation Dr. Candlish had in the St. George's of those great days. And then men like Lord Cowan, and Lord Moncreiff, and Lord Ardmillan, and Murray Dunlop, and Sheriff Spiers, and Sheriff Jameson, and Dr. Bell, and David Maclagan and Samuel Raleigh, and John M'Candlish, and scores of such-like Christian gentlemen, would all frankly tell you that they owed their

own souls to Dr. Candlish's pulpit. And I did not wonder to hear them saying that, for I never heard such soaring, such winning, and such heart-consoling preaching as the third Principal of the New College preached to his privileged.

In my own volume of these Lectures I have underlined and marked more passages than in any similar book in my library. It is not necessary to quote in a preface extended passages of the book which follows, but as an example of Candlish' wonderful interpreting powers, I must whet the appetite of my readers by quoting these lines on I John 5:13-15:

> How then does God himself, having life, this eternal life, in himself, stand related to prayer, or to sacrifice and prayer together? Both must be from within himself. They are alike and equally means of his own appointment or ordination. Sacrifice, the atoning sacrifice of his Son for us, is his own way of opening up communication between himself and us. Prayer, our prayer to him in his Son's name, is his own way of carrying on and carrying out the communication. He, having eternal life in himself, moved from within himself, gives to us this eternal life in his Son. And all the fruit or benefit of it he is pleased to give through prayer. For the eternal life which is now, in a sense, common to him, and us, comes out in prayer. We meet in prayer, he and we together. And we meet, be it said with reverence, on the footing of our joint possession, in a measure, of the same eternal life; life in ourselves; he and we thus meet together.
>
> Thus prayer, as it is here introduced, becomes a very solemn, because a very confidential, dealing with God. It is asking. But it is asking upon the ground of a very close union and thorough identity between God and us, as regards the life to which the asking has respect, and of which it is the acting out. In plain terms, it is our asking as one in interest, in sympathy, in character, in end and aim; — one in short, in life or manner of living with him whom we ask; through his giving us eternal life; that life being in His Son; being indeed the very life of his own Son.

The late G.F. Barbour, in his monumental *Life of Alexander Whyte* says: "Dr. Candlish's writings now rest undisturbed on their shelves." This statement, written over a quarter of a century ago is still true, probably truer today than at that time - with one exception, and I am grateful that an evangelical publishing house is making available again this epochal work, as near to an inspired volume as anything can be outside of the Holy Scriptures. The work has become exceedingly scarce; in fact, I have not seen a copy advertised now for thirty years, nor have I known of anyone who has bought a copy in that time. I have loaned mine so frequently that it had to be rebound, and more than one person has said to me, "I have read much of this on my knees," which is not said concerning many books that fall into our hands these days. I commend this volume to all who love the Lord Jesus, who have longed for a deeper experience through the Holy Spirit of God, and to all seeking a richer understanding of the fathomless words of the beloved apostle.

WILBUR M. SMITH

Pasadena, Calif.

PREFACE TO SECOND EDITION

IN issuing this book anew, I have scarcely anything to add
to what I wrote in issuing it before. I have very carefully
revised it, more than once or twice; not so much, however,
it is fair to say, with a view to its being more learned or
critical, as with a view to its bringing out more clearly what
I thought I had ascertained to be the Apostle's general line
of thought.

I have accordingly—still making my table of contents a
sort of index or analysis of the teachings of the Epistle—
made some slight alterations upon it. I do not think it
possible indeed to reduce this warm outflow of the loving
Apostle's heart into regular and exact logical order; and if
I indicate successive parts, it is with the full apprehension
of the thoughts and feelings brought out in them running
into one another. But I fasten on three emphatic words:
Light, Righteousness, Love; "God is light," "God is righteous," "God is love;" and with a preliminary statement of
the general idea of the Apostolic fellowship, and a fourth
or concluding part about its prevalence over the fellowship
of the world and the wicked one in whom the world lies, I

am inclined to hope that I have indicated somewhat better than I did before the general lie of the country.

It is fair also to say that, in revising these lectures, I have not lost sight of my teaching as to the Fatherhood of God, on which, as I have explained in the Preface to my former edition, the study of this Epistle had a material influence. I hope to follow up this new issue of my Exposition of 1 John, with a corresponding re-issue of my Cunningham Lectures.

PREFACE TO FIRST EDITION

Two " Expositions " of this First Epistle of John came into my hands about the end of last year (1865): the one by the Rev. John Stock, late Vicar of Finchingfield, Essex; the other by Dr. Morgan of Belfast; both published in the course of that year, and both, especially the latter, of great practical interest and value. If they had appeared at an earlier date, I might have abstained from issuing this volume. But in my Lectures on the Fatherhood of God I had previously referred to these discourses of mine on this Epistle, as being completed and ready for publication. And I did not see how I could well draw back, especially as I wished my views on that subject to be looked at in the light of the beloved Apostle's argument in his great Epistle.*

I must frankly add, also, that on a perusal of the two works, I have not found any reason for thinking that mine may not still be a contribution of some value to the theological and exegetical study of this inspired treatise.

* At the risk of a charge of egotism, I may mention that this course of lectures was begun in October 1860, and continued, with frequent interruptions, till January 1864 ; that the lectures, as they were delivered, were carefully written out, in a way tolerably fit for the press ; and that in preparing them for the press now, I have found little or nothing to alter beyond verbal corrections and improvements. They were all finished before the delivery of the Cunningham Lectures on the Fatherhood of God in February and March 1864. And I referred to them, as thus finished, when the Cunningham Lectures were published, about a year after.

I speak of the theological and exegetical study of it. And I do so advisedly. For I am deeply convinced, after years of thought about it, that it can be studied aright exegetically only when it is studied theologically.

Of course I do not mean that a cut-and-dry creed, accepted beforehand, is to rule, or overrule, the critical and grammatical interpretation of the ascertained text. But I think no one is competent to deal in detail with this wonderful book who is not familiar with the evangelical system as a whole, and able, therefore, to appreciate the bearings of John's line of thought in connection with it. I do not speak of the higher qualification of spiritual minded-ness. I make this remark simply as a theologian and an expositor.

The writer to whom I am most indebted is Dr. John H. A. Ebrard, Professor of Theology in the University of Erlangen. I must acknowledge my obligation also to Dr. Friedrich Lücke, of the Prussian University of Bonn. But it is Dr. Ebrard who has helped me most.*

I have not met with English commentators or expositors of much value as bringing out the full sense of this epistle.† There are few separate expositions of it; and when it is handled in a general commentary on the whole Bible or New Testament, it is apt to be handled somewhat per-functorily.

An exception to this remark ought perhaps to be made.

---

* I know both of these works through the translations published by Messrs. Clark; that of Lücke in 1837, and that of Ebrard in 1860. The last is especially valuable, and for an English reader, acquainted with theology, very easily intelligible.

† An exposition of a part of it, the first two chapters, by Dr. Nathanael Hardy, an eminent Puritan Divine (died 1670), has been recently repub-lished in Nichol's Series of Commentaries (Edinburgh, 1865). So far as it goes, it will be read with interest by those who can appreciate the sound, evangelical doctrine and thorough learning of that school of theologians.

Among the "Continuators" of "Matthew Poole's Annota-
tions," we find the name of John Howe, to whom the three
epistles of John were allotted. His notes, however, are
brief, and given verse by verse, without much attempt to
trace the connection of the Apostle's successive lines of
thought. In a spiritual and practical point of view, they
are interesting and edifying; but they do not help much
towards the exegetical interpretation of this book.

For myself, and as regards these lectures of mine, I must
disclaim all intention of presenting to the learned anything
like a critical commentary, properly so called. I do not
quote authors, or discuss their different views and opinions.
I attempt no minute analysis of texts, nor any elaborate
verbal and grammatical construing of them. My object is
a wider and broader one. It is to bring out the general
scope and tenor of the Apostle's teaching, as simply and
clearly as I can.

I do not, therefore, discuss any questions about our
Lord's titles, proper to him in his pre-existent state;—such
as "the Word of Life," or "the Life" (i. 1, 2);—titles which
are better studied in the beginning of John's Gospel, and
which have no material influence on his reasoning in this
Epistle; at least none that does not come out sufficiently in
the course of his argument. For the same reason, I abstain
from other critical discussions. And for an additional
reason also I do so in some cases.

Thus, in regard to the doubtful reading (iii. 16), I rather
evade the question; for I hold it to be of no importance
whatever. I am willing that the disputed words—"of
God"—should be omitted. But then the clause must run:
—"Hereby perceive we this love, because he," the Son of
God (ver. 8), "laid down his life for us." I might notice
other points of criticism, but I forbear.

I have only to say further, that I ask special attention

to the table of contents, as indicating the successive lines of thought which I have tried to trace in this epistle. I cannot say that I am quite satisfied with the divisions I have indicated, although I have followed generally some preceding authorities. Still I would like my book to be read in the light of the table of contents, as giving at least a tentative sketch of the general lie of the country.

INTRODUCTION

1

THE DOCTRINE AND FELLOWSHIP OF THE APOSTLES

"That which we have seen and heard declare we unto you, that ye also may have fellowship with us ; and truly our fellowship is with the Father, and with his Son Jesus Christ." 1 John 1:3
"They continued stedfastly in the Apostles' doctrine and fellowship." Acts 2:42

EVIDENTLY the desire and aim of the writer of this Epistle is to place all to whom it comes in the same advantageous position which he himself and his fellow-apostles enjoyed, as regards the knowledge of God in Christ, and the full enjoyment of the holy and divine fellowship which that knowledge implies. That is his great design throughout ; and this is his announcement of it at the very beginning of his treatise.

Some think that he is here pointing to his Gospel, and that, in fact, this Epistle was meant to accompany that previously-published narrative, either as a sort of supplement and appendix, or as an introductory letter, explaining and enforcing the lessons of his great biography of his Master. It may be so, although I incline, after some vacillation, to my early formed opinion as to that biography being the loved disciple's last work. And here, at any rate, I rather understand him as referring, not to that particular book at all, but to his ordinary manner of teaching, and its ordinary scope ; and as including in the reference all his brethren in the apostleship. When he says, " That which we have seen and heard declare we unto you," I cannot doubt that he means to indicate generally the " apostles' doctrine" (Acts ii. 42)—the common doctrine of all of them alike. " That which we have seen and heard "—all of us alike—" declare we "—all of us alike—in order that we may have you, our disciples and scholars, our hearers and readers, to be sharers with us in our knowledge and in our fellowship. We would have all the privileges of both attainments common between you and us.

In regard, indeed, to knowledge, we cannot make you as well off as we ourselves have been ; not at least so far as knowledge comes through the direct information of the senses, and is verified by their testimony. We have " heard and seen, and looked, and handled " (ver. 1). We have had a personal acquaintance with Jesus in the flesh, and have come into personal contact in the flesh with whatever of God was manifested in him, by him, through him. We have gazed into his face; we have hung upon his lips ;—I, John, have leaned on his breast. We cannot make you partakers with us in that way of " knowing Christ after the flesh " (2 Cor. v. 16) ; nor consequently in the sort of fellowship, so satisfying and soothing, " after the flesh," for which it furnished the occasion and the means.

Even if we could, we would not consider that enough for you—enough for the expression of our good will to you —enough to meet and satisfy the necessity of your case.

For we have ourselves experienced a great change since the sensible means and opportunities of knowledge and fellowship have been withdrawn. That former knowledge of Christ, with the fellowship that accompanied and grew out of it, ranks with us among the "old things that have passed away." We have all learned to say with our brother Paul, "Yea, though I have known Christ after the flesh, yet now henceforth know I him no more" (2 Cor. v. 16). It is not of course that we forget, or ever can forget, all the intercourse we have had in the flesh with our loved and loving Master when he was with us on the earth. Never can we cease to cherish in our hearts the holy and blessed memories of these precious historical years. But the Holy Ghost has come "to teach us all things, and bring all things to our remembrance, whatever Christ then said unto us" (John xiv. 26). That former knowledge does not depart; it is not obliterated or annihilated. But it has become new—altogether new, invested with a new spiritual meaning and power; presenting to the spiritual eye a new aspect of light and love.

It is true that what, under this new spiritual illumination, "we have heard, and seen, and looked at, and handled, of the Word of life," is simply what, "after the flesh," we had "heard, and seen, and looked at, and handled" before. It is nothing else, nothing more. But it is all new; radiant in new light, instinct with new life and love. With new ears, new eyes, new hands, we have listened, and gazed, and felt. It is a new knowledge that we have got, and consequently also a new fellowship. And it is into that new knowledge and that new fellowship, not into the old, that we would have you to enter as joint participators with us.

I. As to the knowledge, "That which we have seen and heard declare we unto you;" that which we have seen and heard of the "Word of life;" "the Life;" which "was manifested;" "that Eternal Life which was with the Father, and was manifested unto us" (vers. 1, 2).

These names and descriptions of the Son undoubtedly refer, in the first instance, to his eternal relation to the Father ; of whose nature he is the image, of whose will he is the expression, of whose life he is the partner and the communicater. But this eternal relation—what he is to the Father from everlasting—must be viewed now in connection with what he is as he dwells among us on the earth. It is " the man Christ Jesus " who is the " manifested life." He is so from first to last, during all the days of his flesh ; from his being " made of a woman, made under the law," to his being " made sin and made a curse " for us, and thereafter, " for his obedience unto death, even the death of the cross, highly exalted ; " from the Baptist's introduction of him to John and others of the apostles as " the Lamb of God that taketh away the sin of the world," to the hour when, as John so emphatically testifies, his side was pierced, and " there came out blood and water." Every intervening incident, every miracle, every discourse, every act of grace, every word of wisdom and of love, is a part of this manifestation. In every one of them " the eternal life which was with the Father is manifested to us." He who liveth with the Father evermore, dwelling in his bosom, is manifesting to us in himself—in his manhood, in his feelings, sayings, doings, sufferings, as a man dwelling among us—what that life is,—not liable to time's accidents and passions, but unchanging, eternal, imperturbable,—which he shares with the Everlasting Father, and which now he shares also with us, and we with him.

In the midst of all the conditions of our death this life is thus manifested. For he who is the life takes our death. Not otherwise could " that eternal life which was with the Father be manifested unto us." For we are dead. If it were not so, what need would there be of a new manifestation of life to us ? Originally the divine life was imparted to man, the divine manner of living; for he was made in the image of God. But now that image being lost or broken and marred by sin, death is our portion, our very nature; death, a manner of being the reverse and opposite of God's; having in it no element of changeless repose, but tumultuous tossings of guilt, fear, wrath, and hatred. Such are we to whom the eternal life which was with the Father is to be manifested. We are thus dead; sentenced by a righteous doom, as transgressors, to this death; already and hopelessly involved in its uneasy, restless darkness. How then can life, the life which is with the Father, be manifested to us, if it be not life that overcomes this dark death,—that is itself the death of it,—that completely disposes of it, and puts it finally and for ever out of the way?

So he who is "the eternal life which was with the Father" is "manifested to us" as "destroying this death." He destroys it in the only way in which it can be destroyed righteously, and therefore thoroughly; by taking it upon himself, bearing it for us in our stead, dying the very death which we have most justly deserved and incurred. So he gives clear and certain assurance that this death of ours need not stand in the way of our having the life of God manifested to us,—and that too in even a higher sense and to higher ends than it was or could be manifested to man at first.

For now that life of God is manifested personally, in one who is himself "the life," being "the Son dwelling in the bosom of the Father." He who so wondrously and so effectually takes our death from us is himself the life,— "that eternal life which was with the Father and is manifested to us;"— so manifested that as he takes our death he gives us his life; he being one with us and we one with him. So, in him who is "the life" we enter into life;—

into that eternal life with the Father wherein there can be no more any element of unquiet guilt or stormy passion, but only trust and love and peace evermore.

"The life was thus manifested" while the Word of life, "made flesh, dwelt among us full of grace and truth; and we beheld his glory"—we, his apostles—"the glory as of the only begotten of the Father" (John i. 14). What we beheld of his glory, as on the mount of transfiguration, we could not indeed then understand, any more than we could understand what we heard Moses and Elijah talking with him about, "the decease to be accomplished at Jerusalem;" or what we witnessed of his agony in the garden, in the near prospect of that decease. What our bodily senses then perceived was all dark to our minds, our souls, our hearts; insomuch that when he was taken away we accounted him lost, and ourselves lost with him, and could but cry woefully—"We trusted that it had been he which should have redeemed Israel" (Luke xxiv. 21). But new senses of spiritual insight, hearing, touch, have been imparted to us, or opened up in us. And the whole meaning of that exchange of our doomed accursed death for his blessed divine life,—which all the while he was among us he was working out,—has flashed upon us; placing in a new light, and investing with new grace and glory, all that presence of our Lord and Master with us, which otherwise must have been to us as a tale that is told.

To have declared to you what we saw and heard, as we saw and heard it at the time, would have been of little avail. The most life-like photographic painting, the most word-for-word shorthand reporting, could only have placed you in the position of our brother Philip, to whom, as representing us all, the Lord had occasion so pathetically to put the question, "Have I been so long with you, and yet hast thou not known me, Philip?" He added, however, then, "He that hath seen me hath seen the Father." And now we can say that we have seen him. All that we witnessed of the grace and truth of which he was full, when as the Word made flesh he dwelt among us, we can now say that we have seen. It is all now before us in its true significancy, as the revelation of "the eternal life which was with the Father and was manifested to us."

What that "eternal life" is; how he is that life with the Father—righteous, holy, loving; how he is that life to us, miserably dead in sin; this is what is manifested in him as he was on earth, and in all that he taught, and did, and suffered. And it is as manifesting this that we, his apostles, "declare unto you that which we have seen and heard." Taught by the Spirit, we would have you to know, taught also by the Spirit, what that eternal life is of which the Lord himself testifies in his farewell prayer for his people, when he says: "This is life eternal, that they may know thee, the only true God, and Jesus Christ whom thou hast sent" (John xvii. 3).

II. So much for the communicated knowledge. The communicated fellowship comes next—"that ye may have fellowship with us." The meaning plainly is, that you may share our fellowship, which truly "is with the Father, and with his Son Jesus Christ" (ver. 3). The object and the nature of this fellowship—"the apostles' fellowship" (Acts ii. 42)—fall now to be considered.

1. The object of this fellowship is the Father and the Son. I say the object, for there is but one. No doubt the Father and the Son may be considered separately, as two distinct persons with whom you may have fellowship. And in some views and for some ends it may be quite warrantable, and even necessary, to distinguish the fellowship which you have with the Father from that which you have with his Son Jesus Christ. As Christ is the way, the true and

living way, to the Father, so fellowship with him as such must evidently be preparatory to fellowship with the Father. But it is not thus that Christ is here represented. He is not put before the Father as the way to the Father, fellowship with whom is the means, leading to fellowship with the Father as the end. He is associated with the Father. Together, in their mutual relation to one another and their mutual mind or heart to one another, they constitute the one object of this fellowship.

The Father and his Son Jesus Christ; not each apart, but the two—both of them—together ; with whatever the Spirit of the Father and the Son may be commissioned to show, and your spirits may be enabled to take in, of the counsel of peace that is between them both; that is what is presented to you as the object of your fellowship.

It is a great idea. Who can grasp it ?

A father and a son among men; both of them wise, upright, holy, loving; of one mind and heart; perfectly understanding one another; perfectly open to one another ; perfectly confiding in one another ; together bent upon some one great and good undertaking; engrossed thoroughly in some one grand pursuit, characterised by consummate genius and rare benevolence ;—that might be an impressive, an attractive picture. To be allowed to make acquaintance with them in their own dwelling where they are at home together ; to be admitted into their study where they consult together; to watch the father's face when the son goes out on any errand or for any work agreed upon between them ; to witness the embrace awaiting him on his return ; to go with the son, as, through ignominy, and suffering, and toil, and blood, and loathsome contact with filth and crime, he makes his way to yonder outcast, and see how it is his father's pity for that outcast that is ever uppermost in his thoughts, how it is his father that he would have to get the praise of every kind word spoken and every sore wound healed; to sit beside the father and observe with what thrilling interest his whole soul is thrown into what his son is doing; and when they come to talk it all over together, when their glistening eyes meet, and their bosoms bound to one another, to be there to see;—that were a privilege worth living for, worth dying for. Such as that, only in an infinitely enhanced measure of grace and glory, is the object presented to you for your fellowship.

For the illustration so fails as to be almost indecorous.

The Eternal Father and the Eternal Son; what the Father is to the Son and the Son to the Father from everlasting; the Father's purpose in eternity to glorify the Son as heir of all things; the Son's consent in eternity to be the Lamb slain; the covenant of electing love securing the fulfilment of the Father's decree and the Son's satisfaction in the seeing of his seed;—then, the amazing concert of that creation-week when the Son, as the Eternal Wisdom, was with the Father, being "daily his delight, rejoicing always before him, rejoicing in the habitable parts of his earth, his delights being with the children of men;"—then, the Son's manifold ministrations as the angel of the covenant on the Father's behalf among these children of men from age to age till his coming in the flesh;—and then, still further—more signal sight still—what the Father and his Son Jesus Christ are to one another, how they feel toward one another, what is the amazing unity between them, all through the deep humiliation of the manger, the wilderness, the synagogues and sea of Galilee, the streets and temple of Jerusalem, the garden and the cross;—what, finally, is that sitting of the Son at the Father's right hand which is now, and that coming of the Son in his own glory and the Father's which is to be shortly;—such is the object of "the apostles' fellowship" and yours. It is fellowship "with the Father and his Son Jesus Christ."

2. The nature of the fellowship can be truly known only by experience. In so far as it can be described, in its conditions, its practical working, and its effects, it is brought out in the whole teaching of this epistle, of which it may be said to be the theme. But a few particulars may here be indicated :—

(1.) That it implies intelligence and insight I need scarcely repeat; such intelligence and insight as the Spirit alone can give. No man naturally has it; no man naturally cares to have it. You may tell me, in my natural state, of tangible benefits of some sort coming to me, through some arrangement between the Father and his Son Jesus Christ, of which somehow I get the good. I can understand that, and take some interest in that. The notion of my being let off from suffering the pains of hell, and of indulgence being extended to my faults and failings, in consequence of something that Christ has done and suffered for me, which he pleads on my behalf, and which God is pleased so far to accept as to listen favourably to his pleading,—is a notion intelligible enough, congenial and welcome enough, to my natural mind. But this is very different from my having fellowship in that matter, even as thus put and thus understood, with the Father and with his Son Jesus Christ. Even while reckoning with reckless confidence on impunity coming to me in virtue of some transaction between the Father and the Son, I may be profoundly and most stupidly indifferent as to what that transaction really is, and what the Father and the Son are to one another in it. In such a state of mind there can be no "fellowship with the Father and with his Son Jesus Christ."

(2.) There must be faith : personal, appropriating, and assured faith ; in order that the intelligence, the insight, may be quickened by a vivid sense of real personal interest and concern. There must be faith : not a vague and doubtful reliance on the chance, one might say, of some sort of deliverance turning up at last, through the mediation of the Son with the Father ; but faith identifying me with the Son, and shutting me up into the Son, in that very mediation itself. There can be no fellowship without this faith ; it is the ground and means of the fellowship ; it is, in fact, the fellowship itself in essence ;—in germ, embryo, or seed. For if I grasp Christ, or rather if he grasps me, in a close indissoluble union, I am to the Father, in a manner, what he is ; and the Father is to me what he is to him. What passes between the Father and the Son is now to me as if it passed—nay, as really passing—between the Father and me. It has all a personal bearing upon myself; I am personally involved in it.

Is it then a kind of selfishness after all ?—selfishness refined and spiritualised, the care of my soul rather than my body, my eternal rather than my temporal wellbeing,—but still the care of myself ? Nay, it is the death of self. For, first, even in the urgency of its first almost instinctive and inarticulate cry for safety—" What must I do ? "—it springs from such a sight and sense of sin and ruin as carries in it an apprehension of the holy and awful name of God and the just claims of God being paramount over all. Then, secondly, in its saving efficacy, it is a going out of self to God in Christ ; an acceptance of God in Christ ; an embracing of God in Christ ; having in it as little of what is self-regarding and self-seeking as that little child's nestling in its mother's bosom has. And thirdly, as the preparation for the fellowship, or as being itself the fellowship, it is the casting of myself, with ever-increasing cordiality of acquiescence and consent, into that glorious plan of everlasting love, in which I am nothing and Christ is all in all ;—of which, when I join the company of all the saved, it will be my joy and theirs to ascribe all the praise "unto him that sitteth upon the throne, and unto the Lamb, for ever and ever."

(3.) This fellowship is of a transforming, conforming, assimilating character. In it you become actually partakers with the Father and the Son in nature and in counsel. For fellowship is participation ; it is partnership. The Father and the Son take you into partnership with them. Plainly this cannot be, unless you are made "partakers of the divine nature ;" unless your nature is getting to be moulded into conformity with the nature of the Father and the Son. For this end in part, or chiefly, that " eternal life which was with the Father has been manifested to you " in your human nature, that through his dwelling in you by his Spirit,—and so being "revealed in you,"—that human nature may become in you what it was when he made it his. Not otherwise can there be community or identity of interest between him and you ; not otherwise than by there being community or identity of nature.

(4.) It is a fellowship of sympathy. Being of one mind, in this partnership, with the Father and the Son, you are of one heart too. Seeing all things, all persons, and all events, in the light in which the Father and the Son see them, you are affected by them and towards them, as the Father and the Son are. Judging as they judge, you feel as they feel. You do so with reference to all that you come in contact with ; all that concerns, or may concern, that great business in which you are partners or fellows, fellow-wishers and fellow-workers, with the Father and the Son. What the business is you know. It is that of which the child of twelve years spoke to his mother and Joseph, " Wist ye

not that I must be about my Father's business?" In what
spirit, and after what manner, the Father and the Son are
" about that business," you also know. You know how, on
the Father's behalf, and as having the Father always going
along with him, the Son went about it all his life-long on
earth. The Father and the Son welcome—nay, they solicit
—your fellowship, partnership, co-operation, sympathy, in
that business. The Spirit is manifesting in you that
" eternal life which was with the Father and was manifested
to us," for this very end, that you may enter with us into
that business which is the Father's and the Son's, with full
sympathy and with all your hearts. It is the business of
glorifying the Father. It is the business of feeding the
hungry, healing the sick, comforting the sorrowful, speaking
a word in season to the weary. It is the business of going
about to do good. It is the business of seeking and saving
the lost. It is the business of laying down life for the
brethren."

(5.) The fellowship is one of joy. Intelligence, faith,
conformity of mind, sympathy of heart, all culminate in joy;
joy in God; entering into the joy of the Lord. For there
is joy in heaven. And if you, receiving what the apostles
declare to you of what they have seen and heard,—receiving
that eternal life which was with the Father and was manifested to them,—have fellowship with them in their fellowship with the Father and his Son Jesus Christ; the end of
all their writing to you is fulfilled, " that your joy may be
full " (ver. 4). Fulness of joy it well may be, if you share
the joy of the Father and the Son: truly a joy that is
"unspeakable and full of glory." Into that joy, as the joy
of ineffable complacency between the Father and the Son
from everlasting to everlasting,—in the counsels of a past
eternity, in the present triumphs of grace, in the consummated glory of the eternity that is to come,—you are called

to enter ; you are to have fellowship in it with the Father and the Son.

Is the thought too vast, indistinct, infinite ? Nay then, in that " eternal life which was with the Father being manifested to you,"—in the Son coming forth from the Father,—you have the joy in which you are to have fellowship with him and with the Father brought home to you with more of definiteness.

When the earth was prepared for man, and for the acting out of all heaven's purpose of grace to man, " I was," says the Son, " by him, and I was daily his delight, rejoicing always before him." When he came in the flesh to execute that purpose, once at least in his humiliation it is testified of him, that he " rejoiced in spirit ; "—it was when he said, " I thank thee, O Father, Lord of heaven and earth, that thou hast hid these things from the wise and prudent, and hast revealed them unto babes : even so, Father; for so it seemed good in thy sight " (Luke x. 21). Into that joy of holy acquiescence in the wise and holy sovereignty of the Father you can enter. And you can hear him and obey him, when bringing home one and another of the poor wandering sheep he came to seek, he makes his appeal to you as knowing his mind and entering into his heart ;—" Rejoice with me, for I have found that which was lost." Rejoice with me. Yes ! Rejoice with me, as my Father calls me to rejoice with him ! " It is meet that we should make merry and be glad, for this our brother was dead and is alive again, was lost and is found."

2

THE JOY OF THE LORD, AND ITS FULNESS

"These things write we unto you, that your joy may be full." 1 John 1:4

THE apostle could not write these words without having full in his memory, and in his heart, the Lord's own thrice-repeated intimation of a similar sentiment in his farewell discourses and farewell prayer: "These things have I spoken unto you, that my joy might remain in you, and that your joy might be full" (John xv. 11); "Ask, and ye shall receive, that your joy may be full" (xvi. 24); "These things I speak in the world, that they"—"those whom thou hast given me"—"might have my joy fulfilled in themselves" (xvii. 13).

It is surely very wonderful that the occasion on which Jesus manifests so intense an anxiety about his disciples having enough of joy, and of his own joy, should be the eve of his last agony. Is it really with him a time of joy? Are the bloody sweat and the cry as of one forsaken by his God the signs of joy? Is that the joy, his joy, which he prays they may have fulfilled in themselves? At all events, his joy, whatever it may be, must be of such a nature that it can be compatible with experience as dark as that. For his joy must be, like himself, "the same yesterday, to-day, and for ever." It cannot be fluctuating and intermittent. It cannot be merely one of many emotions, alternating or taking its turn with others, fitfully swaying the mind at intervals, according to the shifting

breezes of the outer atmosphere. His joy must partake of
his own unchangeableness, as the eternal Son of the Father.
It is true that in his human nature and in his earthly
history he is subjected to the impulses and influences of
this chequered human and earthly scene. He meets with
what may move, at one time to tears, at another time to
gladness. Nor is he unsusceptible of such impressions.
But beneath all these his real joy must be deeper far; a
fathomless, infinite ocean, whose calm repose the wildest
agitations of the upper sea cannot reach or ruffle. " My
joy," he says to the Father, my joy in and with thee, I
would have to be theirs, through their fellowship with
thee and me. Such, in substance, is the Lord's own desire,
as expressed to his disciples and to his Father. And such
is his beloved apostle's aim in his teaching—"that your
joy may be full."

The nature of this joy, as primarily Christ's; the
reality and fulness of it, as Christ's joy becoming ours;—
these are the topics suggested by this text.

i. Joy, as it is commonly understood and exemplified
among men, is a tumultuous feeling; a quick and lively
passion or emotion, blazing up for the most part upon
some sudden prosperous surprise, and apt to subside into
cold indifference, if not something worse, when fortune
threatens change or custom breeds familiarity. "As the
crackling of thorns under a pot, so is the laughter of fools"
(Eccles. vii. 6). It is indeed vanity; an outburst or out-
break of exuberant hilarity, subsiding soon into weariness
and vacancy, the dull cold ashes of a brilliant but passing
flame. All the joy of earth partakes, more or less, of that
character; for it is dependent upon outward circumstances,
and has no deep root in the soul itself. Even what must
in a sense be called spiritual joy may be of that sort.
There may be joyous excitement when the glad jubilee-

trumpet fills the air with its ringing echoes, and an enthusiastic multitude are hastening to keep holiday.   There
may be a real elevation of spirit when some affecting scene
of spiritual awakening is witnessed, or some gracious
ordinance is celebrated, or some stirring voice is heard.
Such joy is like the goodness which, as a morning cloud
and as the early dew, goeth away.   There may be the joy
also of complacency in one's own success in a good and
holy work ; such joy as the Baptist's disciples feared that
their tidings would mar in their master's breast, when they
came to tell him, "Rabbi, he that was with thee beyond
Jordan, to whom thou barest witness, behold, the same
baptizeth, and all men come unto him" (John iii. 26).
His answer is very memorable, and very much to the
purpose of our present inquiry :—" He that hath the bride
is the bridegroom ; but the friend of the bridegroom, which
standeth and heareth him, rejoiceth greatly because of the
bridegroom's voice ; this my joy therefore is fulfilled"
(ver. 29).

It is Christ's joy that is fulfilled in him who is so
truly and heartily the bridegroom's friend ; Christ's twofold
joy ; *first*, his joy as the bridegroom possessing the bride ;
" as the bridegroom rejoiceth over the bride, so shall thy
God rejoice over thee" (Isa. lxii. 9) ;—and, *secondly*, his
joy as the Son possessing the Father ; as the Baptist goes
on to testify so affectionately ; " The Father loveth the Son,
and hath given all things into his hand" (ver. 35).

Now, upon the subject of this " joy of the Lord," this joy
of Christ, this double joy of Christ ; his joy as the bridegroom having the bride ; his joy as the Father's beloved
Son and trusted servant, into whose hand he giveth all
things ;—I would beware of " exercising myself in things
too high for me." I would not venture so much as to
imagine the ineffable joy of the Son dwelling from everlast-

ing in the bosom of the Father, and with the Father and the Holy Spirit ordering the eternal counsels of the Godhead;—the whole vast ideal of creative and providential goodness, all holy and all wise:—and especially the covenanted plan of electing love, for "gathering into one all things in Christ, both which are in heaven and which are in earth" (Ephes. i. 10). Neither dare I do more than touch on what, as the eternal wisdom, he himself says about the Father "possessing him in the beginning of his ways, before his works of old;"—"Then I was by him, as one brought up with him: and I was daily his delight, rejoicing always before him; rejoicing in the habitable part of his earth; and my delights were with the sons of men" (Prov. viii. 22-31).

I come at once to his earthly course, his human experience.

And, first, I see him in the temple, when he was twelve years old. I hear his answer to his mother and Joseph, "Wist ye not that I must be about my Father's business?" How intense his consciousness even already, at an age so tender, of the trust committed to him; his Father's business, the business on which his Father's heart is set, for glorifying that name of his which is light and love, and saving a people to bask in that light and love evermore! "I must be about it." There is deep joy in such a consciousness as that (Luke ii. 49).

Then, secondly, I see him as the disciples left him, faint and wayworn at Jacob's well. On their return they find him fresh and bright. Is it an outward cordial, or is it inward joy, of which he speaks as having revived him? "I have meat to eat that ye know not of: my meat is to do the will of him that sent me, and to finish his work" (John iv. 32 34).

And, thirdly, I find it once, and once only, said in express terms that "Jesus rejoiced in spirit" (Luke x. 21). The statement is a very strong one; it implies inward leaping for joy. And the occasion is remarkable. It is connected with the mission of the seventy. In sending them forth, the Lord has been much exercised with thoughts of the failure, to a large extent, of their ministry and of his own, and the aggravated guilt thus entailed on the highly-favoured objects of that ministry. In receiving them back, he sympathises so far with their delight at finding even "the devils subject to them;" but he adds, "Notwithstanding, in this rejoice not, that the spirits are subject to you; but rather rejoice because your names are written in heaven." "In that hour," and in the view of the names of these his little ones being written in heaven, "Jesus rejoiced in spirit, and said, I thank thee, O Father, Lord of heaven and earth, that thou hast hid these things from the wise and prudent, and hast revealed them unto babes: even so, Father; for so it seemed good in thy sight" (ver. 21). There is here the joy of full, filial acquiescence, for himself, in the gracious and holy will of his Father. And there is added to that the crowning joy of so making known the Father to these babes that they too may acquiesce as he does; "All things are delivered to me of my Father: and no man knoweth who the Son is, but the Father; and who the Father is, but the Son, and he to whom the Son will reveal him" (ver. 22).

Thus "the joy of the Lord is his strength;" prevailing over the diffidence of extreme youth, the exhaustion of nature, and "the contradiction of sinners against himself." Nothing—either in his being a mere child, as when Jeremiah complained, "Ah, Lord God, behold I cannot speak, for I am a child" (Jerem. i. 6); or in his being overcome by distress, hunger, and fatigue, as when Elijah sat down in the wilderness and requested for himself that he might die (1 Kings xix. 4);—or in his being forced to utter triple woes against the cities of his own habitation, as when Isaiah, sent on an errand of judgment to his people, was fain to cry, " Lord, how long?" (Isa. vi. 11);—nothing, I say, in any such trials of his flesh and heart, causes either flesh or heart to faint. At least, when flesh and heart faint, his spirit is refreshed with joy. To be about his Father's business ; to be doing the will of him that sent him, and finishing his work ; to say, " Even so, Father, for so it seemed good in thy sight;"—such joy is his always. Throughout the whole of his painful toil and solitary suffering there may be traced an undercurrent of real joy, without which, I am persuaded, that countenance " so marred with grief " could not have worn, as it did, the aspect of one " fairer than the children of men, into whose lips grace was poured."

Nay, even of his last agony is it not said that " for the joy set before him he endured the cross?" (Heb. xii. 2). There was joy set before him, lying full in his view, in his very endurance of the cross. But what! one says—joy in that dark hour! Over the most excruciating torture of body the brave soul may rise triumphant. But when his soul was exceeding sorrowful even unto death ; when his Father was hiding his face from him ; when the wrath of a holy God and the curse of a broken law were upon him ; when literally the pains of hell gat hold of him ; how could there be joy then? Nay, I cannot tell how. But I bid you ask yourselves if, when he cried, " Father, glorify thy name;" if, when he said, " The cup which my Father, giveth me shall I not drink it?" if, when in his bloody sweat these words came forth, " Father, thy will be done,"—there was no joy in his spirit. More than that, I ask if you can conceive of him, in his utmost extremity of peril, endurance, and expiatory woe, ever for a moment losing the consciousness that he was doing his Father's will and finishing his

Father's work? Could that consciousness be ever interrupted? Could it ever cease to be a source of inward joy? There is joy lying before him, beside him, as he hangs on the accursed tree; not the joy of hopeful anticipation merely, in the near prospect of victory, but the stern joy of battle in the midst of the hot and heady fight, as—true to the trust committed to him by his Father and loving to the last his own whom he came to save—he bares his bosom to the sword awaking in its righteousness to smite the willing victim. That joy no man, no devil, taketh from him; the joy with which he meets the Father's just demand of a great propitiation:—"Lo, I come; I delight to do thy will, O God;"—the joy with which he sees already of the travail of his soul when he says to the dying penitent, "To-day shalt thou be with me in paradise."

Not in heaven only, among the angels of God, but on earth also, in one holy bosom at least, there is in that hour joy "over one sinner that repenteth."

II. This joy, "his joy," is to become ours; it is to "remain in us." "Our joy is to be full" by "his joy being fulfilled in us." Let us notice first the reality, and then the fulness, of this fellowship or partnership of joy between Christ and us.

(I.) Christ would have his joy to be really ours. The bridegroom's friend, standing and hearing him, is to rejoice greatly because of the bridegroom's voice. But that is not all. Something more than the Baptist's official joy, as the bridegroom's friend, waiting upon him as his minister, is to be ours. For the Lord says that "to be least in the kingdom of heaven is to be greater than John the Baptist." In all that constitutes the essence of his own joy the Lord associates us in intimate union with himself.

Thus, first, in his standing with the Father, and before the Father, he calls us to share. The position which he occupies in the Father's house and in the Father's heart is ours as well as his. It is that which opens the way to his joy being ours. And what opens the way to that? His making our standing and our position his. There is an exchange of places between him and us. Our state of guilt as criminals and prodigals, with all its misery, he takes to be his, that his state of acceptance as the Father's righteous servant, and exaltation as the Father's acknowledged Son, with all its joy, may be ours. Hence our sharing his joy begins with our sharing his cross. It begins with our mourning for our sin as piercing him. The very mourning itself has in it an element of joy ; a certain feeling of calm and chastened satisfaction that the strife with God is ended, through our being moved by his Spirit to give in to him. And soon clearer, fuller joy comes. Looking still on that pierced one, pierced for us as well as by us, we see how thoroughly, by putting himself in our place, he has so met and discharged all our liabilities, that we, " being redeemed from the curse of the law," may, by his putting us in his own place, " receive the adoption of sons."

Then, secondly, he makes us partakers of the very same inward evidence of acceptance and sonship which he himself had when he was on earth. The Baptist testified, " God giveth not the Spirit by measure unto him." How much the presence of the Holy Ghost, ever consciously realised, contributed to keep alive in the holy human soul of Jesus, amid all his toil and pain, a joyful sense of his being still the Father's chosen servant and beloved Son— who can tell ?

Thirdly, we have the same commission with Christ ; the same trust reposed in us ; the same work assigned to us. Accepted and adopted in him ; sealed as he was sealed by the Spirit ; we are sent as he was sent into the world. This capital ingredient, this great element of his joy, is ours. It was a deep, secret wellspring of joy in his heart; the feeling, never for a moment lost or interrupted, of his being the Father's fellow, the Father's agent, in carrying out that wondrous plan that had been concerted between them, in the council-chamber of the Godhead, from ever-lasting. There could be nothing, in all his experience, so mean but that this thought must ennoble it; nothing so dark but that this thought must enlighten it; nothing so toilsome or so tearful but that this thought must gladden it. And now, he takes us into his counsels, as the Father has him in his. "All that he has heard of the Father he makes known to us." He does not keep us, as mere servants, in the dark, about what he is doing; prescribing to us our tasks, without information or explanation, to be blindly executed by us in ignorance of what it may all mean. We are "his friends;" the men of his secret; with us he has no reserve; from us he keeps back nothing (John xv. 14, 15). He admits us to his fullest confidence. Some matters, indeed, pertaining to "the times and seasons which the Father hath put in his own power," it may not be for us to know. They are such as he himself, in the days of his manhood, did not care to know. But as to all that is essential, we have the same intelligence that he had, and the same insight. He sends us, as the Father sent him.

Have you, let me ask, duly considered what community of mind and heart between Christ and you all this implies? And what community of joy?

Ah! when you wearily pace the beaten round of certain devout observances; or when you painfully deny your-selves this or that gratification on which your inclinations remain as much set as ever; or when, with half-opened hand, you dole out your measured mite, as you call it, in a good cause, or a cause you cannot venture to put away as bad ; or when you labour hard at your cheerless daily toil, or drag your lazy limbs along in some self-prescribed walk of beneficence, as if you were doing the dullest piece-work for the scantiest wages; and when you count such sort of service religion, as if that were the new obedience to which you are called ;—can you wonder that you have no joy in the Lord ? May not God say to you, as he said once to another, who, however grudgingly, must yet do his pleasure,—"Have you considered my servant Jesus ? " Get something of his acquaintance with me, and with my plans and my ways. Get something of his spirit as he rejoiced to feel always the greatness of the trust committed to him. Get it from himself. Get it in himself. "Take his yoke upon you, and learn of him."

For, fourthly, here is the chiefest element of his joy. He is "meek and lowly in heart;" and therefore "his yoke is easy, and his burden is light;" so easy, so light, that he may count it joy to bear them. It is not an easy yoke in itself that is his; nor a light burden. But his meekness and lowliness in heart makes the yoke easy, and the burden light. The yoke that was laid on his neck when he took the form of a servant was hard indeed ; the yoke of subjection to the law, as broken by us and demanding satisfaction from him. The burden that was lying on his shoulders all the time he was doing the work of a servant was heavy indeed; the burden of bringing in an everlasting righteousness, with full expiation of guilt on behalf of us, miserable sinners. But as the seven years of service seemed to Jacob but one day for the love he bore to Rachel, so the meek and lowly heart of Jesus makes the hard yoke easy and the heavy burden light. In his case, as in Jacob's, the charm is love; love, rejoicing in his Father, whose will he is doing; love, rejoicing over us, whom he is purchasing to be his spouse. For, in a word, it is his self-renunciation, so absolute and entire; his self-forgetting, self-sacrificing affection; his so completely losing himself, merging himself, in the Father whom he serves and the people whom he saves; this is that meekness and lowliness of heart which, making his yoke easy to him and his burden light, moves him, "rejoicing in spirit," to cry, "I thank thee, O Father." We must share that meekness of his; that lowliness of heart. We, like him, must be emptied of self.

For no true joy is or can be selfish. I may hug myself, and applaud myself, and pamper myself, and think to laugh all thought of others, and all care about their thoughts of me, away. I do but kick against the pricks. The task of vindicating my self-sufficiency and asserting my self-will, to my own contentment, against all and sundry, I soon find to be no child's play; but a hard yoke indeed, and a heavy burden. Let me get out of my own narrow self into Christ, and the large heart of Christ. Let me, like him, be meek and lowly in heart; accepting the conditions of my earthly lot; discharging the duty of my earthly calling; meeting the trials of my earthly pilgrimage; not as if I were entitled selfishly to take credit for what I do, or take amiss anything I have to suffer; but simply in loving obedience to my heavenly Father, and loving sympathy with him in his truth and holiness and wide and pure benevolence. That was Christ's way; that was Christ's joy. Then may I have freedom, enlargement, joy, as Christ had, in walking with my Father in heaven always; going about in my Father's name doing good; drinking whatever cup my Father giveth me; and on whatever cross he may see fit to nail me, saying still, as I give up the ghost, "Father, into thy hands I commend my spirit."

(II.) The reality of this joy,—Christ's own joy remain-

ing in us,—may now be partly apparent. But who shall
venture to describe its fulness? "That my joy might
remain in you, and that your joy might be full;" so he
speaks to his apostles. "That they might have my joy
fulfilled in themselves;" so he speaks to the Father concerning them. "That your joy may be full;" such is the
beloved apostle's longing on behalf of his disciples, as it
was his master's on behalf of his chosen ones.

Surely, one would say, it is to the future state, the life
to come, the world beyond the grave, that these expressions point. And that is doubtless true. In its utmost
and ultimate perfection, this full joy belongs to heaven. So
it is with Christ's own personal joy. In heaven he fully
rejoices with the Father and the eternal Spirit over his
fulfilled work of glorious righteousness and grace, and the
fulfilled fruits of it, in the fulfilled salvation of all the
multitude of his redeemed.

Was it something of that joy that Paul caught a glimpse
of in that strange ecstasy of his, when he was caught up
into the third heaven,—into paradise,—and heard unspeakable words, which it is not lawful for man to utter? (2 Cor.
xii. 1-4). Was it Moses and Elias that he overheard, as
on a higher mount of transfiguration, talking with Jesus
about the decease now accomplished at Jerusalem? Or
was it Father, Son, and Holy Ghost; the everlasting
Father, communing with his Son Jesus Christ our Lord,
now in his bosom evermore, and the blessed Spirit plying
evermore his ministry between God and men? But "something sealed the lips" of Paul. Let me, therefore, be silent,
and wait. Let me rather see if there is not some sense,—
some humbler and more practicable point of view,—in which
I have to do with that fulness of joy.

In the 45th Psalm the Messiah, rejoicing over his
church as a bridegroom over his bride, is thus saluted:

" Thou lovest righteousness and hatest wickedness; therefore God, thy God, hath anointed thee with the oil of
gladness above thy fellows. All thy garments smell of
myrrh, and aloes, and cassia, out of the ivory palaces,
whereby they have made thee glad." This gladness of the
anointing oil and the sweet-smelling spices is all associated
with his loving righteousness and hating wickedness. The
secret of his full joy lies in his being, as his Father is, the
holy one and the just.

Hence there can be no discrepancy of thought, or taste,
or feeling, between him and the Father who has sent him.
All things about his mission appear to him as they appear
to the Father; they are to him what they are to the
Father. No painful effort is ever needed to bring his
judgment into subjection to the Father's; or his will into
harmony with the Father's. No lurking tendency of his
own nature toward evil; no insidious suggestion of the
tempter; no impatience of subordination; no secret longing
to taste the liberty of self-will ;—can ever interfere with his
walking in the light as God is in the light. And that is
the perfection of blessedness. To one who is at once a
servant and a son that is " fulness of joy."

Is it attainable by us here ? Yes, in measure, and in
growing measure. Let our nature be assimilated to that
of God; our mind to his; our heart to his. Let our souls
learn the lesson of seeing as he sees and feeling as he feels.
Let sin be to us what it is to him; and righteousness and
truth as well. Let there be a clear understanding between
him and us upon all questions; a thorough identity of
interest and inclination in all points; an entire agreement
of opinion and choice in the great strife of good and evil
going on in the world. That was Christ's own joy. And
it was fulness of joy, even when his personal share in that
strife cost him the tears of Gethsemane and the bitter cry

of Calvary. Let it be ours, more and more, through our growth in grace and in holiness. All misery lies in our judgment not being in subjection to God's; our will not being in harmony with his. Misery ends, and fulness of joy comes, when we think and feel and wish as God does. Therefore fulness of joy may be ours; ours more and more; when "beholding as in a glass the glory of the Lord,"—this glory of his being the Father's willing servant and loyal Son,—"we are changed into the same image, from glory to glory, even as by the Spirit of the Lord."

And now, perhaps, we may see more clearly than we have been accustomed to see the propriety of this "joy of the Lord,"—this "joy in the Lord,"—being represented as not merely a privilege, but a duty. " Rejoice in the Lord; and again I say unto you rejoice." For this joy is not anything like that sort of mysterious incomprehensible rapture into which the spirits may be occasionally thrown under some sudden and irresistible impulse from without or from within. It is not mere excitement. It is not what many call enthusiasm, proper to high festivals. It is a calm and sober frame of mind, suited for everyday wear and everyday work. Neither is its nature recondite, abstruse, and mystical; nor does it come and go in flashes, like the winged fire of heaven. It can be explained and accounted for; analysed and described. Its elements and causes can be specified. Its rise and progress can be traced. It is not therefore an attainment with which we can dispense; it is "our strength." Nor is it a grace for which we may idly wait until it drop upon us unawares from above. We have it in us, the germ of it, the essence of it, if we have Christ in us; if we have the Spirit of Christ. "And if any man have not the Spirit of Christ, he is none of his."

Stir up then the gift that is in you. Do you ask how?

Observe the different connections in which your sharing the Lord's joy stands in the farewell discourses and the farewell prayer ;—as first, with your keeping his commandments and abiding in his love, as he kept the Father's commandments, and abode in the Father's love (John xv. 10, 11); secondly, with your asking in his name as you have never asked before (xvi. 24); and, thirdly, with your being kept in the Father's name, in ever-brightening disclosures of the Father's glorious perfections (xvii. 11, 13). And observe, in the fourth place, the beloved apostle's warm appreciation of this joy as realised in the communion of saints : "Having many things to write unto you, I would not write with paper and ink ; but I trust to come unto you and speak face to face, that our joy may be full" (2 John 12).

Surely this joy of the Lord, as it is thus intimately associated ;—first with obedience,—secondly with prayer, —thirdly with the study of the divine character,—and fourthly with the cultivation of Christian communion ;— is no rare rapture, to be snatched at intervals of excited devotion. It is, on the contrary, a calm and chastened frame of mind ; such as may be realised in every common duty, in every humble supplication, in every devout exercise of soul upon the divine word, in every greeting exchanged lovingly with any of the Lord's people.

Well therefore may the apostolic precept run thus— "Rejoice evermore." For this joy is independent of events and circumstances. The labours you are engaged in may be the hardest drudgery; the people to whom you are seeking to be useful may be the most perverse of all men. Your temper, patience, love, faith, hope, may be tried to the very utmost; all may seem dark ; friends may change, and enemies may be round about you. But Christ is the same, and his joy is the same; the joy of doing and suffering his Father's will. "Rejoice ye if ye are counted worthy to suffer for his sake." "Count it all joy when ye fall into divers temptations; knowing this, that the trying of your faith worketh patience," and that if "patience has her perfect work" ye shall be "perfect and entire, lacking nothing." Let nothing mar or damp your joy. What can mar or damp it if it is Christ's joy remaining in you; Christ's joy fulfilled in you; Christ's joy and yours together in his Father and your Father, his God and your God?

"Although the fig-tree shall not blossom, neither shall fruit be in the vines; the labour of the olive shall fail, and the fields shall yield no meat; the flock shall be cut off from the fold, and there shall be no herd in the stalls; yet I will rejoice in the Lord, I will joy in the God of my salvation (Habak. iii. 17, 18).

That was the prophet's joy, because he apprehended it as Christ's joy, seeing his day afar off, and being glad as he saw it. Let it be your joy also, your joy in him, "whom having not seen you love, and in whom, though now you see him not, you rejoice;" with his own joy fulfilled in you; and therefore "with joy unspeakable and full of glory."

PART ONE

DIVINE FELLOWSHIP—PRIMARY CONDITION—LIGHT
1 John 1:5-2:17

3

THE GROUND OR REASON OF THIS FIRST CONDI-
TION ; LIGHT BEING AT ONCE THE NATURE
AND THE DWELLING-PLACE OF GOD

" This then is the message which we have heard of him, and declare unto
you, that God is light, and in him is no darkness at all. If we say
that we have fellowship with him, and walk in darkness, we lie, and
do not the truth. But if we walk in the light, as he is in the light,
we have fellowship one with another, and the blood of Jesus Christ
his Son cleanseth us from all sin." 1 John 1:5-7

HAVING explained the general aim of his book—to make
his readers, as disciples, partakers of the same fellowship
which he and his fellow-apostles had with the Father and
with his Son Jesus Christ, and of the fulness of joy in the
Lord which that implies,—the writer proceeds to open up
the nature and character of this fellowship of joy. He
begins by laying down the first and primary condition of
it, the fundamentally necessary qualification for its possession, that without which it cannot be. It is light; the
fellowship must be a fellowship in light. He enlarges on

that requirement, and sets it out in various points of view. First, he shows how it rests, not on any merely arbitrary or sovereign divine appointment, but on a holy necessity of the divine nature, admitting of no compromise or evasion (i. 5–7). Thereafter, with a tenderness and faithfulness all his own, he brings the man of simple, guileless spirit into the light, through the door of honest confession and righteous forgiveness (i. 8.–ii. 2). And then, leading him on in the line of intelligent and loving obedience, under the unction and illumination of the Holy Ghost, making him one with the Holy Anointed One, and in him one with all the holy brethren (ii. 3–14);—as well as also in the line of a clear and sharp discrimination between the passing darkness and its passing world on the one hand, and the abiding of the light and of its godliness on the other (ii. 15–17);—he lands the man of guileless spirit in that indwelling in the Son and in the Father which ensures first, stedfastness amid all antichristian defections and apostasies; secondly, the receiving of the promise of eternal life, and thirdly, full confidence in the expectation of the Lord's coming (ii. 18–28).

Such I take to be the topic of this first part of the Epistle; and such the successive aspects in which it is presented.

In the verses now before us (i. 5–7), John gives the ground or reason of his primary and fundamental condition,—that the fellowship must be a fellowship in light; and shows how it rests, not on any merely arbitrary or sovereign ordinance of God, but on his very nature and essential perfection. Accordingly, in that view, we have first a solemn message, next a faithful warning, and lastly a gracious assurance. These are the three steps in this high argument; a solemn message in the fifth verse; a faithful warning in the sixth; and a gracious assurance in the seventh.

I. The form of the announcement in the fifth verse is very peculiar : "This, then, is the message which we have heard of him, and declare unto you." It is not a discovery which we make concerning God, an inference or deduction which we draw for ourselves from observation of his works and ways, and which we publish in that character, and with that weight of influence, to our fellow-men. It is an authentic and authoritative communication to us, from himself. And it is to be accepted as such. It is a message which John and his fellow-apostles have heard of him, expressly in order that they may declare it, as a message, to us. It is substantially Jehovah himself telling us, through the apostles, about himself, what in his own person he told the church of old about himself when he said, " I am holy." For the light is holiness; "I am holy;" "God is light."

The message is twofold. First, positively, "God is light;" next, negatively, "In him is no darkness at all."

1. Positively, "God is light." This is a metaphor, a figure of speech. And in that view, it might suggest a world of varied analogies between the nature of God and the nature of the material element of light. Light is diffusive, penetrating, searching; spreading itself over all space, and entering into every hole and corner. It is quickening and enlivening; a minister of healthy vigour and growth to all living creatures, plants and animals alike, including man himself. It is pleasant also ; a source of relief and gladness to those who bask in its bright and joyous rays.

But there are two of its properties that may be singled out as specially relevant to this great comparison.

In the first place, light is clear, transparent, translucent; patent and open, always and everywhere, as far as its free influence extends. The entrance of light, which itself is real, spreads reality all around. Clouds and shadows are unreal; they breed and foster unrealities. Light is the naked truth. Its very invisibility is, in this view, its power. It is not seen because it is so pure.

For, secondly, a certain character of inviolability belongs to it, in respect of which, while it comes in contact with all things, it is itself affected by nothing. It kisses carrion; it embraces foul pollution; it enters into the innermost recesses of the rottenness in which worms uncleanly revel. It is the same clear element of light still; taking no soil; contracting no stain;—its brightness not dimmed, nor its viewless beauty marred. It endureth for ever, clean and clear.

Now, when it is said, "God is light;" when he says it of himself; when he makes it his own personal and special message to us, which his apostles and ministers are to be always receiving of him and declaring to us;—the one heavenly telegram, or express telegraphic despatch, which they are to be reading to us and we are to be reading to our neighbours, that we may have fellowship, all of us together, with the Father and with his Son Jesus Christ;— let not our imaginations wander in a wilderness of fanciful resemblances. Let these two thoughts be fixed in our minds; first, the thought of perfect openness; and secondly, the thought of perfect inviolability. Let these be our thoughts of God, and of his essential character, as being, and declaring himself to be, "light." Thus "God is light."

2. Negatively, "In him is no darkness at all." I connect this part of the statement with that saying of John in his Gospel; "The light shineth in darkness, and the darkness comprehended it not" (i. 5). In the light itself,

in him who is the light,—even when shining in darkness, the darkness that comprehendeth it not,—there is still no darkness at all.

It must be to some very intimate actual contact of the light—of him who is the light—with darkness; some close encounter and conflict between them, that this second clause of the message refers. Otherwise it is but a repetition of the first; serving only to weaken its force.

"The light shineth in darkness." He who is the light comes, in the person of his Son, to seek and to save us, who are in darkness; who, as to our character, and state, and prospects, are darkness itself. For there is not now in us and around us the element of clearness, brightness, openness, in which we were created at first. Sin has entered; and with sin, shame. There can be pure and simple nakedness no longer. The clear, open sunshine of the presence and countenance of him who is light is no longer tolerable. The covering of fig-leaves, and the hiding-place of the trees of the garden, are preferred. Light henceforth is offensive. The unquiet and unclean soul is like that old chaos, " without form and void ; " and " darkness is upon the face of the deep." With that darkness, the darkness of death, he who is light, the light of life, is brought into fellowship.

And the fellowship is no mere form or name; it is real, actual, personal. The darkness is laid hold of by the light. He who is light enters into the darkness; sounding its utmost depths; searching its inmost recesses. Where guilty fear crouches; where foul corruption festers; he penetrates. He even makes the darkness his own. He takes it upon himself. Its power, " the power of darkness," is upon him ; its power to wrap the sin-laden spirit in a horror of thickest night, in the gloom of hell. Yes !

For our sakes, in our stead, in our nature, he who is light is identified with our darkness.

And yet " in him is no darkness at all." In the very heat and crisis of this death-struggle, there is no surrender of the light to the darkness ; no concession, no compromise ; no making of terms ; no allowance of some partial shading of the light on which the darkness presses so terribly. No ! " He is light, and in him is no darkness at all." All still is clear, open, transparent, between the Son and the Father. Even when the Father hides his face, and " his sword awakes against the man that is his fellow," and the Son cries as one forsaken ; even in that dark hour there is no evasion of heaven's light ; no trafficking with the darkness of earth or hell. There is no hiding then ; no shrinking ; no feeling as if truth might become a little less true, and holiness a little less holy, to meet the appalling emergency. The worst is unflinchingly faced. In the interest of light triumphing over darkness, not by any plausible terms of accommodation, but before the open face of eternal righteousness, pure and untainted, the Father gives the cup and the Son drains it to the dregs. In that great transaction, thus consummated, before all intelligences, between the Father and the Son, it is clearly seen and conclusively proved that " God is light, and in him is no darkness at all."

II. Such being the message in the fifth verse, the warning in the sixth verse becomes simply a self-evident inference : " If we say that we have fellowship with him, and walk in darkness, we lie, and do not the truth." For if it is really into the fellowship of him who testifies of himself that he is light that we enter ; and if it is in and through that wondrous way of dealing with our darkness ; the incompatibility between our claiming fellowship with him and our walking in darkness is so gross that it may well warrant the strong language, "we lie, and do not the truth." The thing indeed is in itself impossible. We cannot, if we walk in darkness, have fellowship with him ; "for what fellowship hath light with darkness? or what communion hath Christ with Belial?" The profession of such a thing is a lie. And it is a practical lie. He who makes it is not speaking, but acting, an untruth. His life is a practical falsehood. The apostle's words are very plain and energetic ; but they are not more so than the case requires : "we lie, and do not the truth."

For what is this walking in darkness? What does it imply?

One answer, in the first instance, must be given, plain and simple enough. All unholy walking is walking in darkness. So far there can be no mistake. The works of darkness are the works of the flesh (Ephes. v. 3–11 ; Gal. v. 19–21). But the matter must be pressed a little more closely home.

The characteristics of light, as has been seen, are, on the one hand, clearness, openness, transparency ; and on the other hand, inviolability, its taking no impression from anything it comes in contact with, but retaining and preserving its own pure nature, unmodified, unmingled, unsoiled, unsullied by external influences, everywhere and evermore the same. Now darkness is the opposite of this light, and is characterised by opposite features. Instead of openness, there is concealment and disguise ; instead of inviolability, there is facile impressibility. Any object, every object, flings its shadow across the benighted path ; shapes of all sorts haunt the gloom.

Now, without making too much of the figure, let the one thought of darkness being that which hides, dwell in our minds ; and by the test of that thought let us try ourselves. Are we living, practically, in a moral and spiritual atmosphere, such as may cause distorted or disturbed vision, and so admit of things appearing different from what they really are? Is the room we sit in so shaded that what we care not to look for may escape our observation, and the somewhat coarse or crazy furniture may be skilfully arranged; its blemishes varnished over; its doubtful beauties magnified and made the most of?

Ah! this walking in darkness! Is it not after all just walking deceitfully? Is it not simple insincerity, the want of perfect openness and transparent honesty in our dealings with God and with ourselves as to the real state of our hearts towards God, and the bent and bias of our affections away from God towards selfishness and worldliness! Is it not that we have in us and about us something to conceal or to disguise; something that does not quite satisfy us; something about which we have at least occasional misgivings; something that, when we think seriously, and confess, and pray, we slur over and do not like to dwell upon; something that we try to represent to ourselves as not so bad as it seems—as indeed, in the circumstances, excusable and unavoidable?

Alas, for this " deceitfulness of the heart!" It is indeed, its "desperate wickedness."

It is not that I seek to shroud myself in a thick cloak, under cloud of night, that, unseen by my fellows, I may wield the assassin's knife,—or hatch with an accomplice some plot against the just,—or with some frail companion do the deed of shame. It is not that I lock myself up alone in my secret and solitary chamber, to gloat over the cruel gains of griping avarice, or nurse in imagination some unhallowed passion. That, doubtless, is walking in darkness. But it is not perhaps the most insidious, or seductive, or subtle sort of such walking. It is when I would have the darkness, more or less thick, to hide me, or some part of me, from myself, and, if it were possible, from my God, that my walking in darkness becomes most perilous; when the secret consciousness that all is not right in me with reference to my Father in heaven—or that my brother on earth may have cause of complaint against me—moves me to get something interposed between me and the pure, clear light of a quickened conscience, and the purer, clearer light of omniscient holiness. It matters not what that something may be. It may be the screen of some better quality on which I flatter myself I am unassailable. Or it may be some good deeds and devout observances which I am almost unawares setting up for a shelter. Or it may be some well-adjusted scheme of self-excuse and self-justification. It is something that casts a shadow. And walking in the darkness of that shadow, however I may say, and even think, that I have fellowship with God, I "lie and do not the truth." I do not act truly, there is guile in my spirit.

It is not merely that my walking thus in darkness is so irreconcilable with my having fellowship with him who "is light and in whom is no darkness at all," that to claim such fellowship is to lie. That is implied in this statement; but it is not all that is implied in it. The walking in darkness is itself the lie ; the acted, not spoken, untruth. It is aggravated, no doubt, by my saying that I have fellowship with him. But my saying so is a mere aggravation ; it is not that which constitutes or makes the lie; if it were, the lie charged would be a spoken, and not an acted untruth. It would consist in my false profession. The charge would be a charge of conscious hypocrisy ; saying that I have fellowship with him while my deliberate walking in darkness proves even to myself the contrary. That charge is not here; at least not necessarily. It is the hypocrisy of practice rather than of profession that is denounced.

I say that I have fellowship with him, not meaning to

profess an untruth. But I walk in darkness; and in so walking I necessarily lie. Apart from anything I may say, my walking in darkness is in itself practical lying. "I do not the truth." I am not acting truly. I am not willing to have all that I do, and all that I am, brought fairly out and placed fully in the broad clear light of truth. I would wish it to be excused, or explained, or somehow obscured or coloured; huddled up or hurried over. I am not for having it exposed in the glaring sunshine. There is something in or about it that to some extent needs and courts the shade. "I lie and do not the truth." And therefore I cannot have fellowship with him who is True, him who is Holy, him who is Light. For it is only "if we walk in the light, as he is in the light," that we can have fellowship one with another; the blood of Jesus Christ, his Son, cleansing us from all sin.

III. From the solemn message in the fifth verse, and the faithful warning in the sixth, the gracious assurance in the seventh fitly follows : "We have fellowship one with another;" God with us and we with God. For it is not our mutual fellowship as believers among ourselves that is meant; the introduction of that idea is irrelevant, and breaks the sense. It is our joint-fellowship with God, and his with us, that alone is to the purpose here.

The expression indeed is peculiar ; it may seem to savour of familiarity ; putting the two parties almost, as it were, on a level; "We have fellowship one with another;" we with God and God with us.

The explanation may be found in the conditional clause— "if we walk in the light, as he is in the light." For that clause associates God and us very intimately together. Observe a certain change of phraseology. It is not "as he is light," but " as he is in the light." It is a significant change. It brings out this great thought, that the same clear and lucid atmosphere surrounds us both. We walk in the light in which God is. It is the light of his own pure truth, his own holy nature. The light in which he is, in which he dwells, is his own light; the light which he is himself. In that light he sits enthroned. In that light he sees and knows, he surveys and judges, all things. And now the supposition is, that we walk,—as he is,—in that light. To us, the light in which we walk is identically the same as the light in which he is. The same lustrous glory of holiness shines on our walk and on his throne. The very same pure medium of vision is common to us both. "We see light in his light." Of old, it was written, respecting the scene at Sinai, "The people stood afar off, and Moses drew near unto the thick darkness where God was" (Exod. xx. 21). But now it is all light! For it is indeed a marvellous community of light that is here indicated as subsisting between God and us; between the Holy One and his redeemed and regenerate people!

To have the same medium of vision with God himself; the same translucent, transparent atmosphere of holiness and truth and love surrounding us; penetrating our inner man and purging our mind's eye, our soul's eye, our heart's eye, that it may see as God's eye sees; illuminating all space to us,—before, behind, above, below,—with the very illumination with which it is illuminated to him; causing all objects, actions, and events, all men and things, all thoughts, words, and deeds,—our own as well as those of others,—to appear to us exactly what they appear to him; thus to "walk in the light, as he is in the light"—who may stand that? Ah me! How shall I ever venture to walk out into that light in which God is? How can I face its terrible disclosures? I can see how this "walking in the light as he is in the light," does indeed open the way to fellowship of the closest sort between him and me.

Literally we see all things in the same light. We therefore cannot but understand one another ; and agree with one another ; and sympathise with one another ; and co-operate with one another ; " we have fellowship one with another." But is it possible that, with respect to all things whatsoever, I can bear to have the same light, the same medium of open vision, that God has ? Sin, for instance ; my sin ; every sin of mine ; every secret sin ; so exceeding sinful ! Oh ! with such sin, and so much, about me, upon me, in me,—how dare I go forth into that very light, so pure and piercing, in which God is ? And yet where else now am I to look for him and find him in peace ?

I thank thee, O my God, O my Father, for that most precious word in season : "The blood of Jesus Christ his Son cleanseth us from all sin." Yes ! it is "a word in season to the weary." For I am weary ; weary of the darkness in which I have been trying to hide or paint deformity, and get up some specious semblance of decency and beauty ; weary of all impostures and all lies ; the poor and paltry lies especially of my self-deluding, or scarcely even self-deluding, self-righteousness ; weary of all attempts to take advantage of the darkness for making evil seem a little less evil, and some show of good look a little more like reality. I would fain step forth from the darkness into light ; into thy light, O God !

Thou mayest, do I hear thee say ?—For, be thy guilt ever so deep and thy heart ever so black, the blood of Jesus Christ my Son cleanseth from all sin. He has answered for all thy guilt. He has purchased for thee a new heart. The fountain filled with his atoning blood is ever freely open and full to overflowing. Wash in that fountain and be clean. Enter into the victory of light over darkness which that blood secures. Let all compromise take end ; compromise is a work of darkness. I invite thee to have fellowship with me; fellowship real, and not merely nominal, with me and with my Son Jesus Christ;— fellowship with us in our plan and purpose of saving mercy,—in all its grace and all its glory;—a fellowship in it with us, of insight, confidence, partnership, sympathy, joy. If it is to be real fellowship, it must be a fellowship of light. I cannot modify, I cannot alter, that condition of the fellowship, any more than I can cease to be what I am— "light." But I do what is far better. I make provision for the removal of every obstacle which your guilt and corruption might interpose in the way of your walking in the light as I am in the light. I give you the assurance that the blood of Jesus Christ my Son cleanseth from all sin.

4

THE PRIMARY CONDITION OF THE DIVINE FELLOW-SHIP FULFILLED IN THE BELIEVING CONFESSION OF A GUILELESS SPIRIT. (Psalm 32)

"If we say that we have no sin, we deceive ourselves, and the truth is not in us. If we confess our sins, he is faithful and just to forgive us our sins, and to cleanse us from all unrighteousness. If we say that we have not sinned, we make him a liar, and his word is not in us." 1 John 1:8-10

THE gracious assurance that "the blood of Jesus Christ, the Son of God, cleanseth us from all sin," suggests the supposition of our "saying that we have no sin." For if we, "walking in the light as God is in the light," could say that truly, we might dispense with the relief which the assurance is fitted to give. But, alas! we can say it only under the influence of self-deception, and such self-deception as implies the absence of that "truth in the inward parts" which God "desires" (Psalm li. 6). Better far to "confess our sins," believing that God "forgiveth our sins," and that he does so in such a way of "faithfulness and justice" as insures our being "cleansed from all unrighteousness" with regard to them,—all unfair and partial dealing with conscience or with God about them. In this full faith let us "confess our sins." For if, after all, even in our confession, there is reserve and guile, trying to make out that in this or that instance "we have not sinned," or not sinned so much as might appear, we are guilty still of an unbelieving distrust of God; "we make him a liar, and his word is not in us."

Such is the line of the Apostle's argument, in three successive steps or stages.

I. "If we say that we have no sin, we deceive ourselves, and the truth is not in us" (ver. 8). It is not deliberate hypocrisy that we are here warned against ; but a far more subtle form of falsehood, and one apt more easily to beset us, as believers, even when most seriously and earnestly bent on "walking in the light as God is in the light."

And yet our venturing to say that we have no sin might seem to be a height of presumption scarcely reconcilable with any measure of sincerity. Any such claim put forward by a child of God the world laughs to scorn. For the world itself makes no such profession. The children of the world are wonderfully ready to chime in with the general acknowledgment implied in the prayer : "Have mercy upon us miserable sinners." Others may set up for saints. We are contented to be, and to be accounted, sinners. We do not deny that we have faults, plenty of faults, some of them perhaps rather serious at times ; although none of them such as we may not hope that a merciful God and Father will overlook and pardon. They too deceive themselves, these children of the world. But their self-deception is not of the same sort as that which John denounces. This last is not, like the former, a vague reliance on indulgence and impunity. It may be the error of a soul working its way, through intense mortification of lust and crucifixion of self, to an ideal of perfection all but divine.

In its subtlest form, it is a kind of mysticism more akin to the visionary cast of ancient and oriental musing than to the more practical turn of thought and feeling that commonly prevails among us. Look at yonder attenuated and etherealised recluse, who has been grasping in successive philosophic systems, or schools of varied theosophic discipline, the means of extricating himself out of the dark bondage of carnal and worldly pollution, and soaring aloft into the light of pure spiritual freedom and repose. After many trials of other schemes, Christianity is embraced by him; not, however, as a discovery of the way in which God proposes to deal with him, but rather as an instrument by which he may deal with himself; a medicine to be self-administered; a remedy to be self-applied. By the laboured imitation of Christ, or by a kind of forced absorption into Christ, considered simply as the perfect model or ideal, his soul, emancipated from its bodily shackles and its earthly entanglements, is to reach a height of serene illumination which no bodily or earthly stain can dim. From such aspirations, the next step, and it is a short and ready one, is into the monstrous fanaticism which would make spiritual illumination compatible with carnal indulgence and worldly lust, and represent it as quite a possible thing for a man wallowing in outward debauchery to be still inwardly pure and sinless; his inward and sinless purity being so enshrined in a certain divine sublimity and transcendentalism of devotion that outward defilement cannot touch it. Church history, beginning even with the apostle's own day, furnishes more than one instance of men thus deplorably "deceiving themselves, saying they have no sin."

Such instances may not be applicable now. But they indicate the direction in which the danger lies. It lies in the line of our sanctification; our purpose and endeavour to "walk in the light, as God is in the light."

When first we come forth out of our darkness into the broad light in which God dwells; when there is no more any guile in our spirits, no more any keeping of silence; when the light of the knowledge of the glory of God in the face of Jesus Christ so shines in us and around us, as to make all clouds and shadows break and fly away, and leave only the bright pellucid atmosphere of God's own nature, which is light, as the medium of vision through which, in and with God, we see ourselves and all things ; ah ! with such discoveries of indwelling sin as then burst upon our quickened and enlightened consciences, how thankful are we for the assurance that " the blood of Jesus Christ his Son cleanseth from all sin." There is nothing then like " saying that we have no sin." On the contrary, we are where Paul was in that deep experience of his, when the law, now loved and delighted in as " holy and just and good," so came home to him by the power of the Spirit as to bring out in terrible conflict its own spirituality and his inherent carnality ;— extorting from him the groan—" O wretched man that I am, who shall deliver me from the body of this death ? " Like him, we " thank God, through Jesus Christ our Lord," for the encouragement we have to believe, and to believe just as we are,—with the mind serving the law of God, but with the flesh still, in spite of the mind, serving the law of sin,—that " there is now no condemnation to them that are in Christ Jesus." Believing this, and apprehending all the relief that there is in believing it, we " walk now not after the flesh but after the Spirit" (Rom. vii. viii.). With enlargement of heart we " walk in the light as God is in the light," and so " we have fellowship one with another,"— he with us and we with him,—the blood of Jesus Christ his Son cleansing us from all sin. Our appropriation of that atoning blood, in all its cleansing efficacy, gives us courage to continue still walking in the light, instead of shrinking back, as otherwise we must be tempted to do, into the old darkness in which we used to shroud ourselves. Such walking with God, in such a fellowship of light, is as safe as it is joyous.

But the risk lies here. It is a sort of walking with God,

which, if we persevere in it faithfully, may become irksome, and be felt to be humiliating. For the old uneasy nature in us, with the rankling suspicions of our old relationship to God, is apt to come in again to mar the childlike simplicity of our faith. For a time the new insight we have got, under that light in which we walk, into the spiritual law of God and into our own carnal selves, keeps us shut up into Christ ; and into that continual sprinkling of his blood upon us, without which we cannot have a moment's peace, or a moment's sense of being cleansed from sin. But gradually we come to be more at ease. We cannot be altogether insensible to the growing satisfaction of our new standing with God and our new feelings towards him. Before the fervour of our first fresh love, inward struggles are hushed. The evil that but yesterday seemed to be so unconquerable ceases to make itself so acutely felt. The crisis is past ; the war, as a war to the knife, is ended ; grace prevails ; iniquity, as ashamed, hides its face.

Ah ! then begins the secret lurking inclination to cherish within myself some thought equivalent to "saying that I have no sin." It may not so express itself. It may not be self-acknowledged, or even self-conscious. It comes insidiously as a thief to steal away my integrity before I am aware of it. Remaining corruption in me ceases gradually to give trouble or distress. A certain lethargic proneness to acquiesce in things as they are creeps over me. I am not conscious of anything very far amiss in my spiritual experience or in my practical behaviour. I begin to "say that I have no sin."

But "I deceive myself, and the truth is not in me." I am fast sinking into my old natural habit of evasion and equivocation, of self-excuse and self-justification. "Guile" is taking the place of "truth," the truth of God, "in my spirit," "in my inward parts." I cease to be as sensitively alive as I once was to whatever in me or about me cannot stand the light. I am thus incurring a serious hazard ; the hazard of being again found walking in darkness, and so disqualifying myself for fellowship with him who is light. And I am apt to lose a very precious privilege : the privilege of continual and constant confession, in order to continual and constant forgiveness. For—

II. "If we confess our sins, he is faithful and just to forgive us our sins, and to cleanse us from all unrighteousness" (ver. 9). This, I say, is a privilege. It will appear to be so if we consider the sort of confession meant, as well as the sort of forgiveness connected with it.

As to the confession, it is the confession of men "walking in the light, as God is in the light ;" having the same medium of vision that God has ; it is the continual confession of men continually so walking, and so seeing. Such confession is very different from the sort of confession in which the natural conscience seeks at intervals a lightening of its guilty burden, and a lessening of its guilty fears. That is the mere emptying of the foul stomach, that it may be filled anew with the vile stuff for which its diseased appetite and corrupt taste continue as keen as ever. This, again, is the laying bare always of the whole inner man to the kind and wise physician who can always thoroughly heal it all.

For the forgiveness, on the faith of which and with a view to which we are thus always to be confessing our sins, will always be found to be a very complete treatment of our case. What is the treatment ?

The sins we confess are so forgiven, that we are cleansed from all unrighteousness with regard to them. This means much more than that we are let off from the punishment which they deserve, and have to answer for them no longer. That is all the absolution for which the church-penitent, at whatever confessional, naturally cares. But that is not what is here held out to us. Our sins are so forgiven as to ensure that in the very forgiveness of them we are cleansed from all unrighteousness,—all unfair, deceitful, and dishonest dealing about them; all such unrighteous dealing about them, either with our own conscience or with our God. The forgiveness is so free, so frank, so full, so unreserved, that it purges our bosom of all reserve, all *reticence,* all guile; in a word, " of all unrighteousness." And it is so because it is dispensed in faithfulness and righteousness; " he is faithful and just in forgiving our sins." He to whom, as always thus dealing with us, we always thus submit ourselves, is true and righteous in all his ways, and specially in his way of meeting the confidence we place in him when we confess our sins.

We open our heart to him; we are always opening it. We spread out our case before him; concealing nothing; palliating nothing. We tell him of all that is sad and distressing in our conflict with indwelling corruption, as well as of all our failures and shortcomings in our strivings after conformity to his law. We speak to him of sloth and selfishness, of worldliness and carnality, damping our zeal, quenching our love, making us miserably indifferent to the good work going on around us, and shamefully tolerant of abounding evil. On the subject of such experiences as these we are coming always to confer with our God, in the light in which he is, and in which it is our aim to walk. We find him always "faithful and just;"—not indulgent merely, kind and complaisant, bidding us take good heart and not be so much cast down;—but "faithful and just." God is true; true to himself, and true to us; so true to himself and to us that all untruth in us becomes impossible.

Ah, brother! you may well trust him with all the secrets of your soul, for well does he requite your trust. He is "faithful;" keeping covenant and mercy; never saying to the seed of Jacob, Seek ye my face in vain. He is "just." He will not, in seeming pity, do you a real injustice. He will not heal your hurt slightly. He will not prophesy smooth things. "He will set your iniquities before him, your secret sins in the light of his countenance." He will keep you in his hand, and under his hand, until all partial dealing—"all unrighteousness" as to any of your sins,—is cleansed out of you. With the charm of true love he will work truth and uprightness in you; so that, as to your whole walk, inner and outer alike, all shall be clear light—light, clear as crystal—between him and you.

That is the sort of intercourse which it is my Father's good pleasure that I should keep up with him continually. It is very different from a mere endless alternation on my part of sin and confession; of confession and sin. It is not on his part a mere capricious oscillation between passion and pity,—between violent wrath and facile fondness;—like what is felt or fancied when I, a slave, offend and ask pardon, and offend again, reckoning on the placability of a weak master, who, however he may be moved to sudden rage, is sure to relent when he sees me prostrate at his feet. In such dealing with me there is neither faithfulness nor justice. Nor is it such dealing with me that will work faithfulness and justice in me. If that is the footing on which I am living with my God and Father, it may be consistent with my saying, in a sense, that "I have no sin;" no sin that need disturb my quiet or distress my conscience. But "I deceive myself, and the truth is not in me." I cast myself off from all that is real and genuine, all that is clear and open, in the fellowship of light that there must ever be between a trusting child and a loving father; especially when that loving father has made such full provision, in so marvellous a way, for the removal of whatever element of dark estrangement my contracted guilt or his violated law might interpose. I refuse to submit myself continually anew to that faithful and just searching of my heart and reins which, if I would but suffer it, must issue continually anew in my being forgiven all my sins, and so forgiven as to be cleansed from all unrighteousness with regard to any of them. Surely such clear, bright, open, confidential fellowship between him who is light and his little child trying to walk in his light, far transcends any poor measure of accommodation which a hollow truce between us might purpose to effect. Let us have that fellowship evermore. All the rather because—

III. If, in the face of such a faithful manner of forgiveness on the part of God, we continue to shrink from that open dealing and guileless confession which our walking in the light as God is in the light implies,—we not only wrong ourselves, and do violence to our own consciousness and our own conscience ; but, " saying that we have not sinned, we make him a liar, and his word is not in us " (ver. 10).

This is a stronger statement than that in the eighth verse. It is not " we deceive ourselves," but "we make God a liar ;" not generally, " the truth is not in us," but very pointedly and particularly, " his word is not in us." The difference is explained by the assurance given in the intermediate verse ;—" If we confess our sins, he is faithful and just to forgive us our sins, and to cleanse us from all unrighteousness."

For that assurance, as has been shown, opens the way to a very confidential intercourse of confession on the one hand, and just and faithful treatment of our case on the other, between us and our Father in heaven. If we think at any moment that we do not need this sort of intercourse, that we can dispense with it and do without it, we labour under a grievous delusion ; we deceive ourselves ; some self-excusing or self-justifying lie is expelling from within our souls the bright clear light of the truth. If again, after all the encouragement which he himself gives, we still at any moment hang back and hesitate, as if we could not venture on the sort of intercourse to which he invites us, surely that is inexcusable unbelief ; refusing to trust God ; giving the lie, not merely to his promises, but to his very character and nature ; not suffering his word to have entrance into our hearts. To prefer now, even for a single instant, or with reference to a single sin, the miserable comfort of wrapping ourselves in fig-leaves and hiding among the trees of the garden, to the unspeakable joy of coming forth naked into the light in which God is, casting ourselves into his open arms and asking him to deal with us according to his own loving faithfulness and righteousness and truth ;—that surely is a high affront to him and to his word, as well as a fond and foolish mistake for ourselves. There can be no fellow-ship of light between us and him if such unworthy senti-ments of dark suspicion and reserve as this implies are again, at any time and in any measure, insinuating themselves into our bosoms.

For, as one indispensable condition of that fellowship,— and indeed the primary and fundamental condition of it,— is that " we walk in the light as he is in the light ; " so an-other condition of it, arising out of the first, is that " we confess our sins." The two indeed are one ; the last is only a particular application of the former. Walking in the light as God is in the light, we must be continually learn-ing to see more clearly as he sees. Our medium of vision being the same as his, our vision itself must be growing more and more nearly the same. Insight and sympathy are ever brightening and deepening. Things come to be more and more in our eyes exactly what they are in his. We ourselves, and our works and ways, are more and more seen by us as they are seen by God.

Can this go on, honestly and really, without ever fresh discoveries and ever new experiences of such a sort as must always make confession, to the earnest and believing soul, a most welcome privilege indeed? It is not merely that I come to perceive in old sins a heinousness and an amount of aggravation that makes me feel as if I had never adequately acknowledged them in time past, but must be ever repenting of them anew, and getting them anew disposed of by their being laid anew on him who is the sin-bearer and the cross-bearer. Nor is it merely that new forms and phases of the ungodliness and selfishness and carnality of my heart,— new shifts and windings of its deceitfulness and desperate wickedness,—must be ever coming up and coming out to vex my quickened spiritual sensibility and damp the ardour of my faith and love. Both these sources of disquietude are, alas! too common. But above and beyond all that,—in my very walking, as God's fellow; being the fellow of his Son Jesus Christ; his fellow-servant, fellow-worker, fellow-sufferer, fellow-heir in his kingdom; as the Holy Spirit gives me an increasing sense and taste of what it is to walk with God in his own light; as I seek to carry that light, and him with whom I walk in fellowship in that light, into all the scenes and circumstances of my outer walk of faith, and all the fluctuations of my inner life of faith; how is my heart troubled! How many fountains of bitterness are ever freshly flowing! And then in the world, with its manifold calls that cannot be put aside, and its troublesome questions of lawfulness and expediency, I am too often at a loss and almost at a stand.

I may try to set aside all such annoyances, as not entering properly into my spiritual experience, and to keep that, as it were, isolated and pure. I may think that when I go to commune with my God and Father; when I enter into my closet and shut the door ; when I seek his face and wait for his salvation ;—I am to leave all my cares and troubles behind me on the threshold, and meet him in some lofty region of spiritual peace, where sorrow and sin are to find no place. But I am deceiving myself. And I am refusing to trust my God and Father, and so I am giving him the lie. From such sin as that may he himself evermore deliver me !

Let me rather, taking him at his word, try the more excellent way of carrying with me always, in the full confidence of loving fellowship, into the secret place of my God, all that is upon my mind, my conscience, my heart; all that is harassing, or burdening, or tempting me ; my present matter of care or subject of thought, whatever that may be. Let me unbosom all my grief. Let me freely and unreservedly speak to him of what is uppermost in my thoughts. There may be sin in it, or about it. There may be something wrong; some wound to be probed; some root of bitterness to be searched out ; some offending right hand or right eye. Be it so. Still, let me open up all ; let me confess all. Let me spread out my whole case. Let me empty and lay bare my whole soul. Let me put myself, and be ever putting myself, thoroughly, nakedly, unreservedly, into his hands. Surely I may rely on his dealing faithfully and righteously with me. Nor would I wish him to deal with me otherwise. He may " chasten me sore, but he will not give me over to death." He may rebuke and convince; he may even smite and slay. But " though he slay me, I will trust in him." I know that he requireth truth in the inward parts. I ask him therefore to lead me into all truth ; into all the truth concerning myself as well as concerning him; however painful the knowledge of it may be to my self-righteous feelings, and however deadly to my self-righteous hopes. I am for no half-measures now, no compromise, no concealment. I would keep back nothing from my God. I will not deceive myself by keeping silence about my sin. I will not make my God a liar,—I will not do my God and Father so great a wrong as to give him the lie,—by refusing entrance into my soul to that word of his which gives light, even the light of life. I will confess my sins, knowing and believing that as "the blood of Jesus Christ his Son cleanseth us from all sin," so "he is faithful and just to forgive us our sins, and to cleanse us from all unrighteousness. "Search me, O God, and know my heart; try me, and know my thoughts; and see if there be any wicked way in me; and lead me in the way everlasting."

5

SINLESS AIM OF THE GUILELESS SPIRIT—PROVISION FOR ITS CONTINUED SENSE OF SIN

"My little children, these things write I unto you, that ye sin not. And if any man sin, we have an advocate with the Father." 1 John 2:1

To obviate, as it might seem, an objection against his doctrine of confession, that it was liable to be turned into an allowance of sin, the Apostle first makes a most emphatic protest as to his real design in setting forth that doctrine; and secondly, puts the manner of restoration, through the advocacy of Christ, on a footing that effectually shuts out all licentious and latitudinarian abuse of it, in the line of practical antinomianism.

His first desire is to make clear the sinless aim of the guileless spirit, about the production of which he has been so much concerned.

And here his appeal is very affectionate: "My little children!" It is the appeal of a loving master to the good faith and good feeling of loving pupils; beseeching them not to misunderstand him, as if he meant to indulge or excuse them in sin. Nay, it is more than that. It is an appeal to their highest and holiest Christian ambition. Far from tolerating sin, I would have you to aim at being sinless. "These things write I unto you, that ye sin not;" that you may make it your express design and determination not to sin.

That is the full force of the Apostle's language, when he says, " I write these things unto you that ye sin not."

I. Let that be your aim, to " sin not." Let it be deliberately set before you as your fixed and settled purpose that you are not to sin ; not merely that you are to sin as little as you can ; but that you are not to sin at all.

For there is a wide difference between these two ways of putting the matter. That in the business of your sanctification absolute holiness is to be your standard, you may admit. A sinless model or ideal is presented to you ; and you acknowledge your obligation to be conformed to it. But is not the acknowledgment often accompanied with some sort of reserve or qualification ? The measure of conformity that may be fairly expected must be limited by what your infirmity may hope to reach ; nay, you even venture to add, by what God may be pleased to give you strength to reach. This is scarcely honest. It is not equivalent to an out-and-out determination not to sin. You do not really mean to be altogether without sin ; but only so far as your own poor ability, aided by the Divine Spirit, may enable you to be so. Or, with reference to some specific work or trial that you have on hand, you do not really mean not to sin in it, but only not to sin in it more than you can help. Is it not so, both generally as regards your cultivation of a holy character, and particularly as regards your discharge of holy duties in detail ? And what is that at bottom, but secret, perhaps unconscious, antinomianism ? You are not in love with sin ; you do not choose sin ; you would rather, if it were possible, avoid it, and be wholly free from it. But that, you say, is impossible. You make up your minds therefore to its being impossible, and reckon beforehand on its being impossible. You wish and hope and pray, that the evil element may be reduced to a minimum. Still it is to be there ; you are quite sure it will be there ; and you must accommodate yourself to what is unavoidable. However you may try, you cannot expect to be without sin, or "not to sin."

This is a very subtle snare. And it is not easily met. For it is founded on fact. It is but too true that in all that we do we come short of the sinless aim. That, however, is no reason for our not only anticipating fault or failure, but acquiescing in the anticipation. Above all, it is no reason why we should take it for granted by anticipation that some particular fault or failure, foreseen and foreknown by ourselves, must be acquiesced in. For the special danger lies there. It is not merely that in entering on any course of holy living, or engaging in any branch of holy labour, I feel certain that I shall sin in it. I have a shrewd suspicion as to how I shall sin in it. I can guess where the breakdown is to take place. I have tried already to keep this law as I see it should be kept, and to keep it perfectly. I will try again, asking God to incline my heart to keep it. I know well enough indeed that I shall fail and fall short. And I know well enough how I shall fail and fall short. Nevertheless, I can but try, and I will try, to do my best.

Is that, however, a really honest determination on my part not to sin ? Am I not reconciling myself prospectively to some known besetting infirmity ? Let us not deceive ourselves. Let us consider how inconsistent all such guileful dealing is with that "walking in the light, as God is in the light," which is the indispensable condition of our fellowship with God and his with us. The very object of all that the apostle writes on that subject is that, at the very least, we rise to the high and holy attitude of determining not to sin. All that he tells us of "the word of life," the life "which was with the Father and was manifested unto us ; " all that he tells us of the divine fellowship for which the way is thus opened up ; all that he tells us of the nature of him with whom our fellowship is to be, and of the provision made through the blood of Jesus Christ his Son which cleanseth from all sin, for our coming forth out of our natural darkness into his light; all is designed to bring us up to this point, that we sin not; that in purpose and determination we are bent on not sinning.

II. But not only would I have you to make this your aim; I would have your aim accomplished and realised. And therefore "I write these things unto you, that ye sin not."

We are to proceed upon the anticipation, not of failure but of success, in all holy walking and in every holy duty; not of our sinning, but of our not sinning. And we are to do so, because the things which John "writes unto us" make the anticipation no wild dream, but a possible attainment.

We must assume it to be possible not to sin, when we walk in the open fellowship of God, and in his pure translucent light; especially not to sin in this or that particular way in which we have sinned before, and in which we are apt to be afraid of sinning again. For practical purposes this is really all that is needed. But this is needed.

I do not care much for any general assurance, even if I could get it, that I am not to sin at all. But, if I am in earnest, how deeply do I care for even a faint hope that, in the particular matter that lies heavy on my conscience, it may sometime and somehow become possible for me not to sin! That is what is pressing. In some hour of calm meditation or divine contemplative speculation, the idea of a serene and stainless perfection of holiness and peace wrapping my spirit in ineffable bliss may have a certain fascinating charm, and may awaken undefined longings and aspirations. They are far too vague, however, to be practically influential. And they do not meet my case. For why am I troubled? What is it that distresses and vexes me? Alas! it is no mere vague consciousness of imperfection. It is some specific "thorn in the flesh" that, as a "messenger of Satan, is buffeting me." "When I would do good, evil is present with me." When I would pray, my soul cleaves to the dust. When I am in my closet, with my door shut against all the world, all sorts of worldly thoughts intrude. When I read and study, I find my mind unfixed. When God speaks to me, my attention wanders. When I should be hearing the voice of his servant, my eyes are drowsy. I take up some branch of God's service,—how soon do I grow weary, or stumble, or offend! I seek to control my temper, and some slight provocation oversets me. Try as I may, I am sure to fail. And then, when, going down to the depths of my inner nature, I seek to have my whole soul purged from lust and filled with love, alas! is there never to be an end of this weary, heartless, fruitless struggle? Is it to be always thus,—sinning and repenting; repenting and going back to sin?

Nay, let me hear John's loving words; "My little children, these things write I unto you, that ye sin not." Believe these things; realise them; act upon them; act them out. They are such things as, if believed, realised, acted upon, and acted out, will make it possible for you "not to sin." For they are such things as, if thus apprehended, change the character of the whole struggle. They transfer it to a new and higher platform. We are brought into a position, in relation to God, in which holiness is no longer a desperate negative strife, but a blessed positive achievement. Evil is overcome with good. The heavenly walk in light with him who is light carries us upwards and onwards, above and beyond the region of dark guilt and fear, in which sin is strong; and places us in the region of peace and joy, in which grace is stronger. Sanctification is not now a mere painful process of extirpation and extermination of weeds. It will no doubt be that still; but it is not that merely. It is the gracious implanting of good seed, and the cultivating of it gladly as it grows. And as we enter more and more, with larger intelligence and deeper sympathy, into the spirit of John's opening words concerning the end and means of our "fellowship with the Father and with his Son Jesus Christ," we come better to know experimentally what is in his heart when he says : "These things write I unto you, that ye sin not." That is what you are to aim at ; and you are to aim at it as now possible.

III. Why then, it may be asked, is provision made for our sinning still after all?—"If any man"—any of us— "sin, we have an advocate with the Father." Let me in reply again appeal to any who are really exercised in resisting sin and following after holiness ; "walking truly in the light, as God is in the light."

For I do not address those who take this whole matter easily ; being quite contented with a very moderate measure of decent abstinence from gross vice and the perfunctory performance of some pious and charitable offices. The present theme scarcely concerns them in their present mood. John assumes that we are in earnest ; that sin is to us exceeding sinful, and holiness above all things desirable. We have purposed in good faith that we will not offend. We rejoice to think that we may now form that purpose with good heart ; not desperately, as if we were upon a forlorn hope ; but rather as grasping the victory, through our Lord Jesus Christ. For he is with us. He cheers us on. He assures us of success. And when, at any time, he sees some lurking apprehension of failure or defeat stealing into our souls again to discourage us ; when he sees that we are getting nervous about the risk of our making some mistake, or meeting with some check or reverse, and that this very nervousness is unhinging and unmanning us; he tells us not to think too much of it, but to press on; for he is beside us, to help us if we should stumble, to lift us if we should fall—" If any of us sin, we have an advocate with the Father."

Shall I then be emboldened to walk heedlessly, presuming on his advocacy? Perish the ungenerous, the ungrateful thought! What! shall I make a mere convenience of that Divine Saviour, and turn his ministry of holy love into a mere pleading for indulgence and purchase of impunity?

Lying priests, false mediators; priests and mediators false to both the parties between whom they mediate, to God's high honour and man's pure peace; false, as not reconciling but alienating, not bringing together but keeping asunder, the yearning Father and his poor prodigal child;—they and their offices may be so used, or abused. But Jesus is an advocate of a very different stamp. He is not content to negotiate, as a third party, between God dwelling in light and us suffered still to continue in darkness. He is one with both the parties whom he makes one in himself. By his one offering of himself, once for all, he brings us, when the Spirit unites us by faith to him, into the very light of God, his Father and ours.

But the light is such as, when our eyes are opened to its brightness, makes our walking in it an affair of extreme delicacy. In good faith, with full purpose, right honestly and heartily to "walk in the light," is to face an ordeal from which a man with renovated principles and sensibilities may well sensitively shrink. True, the tendency of all this marvellous arrangement for placing us on such a footing of light with God,—admitting us into such a fellowship of light and setting us to such a walk of light,— is that we "sin not." And we are assured that if we make full proof of this light, we shall find it no such impossible thing as we might imagine not to sin. But with a growing clearness of vision, becoming more and more alive to the inexpressible lustre and loveliness of the light, and the offensiveness of whatever partakes of the least soil or stain of the darkness which the light exposes ;—how should our advance along the ascending path of heavenliness and spirituality be anything else than one continued discipline of anxious fear ?

Jesus knows our frame, in its worst and in its best state. He knows what to us, with such a frame as ours at the best is, our really " walking in the light as God is in the light " must be. He knows how at every step,—in spite of all the encouragement given us beforehand to hope that we need not, that we may not, that we shall not sin,— we still may shrink and hang back ; fearing with too good ground that even if, in the form we used to dread, our sin shall seem to give way, it may, in some new manifestation of our deep inward corruption, lie in wait to trouble us. Well does our sympathising friend and brother know all this And therefore he assures us that he is always beside us ; " our advocate with the Father." We need not therefore be afraid to walk with the Father in the light. We may walk, alas ! too often unsteadfastly. We may give new offence. We may incur new blame. But see ! There is the intercessor ever pleading for us. " If any of us sin, we have an advocate with the Father."

6

NATURE AND GROUND OF CHRIST'S ADVOCACY AS MEETING THE NEED OF THE GUILELESS SPIRIT

"My little children, these things write I unto you, that ye sin not. And if any man sin, we have an advocate with the Father, Jesus Christ the righteous : and he is the propitiation for our sins : and not for ours only, but for the sins of the whole world." 1 John 2:1,2

THE manner of our restoration, if we fall short of the sinless aim, not less than the sinless aim itself, is fitted to guard against any abuse of John's doctrine of forgiveness. It is through an advocacy altogether incompatible with anything like the toleration of evil. This will appear if we consider the three things here mentioned as qualifying our advocate for his advocacy :—I. He is "Jesus Christ the righteous ; "—II. He is " the propitiation for our sins ; "—III. He is the propitiation " not for our sins only, but also for the sins of the whole world."

I. He is " Jesus Christ the righteous."

Jesus ! The name is as ointment poured forth; fragrant, precious. He is called Jesus because he saves his people from their sins. Jesus ! my Saviour ! my Jesus ! saving me from my sins, from myself ! Art thou indeed my advocate with the Father,—standing by me, pleading for me,—by thy Spirit pleading in me,—when, in spite of my firmest purpose not to sin, and my closest clinging to thee that I may not sin, I must still, under the pressure of sin besetting me, cry, Unclean ! undone ! Then indeed may I hold on walking in the light, and with a sinless aim, if thou art with me. Jesus, save me from my sins!

Christ! the Anointed! whom the Father anoints through the Spirit; whom I also, through the Spirit, in sympathy with the Father, humbly venture to anoint! his Christ and mine!—with thee, O Christ, as my advocate with the Father;—with thee, True Mediator,— Revealer, Reconciler, Ruler,—Prophet, Priest, and King;—I will not, amid all that is discouraging in the experience of my remaining darkness, despair of yet becoming all that he who is light and who dwelleth in light would have me to be; all that thou art, O Christ!

But the emphatic word here is not the proper name Jesus, nor the official name Christ, but the adjective "righteous."

This term may possibly be understood as referring to the righteousness which he has wrought out on our behalf, as our substitute and surety, and which he brings in and presents before the Father as the ground of all his pleading with him as our advocate. For his advocacy is not a mere ministry of persuasion; working as it were on the placibility and fond facility of an angry but weak potentate, an offended but infirm and indulgent parent. It is his submitting to God the Father, as the righteous governor, such a service and satisfaction as may warrant, in terms of strictest law and justice, the exercise of mercy towards his guilty but penitent children. All that is true. But it is not, I think, what John principally has in his mind. For, in the first place, the efficacious and meritorious condition of our Lord's advocacy is sufficiently brought out in the clause which follows, "he is the propitiation for our sins." And secondly, it is awkward to understand the word "righteous" in two distinct senses, as it is used in the same passage, and within the compass of a few verses, first of the

Father (i. 9), and now of the Son (ii. 1). I take it therefore as pointing, not to the legal righteousness which Christ
has—or rather which Christ is—but to the righteousness
of his character, and of his manner of advocacy with the
Father for us. That other meaning need not be excluded,
for the two are by no means inconsistent. But when John
commends our advocate with the Father as " Jesus Christ
the righteous," it is surely upon his benignant equity that
he would have us to fix our eyes.

Such an advocate becomes us ; and such alone. If
we rightly consider the relation to God into which the
gospel message, as John has been putting it, is designed to
bring us ; the footing on which it places us with God ; the
sort of divine insight, sympathy, and fellowship for which
it opens up the way ; and the sort of walk on which it sets
us ; we may well feel that none other than such an advocate
could meet our case.

In any court in which I had a cause to maintain I
would wish to have a righteous advocate. Not less than I
would desire a righteous judge would I welcome a righteous
advocate. I do not want an advocate who will flatter and
cajole me. I do not want one to tell me smooth things
and lead me on the ice ; disguising or evading the weak
points of my plea ; putting a fair face on what will not
stand close scrutiny, and touching tenderly what will not
bear rough handling ; getting up untenable lines of defence,
and keeping me in good humour till disaster or ruin comes.
Give me an advocate who will tell me the truth, and tell
the truth on my behalf ; one who will deal truly with me
and for me, and fairly represent my case. Give me an
advocate who, much as he may care for me, cares for
honesty and honour, for law and justice, still more. Give
me an advocate not afraid to vex or wound me for my

safety, for my good. Whatever his name, let him be the honest, the upright, "the righteous."

Such an advocate is Jesus Christ for us in the high court of heaven; for he is "Jesus Christ the righteous." In the presence of the righteous judge, and at his righteous bar, he thus appears for us; not to bring us off as by some cunning sleight-of-hand manœuvre; not to get the better of strict justice by some dexterous and adroit management, or some plausible and pathetic appeal to pity; but to have the whole controversy sifted to the bottom, and all hidden causes of offence laid bare, and every just demand and outstanding claim met, and all relating to our right standing adjusted,—without any compromise or subterfuge,— upon the terms and according to the principles of perfect righteousness.

Such an advocate is Jesus Christ for us in the high court of heaven. Such an advocate is he also when, in the capacity, as it were, of chamber-counsel, he is with us in our closet, to listen to all that we have to say; to all our confessions and complaints; our enumeration of grievances; our unbosoming ourselves of all our anxieties and all our griefs. He is still "Jesus Christ the righteous;" patient and pitiful, as he bends his ear to our wildest cry or our faintest whisper; yet still righteous; not dallying delicately with our sin or our sorrow; not sparing us; probing us to the quick; giving us no relief till the whole matter is searched into, and spread out, and fairly and justly met. He is "Jesus Christ the righteous."

But it is not only with God as Judge that he is our advocate. He is our advocate with "the Father." His advocacy has respect not only to the Judge's court but to the Father's house. It is the advocacy of the elder brother, who has brought us home to his Father and our Father. It is a home of love and of light; a home of love because it is a home of light. Perfect peace should reign in it, as the fruit of perfect purity. It is not a home in which we can allow ourselves to sin. There is no darkness to hide our sin ; no room for any lie to excuse it. We are brought home, in the marvellous way in which we have been brought home, for the express purpose that we may not sin. Our elder brother, in bringing us home, has suffered enough for our sin to make it very loathsome in our esteem. He has, moreover, so suffered for it that we need have nothing to do with it, nor it with us, any more. And that our connection with the old haunts and associations of our sin may be cut clean away for ever, and we may be placed at once in the best and likeliest position for sinning no more, he concurs with the Father in our being at once embraced as children, invested as children with the robe and ring of honour, and welcomed as children to the children's table. There is to be no reproach ; no upbraiding; no word or look of reference to the past any more. Our elder brother has answered for all, and all is cancelled. There is to be no more any dark servile doubt or suspicion or fear. All is to be holy light and love. There is to be no more sin.

Ah! but more sin, in spite of all this, there is; and there is the apprehension of sin evermore. The Father indeed is light, always light. And we walk in his light; the light of his reconciled countenance ; the light of his pure and loving eye. But how sensitively, on that very account, is our conscience, our heart, alive to all—alas! too much— that is in us and about us still savouring of the dark tastes of our old estrangement.

Where,—we are at every moment constrained to ask,— where is that elder brother who brought us hither, and who alone can keep us here ? We know that he would have us, not to put him in between the Father and us, but to be ourselves, in him, at home with the Father (John xvi. 26, 27).

It should be so; and we seek to have it so. But the home is so holy, and the light is so holy, and he who is in the light is so holy; and we are so sinful, so fain to shrink from the light and court the darkness again, that we cannot stand upright. We cannot keep our ground; we cannot move on; we cannot meet the Father's eye; we stumble; we fall. Ah! we need that elder brother still. We need him to be our advocate with the Father. He must not quit our side. He must not let go our hand. He must be ever leading us in to the Father, and presenting us to the Father, and speaking for us to the Father, and putting us anew right with the Father. And so he is. He is never far off. " We have an advocate with the Father, Jesus Christ the righteous." " The righteous !" For now what sort of advocate with the Father would we have? And what would we have his advocacy to be?

The time has been when, if we cared to live at home in the Father's house at all, we would have been glad of the good offices, say of some upper servant, not very scrupulous and not over strict, who might be disposed to take our part when any breach occurred. It might be convenient to have a friend at court, an advocate with the head and master of the family, ready always to intercede for us; to hide our faults or apologise for them ; to come in between us and the angry glance or the uplifted arm ; to put a specious colouring on the cause of offence, and get us off, no matter how, from dreaded vengeance. But no such advocacy will be welcome now. No such advocate will our elder brother be. For he is our advocate with the Father, as "Jesus Christ the righteous." Yes! in dealing with us, as well as in dealing with the Father for us, he will deal righteously, truly, justly. He will so ply his office, and travail in his work, of advocacy between the Father and us, as to preserve the right understanding which he has himself brought about, and obviate the risk of renewed separation. He will make it all subservient to our more thorough cleansing from sin, and our closer walk with God;—our being "holy as he is holy." For—

II. "He is the propitiation for our sins." He is so now. He is present with us now as our advocate with the Father; and it is as being the propitiation for our sins that he is present with us.

It is not needful to settle in what precise aspect of the sacrificial service Jesus is here spoken of as the propitiation; whether with reference to the sacrificial victim slain, or the altar on which it was burned, or the mercy-seat on which its blood was sprinkled. Jesus is all three in one; the lamb slain, the altar of atonement, the blood-baptized mercy-seat. The important lesson is this, that it is as the propitiation for our sins that Jesus Christ is our advocate with the Father. Whenever he acts as our advocate, whether to satisfy the Father anew or to pacify our consciences anew, he acts in virtue of his being—not having been but being —the propitiation for our sins. The two, in fact, are one; his advocacy with the Father is his being the propitiation for our sins. In every instance in which it is exercised, it is simply a new and fresh application to our case of the virtue of his being the propitiation for our sins.

For what does he do when, in some dark hour, he ministers to me and in me as my advocate with the Father? He draws near; the Spirit so taking of what is his and showing it to me as to bring him near. He is beside me, with me, at my right hand. He is here with me now, the propitiation for my sins now, precisely as he was on Calvary. I see him, invisible as he is, now and here, exactly as he was then and there; thorn-crowned, bleeding, in agony; bowing his head; giving up the ghost; pouring out his soul an offering for sin. Yes! that is my advocate with the Father;

and that is the manner of his advocacy! Can it be other than a righteous advocacy? Can he be other than a righteous advocate? When my sin, grieving the Father's heart and vexing his Holy Spirit, has pierced his Son Jesus Christ anew, and he hastens, with blood and water freshly flowing from the re-opened wound, to wash me anew, and anew present me to the Father; is that a sort of ministry that can lead to sin? Can I touch these hands which I have been nailing again to the accursed tree, or feel them touching me again to bless me, without my whole frame thrilling as the voice runs through my inmost soul—"Sin no more;" "Thou art dead to sin"?

III. There is a supplement added which still further explains the sort of advocacy which Jesus Christ the righteous carries on. He is "the propitiation for our sins; and not for ours only, but also for the sins of the whole world." This is added, as it would seem, for this very end, to preclude the possibility of a believer thinking that, if he lapses, it is under some method of recovery different from that which is available for all mankind. Otherwise, it comes in awkwardly and irrelevantly.

For it is out of place here to introduce the subject of the bearing of the propitiation on mankind at large; for the purpose of considering that subject for its own sake, or settling any doubtful question regarding it. It is very much in point, however, and very much to the purpose, to make a passing reference to the world-wide scope and aspect of the propitiation which Christ is; and so to guard against the notion of there being anything like favouritism in what he does on behalf of his true followers and friends.

There is no new specific for meeting our case when we who walk in the light fall into sin, no specific different from what is provided for meeting the case of all sinners—of the whole world. We have no special fountain opened for our cleansing, but only the fountain opened in the house of David for all the inhabitants of Jerusalem indiscriminately; for all the world, and all its sin, and all its uncleanness. There is no way in which we can get rid of that sin of ours,—its guilt and curse, its deadly blight and canker, eating out the very life of our soul,—except that way, patent and open to all, in which all the world, if it will, may get rid of all its sins. Doubtless when we sin we have an advocate with the Father to stand by us, and lift us up, and plead our cause, and place us again on a right footing with the Father. But he can do all this only by interposing himself as "the propitiation for our sins," in the very same sense and manner in which he interposes himself as the propitiation "for the sins of the whole world."

Where, then, ye children of the light and of the day,— ye fellows of the Father and of his Son Jesus Christ,— where is your peculiar privilege of sinning lightly and being easily restored? What is there in that sin of yours that should make it lie less heavily on your conscience, and afflict your souls less grievously, than the sins which, when you were of the world, you committed; of which you repented; and for which you sought and obtained forgiveness, when you came out of the world's weary wilderness, and were brought home to your Father's house? Is your sin now less heinous than were your sins then? Are there no aggravations to enhance its guilt, and to stamp with a deeper dye its exceeding sinfulness? Does it demand fewer tears and less poignant searchings of heart, less of godly sorrow, less of bitter weeping?

What! when that eye which looked on Peter—that eye not of reproach so much as of silent unutterable woe—the eye that smote him with a mortal stab,—when that eye catches mine—yes! as he is in the very act of hastening to the rescue lest my faith fail, coming quickly to be my advocate with the Father—when, fallen as I am, I feel his touch, and that open calm look of his arrests and rivets me,—Jesus! I cry, my Lord, my God, dost thou yet care for me? Wilt thou yet comfort me; me, a sinner; a sinner worse than ever; sinning more inexcusably than ever in all the days of my ignorance I sinned; more inexcusably than all the world in its ignorance can sin? Can such a one as I yet live? I ask no special favour; I plead for no partial exemption. Let me only anew,—not as a saint,—not as a child of God,—but only as a sinner,—of sinners the chief,—betake myself to thee, the propitiation for my sin!

Yes! I may, I do. And I find thee still the propitiation for my sin, because thou art the propitiation for the sins of the whole world. Not otherwise could I take the benefit of thine advocacy. It is not as a propitiation peculiar to me that I grasp thee in my distress; as if I had any peculiar claim to thee; as if others were sinners more than I, or I less than they. Alas! no. My only hope is in grasping thee as "the propitiation for the sins of the whole world." That wide charter will take me in when nothing else can. "It is a faithful saying, and worthy of all acceptation, that Jesus Christ came into the world to save sinners, of whom I am chief."

This, and this alone, is thy refuge and revival, O poor soul! Thou sinnest;—as a child of God, walking in the light, thou sinnest. And in the light in which thou walkest thy sin finds thee out. Thou art overwhelmed. Can such sin as thine be forgiven? Yes, brother. But not otherwise than through the advocacy of Jesus Christ the righteous, who is the propitiation for thy sins. Thou must have recourse to him in that character. But not as if thy case were peculiar, and demanded or could receive peculiar treatment. No. Thou must be content to take thy place among the whole body of the sinners of mankind, for the very worst of whom the propitiation is available precisely as it is for thee; for them as fully as for thee; for thee as fully as for them. That indeed is the very consideration which revives thee. He is the propitiation for all sinners and for all sins. No sin, no sinner, is at any time beyond the reach of that great atonement. It meets the case of all mankind, of all the world; and therefore it meets thy case, be thy backsliding ever so grievous, thy guilt ever so aggravated. Thou couldst not venture to appropriate Christ as the propitiation for thy sins, otherwise than as he is the propitiation for the sins of the whole world. It is only because thou believest and art sure that no sin, no sinner, in all the world, is debarred from that wondrous fountain filled with blood, that thou canst summon courage to plunge in it thyself afresh. Even to the last, it is not as isolating thyself from sinners of mankind, but as associating thyself with them,—feeling thyself to be the chief of them,—that thou lookest, when thou hast sinned, to " the Lamb of God that taketh away the sin of the world." *

---

* In my book on the Atonement (edition 1861, pages 66-71), I suggest an explanation of this passage that may seem to differ from that given here. The difference, however, is merely apparent. I here protest against believers, when they fall into sin, having any method of recovery to which they may have recourse, different from, or going beyond, what all sinners called to repentance have within their reach, as freely offered to them in the Gospel. My meaning there is substantially the same. It maintains the applicability of the propitiation, as bearing on the back-slidings of believers, not only to the disciples to whom John wrote;— that is to himself and his fellow disciples;—but generally to all and sundry in the like case. The only new idea which I throw out here is one which seems to me to enter into the heart of the text,—and into the heart also of any spiritual experience on which the Spirit brings the text to bear;—the idea, namely, that no true Christian, under a sense of sin, can ever recover his footing in the free grace of God, through any propitiation that is not common to him with " the whole world."

The worst enemies of Calvinism are those who challenge such statements. So far as their views are at all intelligent and logical, they make faith impossible; faith, that is, resting on a free Gospel, and without the warrant of an express personal sign, inward or outward. Whether as a sinner called, or as a backslider recalled, I can build no hope on any propitiation presented to me as peculiar to a class, and not open to the race at large. I am thankful therefore for the assurance that, "if any man sin, we have an advocate with the Father, Jesus Christ the righteous, who is the propitiation for our sins, and not for ours only, but also for the sins of the whole world."

This is my answer to certain critics who have founded on garbled extracts from this passage the charge of an unguarded and objectionable mode of expression as to the nature and extent of the atonement.

7

THE GUILELESS SPIRIT REALISING THROUGH OBE-
DIENCE THE KNOWLEDGE OF GOD AS THE
MEANS OF BEING AND ABIDING IN GOD

"And hereby we do know that we know him, if we keep his commandments. He that saith, I know him, and keepeth not his commandments, is a liar, and the truth is not in him. But whoso keepeth
his word, in him verily is the love of God perfected: hereby know
we that we are in him." *   1 John 2:3-5

THIS is a more literal explanation of the divine fellowship,
considered as a fellowship of light, than has been given before. The light which is the atmosphere of the fellowship,
or the medium of vision and sympathy through which it is

---

* A doubt may be suggested as to what Divine Person is meant here
when the third personal pronoun is used. Is it the Son or the Father?
One might at first be inclined to say it is the Son; for it is he who is
spoken of in the immediately preceding verses (1, 2). But throughout
this whole passage John is speaking of God the Father as the object of
knowledge and fellowship. It is with God in Christ that he summons us
to have communion. The Son is brought in separately (i. 7, ii. 2), only
to show how his ministry of sacrifice, intercession, and propitiation, by
providing for our not sinning, or not sinning beyond the hope of repentance and revival, makes such communion possible. That end being
served, the discourse returns to its original channel. On this account, as
well as on grammatical grounds, I lean to the opinion of those who think
that God the Father is the Divine Person referred to. And I do so the
rather because in the verse that follows (6),—"He that saith he abideth
in him, ought himself also so to walk, even as he walked,"—there is a
remarkable distinction of pronouns. It does not appear in our translation; and indeed the English tongue scarcely admits of its appearing.
But it is clear in the finer idiom of the original Greek. The "he" in the
last clause is different from the "him" in the first; which again agrees

realised, is the light of knowledge, the light of the knowledge of God. For the fellowship is intelligent as well as
holy—intelligent that it may be holy.

But of what sort is that knowledge? And how is it to
be got hold of and made sure of? These are the questions
with which John now proceeds to deal. And in the verses
that form our text he introduces them very emphatically,
as questions personally and practically affecting us, with
reference to our claim and calling to be walkers in the
light.

For, first, he would have us to " know that we know
God " (ver. 3). He raises the question of the trustworthiness of our knowledge of God. It is as if you asked me
about one of my familiars, whose name I am fond of using,
whose opinions I am apt to quote, whose patronage I
rather boast of ;—" But do you know that you know him?
Are you sure that you understand him?" The abrupt question takes me somewhat aback. I think I know him. But
your doubt startles me. I must inquire and see. Again,
secondly, John would have us to "know that we are in
God" (ver. 5). This suggests still more hesitancy. I have
had the idea that I am in him, in the sense of being united
to him in the bonds of faith, fellowship, and friendship.
But you raise misgivings. Do I indeed know that I am in
him?

The two inquiries may be treated as one ; requiring the
same examination and admitting of the same proof.

There comes in, however, thirdly, an intermediate
thought : " whoso keepeth his word, in him verily is the

with the "him" and the "his" in the verses now before us (3–5). Surely
this marks a change. The person indicated in the end of the sixth verse
is not the same as the person indicated in the beginning of that verse,
and in those that precede it. But the person indicated in the end of the
sixth verse is clearly the Lord Jesus. It must therefore be God the
Father who is indicated in the verses of our text.

love of God perfected" (ver. 5). This expression denotes a fact accomplished. The word "is perfected" points to something done; and the word "verily" or "truly" marks the reality and thoroughness of what has been done and of the doing of it.

Now it is love that is here said to be thus perfected; the love of God. This can scarcely mean here the grace or affection of love; as the love of God to us, or our love to God; but rather the fellowship of love between him and us. "In the keeping of his word" that fellowship of love, so far as we are concerned, finds its completion, or "is perfected."

Most fitly does this thought come in between the other two. I. To know God; II. To have his love verily and indeed perfected in us; III. To be ourselves in him; that is our thrice holy standing, our thrice blessed privilege, in his Son Jesus Christ. If we would make sure of it, in our experience, it must be by keeping his commandments,—keeping his word.

I. There were those in John's day who affected to know God very deeply and intimately, in a very subtle and transcendental way. They laid great stress on thus knowing God; so much so that they took or got the name of knowing ones, or Gnostics. All about the essence of God, or his mysterious manner of being, they knew. All his attributes, and inward actings, and outward emanations, they knew. The forthgoings from everlasting of all his thoughts and volitions they knew so familiarly, and by so sublime an insight, that they could give to every one of them a local habitation and a name. They knew how heaven swarmed with these divine effluences or outcomings, as it were, of God's inner nature; to which they ascribed a sort of dreamy personality; associating them into a spiritual or ghostly hierarchy, in whose ranks they dared to place the very Son of the Highest himself. So they, after their own fashion, knew God. And through this knowledge of him, they professed to aspire to a participation of his godhead; their souls or spiritual essences being themselves effluences and emanations of his essence; and being therefore, along with all other such effluences or emanations, ultimately embraced in the Deity of which they formed part. So they "knew God."

But how did they know that they knew him? Was it because they kept his commandments? Nay, their very boast was that they knew God so well as to be raised far above that commonplace keeping of the commandments which might do for the uninitiated, but for which they had neither time nor taste. Their knowledge of God was too mystical and ethereal—too much of a rhapsody or a rapture —to admit of its being tested in so plain and practical a way. It was a small affair for them to keep the commandments, and a small affair also to break them. They were occupied with higher matters. Their real life was in a higher sphere. They cared for nothing but "knowing God."

John denounces strongly their impious pretence,—"He that saith, I know him, and keepeth not his commandments, is a liar, and the truth is not in him." The language is more forcible than ever. He not merely "lies" (i. 6); but "is a liar." Not merely does he "not do the truth," but in that man "the truth is not." To affect any knowledge of God that is not to be itself known and ascertained by the keeping of his commandments,—to dream of knowing God otherwise than in the way of keeping his commandments,—is to be false to the heart's core.

For, in fact, the question comes to be, Do I know God as a mere abstraction, about whose nature I may speculate? Or do I know him personally, as a man knows his friend? This last is the only kind of knowledge of God which John

can recognise and own. It is what he starts with; his
fundamental position; his postulate or axiom. God is
known through or in the incarnate Word of life, as he was
heard, looked upon, handled, by those who lived familiarly
with Jesus. Whosoever hath seen him hath seen the
Father. "No man knoweth the Father but the Son, and
he to whom the Son will reveal him." God is known in
Christ. And he is known in Christ as personally interested
in me, and personally dealing with me; kind to me; com-
passionate to me; waiting to be gracious to me; opening
his arms to embrace me; seeing me afar off; meeting me;
falling upon my neck and kissing me. When the Spirit
opens my eyes, it is thus that I know God. And how may
I know that I do really know him thus? How otherwise
than by my keeping his commandments? For this knowledge is intensely practical; not theoretic and speculative
at all; but only practical. I know God in the giving of
his Son to me and for me; in his giving him to be my friend
and brother; my surety and redeemer; giving him to die
for me on the accursed tree. With the new mind and the
new heart created in me by his own Spirit, I know God
now in Christ, as washing me from all my guilt; taking me
home; making me his child and heir. I know him by the
fatherly benignity of the look he bends on me, and the
fatherly warmth of the grasp in which he holds me. And
I may assure myself that in any tolerable measure I thus
know him, only if I keep his commandments.

Let me bless his name for that simple practical test. I
am not sent to any Gnostic school to seek a certificate of
scholarship from any of these knowing ones. I have not to
graduate in any of their colleges. I need not aspire to any
mystic insight, or visionary rapture, or sublime beatific
ecstasy. A lowlier path by far is mine. I am ignorant of
many things; ignorant of much even that it concerns me to

learn of God and of his wondrous love to me ; far, very far, from knowing him as I ought. But do I so know him as to make conscience of keeping his commandments—keeping them as I did not care to keep them once ? Is my proud will subdued and my independent spirit broken ? Moved and melted by what I know of God, do I, as if instinctively, cry, "Lord, what wouldst thou have me to do ?" Then, to me, this word is indeed a precious word in season ; "hereby we do know that we know him, if we keep his commandments" (ver. 3).

II. For while " he that saith, I know him, and keepeth not his commandments, is a liar, and the truth is not in him " (ver. 4) ; "whoso keepeth his word, in him verily is the love of God perfected " (ver. 5).

The change of expression here is surely meant to be significant. "His commandments," which may be many and various, are reduced to what is one and simple—"his word." The meaning is doubtless in substance the same ; but there is a shade of difference. This keeping of his word is, as it were, the concentrated and condensed spirit and essence of the keeping of his commandments. The thought suggested is not so much that of the things commanded, as of the command itself. It is not commandments, but God commanding ; not speech, but God speaking ; his word. The knowing ones stigmatised as liars pretended to know God, not as speaking, but simply as being ; not by communication from him, but by insight into him ; not by his word, but by their own wisdom. But you know him by his word. And that word of his, when you keep it, perfects the good understanding, the covenant of love, between him and you.

For indeed it must always be by word that love is truly perfected between intelligent parties ; by the plighting of troth ; by the interchange of pledge or promise expressed or understood; by word given and kept. How is it, when I know a friend, that his love is truly perfected in me? He gives me his word, and I keep it. I have nothing else for it but his word; his bare and naked word. I need nothing else; I desire nothing else. I keep that word of his; I keep it firm and fast. And as he is true to me, and I am true to him, I find that mere word of his, so kept by me, a sufficient warrant and assurance of all being right, and there being nothing now between us but true and perfect love, a true and perfect state of amity and peace.

When God is the party concerned, the keeping of his word on my part may well suffice for his love being thus truly perfected in me. For that word of his, the sum now to me of all his commandments, is his one simple assurance of good will in his Son. It is his word of reconciliation in Christ. It is, one might say, Christ himself, the reconciler. It is "God in Christ reconciling the world unto himself, not imputing unto them their trespasses." It is a word of very complete and comprehensive sweep: embracing all on God's part that is sovereign, efficacious, and authoritative, in the gift of his grace and in the obligation of his law; and all on our part that is humble, submissive, and obedient, in our trusting acceptance of the gift and cordial compliance with the obligation. It is a word making over to us freely from God all that is his; for "he that spared not his own Son, but gave him up for us all, how shall he not with him also freely give us all things?" It is a word winning over to God freely from us, ourselves, and all that is ours; for "we are not our own, but bought with a price," and so bound to "glorify God in our bodies and in our spirits, which are his." So full, complete, perfect, is this word on both sides. Only let it be kept. Kept on God's side it cannot fail to be. Let it be kept on ours. God is faithful to keep it to us. Let us be faithful to keep it to God. Kept by us, as it is sure to be kept by him, it does indeed ratify a perfect treaty of love.

III. And thus "we know that we are in him" (ver. 5). This, as it would seem, is the crown and consummation of all; first, to be in him; and, secondly, to know that we are in him.

First, to be in him; in a God whom we know, and between whom and us there is a real and perfect covenant of peace and love;—that must be an attainment worth while for us to realise; worth while for us to know or be sure that we realise.

To be in him! This cannot mean to be in God in any mystical sense of absorption; as if we were to lose our distinct personality, and be swallowed up in the ocean of the divine essence. All such ideas are precluded by the clear and unequivocal recognition of personal dealings, as between one intelligent being and another, implied in our knowing God, and in his love being truly perfected in us. But short of that wild and impious dream, it is not easy to urge too far the almost literal significancy of the expression,—" we are in him." Certainly it is something very different from merely being in what is his; as in his church, his house, his family, his kingdom. It is being in himself. What, on his part, that implies is among "the things which eye hath not seen, nor ear heard, nor heart conceived, but which God hath prepared for them that love him." Even to them it cannot be described beforehand. It transcends all that in imagination they could previously grasp. It is so prepared for them that love him that only in loving him can they apprehend and prove it. To be in him! What a covering of them with his wings—what a wrapping of them round with his own divine perfections—what an identifying of them with himself, of their interests with his, their triumph with his, their joy with his; what an identifying of himself with them, his grace with their guilt, his strength with their weakness, his glory with their salvation! To be in him! What a surrounding of them on all sides as with eyes innumerable and arms invincible; clothing them, as it were, with his own omniscience, his own omnipotence! Truly " as the mountains are round about Jerusalem, so the Lord is round about his people." They are in him. " He that dwelleth in the secret place of the Most High shall abide under the shadow of the Almighty."

But it is rather what on our part this phrase implies that we are here led to consider. What insight! What sympathy! What entering into his rest! What entering into his working too! What a fellowship of light!

We are in him! We are in his mind. He lets us into his mind. If I have a friend whom I know, and between whom and me there is a truly perfected love, I long to enter into his mind; to be partaker with him in all his mental movements and exercises, as he reads, and meditates, and studies; as he lays his plans and carries them into effect. I would be so in him that there should be, as it were, but one mind between us. Oh to be thus in God, of one mind with God!

We are in his heart. He lets us into his heart,—that great heart of the everlasting Father so warmly and widely opened in his Son Jesus Christ. To be in him, so that that heart of his shall draw to itself my heart, and the beating of the two shall, as it were, be in unison, and the throbbing of the two shall be blended in one;—and the Father's deep earnestness shall be mine; and the Father's holy wrath shall be mine; and the Father's pity shall be mine; and the Father's persuasive voice shall be mine; as I plead with my fellows;—" Turn ye, turn ye; why will ye die?" —what a thought! To be thus in God through our knowing him, and through his love being perfected in us! Surely that is about the highest reach of our fellowship with the Father and with his Son Jesus Christ.

And therefore, secondly, to know that we are thus in God cannot but be a matter of much concern. Who, on such a point, would run the risk of self-deception—nay, of being found "a liar, not having the truth in him"? To have some tolerable confidence, tolerably well grounded, that my being in God is a reality; that surely is desirable if it can be attained. And how am I to seek it? How am I at once to aim at being in him, more and more thoroughly and unequivocally, and also to aim at verifying more and more satisfactorily and surely my being in him? For these two aims must go together; they are one. Keep his word, is the reply. Is that then all? I may be tempted to ask. Am I to look for no clearer token, no more decisive mark and proof of my being in him? Is there to be no tangible evidence in my experience, no sign from heaven, no voice, no vision, no illapse or sliding into my soul, I know not how, of some sensible assurance, I know not what, to attest my being in him? Nay, to have such confirmation might only mislead me. I might content myself with the sign, instead of striving to realise more and more what it signifies. Better, safer, is it, that I should be directed to a humbler method, the keeping of his word. But is that enough? Yes; for in the keeping of his word his love is truly perfected in us who thereby know him.

Let us keep his word in that view of its power and virtue; as the seal and bond of a perfect understanding and a perfect state of peace between him and us. Let us cultivate what is the vital element of all intelligent and loving fellowship between him and us, the spirit which prompts the cry, "Speak, Lord, for thy servant heareth." In that spirit let us keep his commandments; the com mandments in which his word is broken up in detail; the commandments which assure us of his love to us; the commandments which exercise our love to him. Let us keep the commandments of his word; which, in our keeping of them, assure us of his love to us. " Ho, every one that thirsteth, come ye to the waters," " come now and let us reason together," " this is my beloved Son, hear him." Let us keep also the commandments of his word, which, in our keeping of them, exercise our love to him;— "Humble yourselves under the mighty hand of God," "risen with Christ, seek the things which are above," " come out and be separate, and touch not the unclean thing; and I will be a Father unto you, and ye shall be my sons and daughters." So keeping his word and his commandments, we more and more completely apprehend his love as truly perfected in us. We more and more clearly, brightly, hopefully, ascertain that we do know God and are in God, in some measure as he knows God and is in God, who while on earth could truly say, " The Father knoweth me, and I know the Father;" " Thou, Father, art in me, and I in thee."

8

THE CHRISTLIKE WALK OF ONE WITH GUILELESS SPIRIT ABIDING IN GOD

"He that saith he abideth in him [God], ought himself also so to walk even as he [Christ] walked." 1 John 2:6 (See foot-note, pp. *77, 78*.)

To " walk as Christ " walked is essential to our " abiding in God ; " not merely " being in God," as it is put in the previous verse, but being in him permanently ; continuing or abiding in him. It is therefore the test of our truth when we " say that we abide in God ; " it is the very means by which we abide in him. Jesus tells us (John xvi. 10, 11) that he continued or abode in the Father's love by keeping the Father's commandments. That was his walk, by which he abode in God. If we would abide in God as he did, we must walk as he walked, keeping the Father's commandments as he kept them. Thus this verse fits into those that go before, and completes, so far, the apostle's description of the divine fellowship, viewed as a fellowship of holy light, and transforming, obedient knowledge.

The walk of Christ, abiding in God, is therefore to be considered as our study and our model.

I. It is sometimes said of Christ simply that he walked, without anything to define or qualify the expression. ' After these thing Jesus walked in Galilee ; for he would not walk in Jewry, because the Jews sought to kill him " (John vii. 1). He says it of himself ; " Nevertheless I must walk to-day, and to-morrow, and the third day, for it cannot be that a prophet perish out of Jerusalem" (Luke xiii. 33). Again he says, "Are there not twelve hours in the day? If any man walk in the day he stumbleth not, because he seeth the light of this world. But if a man walk in the night he stumbleth, because there is no light in him" (John xii. 9, 10).

Jesus then walked. His life was a walk. The idea of earnestness, of definiteness of purpose, of decision and progress, is thus suggested. Many men live as if they were not really walking, but lounging and sauntering; or running fitfully and by starts, with intervals of aimless, listless sloth; or musing, or dreaming, or sleep-walking. Some are said to be fast-livers; their life being not a walk, but a brief tumultuous rush of excitement, ending soon in vacancy, or something worse. Others again live as if life were to be all, instead of a walk, a gay and giddy dance; alas! they may find it the dance of death. It is something to apprehend and feel that life is a walk; not a game, or pastime, or outburst of passion; not a random flight, or a groping, creeping, grovelling crawl, or a mazy labyrinthine puzzle; but a walk; a steady walk; an onward march and movement; a business-like, purpose-like, step-by-step advance in front; such a walk as a man girds himself for, and shoes himself for, and sets out upon with staff in hand, and firm-set face, and cap well fixed on the head, and holds on in, amid stormy wind and drifting snow; resolute to have it finished and to reach the goal. Such a walk is real life; life in earnest. Such a walk pre-eminently was the life of Jesus. No dilettante trifler was he; nor a visionary; nor a loiterer; nor a runner to and fro; nor a climber of cloud-capped heights; but a walker; a plain pedestrian walker; a determined walker, whom nothing could turn aside or turn back. It is said of him, on one occasion, that he "stedfastly set his face to go to Jerusalem." That was his way, his manner always. He walked. He stedfastly set his face to walk. On, still on, he walked, unflagging, unflinching; he walked right on. It is a sublime spectacle to gaze on; this Jesus, Son of God, Son of man, thus walking; in Galilee; in Jewry; his face stedfastly set to go to Jerusalem.

Now, "he that saith he abideth in God, ought himself also so to walk even as Jesus walked." It was as always "abiding in God" that he "walked." It was his abiding always in God that constrained him to walk; to be always walking. It was that which would not suffer him either to stand still or to make haste; either to pause and fall behind, or to run too fast before. He abode in God. He walked as one who was abiding in God all the while he walked. While his feet were busy walking, his soul was resting in God. Outward movement, inward repose;—the whole man Christ Jesus bent upon the road,—mind, spirit, heart, all bent upon the road;—and yet ever, at the same time, the whole man Christ Jesus dwelling in the Father's bosom,—mind, spirit, heart, all dwelling in the Father's bosom; as calmly, tranquilly, quietly, as in that unbroken eternity, ere he became man, he had been wont to dwell there;—so he walked, abiding in God.

So you also ought to walk even as he walked;—"abiding in God." Ah! this blessed combination! Outward movement, inward repose; the feet busy, active, alert—the soul resting in God; incessant marching up through the wilderness, amid fightings and fears, but always peace within, peace with God, peace in God; noise and uproar often to be encountered on the open way, but silence evermore in the hidden part, the deep holy silence of God's own secret place!

Oh! to walk as one abiding in God; abiding in him all the while we walk! Who can look at Jesus walking without feeling that it is the walk of one abiding in God ? He speaks of himself as "the Son of man which is in heaven" (John iii. 13);—not which was, but which is, in heaven. It is as the Son of man who is in heaven even when he is on earth that he tells of heavenly things. It is as the Son of man who is in heaven that he walks on earth. Hence his life is indeed a walk. His being, all the while he is walking on earth, himself in heaven; abiding in God; imparts that clear outlook and that calm confidence, without which there may be wandering up and down, but not real steady walking. Therefore he is neither as one blindly feeling his way, nor as one in doubt or in despair trying every or any path. He walks, "not as uncertainly,"—even as he fights, "not as one that beateth the air." He walks as one who has "the mastery." For he walks, abiding in God.

But some one may say, Is not this too high an ideal ? Is it not the setting up of an inimitable model ? Jesus, the Son of man, while walking on earth, is still in heaven, in a sense in which that cannot be said of any of us. His being still the eternal Son of the Highest as well as the son of Mary, may well be supposed to give him such divine insight and assurance as to make his life more like what life should be, a real walk, than ours can be expected to be.

Not so. For, first, he fully shares with us whatever disadvantage, as regards his walking, may be implied in his being a son of man. And, secondly, he would have us fully to share with him whatever advantage there is in his being the Son of God. For both reasons, our life may be as much and as truly a walk as his was.

First, it is a man whom we see walking ; one who is true and very man. His being God also gives him no exemption or immunity from any of those annoyances, or difficulties, or dangers, which might be apt to turn the walk into some sort of movement more irregular and less becoming. On the contrary, what he saw, and knew, and felt, as the Son of God, made these trials of his walk all the more formidable. He, in his walk, met with far more that was fitted to make his feet stumble and his courage fail, than any of us can ever meet with in ours. And as his divine knowledge gave him a clearer sight, so his divine holiness gave him a keener sense, of it all. If ever this great walker's firm step might totter, and his gait grow staggering, and his eye irresolute, it might well be when, with the full and vivid apprehension he had of their real meaning and awful horror, he found his walk lying through the wilderness of satanic temptation, the garden of overwhelming agony, the shame and curse of Calvary. Truly he was no privileged walker amid earth's dark scenes of misery and sin ; having for his own share to endure the contradiction of sinners against himself, and, before all was over, to taste the bitterness of death, with its cruellest sting, for the very men who cried out, "Crucify him, crucify him!" Think you not that it might have been easier for him to walk calmly and with composure if, when he was led as a lamb to the slaughter, it had been possible for him to be led blindfold ? No. There was no royal road for him to walk in. His walk was on the billows of the angry sea.

Then, secondly, if there is any advantage in the way of imparting firmness and fixedness to his walk in his being the Son of God, is he not sharing that advantage with us ? Is it his being in God, and abiding in God, as the Son in the Father's bosom, all the time he is walking here below, that makes his walk so admirable for its serene and settled heavenliness ? Does he keep that position to himself ? Does he not make it freely ours ? Is it not as abiding in God, even as he abides in God, that we are exhorted and expected to " walk even as he walked ?"

II. Let some particulars about this walk be noticed.

1. If we say that "we abide in God," we ought to walk as seeing God in all things and all things in God; for so Christ walked. Nothing is more conspicuous in the general bearing of his conduct, and in every detail, than his constant reference to God. "All things" to him "were of God" (2 Cor. v. 18). It was not that he so identified the world around him with God as to reckon devotion to the world equivalent to devotion to God; making the world's business God's worship. It was rather that, abiding in God, he so identified himself with God, that every object, every event, presented itself to him in its relation to God. What is it in God's point of view?—what does it mean as regards him?—what are its aspects towards him?—what is his estimate of it and his mind concerning it?—that is always the uppermost, the only question. And it is the same with persons as with things and circumstances. No man is known after the flesh (2 Cor. v. 16). The young man, with all his natural amiability and attractiveness, of whom it is said that "Jesus beholding him, loved him" (Mark x. 21), is yet not known after the flesh ; Jesus will know him only in God, in whom he himself abideth. Even though he has to let him go away sorrowful,—himself more sorrowful still for having to let one so lovable go away,—he will walk towards him as himself "abiding in God." Neither the youth's great possessions, nor his all but resistless winning qualities, will counterbalance in Christ's mind what is due to the paramount claims of God and his kingdom. His walk is still not manward at all, however strong the temptation to decline a little, a very little, in that direction, but Godward alone, Godward altogether. It is still always God and not man who is in all his thoughts. Is a woman who has been a sinner behind him, washing his feet with her tears?—or

before him alone, abashed, all her accusers having gone
out? Not a thought of what men may think or say is in
his mind; but only how his Father will feel, and what his
Father will have him to do. So he walked, abiding in
God. And "he that saith he abideth in God ought himself also so to walk."

2. He ought to walk as one subordinating himself
always in all things to God; submitting himself to God;
committing himself to God. Abiding in God, he ought to
walk as being himself nothing; God, in whom he abides,
being all in all. So Christ walked. He did not seek his
own glory, or do his own will, or find his own meat, or
save his own life, or plead his own cause, or avenge his own
wrong. Self is never a consideration with him, but always
God his Father, in whom he abides.

It is not that he is either a mad fanatic, prodigally
reckless of God's gift of life and of life's loving comforts;
or a mad enthusiast, dreaming of one knows not what
absorption of individual personality in some vast and vague
idea of the Godhead. He shared the joy of the marriage-
feast and the hospitality of the common meal. In the
home of Bethany he loved to be with Martha, and her
sister, and Lazarus. He was ever, as the Son, distinct
from the Father; and as the servant, subject to the
Father.

But abiding in God, he walked as having no mind of
his own, but only to know the mind of God, and to have it
done at whatever cost. It was not self-denial merely, and
self-sacrifice. It was the self-denying and self-sacrificing
surrender of himself to God. It was, "Lo, I come; in the
volume of the book it is written of me; I delight to do thy
will, O God" (Ps. xl. 7, 8; Heb. x. 7–10).

To walk in this respect as Christ walked, abiding in
God as he did, is indeed to be emptied of self. But it is

not that only. It is to be filled with God. It is to walk humbly, meekly, patiently, cheerfully;—"seeking not our own, not easily provoked, bearing all things, enduring all things;"—not as being insensible to pain and grief, or as if we affected the stoical pride of indifference to such things; but simply as "learning obedience," where Jesus learned it, in the school of suffering and submission.

3. "He that saith he abideth in God" ought to walk in love. If we abide in God, we abide in the great source and fountain of love : in the infinite ocean of pure and perfect benevolence.

It was thus that Jesus, "abiding in God," walked abroad among men; the very impersonation of benevolence; "a man approved of God, who went about doing good." His whole walk was one continuous manifestation of good will to men. And it was of the Father's good will to men that his walk was the manifestation; for he was ever abiding in God. No good will to men's principles and practices, while at enmity with God, did his walk manifest : no such good will as would have their principles and practices tolerated and indulged at the expense of the honour and the law of that God and Father in whom he was continually abiding. But good will to their persons, to themselves, —ah ! how intense, how unwearied, how inexhaustible,— was that walk of his incessantly exemplifying !

Can we say that we "abide in God" as Jesus did, if our walk is not what his was; a walk of active benevolence, practically proclaiming our Father's good will to men as our brethren ? Ah ! let us not forget to do good, to distribute, to be kind, to carry food to the hungry, healing to the sick, comfort to the sorrowful, hope to the sinful; to speak a word in season to the weary ; to visit the fatherless and widow in their affliction, while we keep ourselves unspotted from the world.

4. "He that saith he abideth in God ought," in a word, to walk in unity with God, as being of one mind with God, and of one heart. So Jesus walked. For with reference to his human walk on earth quite as much as to his divine nature, or his being in heaven, he could say "I and my Father are one." He had no separate interest from his Father; no separate occupation; no separate joy. Whatever touched the Father, equally and in the same way affected him. "The zeal of thine house," he cried, "hath eaten me up." He pleased not himself; but, "as it is written : The reproaches of them that reproached thee fell on me." This harmony of sentiment, this conscious unity of desire and aim between him and the Father who appointed his lot,—the result of his "abiding always in God,"—made his life a walk indeed. It was not a walk through pleasant places. It was no holiday excursion; no easy ramble. And yet the sense of a high and intimate community of motive, means, and end between him and the Father, which his abiding ever in God must have inspired, could scarcely fail to invest the scenery through which he passed, at its very wildest and darkest points, with a certain charm of divine majesty and awe; as well as also to impart to his soul, in passing through it, I say not equanimity only, but a measure also of deep and chastened joy.

For in fact, with all its trials and terrors, its agonies and griefs, I cannot imagine that even to the man of sorrows his walk through life was what could fairly be called unhappy. When the road led through Bethany's peaceful shades, and allowed a night's tarrying in the home he loved so well, the hallowed repose of that familiar friendly circle must have been very sweet to his taste; all the sweeter for the thought that, abiding in him who put so welcome an entertainment, so congenial a solace, in his way, he was not solitary in the enjoyment of it; the relish of it being common to the Father and to him. And even when in his walk he had to "tread the winepress alone;" yet not alone, for the Father was with him; when flesh and heart fainting would have moved him almost to put the cup away from him;—is it conceivable that, abiding in God, he could ever lose the apprehension of the unity of counsel between them in the great design for which he came into the world? It could not be with any other feeling than that of relief, of acquiescence, I will say of intensest satisfaction, that, overcoming in the Spirit the weakness of the flesh, he gave himself up to him in whom, in that dread hour, he was abiding, if it were possible, more closely, more intimately, more lovingly than ever;— " Father, thy will be done ; "—" Father, glorify thy name ;" —" Father, into thy hands I commend my spirit."

So he walked. And so it is our privilege to walk, abiding, by the power of the Spirit, in God as he did; saying always, " Not my will but thine be done."

" Who then is among you that feareth the Lord, and yet walketh in darkness, seeing no light? Let him trust in the name of the Lord, and stay himself upon his God " (Isaiah l. 10, 11). Walk on still, in darkness if it must be so, but abiding still in God. The darkness will not last for ever. " Weeping may endure for a night, but joy cometh in the morning." Walk still on, I say, abiding in God as he did, who, when his walk was as of one forsaken,—through the hell which your sins and mine deserved,—cried still: " My God, my God!" My God, I abide in thee! Though thou slay me, I will trust in thee.

Who says now, I abide in God? See that you really

walk as he walked, who alone is the perfect pattern and example of abiding in God. Ah! the notion of any other sort of abiding in God, or any other way of abiding in God, than his sort and his way of it, which his walk so fully verified, is wholly false and vain. You cannot hope to abide in God, and in God's love, otherwise than as he did;—by keeping his commandments.

I charge you, then, all of you, to keep the commandments of God; to walk in the way of his commandments; that you may have fellowship with him and he with you. That is the true apostolic fellowship—fellowship with the Father and with his Son Jesus Christ. I ask you, every one of you, how are you walking? How, and whither? Are you "walking after the course of this world?" Then I have to tell you,—or rather Paul tells you,—that you are really "walking after the prince of the power of the air, the spirit that now worketh in the children of disobedience." That is your fellowship, the fellowship of the devil, if that is your walk, after the course of this world. "And I would not that ye should have fellowship with devils." But walk in the light, as God is in the light, and have fellowship with him and he with you, the blood of Jesus Christ his Son cleansing you from all sin!

9

THE COMMANDMENT AT ONCE OLD AND NEW TO ONE WALKING WITH GUILELESS SPIRIT IN THE LIGHT — THE DARKNESS PASSING — THE TRUE LIGHT SHINING

"Brethren, I write no new commandment unto you, but an old commandment, which ye had from the beginning : the old commandment is the word which ye have heard from the beginning. Again, a new commandment I write unto you, which thing is true in him and in you ; because the darkness is past, and the true light now shineth." 1 John 2:7,8

WHAT commandment does John mean ? Is it the same commandment throughout ? If so, in what sense is it at once old and new ?

Some will have it to be the commandment of brotherly love, introduced at the ninth verse. There is an awkwardness, however, in thus making these two verses describe a commandment not yet mentioned. It is an unnatural mode of writing. And it is unlike the apostle's usual simplicity, to be as it were sounding a trumpet of preparation for the precept which he so commends, with a sort of rhetorical paradox about its being not new but old, and yet again new, and all this before the precept itself is indicated. And the last clause of the seventh verse seems conclusive against that view. The apostle tells what the commandment is. It is " the word which ye have heard from the beginning." Surely this may best be understood as referring back to the word of life (i. 1), which the apostle says he and his fellow-apostles had from the beginning heard and seen and handled, and which, he adds, we declare unto you. Is not that what he means here by "the word which ye have heard"?

It is not new but old, as old as the first preaching of the gospel. I am no setter-forth of novelties or strange doctrines. What I write (1.) concerning the fellowship of light and joy with the Father and the Son into which your believing knowledge of the word, through the teaching of the Spirit, introduces you; (2.) concerning the indispensable condition of that fellowship, your walking in the light as he is in the light; (3.) concerning the sacrifice and advocacy of Jesus Christ, as meeting that sense of sin and shortcoming which otherwise must be ever fatally dimming the light, and marring the joy, of the fellowship; and (4.) concerning the obligation of a sinless aim, an obedient heart, a Christlike walk, if you would really know God, and have his love perfected in you, and be in him;—all that, which I am writing to you, is old. It is no new discovery, no new despatch from heaven. It is "an old commandment, which ye had from the beginning."

But what of the intimation that follows,—"a new commandment I write unto you"? It is not merely a thrice-told tale that I am writing to you about. There is something fresh and new about it. And what is that?

It is the realising of this fact, or this thing, as true, first in Christ and then in yourselves, that "the darkness is past," or is passing, "and the true light is now shining."

For so this clause really runs. It is not a reason for the thing which is true; it is the very thing itself;—"which thing is true, in him and in you; this, namely, that the darkness is past, or is passing, and the true light now shineth."

This is what constitutes the newness of the old commandment. It is a new thing to have this fact becoming matter of consciousness;—the fact of its being true, in Christ and in you, that the darkness is passing and the true light is now shining. The obligation to make this good is emphatically a new commandment. It commands, or commends, what must ever be felt to be a novelty.

Thus viewed, this new commandment may bring out a singularly close parallelism or identity between Christ and all who, abiding in God, walk as Christ walked.

I. In Christ personally this is true, "that the darkness is passing and the true light is shining." In so far as this is a continuous process, or progressive experience, it is true of Christ only as he walked on earth. Look at him, then, in his human life.

A new commandment is given to him, a new charge or commission from above. Something new is given to him to be learned as a message or lesson. It is the message or lesson of its being true in him that the darkness passeth, and the true light now shineth. He is placed in new circumstances. He is plunged into the very thickest of the fight that is evermore waged here below between the two. On the one hand, darkness—the darkness that is opposed to the light which God is, and in which God is, the light which is at once his nature and his dwelling-place,—that darkness is no stranger to him ; he no stranger to it. Neither outwardly in his history, nor inwardly in his inmost soul, is he a stranger to it or it to him. Darkness is upon him, around him, in him ; the darkness of the sin with which he comes in contact, the sin which, in its criminality and curse, he makes his own. But, on the other hand, the true light is ever shining upon him, around him, in him ; the light of the Father's loving eye bent upon his suffering Son ; the light of his own single eye ever bent upon the Father's glory. In him this darkness and this light are incessantly meeting; present always, both of them, vividly present to his consciousness; felt to be real, intensely real;—the darkness, however, always as passing; the true light always as now shining.

For this is the peculiarity of the position. The darkness is on its way to the oblivion in which all the past lies buried, because there is now true light shining. It is no longer a doubtful struggle, or one that might issue in a drawn battle. The seed of the woman is bruising the head of the serpent. The true light now shining is causing the darkness to pass. So Jesus perseveres. Otherwise he must have given way. In him, even when in his experience and to his agonised consciousness, the darkness is deepest, it is still a darkness which is passing, and is realised as passing. In him, even then, the true light is shining. It is a present shining; it is the true light shining now. It is not merely that there might be in him, amid the darkness, some memory of the true light shining once, of old, from everlasting; or some anticipation of its shining again soon, to everlasting. But the true light is shining in him now; the light of conscious victory over the passing darkness. Therefore "for the joy that was set before him he endured the cross."

II. What is true in him should be true in us, and should be realised by us as true in us as in him. That is the apostle's new commandment. For we enter into the position of him in whom, in the first instance, that is true. The commandment to us is to enter into his position. And it is a new position. It is new to every one with whom the commandment finds acceptance, and in whom it takes effect. It is a new thing for me, in compliance with this commandment, to apprehend it to be true, in Christ and in me,—in me as in Christ,—that the darkness is evanescent, vanishing, passing, and that the true light is now shining. Nay more, it is a new thing for me every moment. Not once for all, but by a constant series of believing acts and exercises of appropriation, I recognise it as true in him and in me, that the darkness is passing and the true light is now shining.

1. "The darkness is passing." Is it so with me, to me, in me? Then all that pertains to the darkness, all that is allied to it, is passing too. It is all like a term in course of being worked out in an algebraic question; a vanishing quantity; a fading colour. Is it thus that I practically regard the whole kingdom of darkness, and all the works of darkness, and all the terrors of darkness; the power of darkness; the darkness of this world and the rulers of it?

Plainly there is here a thoroughly practical test. What is the darkness to me as regards my relation to it and my esteem of it? Or the things of darkness—what are they? I know well enough what the darkness, in this use of the word, means; what it is. It means, it is, the shutting out of God. For darkness is the absence of light. But God is light. This darkness therefore is the absence of God, the shutting out of God. In whatever place or scene or company God is shut out there is darkness. Whatever work or way God is shut out from, that is a work or way of darkness. Whoever shuts out God from his thoughts is a child of darkness. Now I come into contact with this darkness on every hand, at every point. Places, scenes, companies, from which God is shut out; works and ways from which God is shut out; people from whose minds and hearts God is shut out;—I am in the midst of them all; they press upon me; I cannot get rid of them. Tempting, flattering, cajoling; or trying, threatening, persecuting; they are on me like the Philistines on Samson. Worse than that, they are in me, as having only too good auxiliaries in my own sinful bosom. How do I regard them? Do I cleave to them, to any of them? Would I have them to abide, at least a little longer? Would it pain me to part with them and let them pass? Or is it this very feature about them all that they are passing,—that the darkness which owns them all is passing,—that I fasten upon for relief and comfort? Is it that which alone reconciles me to my being still obliged for a season to tolerate and have dealings with the darkness?

For dealings with this darkness I cannot but have. I have to go down into its depths to rescue, if it may be, its victims. And I have to resist its solicitations when its ministers come to me disguised as angels of light. My soul, like the righteous soul of Lot, must be vexed with the evil conversation and ungodly deeds that the darkness covers in Sodom. I have to stand its assaults; and when reviled, revile not again. So this darkness, this shutting out of God, with its manifold influences and agencies, besets me. How do I feel towards it? Have I still some sympathy with it in some of its less offensive aspects? Am I still inclined to make terms with it, so as to disarm its hostility, and even taste, in some safe manner and degree, its friendship? Would its instant and thorough disappearance from before me,—would my instant and thorough removal from beside it,—be altogether welcome? Would I have it stay with me or pass from me? Is the darkness of this world, with its pursuits and pleasures and amusements, its seductions, its associations, its customs and fellowships,—in which God is not, and therefore light is not,—is it a lingering friend to me, or a departing stranger, a retreating foe?

"The darkness is passing." Is that true in me, as in Christ, with reference not merely to the darkness of this world that has such a hold on me, but also and chiefly to the darkness of my own shutting out of God; the darkness of my shutting out of God from my own conscious guilt and

cherished sin ? That is darkness indeed. Is it passing ?
Am I glad of its passing ? Or am I somehow, and
in some measure, loving it still ?—so loving it that I
would not have it altogether or all at once pass ? Say
that my sin is finding me out ;—the sin, generally, of
my state and character before God, or some particular sin.
Say that I am falling away from my first love, or coming
again under the dominion of some form of evil ;—that, in
some particular matter, my heart is not right with God.
So far as that matter is concerned, I would shut out God.
I would put in something between him and me ; some
excuse ; some palliating circumstance ; some countervailing
aspect of goodness ; some plea of self-justification of some
sort. That is the darkness which, in such a case, I naturally
love. And I feel myself drawn to love it, even in spite of
my experience of the more excellent way of guilelessness
on my part towards God, and grace on God's part towards
me. But is it passing—this darkness ? Is it passing with
my own consent ? Do I make it free and right welcome to
pass ? Or do I cleave to it as if I would still have a little
of it to abide with me ? Ah ! this darkness, this shutting
out of God ! How apt am I, if not to ask it, at least to
suffer it, to return and remain. " Search me, O God, and
know my heart ; try me, and know my thoughts ; and see
if there be any wicked way in me, and lead me in the
way everlasting."

" The darkness is passing." Is this my stay, my hope,
my joy in the hour of its fiercest power ? When it gathers
thickest and falls heaviest, hiding God's face from me ;
when all about me and in me is so dark that I cannot see
my signs ; when a sense of guilt sinks me as in a dark pit,
and " the sorrows of death compass me, and the pains of
hell get hold upon me, and I find trouble and sorrow ; "—let
me fasten on this " thing which is true in Christ and in me,

that the darkness is passing." I am suffering with Christ, undergoing a kind of crucifixion with him. To me, as to him,—to me conscious of sin, my own and not another's,—the cup of wrath is presented. On me, as on him, the awful blackness of that day of doom settles down. To me, as to him, sin is indeed exceeding sinful ; and the death, which is its wages, terrible. Sold under sin, I am consciously, with a keen and nervous sensitiveness of conscience, dying that death. My faith is failing. Unbelief all but has the mastery. But a new commandment is given me, and a new power, at the critical moment, to realise it as a thing true in Christ, and therefore true in me, that this darkness is passing. In him it is true only through his draining the cup of wrath, dying the accursed death for me. O my soul, bless thou the Lord, that it is already and most graciously true in thee, because so terribly true in him, that, without cost to thee, though with infinite cost to him, this great darkness passes away for ever !

2. " The true light is now shining." This " thing also is true in Christ and in you ; " in you as in Christ ; in you because in Christ. And it is to be apprehended and felt as true now. The true light now shineth. It is not said that this true light is to shine hereafter. This is not represented as a benefit to be got, or as a reward to be reached, after the darkness shall have passed. It is a present privilege or possession,—a thing which is true in Christ and in you,—that all the time the darkness is passing the true light is shining. " Arise, shine ; for thy light is come, and the glory of the Lord is risen upon thee." That is the gospel call to the Church and to every member of it. It is true, as a great fact, in you as in Christ, that the true light now shineth. Its present shining is in you, as truly as in him, a blessed reality.

For this true light now shining, which is a true thing

in you as in Christ, is simply what Christ found it to be ; God's loving eye upon you, and your single eye towards God. That is the true light now shining. And the fact of its now shining while the darkness is passing, is the thing which is to be recognised as true, in you as in Christ.

That is the "new commandment ;" a commandment always new ; conveying in its bosom an ever-fresh experience, pregnant with ever-fresh experimental discoveries of him who is light, and who dwells in light. Only act up to this commandment; be ever acting up to it more and more. Enter into the spirit of it, and follow it out to its fair and full issues. The newness of it, its constant novelty, will be more and more apparent, or at least more and more felt and relished. A loving Father's eye ever fixed upon you, and a filial eye in you ever fixed upon him ;—that, I repeat, is the true light now shining in you as in Christ. It is not outward revelation only ; it is inward illumination as well. It is the Spirit that dwelt in Christ dwelling also in you ; shedding abroad in your hearts the love of God, and calling forth the simple response of obedient love in return. Let no child of God say that this shining of the true light must be reserved for the future. The true light shineth in him as in Christ now. The new commandment concerning it is in force now. It is a great fact, a thing which is true in Christ,—not in Christ considered as glorified, but in Christ humbling himself, in Christ walking, in Christ crucified,— that not only is the darkness passing, but the true light is now shining. It is, it should be, it must be, it shall be, a great fact, a thing that is true, in you also. Is it not so ? Why should it not be so ? Is not that great, open eye of your Father in heaven continually beholding you ? Yes ! Even when in a little wrath he hides his face from you, even when he smites you with the rod, are you not under that benignant eye ? And on your part, through grace, may not this voice be ever going upwards to the throne of grace? "Behold, as the eyes of servants look unto the hand of their masters, and as the eyes of a maiden unto the hand of her mistress; so our eyes wait upon the Lord our God, until that he have mercy upon us" (Ps. cxxiii. 2).

Thus it is "true in him and in you, that the darkness is passing, and the true light shineth." And it is ever a new oracle of divine grace. It will always be so to the pilgrim on his way through the dark wilderness to divinely lighted Canaan. It will always be so, at every step, to you who, abiding in God, walk even as Christ also walked. When faint and weary because of the way, tempted almost to give up, and to give in, as if your striving against sin were all in vain, and your endurance of the contradiction of sinners against yourself more than flesh and blood can stand, call to mind this word—"Which thing is true in him and in you, that the darkness is passing, and the true light now shineth." It is a new word to you then, a new assurance, a new appeal. It dissipates the gloom that is enshrouding all things to your view. "Lo! they are all new in the true light that is shining. Whenever the old shadows are flinging themselves again across your path, the old misgivings and questionings, the old doubts and fears, the old partial dealings with God's promises in the word of his gospel, the old hesitancies about the freeness of his grace, and the sufficiency of his great salvation, and your title to believe in the forgiveness of your sins; call to mind this word: "Which thing is true in him and in you, that the darkness is passing, and the true light now shineth." It rings as a new Jubilee trumpet. It breathes new life into you. For "in that day thou shalt say, O Lord, I will praise thee: though thou wast angry with me, thine anger is turned away, and thou comfortedst me. Behold, God is my salvation; I will trust, and not be afraid: for the Lord

Jehovah is my strength and my song : he also is become
my salvation." Are old frames coming back upon me :
old ways of thinking and feeling about the service of God,
and the troubles of life, and the terrors of death ; the old
ideas as to God being an hard master, and his commandments being grievous ; the old spirit of bondage, the old
servile grudging, the old rebelliousness, that makes duty
irksome, and self-denial hard, and labour thankless, and the
whole doing of God's will a dull routine or dreary task ?
Let me call to mind this word : "Which thing is true in
him and in you, that the darkness is passing, and the true
light now shineth." Is it not a new and spirit-stirring
summons to me ? Is it not a new gospel to me ? Is it not
a new quickening, a new awakening ? Is it not a new
prayer that it prompts ?—"Create in me a clean heart, O
Lord ; and renew a right spirit within me."

And now, connecting the two verses which we have been
considering separately, we may see how John, being "a
scribe instructed unto the kingdom of heaven," is "like
unto a man that is an householder, which bringeth forth
out of his treasury things new and old." He probably had
in his view a class of men, not uncommon in his day, who
thirsted for novelties, if not in the doctrines of the gospel
themselves, at least in the way of setting them forth ; upon
whom the primitive simplicity that is in Christ was beginning to pall ; by whom the commonplace preaching of the
cross was felt almost to have become effete, and to have
lost its stimulating power. John will not pander to such
a taste. He has been discoursing about high matters ; but
he is careful to assure his readers that they are not the sort
of novelties for which some have a craving. There is
nothing really new in his teaching. It is the old word
which has been heard from the beginning ; the same word

that " Paul and Apollos and Cephas " proclaimed ; the same word that John has been always reiterating. But if any will have novelty, here is a safe receipt for it. Let them make the old word new in their own experience by the ever-fresh practical application of it, in the ever-fresh practical apprehension of the " thing which is true in Christ and in them, that the darkness is passing, and the true light now shineth." For though doctrinal Christianity is always old, experimental Christianity is always new. The gospel preached to us is old ; but the gospel realised in us is always new. Christ set forth before our eyes is always old ; but " Christ in us the hope of glory,"—" Christ dwelling in our hearts by faith,"—Christ becoming more and more, through the Spirit's teaching, part and parcel of our whole inner man—This Christ is always new.

10

BROTHERLY LOVE A TEST AND MEANS OF BEING AND ABIDING, WITH GUILELESS SPIRIT, IN THE LIGHT, INSTEAD OF WALKING IN DARKNESS

" He that saith he is in the light, and hateth his brother, is in darkness
even until now. He that loveth his brother abideth in the light,
and there is none occasion of stumbling in him : but he that hateth
his brother is in darkness, and walketh in darkness, and knoweth
not whither he goeth, because that darkness hath blinded his eyes."
1 John 2:9-11

" HE that saith he is in the light" is one who professes to
obey the "new commandment;" to realise in himself, personally, the new position or state of things implied in its
being "true in Christ and in him,"—in him as in Christ,—
"that the darkness is passing and the true light is now
shining." He says he is in the light which is now shining
and chasing the darkness away. But he hateth his brother ;
one who says the same thing ; one in whom, as in Christ
and in him, the same thing is true. He refuses to recognise him as a brother, or to regard him with brotherly love.
And that is enough to prove that he cannot really be himself one of those in whom, as in Christ, "this thing is true,
that the darkness is passing and the true light is now
shining."

On the other hand, "he that loveth his brother,"—he
that loves as his brother one in whom, as in Christ and in
himself, "this thing is true, that the darkness is passing
and the true light is now shining,"—not only shows
thereby that he speaks truth when he says he is in the

light, but takes, moreover, the most effectual means for securing his continuing in the light; so abiding in the light that there shall be in him nothing to occasion stumbling.

But let him be warned. If he is destitute of this brotherly love, he cannot be in the light, the true light which is now shining. He is in darkness; the darkness which, in all that are Christ's, as in Christ himself, is passing. And according to the darkness in which he is, must his walk be. It cannot be the walk of one in whom there is no occasion of stumbling. It must be the walk of one who is darkly groping his way, not knowing whither he is going. Nor is this his misfortune; it is his fault. There is light enough, but he refuses to see it; he allows the darkness to blind his eyes.

This cursory analysis of these verses may suggest for consideration the following particulars respecting brotherly love :—I. Its nature as being a brotherhood of light; II. The reasonableness of its being made a test of being in the light; and III. The fitness of its continued exercise to ensure continued abiding in the light.

I. Brotherly love consists in this, that they in whom, as in Christ, this thing is true, that the darkness is passing and the true light is shining, recognise one another as, in that character, and on that account, brethren. That is the first aspect of brotherly love suggested in this Epistle.

Look again, in this connection, at " this thing which is true."

See the vast cauldron or wide ocean of darkness; restless, tumultuous, angry. It is the chaos of moral evil; the wild anarchy of ungodliness; in which, God being shut out, spirits made in his image " wander up and down for meat, and grudge if they are not satisfied" (Ps. lix. 15). Into this darkness, into the thick of it, one plunges himself, who has no affinity with it, and over whom it has no power. But he is in it; acquainting himself with all its terrors and sounding its utmost depths. He ransacks the chambers of the darkness. Its powers and principalities he defies; its works and ways, its poor expedients of relief, its miserable comforters, its refuges of lies, he remorselessly lays bare. But more than that he does. He marches straight up to the fountain-head of the horrid stream that has made so vast a desolation. That shutting out of God, which is the real blackness of this darkness, he deals with. To make reconciliation, to make peace, he takes upon himself my dark death, in order that the Holy Ghost, the Spirit of life and light, may quicken and gladden me in him.

Yes! the darkness is upon him. Its death is upon him; the death in which there is sin's dark sting and God's dark curse.

But it is passing; and already the true light is shining. The eclipse is over; and lo! a bright cloud! a glorious Shechinah! The righteous God glorified! The loving Father well pleased! The Son himself,—yet not for himself, but as "seeing his seed,"—rejoicing and giving thanks!

Now it is with us as with Christ, when in us, as in Christ, "this thing is true, that the darkness is passing, and the true light is shining."

For, first, in Christ, our position with reference to that darkness is changed from what it naturally is. It is reversed. The terrible flood is not now carrying us away; we stem it holding him—he holding us. We see it passing.

Yesterday it was hurrying me along in its strong deep tide, to what ocean I knew not, and scarcely cared, or did not venture, to ask. Shutting my eyes, I was content to follow the stream. Or if at times some rude shock or some eddying whirl gave me pause, and a momentary alarm seized me as I saw signs of wreck and ruin on every side, I could but catch convulsively some frail stem or slippery rock; or desperately toss and struggle like some "strong swimmer in his agony."

Now all is changed. By grace in Christ, I am in a new way. My head is turned up the stream, and against it.

At first it is a fearful struggle. What waves and billows go over me. No breath, no life is in me. I am lost, I perish!

But lo! Christ is with me; he who "liveth and was dead, and is alive for evermore." He grasps me, and I grasp him. Together we rise, through such a death as I never thought I could survive, to such a life as—how shall I describe it? How but in inspired words, "Eye hath not seen, nor ear heard, neither have entered into the heart of man, the things which God hath prepared for them that love him."

"The things which God hath prepared for them that love him?" Yes! For they are prepared in order to their being presently realised. "The true light now shineth." As my head is raised, leaning on his shoulder and his bosom; as my feet begin to touch the rock on which, though fierce floods may still try to drown me, my goings are to be established; as I feebly open my heavy eyes in the upper atmosphere I am now beginning to breathe; what bright warm beam is that which lightens up the face of him in whose arms I am, and lightens up my heart as I look and gaze on him, and cling and grow to him! It is the Father loving me as he loveth him. It is "the darkness passing and the true light now shining."

Then, as the first confused and rapturous joy of my own narrow escape becomes collected and calm, I look around. And I see him—for he multiplies himself and is everywhere— I see him doing the same kind office to one, and another, and another still, that he is doing to me. Here, close beside me,—there, a little farther off,—is a man like myself, in whom as in me ;—because in his Lord and mine ;—"the darkness is passing and the true light is shining." I look still, and my sight grows clearer as the light grows brighter. Here and there, all over, the surface of the dark ocean-stream is studded with miracles of saving mercy, as stupendous as I am myself ; I, the chief of sinners, saved by special and as it were chiefest grace. At first I feel as if all around were still thick impenetrable gloom ; and I alone were in the fond embrace of one who " loved me, and gave himself for me." But he tells me that he has others ; and I see that he has. I see him embracing them because he loved them, and gave himself for them. Shall I not hail them as my brethren ? Can I hate, or refuse to love, one who is my brother on such a footing as that ? Can any cause of coldness or estrangement have more power than the tie that should thus unite ?

II. Hence it is that the existence of this brotherly love is a fitting test of our being " in the light." At all events, the absence of it is conclusive proof that we are not.

For, consider what this hating, or not loving, our brother is ; and what it involves.

Here is one who but yesterday was, as we once were, carried helplessly on in the darkness that, as it passes, sweeps so many to destruction. But he has been arrested, and has got a' footing. In his experience " the darkness is passing," but he is not now himself passing along with it. He stands against it and stems it. His head being raised above it, catches the cheering beams of heaven's light. And yet we who say that this is exactly our case, as we admit it to be his, hate that man ; look coldly or cruelly on him ; refuse to count him a brother !

I do not ask if this is consistent. The question is

rather—Is it possible? The apostle says it is not. But why not?

It does not always follow that experience of a common danger and a common deliverance makes men brothers. Perhaps it should; where it does not, there is probably something wrong. The bitterest enemies, rescued in their strife from Niagara's Falls, will scarcely have the heart or the hardihood instantly to renew the fight. If they do, all around will cry shame on them. But there is really nothing in what they have undergone together that has any power, in its own nature, to alter their relations to one another, or their feelings towards one another. They are the same men that they were before; and no one has made peace between them. Here, however, there is a peacemaker. First, I find myself individually and personally embraced by him, lifted up by him out of the darkness of my deep estrangement from God, into the light of God's reconciled countenance; the light of the love of his Father and my Father, his God and my God. Next, I see him dealing with you, my late companion in the darkness,—my late antagonist, if you will, in some of the darkness's deadly strifes,—exactly as he deals with me. I see him embracing you as he embraces me; lifting you up, as he lifts me, out of the same dark dread and dislike of God into the same light of his love. Do I love him who has me in his arms; keeping me so that it continues to be ever "true in him and in me that the darkness is passing, and the true light is shining?" And do I still hate you whom he has in his arms as he has me, and whom he keeps out of the darkness and in the light as he keeps me? It cannot be. I can no more hate you than I can hate him. I may say that I am in the light; but if I hate you who also are in the light, I am "in darkness even until now."

Light is in itself—in its very nature and bare shining—
a great extinguisher of hatred; especially of hatred among
those who should be brethren. It is in the darkness that
mistakes occur, and misunderstandings arise. It is in the
darkness that injuries are brooded over, and angry passions
nursed. If you, brother, and I, are at variance, it is almost
certain to be because there is some darkness about us that
hinders us from seeing one another clearly. Hence we
imagine evil of one another, and impute evil to one another.
Let in the light. Let us see one another clearly. Differ-
ences between us may still remain; our views of many
things may be wide as the poles asunder. But we see that
we are men of like passions and like affections with one another. The light shows us that we are true brethren in
spite of all.

The light here is the light which God is (i. 5), the light
in which God is (i. 7). It is the light which is at once his
nature and his dwelling-place.

First, the light is the divine nature; "God is light."
If I am in the light, I am a partaker of the divine nature;
my moral nature becomes the same with that of God. This
identity is very specially realised in the department of the
affections, in the region of the heart. I cannot be in the
light—meaning by the light the nature of God, or what
God is—without my heart being like his. To be in the
light is to be in a high sense Godlike in our preferences, as
Christ showed himself Godlike in his preferences when he
was here. We know what his preferences were; they were
the same as his Father's. Could it have been said truly of
him that he was in the light, if they had been otherwise?
Can I say truly that I am in the light if mine are otherwise?
What then are my preferences? Whom do I prefer and
choose? Is it they whom Christ would have preferred and

chosen ? Is it they whom his Father and mine prefers and chooses ? Are the same persons, and the same qualities in persons, likeable and lovely to me that would have been likeable and lovely to Christ,—that are likeable and lovely to God ? If not, let me beware lest, though I say I am in the light, I may be in darkness even until now.

Again, secondly, the light is God's dwelling-place; "God is in the light." If therefore I am in the light, then I have the same medium of vision, as well as the same nature, with God. Objects appear to me as they appear to God. And so also do persons. This world's darkness obscures features and confounds distinctions. The "ruler of its darkness," the "prince of the power of its air," makes that air of such a dense thickness and of such an artificial hue, that men and things look different from what they are : softened, shaded, subdued ; or else distorted and discoloured. If I am in the light, that darkness is passing. I am as Christ was, in whom, even when he was in the midst of that darkness, it was passing, and the true light was shining, showing him men and things in the light in which his Father sees them. Is it so with me ? Does that poor God-fearing man appear to me as he would have appeared to Christ, as he appears to God ? Do I look at the same things in him that Christ and his Father look at ? Do I fasten upon the same characteristics of the man that Christ, if he were in my place, would fasten upon, that his Father and mine is fastening upon ? Do the same qualities or adjuncts of the man bulk in my eyes that bulk in theirs ? His rags, his unwashed limbs, his sores, as I see him lying a beggar at the rich man's door ; or his ungainly aspect and uncouth manners, as he, a clownish rustic, meets me in my dainty path ; things in him and about him that are repulsive or annoying ; causes of irritation and offence, for which, right or wrong, I hold him responsible : these I dwell on, and single out for contemplation, and magnify and exaggerate. Counterbalancing excellencies, redeeming virtues ; graces flourishing in circumstances in which mine would languish ; exercises of patience, meekness, self-denial, charity, that might put all my easy goodness to shame ; escape my notice. They are overlooked, or perhaps disparaged and depreciated. These things ought not so to be. They would not be so with him who is the light of men, if he were in my place. They cannot be so with me, if I am really abiding in the light.

III. The exercise of brotherly love is fitted to be the means of our continuing in the light, so as to avoid the risk of falling (ver. 10). Two benefits are here.

First, positively, by means of brotherly love we abide in the light. The law of action and reaction is here very noticeable. Being in the light begets brotherly love, and brotherly love secures abiding in the light. For this brotherly love is simply love to the true light, as I see it shining in my brother as it shines in Christ. And such love to the true light, wherever and in whomsoever it is seen shining as it shines in Christ, must needs cause me to grow up more and more into the true light myself; to grow up into Christ, and God in Christ.

There is a well-known principle in ethics that may furnish an illustration here. It is that of sympathy ; according to which it is found that our moral instincts, judgments, and emotions, are largely developed by our putting ourselves in our neighbour's place, so as to see with his eye and feel with his heart. It is a most wholesome corrective of our sentiments on all questions of duty that is thus obtained. But it is more. It is a stimulus and incentive impulse also. If I wrap myself up in myself, becoming a sort of isolated being, bent chiefly or exclusively on the preservation of my own virtue and the cultivation of my own character; my sense of obligation, however sound and alert originally, will be apt to get warped or to grow torpid. Keeping thus aloof from my fellows—self-studious, self-contained,—not only is my conscience towards man dwarfed and dimmed, but my conscience also towards God. I am by no means so sensitively alive to what he claims and what I owe, as when, even in imagination, I associate with myself a brother, and make his mind and soul, as well as my own, my standing-point.

Within the domain of spiritual light and love, a similar fact is to be noted; a similar law or principle holds good. A selfish religionist is sure to become either morbid or stupid. It is by sympathy and brotherhood that the fire of personal Christianity is fanned. For one thing, it is always refreshing to see how the gospel works in others after it has been working, say for years, in us. To observe the process of fresh conversion or quickening, simply as a spectacle,—to watch it as an experiment,—is both interesting and edifying.

We look on, in a time of general and remarkable awakening. We read or listen to the details of some well-marked missionary movements. Here are new and fresh specimens of people born of the Spirit; men and women created anew in Christ Jesus the Lord. Surely it is good for us to have such specimens presented to us; especially if at any time we have been beginning to lapse into a low and languid apprehension of what living Christianity is, and almost to forget the power of a first sense of sin, and a first sight of Christ;—a first prayer and a first love. And here brotherly love is all in all. Without it, the brightest and most vivid displays of grace, passing before our very eyes, will be all in vain. If we coldly gaze, or curiously inquire,—to criticise, to speculate, to theorise or syste-

matise ; we simply become frozen up in our apathy more
and more. Let it be assumed, however, that where God's
work is hopefully going on, there our heart is ; that it is
there, as a brother's heart, in full brotherly sympathy with
all who are engaged in it, and with all whom they are
instrumental in saving ;—that our fraternal fellow-feeling
goes along with the evangelist, even in that warmth and
enthusiastic zeal which may occasionally transgress the
bounds of prudence or of etiquette ;—and that the young
converts and newly-enlisted recruits, even in the extremes
of their grief and joy, touch a chord within us that awakens
the melody of heaven's home. In a word, let brotherly
love be in exercise where brethren are seeking brethren, in
the Lord, from among the crowd of the ungodly in the
world. Let a lively interest be felt. Let reports be
earnestly pondered. Let individual cases be made the
subjects of special prayer, and let individual souls be embraced as old familiar faces. We catch the contagion of
the excitement into the midst of which we throw ourselves. We get a new and fresh idea of what the Spirit's
movement is. The light in which these apostles and disciples of a new Pentecost dwell becomes the light in
which we also dwell. Its " clear shining after rain " dis-
pels a world of mists and vapours in our otherwise too still
and stagnant firmament. Our abiding in the light is
thus more vividly realised, the more our brotherly love is
exercised.

It is so, even when from necessity we are listeners and
spectators merely. Many a disabled child of God, lying
wakeful upon his bed in the night season, feels himself to
be all the more sensibly, consciously, rejoicingly, abiding
in the light, for the brotherly thought and brotherly
prayer he sends far across the ocean ;—to yonder missionary with burning lips, preaching Jesus to some stricken

soul,—or to some saved sinner, full of a newly-found Saviour, and shouting aloud for joy.

Much more may this be the effect when we are permitted personally to take part, as fellow-workers and fellow-helpers with the Son, in what he is doing on the earth for the scattering of hell's darkness and the spreading of heaven's light. My own soul prospers as I care for the souls of others. My abiding in the light myself is more and more to me a matter of actual joyous experience and assurance, for every brother into whose being in the light and abiding in the light I, as a brother, enter. It is as if his abiding in the light were added to mine. I appropriate his soul-exercise and make it mine. All different ways of abiding in the light may thus become mine, and I may have the good of them all. How wide and potent is the spell which my brotherly love may thus wield! It lays its hand on the dead; and I have brotherhood with Paul, and John, and Peter; and a whole host of worthies; and a dear cherished friend or two, but yesterday called home. They all abode in the light; in them all the true light shone, as in Christ. But no one of them was in this exactly as any other. They are all, however, available to enhance and intensify my abiding in the light. The sympathy of brotherly love gives me an insight into all their frames, and a fellowship with them in all their feelings. But "the living, the living, they praise God!" Let my brotherly love carry me out to living Christians, and lay me alongside of them, and win for me entrance into their hearts. Let me share their abiding in the light as they may share mine. Let me be helpful to my brother as regards his abiding in the light. Let me, with a brother's tender hand, remove whatever trouble or sorrow or want may interfere with the bright clearness of the light in which he abides. Let me, with a brother's

wise affection, win him more and more into the light's
meridian glory. Let me do him all brotherly offices by
which his abiding in the light may become less embar-
rassed and more free and joyous. The whole good is mine
as much as his. Thus "he that loveth his brother abideth
in the light." This is a positive benefit to himself. And
it implies another benefit.

For, secondly, "there is none occasion of stumbling
in him." This is a negative advantage; but it is great.
Its greatness will appear if we consider the case of him who
is described as wanting it. " He that hateth his brother is
in darkness, and walketh in darkness, and knoweth not
whither he goeth, because that darkness hath blinded his
eyes" (ver. 11).

The case put must be viewed as that of one who is so
far in earnest as to be really aiming heavenward. He
may be even a most painstaking seeker of the heavenward
way, and a plodding walker in whatever way he takes to
be it. Such was many a Pharisee, like Paul in his days of
elaborate self-righteousness. Such was many a Gnostic, or
knowing one, among those whom John, I doubt not, had in his
view when he was writing this verse. Take a devotee of that
sort, engrossed in some self-purifying and self-perfecting
spiritual discipline. "He hateth his brother." That means,
in John's phraseology, he is destitute of brotherly love. He
has no warm brotherly sympathy with other believers. He
may have no positive ill-will to any man; on the contrary,
in a sort of vague and general way he may think he wishes
all men well. But he has no special affection for godly
men as such, for children of the light. He is taken up
with the care of his own soul, and his preparation for
serving and enjoying God now and afterwards. I purposely state the case in its most favourable aspect. Now
how does such a man really walk? One might suppose

that, having nothing to do but to mind his own steps, he must walk very wisely and surely. But alas! the dreary, dismal records of ascetic and monastic piety prove that its walk is a terrible groping in the dark. Was ever the path of any of these recluses, even the holiest, " like the shining light that shineth more and more unto the perfect day? " Is it not rather a desperate plunging and floundering through mire and filth, amid stones and pitfalls, in the face of grisly phantoms of sin and hell? The man is bent on righting himself; ridding himself of lust; leaving behind him the world, the devil, and the flesh; working himself up into a state of serene and passionless equanimity, like that transcendental quiescence and repose in which he supposes God to dwell. It is a high though a visionary aim. For the attainment of it what efforts will he not put forth! what sacrifices will he not make! to what self-flagellation, self-laceration, bodily and spiritual, will he not submit! And yet what is it all but wandering as in a starless night? Incessant failure; disappointment after disappointment; new expedients resorted to in vain; now, for a moment, a supernatural trance, an ecstatic rapture, to be followed instantly by a fierce gust of unhallowed passion, or some horrid St. Anthony's temptation! Truly the man knoweth not whither he goeth. His eyes become so blinded that the very light is to him as darkness. The light of the glorious gospel itself fails to illuminate and enlarge his soul. The absence of sympathy; brotherly sympathy; first with the elder brother, and then with the little ones in him, explains it all.

For now let brotherly love abound. Try the more excellent way, not of working in upon yourselves that you may be perfect, but of going out after Christ the Shepherd, and going forth by " the footsteps of the flock." Leave the cell, the cloister. Quit even the too exclusive use of the study, the closet. Or at least learn to make the study as wide, the closet as capacious, as the great heart of him with whom you commune in the study, to whom you pray in the closet. For that is brotherly love. It is your loving whom your Father loves; and loving as he loves. It is the elevating, sanctifying, expanding of your heart, till it becomes, in a sense, of the same character and compass with the holy, loving heart of your Father in heaven. You are not shut up in self, any more than he is. You are abroad among men as he is. There is no longer in you that painful spirit of bondage which is for ever causing offences and the fear of them; occasioning stumbling-blocks at every turn; making every step nervous and uneasy. Saved yourselves by grace, gratuitous and rich and full; loved with an everlasting love; grasped in the arms, in the bosom, of him in whom and in you, as now one, "the darkness is passing and the true light is now shining,"— your spirit is free; your heart enlarged. Being loved, you love. The scales of selfishness fall from off your eyes. Christ sends you to his brethren : "Go tell my brethren." And as you go to them with Christ's message and on Christ's errand, and make them more and more your brethren as they are his, you clearly see your way. He makes it clear. And you walk at liberty when you have respect to all his commandments; "loving your brother, and so abiding in the light."

One thought may be allowed, in closing, as to the peculiar blessedness of there being no occasion of stumbling in you. Occasions of stumbling there will be, enough and to spare, till the end of your course on earth. "It must needs be that offences come." Even Jesus had his stumbling-blocks, his occasions of stumbling, in his path. Peter was one of these when he withstood his going up to Jerusalem. Even the brother you love may be an offence, an occasion of stumbling, to you by the way. But it is something to have none occasion of stumbling within; to be purged of malice and partial counsel; to have the narrowing and blinding influence of the love of sin and the love of self exchanged for the broad, clear, free vision and action of the love of God, and Christ, and the brethren, and all men; to have "the eye single" and "the whole body" therefore "full of light."

11

THE GUILELESS SPIRIT ABIDING IN THE LIGHT
IN ITS THREEFOLD ASPECT OF CHILDHOOD,
FATHERHOOD, AND YOUTH

"I write unto you, little children, because your sins are forgiven you for
his name's sake. I write unto you, fathers, because ye have known
him that is from the beginning. I write unto you, young men,
because ye have overcome the wicked one. I write [have written]
unto you, little children, because ye have known the Father. I have
written unto you, fathers, because ye have known him that is from
the beginning. I have written unto you, young men, because ye are
strong, and the word of God abideth in you, and ye have overcome
the wicked one." 1 John 2:12-14

THESE verses form, I think, a break or interruption in the
apostle's line of argument. There is, as it were, a pause.
John calls upon those to whom he writes to consider, not
only what he is writing to them, but what they themselves
are to whom he is writing; what is their character and
standing; what he is entitled to assume in and about them
as likely to ensure a favourable reception of his message.
This is a common apostolic method. It is a courteous and
complimentary way of insinuating advice; taking for
granted the attainments to be enforced. But it is far more
than that; and it is so emphatically here. It is a trumpet-
call, summoning all the faithful to a recognition of their
real and true position before God; and that with a view
to their receiving aright what his servant is now writing
to them—or, it may be, before this letter reaches them,

has written to them—of the divine fellowship of light and love.

How then does John address us here ? As "little children," "fathers," "young men." These triads or triplets come in twice. There are two sets of propositions or statements, each of them three in number, and evidently corresponding and parallel to one another. The one set of three is introduced by the verb in the present tense, "I write ; " the other set of three by the verb in the past tense, "I have written." For the authority of manuscripts, critically weighed, as well as the whole structure and symmetry of the passage, requires us so far to amend our present text as to make the last clause of the thirteenth verse consistent with the fourteenth, "I have written unto you, little children."

Clearly there are two parallel lines running thus :—

I. "I write unto you, little children, because your sins are forgiven you for his name's sake."

"I have written unto you, little childen, because ye have known the Father."

II. "I write unto you, fathers, because ye have known him that is from the beginning."

"I have written unto you, fathers, because ye have known him that is from the beginning."

III. "I write unto you, young men, because ye have overcome the wicked one."

"I have written unto you, young men, because ye are strong, and the word of God abideth in you, and ye have overcome the wicked one."

In either series, in each of the two, "little children" is the endearing term first employed. It is not indeed the same word in the original in both instances ; but the words are of the same import, and can scarcely be rendered differently. They are the words usually employed by John, and employed by him indiscriminately, when he is tenderly and affectionately addressing believers. They are, both of them, his common and customary words of love ;—"little children," or babes, "children," or boys. Children, little

children, they all are; all alike to whom, as he says, he
writes or has written. As such, as little children, he first
addresses them all, and appeals to them all collectively.
But then, secondly, he separates them into two classes,—
"fathers" and "young men,"—old and spiritually exercised
Christians on the one hand, and on the other hand, those
who are in the fresh and vigorous prime of recent but yet
manly Christian experience. All alike are "little children;" but some are "fathers," ripe for glory; others are
"young men," strong for work. Such, as I apprehend,
is the real primary meaning of this threefold appeal of
John.

But what of the repetition of it?—and the repetition of
it with a change of the tense from the present to the past?

It is a very emphatic reiteration; having in it a pathos
that should be very affecting. The apostle first realises his
own position as he is writing now, "I write." Then he
realises what may be the position of those to whom he
writes when they receive what he is writing now. To you
it may come as what "I have written;" the writer having
himself been taken home. I am now writing to you as
"little children;" to all of you alike I am writing thus
lovingly. To some of you, however, I write as to "fathers;"
to others of you I write as to "young men." Let all that
be marked and felt when you come to read what I am now
writing. All the more because you may have to read it as
what I have written; as my parting words to you. The
present tense answers well enough now, when I am writing.
But I am an old man; and the past tense may be the right
one very soon, even before you can be reading what I am
now writing. In any view receive it as what I solemnly
and deliberately write; or, if I am gone, as what I have
solemnly and deliberately written; my last legacy, my
dying charge. Receive it as my full and final testimony to

you, on the subject of what you ought to know, and to be and to do, as "little children," as "fathers," as "young men." It is all I have to write: and I write it with all the earnestness of one who, before you read it, may have passed away. I write it as my farewell word.

Thus viewed, the appeal in these verses is surely very impressive and affecting. Let us look at it, first in itself, and secondly in the connection in which it stands.

I. Considered in itself, the appeal recognises, on the one hand, a common character in all believers, that of " little children," and on the other hand a distinction between " fathers " and " young men."

1. In addressing us all as little children, John makes a distinction between his first and his second appeal. In the first it is " because your sins are forgiven you for his name's sake ;" in the second it is " because ye have known the Father." In addressing us as separated into two classes,— as fathers and youths respectively,—he merely repeats in the second appeal almost literally what he had said in the first. But in addressing us all as his beloved little ones, he varies the thought. The variation, however, is slight. It is the same thought in reality, only put in somewhat different lights. For the Father is truly known, only in the forgiveness of our sins for his Son's name sake. It is when we suffer the Son to take us by the hand and lead us home to the Father, and when we discover, in our experience, how the Father deals with us when the Son presents us to him, saying, " Behold I and the little ones whom thou hast given me,"—it is then, and then only, that we begin to know the Father. Up till that time we have not known him ; we have worshipped him perhaps, but it has been ignorantly ; we have misunderstood him, and done him great injustice in our esteem of him. We have had hard thoughts of him ; of his character and government and law ;

of his treatment of us and his requirements from us; of his ways and his commandments; nay, even of his very mercy itself. But we are moved to trust in the name of Jesus, and to make trial of the power of that name with the Father. And what a gushing tide of forgiveness and fatherly love does it cause to rush in upon our souls! How rich and free is the measure and manner of the Father's pardoning grace! We do thus really know the Father; for we know him through our sense and experience of his fatherly love in the forgiveness of our sins for his Son's name's sake.

2. The appeal is next made to the two classes or companies into which we may be divided; those who are fathers in Israel; and those who are young men.

Ye fathers in Israel! the argument with you is, that " ye have known him that is from the beginning." You have reached a higher, deeper, more satisfying knowledge of Christ, as " him that is from the beginning," than that which is common to all the household of faith, all the little ones given to him by the father. Your clear and calm insight into the glorious person of him for whose name's sake your sins are forgiven, and who thus introduces you to the knowledge of the Father; your mature acquaintance with him, in his eternal relation to the Father and oneness with the Father from the beginning;—should move you to give the more earnest heed to this writing or epistle of mine both now and when I am gone.

Ye youths, ye young men, the flower of the army of the Lord of Hosts! I have a hold on you also. You I summon, "for ye have overcome the wicked one " (ver. 13); " ye are strong, and the word of God abideth in you, and ye have overcome the wicked one" (ver. 14). As good soldiers of Christ, I would remind you of your high vocation; of what is committed to you; of what is expected of you. Your sphere is the field of battle. The quiet of contemplative study may best suit aged saints, advanced disciples, " fathers ; " who may best serve the cause by enlarging, under the Spirit's teaching, their own and the Church's knowledge of the Eternal Word ; elevating their own and the Church's views of the Son in the bosom of the Father. But the vigour of spiritual youth points to the never-ending conflict between the seed of the woman and the seed of the serpent, as your special department. For you are called to wage war with the wicked one. And you have every encouragement to do so. You have overcome him already in Christ, for he has overcome him. You have but to follow up and follow out the conquest. You are strong, and the word of God abideth in you. And through that word which testifies of Christ's victory abiding in you, the foe is already vanquished. You have overcome the wicked one.

To believers of all ages, to Christians in every stage of advancement, the apostle thus appeals. He first urges arguments and considerations applicable to all alike as little children ; and then such as are proper to fathers, and such as are proper to young men. By these various and accumulated motives, he conjures us to give heed to his teaching in this epistle. It is a very solemn, as well as a very full and comprehensive appeal. And the place in which it stands in the epistle renders it still more emphatic.

II. It stands between two opposite precepts ; the one positive ; the other negative ; " Love the brotherhood " (vers. 9–11) ; " Love not the world, neither the things that are in the world " (ver. 15). To love the Father, and the brethren as the Father's family ;—not to love the world lying in the wicked one ;—these are the contrasted commands between which the apostle's earnest and affectionate appeals occur. Doubtless these appeals cover the whole epistle ; all that John is writing ; all that they to whom he writes are to regard him as having written, when the writing reaches them, perhaps after the writer is no more. But they bear immediately on loving the brethren, and not loving the world.

The distinction is created by what John has just been dwelling upon ; the " thing which is true in Christ and in you, that the darkness is passing, and the true light is now shining." For light is a divider. It was so at the first creation (Gen. i. 3, 4) : " God said, Let there be light : and there was light. And God saw the light that it was good : and God divided the light from the darkness ; " he divided between the light and the darkness. It is so in the new creation. The entrance of the light into the world : its entrance into the hearts of as many as are in Christ ; necessarily causes a division. It unites by a new bond of brotherhood the children of the light among themselves. And it separates between them and the world. The separation, or distinction, is not of their own making, but of God's. He is in the light. He is himself the light. It is he who is the divider, and not they. Nor is the distinction of such a sort as to feed or nurse vaingloriousness on our part, or to be invidious as regards the world. Far otherwise. It is fitted to humble us in the very dust, as often as we think,—and when do we not think ?—of what we are in ourselves, and but for sovereign mercy must ever have been ; of what many, very many, around us are ; less guilty, by many degrees, than we ; and more likely than we to win, not only earth's approval, but, one would almost say, even heaven's favourable regard too. What am I ? And what are they ?

Ah ! it is in no spirit of supercilious self-complacency, or self-congratulation, that we associate together as brethren in the Lord, if indeed the true light is shining in us as in Christ, so as to show us the blackness of the darkness that is passing, and in its passing is hurrying to a fatal shipwreck so much that is fair and generous and lovely. No! nor is it with cool indifference that we look on and see its victims struggling in its fierce tide, or sinking lethargic in its quieter and deadlier eddies—feeling, as we do, that there is not one among them who deserves the horrid doom so much as we; and knowing as we do that there is not one whom grace may not make, as grace alone makes any one of us, a member of the brotherhood of light. The division which the light occasions assuredly affords no ground of boasting or of disdain. Nevertheless, it is to be recognised and realised; we must apprehend and feel it. One great design of John, in this whole epistle, is to bring us to a full apprehension and feeling of it; of what it is; and of all that it implies. The line is sharp; the preference must be decided. We have to choose whom we are to love and like, the brethren, or the world.

Now it is for the enforcing of a firm choice and a decided preference on the right side, that John makes his double, and doubly emphatic, appeal to us, as little children, fathers, young men. It is not for our consolation merely, our personal satisfaction and comfortable assurance, that he reminds us of the exceeding great privileges which, as little children, as fathers, as young men, we possess; as little children, having our sins forgiven for the Son's name's sake, and in that way knowing the Father; as fathers, knowing him that is from the beginning; as young men, having overcome the wicked one. These are all high and blessed attainments, and the consciousness of our right to them in Christ is doubtless a legitimate source of humble, holy, thankful joy. But it is not merely in order that our joy may be full that John dwells so earnestly on these elements of our oneness with Christ in the light. It is for a more practical purpose; that we may be roused to some adequate sense of the duty of love which we owe to every brother in whom, as in Christ and in us, the darkness is passing and the true light is now shining; and of the attitude which it is best for us to maintain towards the world; best with a view to our own consistency and safety; best also in the view of what is true kindness and faithfulness to the world itself.

Let us look then again at these appeals, in the light in which John's practical design or object in introducing them may seem to place them. In so looking at them, it is not necessary now to consider the apostle as formally classifying us, according to our different stages-of advancement, either in the life natural, or in the life spiritual. We all are, we all should be, little children, fathers, young men;—all three together;—little children, in respect of our having our sins forgiven for the Son's name's sake, and so knowing the Father; fathers, in respect of our loving insight into the mystery of the Son's being from the beginning; young men, in respect of our overcoming the wicked one. By what we are, in all these three aspects of our spiritual history and experience, John solicits our attention to this letter of his and to its teaching; specially that we may love our brother, and not love the world.

I. We are little children, and it is the instinct of little children to cling to home, and shrink from the strange world outside. What makes us little children? What but our being moved and made willing to accept the forgiveness of our sins for the Son's name's sake, and our coming, in that way, to know the Father? The Lord says, " Except ye be converted, and become as little children, ye cannot enter into the kingdom of heaven." Our conversion therefore makes us little children. For in our conversion the Spirit takes out of us the proud, cold, hard heart of manhood: and creates in us the meek heart of childhood, of "the holy child Jesus." For manhood's heart in me, hackneyed in suspicion and selfishness, recoils from subjection to God, and resents the idea of dependence and indebtedness. I must needs justify myself; I will do something to put myself right. Even when I arise to go to my father, it is with the purpose of asking a hired servant's food in recompense of a hired servant's work. I am only thoroughly subdued when I suffer my Father to forgive me freely, and take me more lovingly to his bosom than he would have done if I had never gone astray.

Then I am indeed a little child. All the pride of manhood's self-righteousness, all the stubbornness of manhood's self-will, is gone out of me. I am fain, as when I was an infant at my mother's knee, to have my burdened and broken heart relieved by a flood of penitential tears, as I confess all, and am clasped in an embrace that assures me, oh how feelingly! that all is pardoned. Then, at last, I know the Father,—what sort of Father he is,—when thus, for his Son's name's sake, who has got me, ah with what difficulty! to let him relieve me of my load of guilt and grief, and bring me home to his Father and mine,—that Father pardons all my iniquities.

Is it so with me? Then where now will my heart be? A little child's heart is in the home of loving parents, and brothers, and sisters; away from that home he is uneasy and unsatisfied. Houses of rarest splendour, scenes of fairest beauty, will not reconcile him to prolonged absence from home, and prolonged residence elsewhere. He pines for his father's well-known smile, and for the companionship of those who share that smile with him. As to all else on earth, he is a stranger among strangers. You are little children—are you not?—converted and become as little children; suffering Jesus to bring you to the Father, to receive his forgiveness and to know his love. You are all of you little children; for such treatment cannot but make you little children. And it is as little children that you are exhorted to love your brother, and not to love the world.

II. You are fathers. Babes in Christ, new-born babes at first, and in a sense always so, for you are always renewing the experience in respect of which you are little children,—yet, " as new-born babes, you desire the sincere milk of the word that you may grow thereby." Continuing to be children always in respect of malice, the malice of self-conceit and self-seeking, you yet in understanding are men. Nay, you are fathers; you attain to the wisdom and insight proper to those who are of full age, as you grow in grace and in the knowledge of your Lord and Saviour Jesus Christ.

What makes you fathers is your knowing him that is from the beginning; knowing what we, his apostles, declare to you of that eternal life which was with the Father, and was manifested to us (i. 1–3). It is your being taught and enabled, by the Spirit, to trace up what you experience in time,—when as little children you receive forgiveness of your sins for the Son's name's sake and so know the Father,—to its source in the eternal counsels of the Godhead; in what the Son is to the Father from everlasting. For now you not merely look to Jesus as accomplishing for you a great work, effecting on your behalf a great deliverance, and ministering to you a great benefit. You delight to connect all this with his being from the beginning; with the love with which the Father has from the beginning loved him ; and "the glory which the Father giveth him because he loved him before the foundation of the world." You rise to a believing apprehension of the ultimate ground and reason of the whole vast economy of redemption in the deep, unfathomable, unchangeable nature of Jehovah; in the purpose of the Father's good pleasure to constitute the Son heir of all things; in the covenant securing from of old to the Son, in requital of his humiliation and obedience and death, a people in whom he is to see of the travail of his soul and be satisfied, and for whom as his body he is to be head over all things. It is such knowledge as that, of him who is from the beginning, that should make you fathers in Israel. It is when you rise, by the Spirit's teaching, to views like these of Christ and his salvation; contemplating the gospel plan, not as a mere afterthought and expedient, to meet an emergency and serve a purpose in time, but as the bright and blessed unfolding to all eternity of what from all eternity the Son is to the Father; dwelling in his bosom; declaring his name; glorifying the Father as the Father glorifies him: it is then, and in that way, that your Christian character acquires a certain ripe and mellow fulness, and your Christian standing comes to partake of the very stability of the Son's own position, as being from the beginning. You enter into the very mind and heart of God; Father, Son, and Holy Ghost. You are no more little children merely; apt to be tossed about, and to be unstable. You are fathers.

The fresh feelings of childhood, it is true, must ever continue; for its experiences are ever freshly revived. But along with these there is now the staid fixedness that should distinguish those who have a sort of fatherly place in the house, and take a sort of fatherly view of its inmates and its affairs. And so literally you do, when you know him who is from the beginning. You look at the family, the whole family in heaven and earth named of him, not now merely from a little child's standing-ground or point of view, but from a father's standing-ground or point of view; even

from the standing-ground or point of view of the great
Father himself. Yes! you come to see Christ the Son as
the Father sees him; not as it were from before only; from
the front; from where your foot is at this moment planted;
but from behind, from where the Father sits enthroned in
his eternal majesty. Your fatherhood is thus, in a sense,
your participation, or at least your sympathy, with the
Father in his. You are fathers when, knowing him who is
from the beginning, you contemplate the whole of his
mighty undertaking, with its results and issues, not merely
in the aspect presented to poor sinners on earth, but in the
aspect presented to the Eternal Father in heaven. As
little children, you let the Son lead you up to the Father,
that you may receive forgiveness for his name's sake, and
so may know the Father. As fathers, able now to sympathise with the Father, you find him giving you new
knowledge of the Son, as being with him from the beginning. For as "no man knoweth the Father but the Son
and he to whom the Son will reveal him," so "no man
knoweth the Son but the Father." And you, when as
fathers you know him who is from the beginning, become
truly sharers of the Father's knowledge of the Son. This,
I repeat, is your fatherhood. It is your entering in a sense
into the fatherhood of God.

Need I take any pains to show how such a fatherhood
as this may well be appealed to as a reason why every one
of the family should be to you a brother beloved, and you
should not love the world that knows not either the
Father or the Son? A father's intelligent interest, as well
as a child's loving instinct, must keep your affections always
at home.

III. You are young men. As such, you are strong.
The vigour of manly prime is yours. And you need it all.
For the home of brotherhood which you are to love, and

the world which you are not to love, are not far apart; at least not yet. They shall be one day, when there shall be a great impassable gulf between them. But they are near one another now. They meet; in my heart within, as well as everywhere without and around me, they meet. Hence, for myself, I have a constant battle to fight, to keep the world out of my heart. Ah ! how may that be ? How but by the word of God abiding in me ? Let that word dwell in me richly. Let it so richly dwell in me that the world when it comes to solicit admittance, or to challenge surrender, or to make a breach, or to spring a mine, shall find no access, no open door, no weak defence, no treacherous longings and lingering likings for some of its good things, ready to betray the citadel, and capitulate to the foe.

But alas for me ! The world is so strong; so apt to draw me away from loving my brother and his fellowship; to draw me into conformity to its own still too congenial ways !

Shall I then faint and grow weary and cease to resist ? Nay, let me be strong, and quit me like a strong young man : the word of God abiding in me. For, let me remember, I have overcome the wicked one. He is the prince of this world ; it lies in his arms ; it is he who, by means of it, is strong to overcome me. But I have overcome him.

So I am assured by that word of God which abideth in me. He has nothing in me now, any more than he has in Christ. He cannot accuse me now ; he has no right to rule me now. I am not now at his mercy, fain to comply with his terms; to win a delusive peace by some poor compromise with him; to be dependent on his lies for a wretched respite from the stings of conscience. I stand now in God's favour, and may bid defiance to the charges and assaults of the wicked one. And therefore I can afford and venture to break all terms of truce or amity with the world which lieth in him, and to avow henceforth that I love the Father and the Son and the brethren, in the Holy Spirit. By my youth and manhood, I am summoned to maintain this attitude always. And that not for myself only; that the home of my childhood and fatherhood may be kept from the invasion of the world; but for the sake of other little children, who are still such as I once was, and who are struggling in the dark flood, as I once did. The wicked one would claim them as his own. Let me claim them for my Father. And in stretching out to them a helping hand, let me hear John exhorting me, as a young man, to do so resolutely, because, as he reminds me, " I am strong, and the word of God abideth in me, and I have overcome the wicked one."

To sum up all, I can imagine John, at the point at which he has arrived in the composing of this letter,—the point of enforcing the brotherhood of believers and its antagonism to the world,—pausing to ask himself, Will these counsels of mine be understood and obeyed? Will those to whom they are addressed receive them as they are given, in faithfulness and affection? He is moved to make an earnest, and what may be a last appeal to them.

What I am writing to you, I write in the fulness of my heart. I know that you believe in Jesus; I give you all credit for being Christians indeed. I appeal to you, by all the motives and considerations that should weigh with you as such. I appeal to you in every view of your Christianity, as little children, fathers, young men. And by all that is implied in your being little children, fathers, young men, I beseech you to hear me. So " I write unto you." Take kindly what I write unto you, as little children, fathers, young men.

But, it occurs to him to think, I am old, John the aged. Before the ink I am now using is dry I may have been summoned to my rest. Be it so. Then take it, O my beloved, as what " I have written ; " as my last legacy to you. Take it as what I wrote when I felt as if I was bidding you adieu. Take it as my final parting testimony and prayer.

As little children, knowing the Father by ever-fresh experience of his rich and free love in forgiving you for his Son's name's sake; as fathers, entering intelligently and sympathisingly into the Father's knowledge of the Son as being from the beginning in his bosom; as young men, strong in him who is the Lord your righteousness, and therefore the Lord your strength; fortified by his word always abiding in you richly; bold and brave in asserting the victory over the wicked one that is already yours as it is Christ's ; by all that is simple in your childhood, by all that is godlike in your fatherhood, by all that is divinely strong in your manhood; be persuaded to give heed to what I write or have written; to love the brotherhood; and not to love the world.

12

THE GUILELESS SPIRIT LOVING NOT THE WORLD, WHICH IS DARKNESS, BUT GOD, WHO IS LIGHT

" Love not the world, neither the things that are in the world. If any man love the world, the love of the Father is not in him. / For all that is in the world, the lust of the flesh, and the lust of the eyes, and the pride of life, is not of the Father, but is of the world."
1 John 2:15-16

THE love of the world is here declared to be irreconcilable with the love of the Father. " If any man love the world, the love of the Father is not in him " (ver 15). And the declaration applies to " the things that are in the world," comprehending " all that is in the world." These are represented under three categories or heads, " the lust of the flesh, the lust of the eyes, and the pride of life " (ver. 16). They are afterwards reduced to one, " the lust of the world " (ver. 17); but in the meantime we have to consider them as three. And, in that view, the sixteenth verse is to be regarded, not as giving the reason for the command in the fifteenth, but rather as explanatory of its nature ; bringing out the contrast between the two incompatible objects of love, the Father on the one hand, and on the other hand the world, whatever form its lust may take.

Plainly the world is here represented as an order of things very thoroughly complete in itself; self-contained and self-developing. " All that is in the world " is " of the world." No foreign elements are suffered to intrude ; or if they do, the world speedily accommodates and assimilates them to itself.   For the world,—what is it ?   Fallen human nature acting itself out in the human family ; moulding and fashioning the framework of human society in accordance with its own tendencies.   It is fallen human nature making the ongoings of human thought, feeling, and action its own.   It is the reign or kingdom of " the carnal mind," which is " enmity against God, and is not subject to the law of God, neither indeed can be."   Wherever that mind prevails, there is the world.

" The things that are in the world " correspond in character to the world itself.   The love therefore of any of them is equivalent to the love of the world.

I may seem to be, and may suppose that I am, separated from the world.   I may have renounced companionship with that visible outstanding circle, in regard to which, as a whole, it may be too plainly seen that it does not admit the true light to shine in it, but is still in the darkness which that light chases away.   For there is a circle which may be thus collectively identified.   There is a tolerably well-defined mode of life which a spiritual man cannot but recognise as worldly ; and there are a set of people who so manifestly conform themselves to that mode of life, and that alone, as to make it impossible for the most tolerant Christian charity to characterise them otherwise than as worldly persons. Let that then be the world, broadly considered.   Now I have withdrawn myself from that world ; I have no sympathy with its general tone and spirit ; I am attached to another order of things.   So far, I think I may say that I do not love the world.   In its corporate capacity, as it were, it has lost its hold over me.

But " the things that are in the world," viewed separately and in detail, may have attractions for me still.   I may love them, or some of them, or one of them.   If so, it is the same thing to me as if I loved the world itself in the mass. The love of what is in the world, is really the love of the world. Hence the necessity for breaking up the general notion of "the world" into its contents, "the things that are in the world."

The things that are in the world which may attract love, as distinct objects of desire, even when the world as a whole seems to be discarded, are too manifold to be enumerated. But they may be classified; if not according to their own properties or qualities ; at any rate, according to the inward dispositions to which they appeal. The apostle thus classifies them under three heads. "All that is in the world" is distributed into "the lust of the flesh, the lust of the eyes, and the pride of life." To these three harpies of the soul the world ministers.

First, there is " the lust of the flesh." The genitive or possessive here—" of the flesh "—denotes, not the object of the desire, but its nature. It is lust of desire of a carnal sort; such as the flesh prompts or occasions. It is the appetite of sense out of order, or in excess. It is not, of course, the appetite of sense itself; that is of God, as the provision for its satisfaction is also of God. The appetite for which food is God's appointed ordinance, and the appetite for which marriage is God's appointed ordinance,—the general needs and cravings of the body which the laws of nature and the gifts of providence so fully meet,—the higher tastes which fair forms and sweet sounds delight,—the eye for beauty and the ear or the soul for music ;—these are not, any of them, the lust of the flesh. But they all, every one of them, may become the lust of the flesh. And in the world they do become the lust of the flesh. It is the world's aim to pervert them into the lust of the flesh, and to pander to them in that character, either grossly or with refinement. All its arrangements, its giddy sports and anxious toils, tend in that direction. Sensuality, or that modification of it now spoken of as sensuousness, enters largely into the world's fascinating cup. And it may be detached plausibly from what is avowedly and confessedly the world; it may be covertly loved, while the world, as such, is apparently hated. Gluttony, drunkenness, uncleanness; the rage for physical or æsthetical excitement which the ball, the theatre, the gaming-table, if not worse excesses, must appease;—these forms or modifications of the lust of the flesh may not be for us the most insidious. It may creep into our affections disguised almost as an angel of light. A certain fondness for the good things of this life, an unwillingness to forego them, a pleasant feeling of fulness in the enjoyment of them, a growing impatience of any interruption of that enjoyment,—how soon may such a way of tasting even the lawful gratifications of sense grow into selfishness and sin! And then how readily does the imagination admit ideas and fancies the reverse of pure! Through how many channels, the news of the day, the gems of literature, the choicest trophies of the fine arts, poesy, sculpture, song, may unholy desire be kindled! I may be out of the world; but this that is in the world, "the lust of the flesh," may not be out of me.

There is, secondly, "the lust of the eyes." This must be distinct from the lust of the flesh. It cannot therefore be that "looking on a woman to lust after her," which the Lord holds to be the commission of adultery in the heart; or that "looking upon the wine-cup when it is red," against which Solomon warns us. The lust of the eyes is something different. It is lust or desire having its proper seat in the region of contemplation, or of onlooking. It is not merely that the flesh lusts through the eyes, or that the eyes minister to the lust of the flesh. The eyes themselves have their own lust. It is lust that can be satisfied

with mere sight; which the lust of the flesh never is, nor
can be. It is a feeling of such a sort that a bare look or gaze
may please or may offend it. For example, I cannot stand
the sight of more good in my neighbour's possession than
in my own. I would be relieved if I saw him worse off
than I am. That is to a great extent the instinct of corrupt humanity; it is the way of the world. And it is one
of the world's ways that, even when I renounce the world,
I am still apt to follow, or that is apt to follow me. I may
be one in whom the world's sensual or sensuous delights no
longer stimulate the lust of the flesh. But my eyes are
pained when I see the giddy crowd so happy and secure.
My bosom swells and my blood boils when I am forced to
look on villany triumphant and vice caressed. It may be
all righteous zeal and virtuous wrath; a pure desire to witness wrong redressed and justice done. But, alas! as I
yield to it, I find it fast assuming a worse character. I
would not myself be partaker of the sinful happiness I see
the world enjoying; but I grudge the world's enjoyment of
it. " I was envious," says David (Ps. lxxiii.), " at the foolish, when I saw the prosperity of the wicked." That was
his temptation; it was his infirmity; it formed the sad
burden of more than one of his most plaintive Psalms.
It was the love of the world in one of its most
stealthy and dangerous forms, winning its way into his
heart, and supplanting there, for a time, the love of
God.

Once more, thirdly, there is "the pride of life." Self-
indulgence, or "the lust of the flesh," and envious grudging, or "the lust of the eyes," might seem to exhaust "all
that is in the world." The whole substance of "the world
and the things of the world" is reducible to these two heads,
or may be regarded in these two lights: what I long to
possess and enjoy myself, and what I cannot calmly bear to

see possessed and enjoyed by another. These two views of
it exhaust the whole of what is substantial in the world.
But the show, the shadow, the semblance, as well as the
substance, is something to the world's vanity, or to my
vanity with reference to the world. Nay, it is much; the
world's manifold conventionalisms, for they are indeed
manifold, prove it to be much. What pains are taken in
the world to save appearances and keep up a seemly and
goodly state! It is a business all but reduced to system.
Its means and appliances are ceremony and feigned civility.
Life is to be ostensibly, nay even ostentatiously, all right.
All is to be in good taste and in good style; correct, credit-
able, commendable. It is the world's pride to have it so.
What is otherwise must be somehow toned down or shaded
off; concealed or coloured. Falsehood may be necessary;
a false code of honour; false notions of duty, as between
man and man, or between man and woman; false liberality
and spurious delicacy. Still the world does contrive, by
means of all that, to get up and keep up a proud life of its
own; a life grand and graceful; having its decencies and
respectabilities; yes, and its charities, courtesies, and
chivalries too; all very imposing in themselves, and altogether contributing to make the world's life very imposing
as a whole.

That I take to be the "pride of life" in the world. In
one aspect, it is undoubtedly mean enough. It sets in
motion a game of diplomacy and a race of emulation most
destructive of all the truer and finer instincts even of unrenewed humanity. It debauches conscience, and is fatal
to high aims. It puts the men and women of the world on
a poor struggle to out-manœuvre and outshine one another,
to outdo one another, for the most part, in mere externals;
while, with all manner of politeness, they affect to give one
another credit for what they all know to be little better

than shams. Nevertheless, the general effect, I repeat, is imposing. The world's "pride of life" is something to be proud of after all.

Now of this "pride of life" it is by no means easy even for those who do not love the world to keep themselves altogether clear. It is, as it were, their last worldly weakness. The lust of the flesh may be mortified, crucified, nailed to the cross of Christ; the lust of the eyes may be overcome by the mighty power of love, the love which "envieth not;" and yet the pride of life may cleave to me. It is so difficult to have done with the world's seemings, and to come out simply as what I am.

Need I suggest how many sad instances of religious inconsistency and worldly conformity spring from this source? I may acquit you of sensuality or sensuousness, and of selfish jealousy; you are free, as to both of these instruments of the world's power. But what of its opinion? Have you learned to defy it, or to be independent of it? Can you dispense with the world's approval and brave its frown? Do you not sometimes find yourselves more afraid or ashamed of a breach of worldly etiquette,—some apparent descent from the customary platform of worldly respectability,—than of such a concession to the world's forms and fashions as may compromise your integrity in the sight of God, and your right to acquit yourselves of guile? The opinion of the world! What the world will think or say! Ah! that pitiful consideration may often sway or embarrass you when you have no selfish longing or envious grudge to gratify. To a large extent, it is identical with that "fear of man which bringeth a snare." It puts you at the mercy of the idle thoughts and idle words of any onlooker who may presume to judge you. You cannot acquit yourselves altogether of the love of the world so long as you have in your hearts that liking for the world's good report, or that sensitiveness to the world's censure, which "the pride of life" implies.

And now, for practical use, let three remarks be made.

1. Of "all that is in the world" it is said that "it is not of the Father, but of the world." This may be true of things good in themselves, the best things even, when they come to be things "in the world." They may be of the Father originally, in their true and proper nature; but the world appropriates them and makes them its own; and so they cease to be of the Father, and are now simply of the world. The choicest blessings of home, the holiest ordinances of religion, the very gospel itself, may thus come, when once "in the world," to be "of the world." Be not then deceived. Much that meets your eye, as you look on the world and the world's ways, may seem fair and excellent; graces most attractive, devotions most comely and fervent, amenities most winning, philanthropies most admirable. But God is not really in them all. They "are not of the Father." A pure and simple regard to his will is not their animating spirit. They are "of the world." There is nothing in them that rises above the natural influences of self-love and social, as these are blended "in the world."

Again, 2. "All that is in the world is of the world," wherever it may be found. The three world-powers or world-principles are, always and everywhere, "not of the Father but of the world." They may be in the Father's house; they may be in the hearts of the Father's children; but they are none the better for their being there. They are not themselves cleansed or hallowed by what they come in contact with, however pure and however holy. But all that they touch they smite with leprosy and wither into impotent paralysis. Let us beware then of letting into the sanctuary and shrine of our soul, now become the dwelling-place of God by his Spirit, anything that savours of the world's sloth and self-indulgence, or of the world's jealousy and envy, or of the world's vain pomp and pride. No matter though, as we think, we do not now love the world, but are separated from its friendship, if still we love any of the things of the world. For "all that is in the world is not of the Father, but of the world." And "if any man love the world, the love of the Father is not in him."

Finally, 3. Let us remember that the world which we are not to love, because "all that is in it is not of the Father but is of the world," is yet itself the object of a love on the part of the Father, with which, as his children, having in us his love, we are to sympathise. "God so loved the world, that he gave his only begotten Son, that whosoever believeth in him should not perish, but have everlasting life." This is said of the very world which we are commanded not to love; and of that world viewed in the very aspect on account of which we are commanded not to love it; as having nothing in it that is really "of the Father." "God so loved this world," this very world, thus viewed, having nothing in it or about it that he can recognise as his own, as what he made and meant it originally to be, "that he gave his only begotten Son" on its behalf. And he calls upon us so to love it too; with the same sort of love, and with love moving us to the same sort of effort and the same sort of sacrifice. And it is our so loving the world as the Father has loved it, that will be our best security against loving it as the Father forbids us to love it. Let the world be to us what it is to the Father. Let us look at it as the Father looks at it; as a deep dark mass of guilt, ungodliness, and woe. Let us plunge in to the rescue. Let us lay hold of that young man, whom, as we behold him, like Jesus, we cannot help loving. Let us snatch him, for he is not safe, as a brand out of the burning. If we love the world as God loves it, we will have no heart for loving it in any other way. Its attractions, its fascinations, its amiabilities, its sentimentalisms, will have no charm for us. We see in them only snares to catch and ruin souls that we,—that God,—would have to be saved. We cannot love, with any love of complacency, the world which we love in sympathy with him who " sent not his Son into the world to condemn the world ; but that the world through him might be saved."

13

THE GUILELESS SPIRIT, AMID THE DARK WORLD'S FLOW, ESTABLISHED IN THE LIGHT OF GODLINESS

" And the world passeth away, and the lust thereof : but he that doeth
the will of God abideth for ever." 1 John 2:17

THE expression here used concerning the world and its
lust, is the same as that used in the eighth verse concerning
the darkness : it is " passing away." The world, with its
lust, is in this respect identical with the darkness. They
partake at least of a common quality or property; they
pass, or are passing.

There is more meant here than merely that " the
things which are seen are temporal." The fleeting nature
of this whole earthly scene is doubtless a useful topic of
reflection ; but it is not exactly what is suggested in this
verse. The idea of the darkness being a vanishing element is still the leading thought. The prince of darkness,
though he may keep up appearances for a while, is like a
beaten foe, drawing off from the disputed territory. Through
the shining of the true light, the darkness is passing ; and
in the same sense " the world passeth away, and the lust
thereof." " But he that doeth the will of God abideth for
ever," for he is one in whom, as in Christ, " the darkness
is passing, and the true light now shineth."

1. The characteristic of the world is that it does not

"do the will of God;" it is the sphere or region in which the will of God is not done. The lust of the world is not doing the will of God. Take it in any of its forms. Let it be the lust of the flesh; as "lovers of pleasures more than lovers of God," you are doing your own will and not God's. Let it be the lust of the eyes, envying others who prosper more than you; then it is the thwarting of their will, not the doing of God's will, that your mind is bent on. Let it be the pride of life, hanging on opinion's idle breath; you have no freedom to do the will of God, for you are at the mercy of the will of your fellow-men.

As not doing the will of God, the world and its lust must pass away; for it is identical with the darkness which is passing. Passing! Whence? and whither? Whence, but from off the stage of this redeemed earth, the final blessed meeting-ground of all the Lord's children? And whither? I cannot tell. This only I know, it must be to where it shall do no harm any more for ever. I read of everlasting fire, prepared for the devil and his angels. Is that the final resting-place of the darkness?—of the world and its lust? There it is to be no longer passing, but permanent, abiding. "The worm dieth not, and the fire is not quenched."

O ye lovers of the world, or of what is in the world, have you considered what the end is to be? It may well move you to be told that the whole of that economy with which you are mixed up is fleeting, transitory, evanescent. "What shadows you are and what shadows you pursue!" It is a deep knell that is rung over the grave of all merely temporal prosperity, all earthly hope and joy; "the world passeth away, and the lust thereof." But it is a knell that, ringing out life's present and precarious dreams, rings in a terrible reality. The world, with its lust, is passing here; apssing and changing always. But it is passing to where it will pass no more, but stay; fixed unchangeably for ever.   It is not annihilated; it does not cease to be; it only ceases to be passing.

Have you ever thought how much of the world's endurableness; I say not its attractiveness but its endurableness; depends on its being a world that passes, and therefore changes?   Is it not, after all, its being changeable that makes it tolerable even to you who like it best ?   Can you lay your hand, your memory's hand, on any one feeling you have ever had of intensest worldly gratification, and say that you could be content, with that feeling alone, to spend eternity ?   Is there any sensation, any delight, any rapture of worldly joy, however engrossing, that you could bear to have prolonged, indefinitely, for ever, unaltered, unalterable ?

But I put the case too favourably.   I speak of your finding the world with its lust, not passing but abiding, in the place whither you yourselves pass, when you pass hence.   True, you find it there.   But you find it not as you have it here.   There are means and appliances here for quenching by gratification, or mitigating by variety, its impetuous fires.   But there you find it where these fires burn, unslaked, unsolaced; the world being all within, and the world's lust; and nothing outside but the Holy One.

Again I ask—Have you ever thought how much of the world's endurableness depends on the fact that, with its lust, it has its seat for a while here in the midst of a transition process, as it were, which is going on, "the darkness passing and the true light shining?"   What keeps this earth from being, at this moment, hell, or a part of hell?   What but its being a place of preparation for heaven; destined ere long to become to myriads of the saved heaven itself?

When in that heaven where the angels dwell, sudden

darkness sought to dim the light, and wilful creatures would not do the will of God, not an instant was lost. Swiftly, summarily, the world is cast out, and its lust. There is no room for it there, no, not for an hour. The lovers of it, and of its lust ; the doers of another will than God's ; their own, or their leader's ; are no more found there ; but somewhere else in the universe of God, where they are "reserved in everlasting chains, under darkness, unto the judgment of the great day." That holy heaven is full of light alone, and in it is no darkness at all. The will of God is always done there.

We are taught to pray that his will may be done on earth as in heaven ; and we believe that it shall be so. But the time is not yet. The darkness is only passing, not past; "the world is passing away, and the lust thereof." For it has pleased God not to deal with this earth where we dwell, as he dealt with that heaven where the angels dwell. If he had, he must have left it empty. The darkness must needs be tolerated ; the world, with its lusts, not doing the will of God, must be allowed to continue ; till the race for whom the earth was made, the family of man meant to fill it, is complete. But all is not to be darkness ; a world lusting its own lust and not doing the will of God. There is to be light; there are to be children of the light. For the light and its children, as well as for the darkness and its world, the earth is to be adapted. Its order and laws ; its arrangements and accommodations ; must be such as suit its present mixed occupancy. And such also must be God's general providence over it. Hence you who love the world and its lust, and do not the will of God, find yourselves in a position here, under these conditions, which does not give the world and its lust full swing ; or, as it were, "ample scope and verge enough."

Not to speak of the direct shining of the light, in gospel means and ordinances, which tells upon you in spite of

yourselves, in some vague way, for your partial respite from
the pangs of conscience ; I point to the elements of good
that there are in the institutions which God has sanctioned,
and which he blesses, for alleviating pain and giving
happiness on this earth on which he suffers you to dwell
for a season with the righteous ; healthy labour, alternating
with such sleep as God gives his beloved ; family relation-
ships ; social ties ; domestic endearments ; spheres also of
public activity and usefulness and generous ambition ; out-
lets for native energy and amiability, and lofty thought and
fine feeling, and the stirrings of kind pity, and the flights of
genius.   Do not imagine that these form part of the world
or its lust, which you are to carry with you when it and
you together pass hence.   This earth is not furnished with
these conveniences for your sakes, but for their sakes who
find in them the choicest apparatus and machinery for doing
the will of God.   You have the use, you have the benefit
of them, for a brief space.   Your world, with its triple lust,
is permitted for a little to have to do with these contrivances
of God for making earth a school for heaven.   Alas ! what
harm does it often work among them ; blighting what is
pure, blasting what is peaceful, desolating hearths and
homes and hearts.   Still your loved world, and you who
love it, are the better and the happier for your contact with
what on earth is even now allied to heaven.

But have you ever thought what it will be to pass hence
and go where nothing of all that can follow you ?   No holy
beauty ; no virgin innocency ; no guiltless, guileless love
of parents, spouse, child, brother, friend ; no virtue ; no
decency even ; none of the decorum which at least serves
to make vice less hideous ; no soothing balm of pure hand
laid on the fevered brow ; no faintly-whispered hope or
wish of pure lips blessing you in your despair ; nothing of
the sort of comely veil which, down to the last breath of

the dying sinner's godless career, may hide the real truth from his view.

Let that real truth burst upon you. Place yourself, with your loved world and its cherished lust, where you and it and God are alone together, with nothing of God's providing that you can use or abuse for your relief. Your creature comforts are not there with you. Nothing of this earth, which is the Lord's, is there; nothing of its beauty or its bounty; its grace or loveliness or warm affection; nothing of that very bustle and distraction and change which dissipates reflection and drowns remorse; nothing but your worldly lust, your conscience, and your God. That is hell; the hell to which the world is passing, and its lust; and whence it never passes more; a dreary monotony of banishment from all that God has made to be chosen and enjoyed. It is yourselves, ye lovers of the world, filled with the lust of the world, its vulture appetites and stormy passions; shut up for ever in the darkness, as it were, of empty space, the desolate unfurnished prison-house of eternal justice.

II. But now let us turn to a brighter picture. "He that doeth the will of God abideth for ever." Suppose that the world has passed away and the lust thereof. Does it follow that the earth is dissolved or perishes? Nay, it remains. And whatever in it or about it is of God remains. There may be a temporary baptism of fire, to purge away the pollution contracted while the world has been tolerated in it and the world's lust; to regenerate it and transform it into the "new heavens and new earth wherein dwelleth righteousness." But the earth thus cleansed and renovated does not pass away. It surely must continue, under the condition of the petition, at last fully answered; "Thy will be done in earth as in heaven." For surely that is a petition which is yet to be fully answered; and not in time only, but for eternity. This abode of men is to be assimilated thoroughly to yonder abode of angels, in respect of the will of God being alike done in both. That at all events is the heavenly state, let its localities be adjusted as they may ; that is its eternal crown and joy ; angels and men together doing the will of God ; they in their heaven, we in our earth. That is the blessed consummation to which the apostle would have us to look forward when he urges this encouragement and motive : " he that doeth the will of God a bideth for ever.

But the precise point of his statement is not adequately brought out unless we connect and identify the future and the present. It is not merely said that he who doeth the will of God may hope to be hereafter in a place or in a state in which he shall abide for ever. It is plainly implied that he is in it now. The world, with its lust, is passing ; but he is in possession. The world, as it were, has forfeited its title, and is tolerated on sufferance merely, for a time and for a temporary purpose ; he is a proprietor, having a good and valid right to remain for ever. The world must go, he stays ; it has notice to quit, he abides. Doing the will of God, therefore, you are already in your abiding state ; in the state in which you are to abide for ever. No essential change is before you. There may be stages of advancement and varieties of experience ; a temporary break, perhaps, in the outer continuity of your thread of life, between the soul's quitting the body to be with Christ where now he is and its receiving the body anew at his coming hither again. But substantially you are now as you are to be always.

For there is this difference between you in whom the love of the Father is, and those in whom there is only the love of the world. The world which they love, with its lust, is a foreign element in this earth, considered as the creation of God, and an element, therefore, which must be cast out, as the land of Canaan is said to have "vomited out" its inhabitants when their "iniquity was full." There is really nothing of hell in this earth viewed as the creation of God, or in its arrangements viewed as God's ordinances; however much there may be of hell in the world with its lust, which is not God's creation or God's ordinance, but fallen man's, or his tempter's. From all that is of God's making or of God's ordaining in the earth, they who love the world must pass, with the world and its lust; carrying no good of it hence; quitting it all, and going to be with devils in eternal, unquenchable fire. But in this earth as God's creation, and in its arrangements as God's ordinances, what may there not be of heaven? And whatever of heaven is in it, and in them, is yours, if you are doing the will of God. Neither does it pass from you nor you from it. You and it together abide for ever.

Here, therefore, is the great alternative between "loving the world and its lust" and "doing the will of God." Here is the solution of what we are sometimes apt to regard as a hard problem in Christian morals. What is that separation from the world which I must keep up, if I would prove myself to be one who does not love the world, but who does love the Father? A hundred minute points of detail may come into discussion here. Is it lawful? is it expedient? might be asked to weariness, of this or that pursuit, this or that pleasure, this or that party, or company, or occupation. I meet these and all similar inquiries with the broad appeal to consciousness and conscience: Are you doing the will of God? It is not—Are you doing what, as to the matter of it, may be consistent, or not altogether inconsistent, with the will of God? But are you, in doing it, doing the will of God? You may be where the will of God would appoint or allow you to be. Are you there because it is the will of God that you should be there? Are you there on set purpose, there and then to do the will of God? This test will carry you through all entanglements, and raise you above all compromises. Only be sure that you apply it fairly. For, in this matter, the prince of this world is very wily. If possible, he will have you to substitute something of God's instead of what is his, as being what you are not to love. He will allow and encourage you to abstain from meats and from marriage; to withdraw from your fellows and retire into the desert; to abandon the affairs of active life; to assume an ascetic severity, frowning on the ordinary ongoings of society. He is pleased when he sees you counting that to be coming out from the world. For he knows that all the while it is really God's creation and God's ordinance, and not his world with its lust, that you are putting away.

Ah! it is a great thing to draw the line clear and sharp between what here and now is "of God," and what is "of the world and its lust." And if the line is to be drawn clear and sharp, it must be drawn, not from without, but from within. It must be drawn, not by external routine or regulation, but by a living spirit in the inner man; the spirit of love and loyalty to the Father; the spirit that moved Jesus to say, "I came not to do my own will, but the will of him that sent me." He had no perplexities, no misgivings, in going in and out among his fellow-men. He moved freely where the Pharisees were censorious and straitlaced. For everywhere and always, wherever he was, in the house, on the road, at the hospitable table, beside the open grave; with whomsoever he met, publicans, sinners, harlots, as well as Scribes, and Sadducees, and Herodians; he was doing the will of God; he was about his Father's business; doing his will. It was not with him —Where shall I go? whom shall I meet? so much as,—Go where I may, meet whom I may, what business would my Father have me to be about? Something surely bearing on the great work for which I came intot he world; something to glorify my Father; something for the saving of lost sinners; something for the comfort of weary souls. Ah! let this same mind that was in him be in you. Let it become a delight with you, as well as a business, to be everywhere and always doing the will of God. That, and that alone, is "not loving the world, nor the things of the world."

For the world which, with its lust, is passing away, is just the darkness whose passing you are to apprehend as a thing true in you as in Christ. And the doing of the will of God, which is your abiding for ever, is just the true light now shining; which shining of the true light, as well as the passing of the darkness, you are also to apprehend as true in you as in Christ.

There is a twofold movement going on in the earth; the moving off of the darkness, or of the world and its lust, and the moving in of the true light and its gracious, glorious kingdom. Christ, and all of you in whom, as in Christ, "that thing is true, that the darkness is passing and the true light is now shining," are engaged in the advancing movement and identified with it. It is the movement that is regaining, reconquering, recovering the earth for God. Into that movement you are to throw yourselves. With all who are in it you are to have a common brotherhood, and to make common cause. That is the will of God which you are to do. With the other movement, the moving off from the stage of the darkness and the prince of darkness, with his trappings and troops, you have nothing to do, save only to rescue, in the Father's name, all whom you can reach, ere that movement carries them away. For yourselves you have no concern with it. You love not the darkness, nor anything in it or about it. Your whole soul is bent on doing the will of God, and so falling in with the advancing march and movement which is to issue ere long in the universal shining of the true light over all the earth.

Surely that is a noble course for you, and one that must ensure your abiding for ever. It may seem indeed that you have no abiding place here. You may be called hence quickly at any time, while the darkness may seem to be passing very slowly; and the world with its lust may be still holding its ground stoutly, and showing an imposing front. But you lose not the fruit of your doing the will of God. " Blessed are the dead who die in the Lord; they rest from their labours, and their works do follow them." You have cast in your lot with a cause which does not pass away, but abideth for ever ; and a leader who does not pass away, but abideth for ever,—" the same yesterday, and to-day, and for ever." It is but a little while. Lo, he comes quickly, and you who have departed to be with him come in his train. He comes, and you come, to triumph over the complete and final passing away of the darkness, of the world and its lust, of all doing of any will but the will of God ; and to abide for ever in the earth, in which thenceforth for ever the will of God is to be done, even as it is in heaven.

14

THE GUILELESS SPIRIT, AMID ANTICHRISTIAN DE-FECTIONS, ESTABLISHED BY A MESSIANIC UNC-TION AND ILLUMINATION

" Little children, it is the last time: and as ye have heard that antichrist shall come, even now are there many antichrists ; whereby we know that it is the last time. They went out from us, but they were not of us ; for if they had been of us, they would no doubt have continued with us : but they went out, that they might be made manifest that they were not all of us. But ye have an unction from the Holy One, and ye know all things." 1 John 2:18-20

" Ye have an unction from the Holy One, and ye know all things." This is represented as our security against such apostasy or desertion as John has occasion to lament. We live, he says, in perilous circumstances. What has been foretold as characteristic of the last time may be seen virtually realised in our own day. The warning against antichrist need not be put off to a distant date. Already, in too many instances, the spirit of antichrist is discovering itself. To all practical intents and purposes, it is even now the last time to us. It is proved to be so by the prevalence of the very sort of opposition to Christ which in some gigantic shape is to signalise that era. We need not be setting up the phantom or ideal of a coming antichrist that is to torment and try the church of the future. We have enough of antichrists around and beside us now. And they are very near and close ;—almost of kin with us. But yesterday they were among us ; one with ourselves in

privilege, profession, and outward character. The keenest
eye could not discriminate between us and them. True,
their having gone out from us is a presumption, and indeed
a proof, that they were not really of us. That very fact,
however, making it plain that they who are still among us
are not all of us, may not unnaturally cause uneasiness as
to our own standing. But it need not. For there is a
difference ; " Ye have an unction from the Holy One,"
which they have not, " and ye know all things."

I do not at this stage inquire either into the nature and
character of the coming antichrist, or into the common feature identifying all antichrists. I wish rather to dwell upon
the ground of confidence here indicated, with special reference to trying times ; and in that view I notice these four
particulars : I. The anointing or unction ; II. The knowledge connected with it ; III. The nature of the connection ;
and IV. The security afforded by the unction and the knowledge against heresy and apostasy.

I. I begin with the anointing : " Ye have an unction,"
or the unction, or generally, unction. The term may literally denote anointing oil ; so that having unction may mean
being anointed with oil. This anointing, or being anointed
with oil, you have "from the Holy One ; " from Christ Jesus
our Lord. For it is he who is meant. The title indeed of
" the Holy One " may with all propriety be applied to God
absolutely ;—to the undivided Godhead, Father, Son, and
Holy Ghost. And if the persons are distinguished, it may
be applied to the Father and the Holy Ghost as well as to
the Son. But the sense of the passage, as well as the general usage of Scripture, points to the Son. In his humiliation, the devils acknowledged him as the Holy One (Mark
i. 24). In his exaltation Peter preaches him as such (Acts
iii. 14). And indeed, before his incarnation, the people
worshipped him in his divinity, and the prophets foretold

him in his humanity, as the Holy One; the Holy One of God; the Holy One of Israel (Psalm xvi. 10, etc.) The same application of the term best suits the present text. The Holy One is Christ; the unction or anointing is from Christ, who is himself, as Christ, the anointed One.

There is great significancy in the unction thus viewed as coming from this Holy One. Antichrists are spoken of. These are antagonists to Christ; to the anointed One; to him who is anointed to be the Holy One. You, on the other hand, have anointing from him. The unction which he himself receives, he communicates to you; consecrating you to be holy ones, as he is the Holy One. Thus you are joint-christs with him, while they are antichrists. They are against the anointed Holy One: you share with him in his anointing as the Holy One. They set at nought the unction which he has as the Holy One: you have this very unction from him. Such really is the antithesis. They are anti-christs, you are joint-christs; for you have an unction from him as the Holy One, making you "holy as he is holy."

The holiness here meant is consecration. It is what the Lord indicates in his farewell prayer: "Sanctify them through thy truth: thy word is truth. As thou hast sent me into the world, even so have I also sent them into the world; and for their sakes I sanctify myself, that they also might be sanctified through the truth." This is the unction which you have from the Holy One; from him whom "the Father hath sanctified and sent into the world."

The anointing is with the Holy Ghost. He is the anoint-ing oil; the oil of gladness with which God has anointed Christ above his fellows; the precious ointment poured out upon him, as the head, that runs down over all his body, even to the skirts of his garments. The unction therefore which "you have from the Holy One" is his own unction;

it is identically the same with what was his. He sheds forth upon you and in you the very same presence, power, and influence of the Holy Ghost that was shed forth upon and in himself, when he was about the business for which, as the Holy One, he was consecrated.

In his case that unction was real, sensible, manifest. If we have it from him, it must be so in ours also. It was in him and to him the seal of his acceptance, and the witness of his Sonship; for when the voice from heaven proclaimed him to be the Father's beloved Son in whom he is well pleased, "the Spirit descended on him like a dove." We have acceptance in him, and the adoption of sons. And the unction which we have from him is our being sealed, as justified ones, by "the Holy Ghost shedding abroad in our hearts the love of God;" and our receiving, as sons, "not the spirit of bondage again to fear, but the Spirit of adoption, whereby we cry, Abba, Father,—the Spirit witnessing with our spirits that we are the children of God."

In Jesus this unction was, on the one hand, his having always the Holy Spirit helping, comforting, and strengthening him; imparting to him, amid all his toils and tears, such fresh communications out of his Father's heart, such assurances of his Father's love and his Father's nearness to him, as never failed to nerve his soul for its utmost trial; to keep him trusting still in God; and to turn every prayer of nature's prompting : "Father, if it be possible, let the cup pass," into the resignation of filial obedience : " Nevertheless, Father, not my will but thine be done." The unction which we have from him as the Holy One, is our being in the same way upheld by the Holy Spirit in all our goings; our being enabled therefore to show "the meekness and gentleness of Christ;" our making it thus manifest that "the same mind is in us that was also in him."

Again, on the other hand, in Jesus the Holy One, this

unction was his constant and abiding apprehension or realisation of the Spirit moving him to the work for which he
was sent into the world. That work was to do the will of
him that sent him ; to preach glad tidings to the meek ; to
bind up the broken-hearted ; to fulfil all righteousness ; to
suffer, the just for the unjust; to give his life a ransom
for many. The unction which we have from him, that we
may be consecrated to be holy ones as he is the Holy One,
is our feeling and owning the inward call of the Holy Spirit,
moving us in our sphere to give ourselves to the same life-
work that always occupied him ; to carry out the great
design of his coming into the world ; to be his wholly
and unreservedly, as he was always and altogether the
Father's.

Thus, in all that it can be held to imply of consciously
apprehended and sensibly enjoyed favour and fellowship
with God, as well as of sacred destination and devotion to
God, we share with Christ his own very unction. Whatever is implied in his being anointed with the Holy Ghost
we are to realise in ourselves, as having "an unction from
the Holy One." Thus we are christs, as he is the Christ ;
anointed ones, as he is the Anointed One ; the Lord's
anointed, the Lord's christs, in somewhat of the same sense
in which he is so. For we share his anointing ; we "have
unction from the Holy One."

II. As thus anointed, we "know all things." This is
not of course omniscience ; but full and complete knowledge
of the matter in hand, as opposed to knowledge that is
fragmentary and partial. The question is between Christ
and antichrist ; between the truth of Christ and the lie of
antichrist. That lie is a denial of Jesus as the Christ ; and
therefore a denial of him as the Son, involving necessarily
a denial of the Father also (ver. 22, 23). But we know
the truth ; we "know all things" about it. The whole

truth concerning Jesus as the Christ, the Son of the Father, in all its relations to the divine character and counsels as well as to human experience and hope, we know. We have mastered it, not piecemeal, but entire ; or it has thus mastered us. Not a corner of the field, but the field itself, is ours. We know Jesus as the Christ, the Son of God, in all the rich and ample significancy of these titles or designations. So we know all things ; all things concerning the truth that Jesus is "the Christ, the Son of the living God."

This, in one view, may not be knowing much ; but it is knowing what we do know well and thoroughly. And much depends on our knowledge being of that sort ; not universal in its range ; but, be its range ever so limited, universal in its kind, so far as it goes ; universal—full-orbed, as it were, and all round,—as opposed to what is one-sided. The anointing of Jesus, his being the Christ,—what it is, and what it means ; his consecration as the Holy One ; his oneness as the Son with the Father ; all that we know. And we know it, not by catching at some one aspect of the mighty plan,—the great " mystery of godliness, God manifest in the flesh,"—that may happen to suit our convenience, or to strike our fancy, but by a calm, clear, and comprehensive insight into all that it unfolds of the highest glory of God, and all that it contemplates of highest good to man. We look at this great theme, or rather this great fact, in all its bearings ; as it vindicates the righteous sovereignty of the Lord of all, while it secures full and free salvation to the worst and guiltiest of his creatures, if they will but own that sovereignty and submit to it.

Hence it is a knowledge having eyes, as it were, on all sides, all round ; open to what touches the prerogatives and rights of heaven, no less than to what concerns the interests of earth ; full of thoughtfulness about God and what is due to God, as well as about sinful man and what sinful man requires; well balanced, therefore, and guarded against both extremes, the extreme of mere arbitrary rule, or a sort of fatalism, ascribed to God, on the one hand, and that of accommodation and compromise, assumed to meet man's case, on the other.

We know all things; all the principles of God's government, all the attributes of his nature, all the features of his character : as well as all the miseries and necessities of man's lost and guilty state ; so as to take them all into account in forming our conception of the plan of mercy, the reign of grace, the method of redemption and salvation. Hence our conception of that economy of righteous love, however far from being perfect, is yet, to the extent to which it carries us, consistent, and, from its consistency, sure and satisfying. We know indeed only in part after all. All the things that we know, we know only dimly and faintly. We know none of them fully, or as we hope to know them one day, when we shall know even as you are known. But still we know them all. For, as Paul testifies (1 Cor. ii. 9–12), although " eye hath not seen, nor ear heard, neither have entered into the heart of man, the things which God hath prepared for them that love him," yet " God hath revealed them to us by his Spirit ; for the Spirit searcheth all things, even the deep things of God." And " we have received, not the spirit of the world, but the Spirit which is of God, that we might know the things that are freely given to us of God." We thus know them all, the deep things of God, the things freely given to us of God, in virtue of the unction which we have from the Holy One.

III. For the unction which we have from the Holy One, and our knowing all things, are intimately connected.

One might imagine perhaps, that the knowledge which

I have been describing as so comprehensive and complete, must be the fruit of leisurely and learned study ; of academic training and scholarly research. But it is really not so. If it were, it would be but little trustworthy, especially in any advent or development of the last time, in which antichrist may be coming, or there may be already many antichrists. All experience proves, that of our own day as well as of older ecclesiastical history, that the knowledge of the schools, even when it seems almost to be, humanly speaking, omniscience, is no security for those who have it continuing with us, as John puts it, in our genuine apostolic fellowship. Much study may be a weariness of the flesh, without being either strength or stedfastness to the spirit. The knowledge which alone can be relied on, must be not only the knowledge of all things ; but such a knowledge of all things as only unction from the Holy One can give.

In fact, we cannot have true knowledge of any of these things unless we have it by unction from the Holy One. For "the natural man receiveth not the things of the Spirit of God ; for they are foolishness to him ; neither can he know them ; because they are spiritually discerned" (1 Cor. ii. 13). It is only "he who is spiritual" who "judgeth all things," who can know them so as to judge them. For he alone is in a position and has the capacity to form a fair estimate or judgment of the relations among the things of God. And it is by their mutual relations that things are really known and judged.

This is a maxim true in all sciences ; and not least manifestly so in the science of divinity. If, in the science of astronomy, we would know all its things, all its truths, to any satisfactory end, theoretical or practical ; we must get, not the eye of a clown or vulgar stargazer, nor that of Chaldean sage or poetic dreamer, nor that of one to whom the clear calm midnight sky is a confused galaxy of bright

gems, a brilliant shower of diamonds shed in rich disorder
on the dark brow of nature's sleeping beauty, but the eye
of Newton's scholar and Laplace's, who has learned of them
to calculate planetary magnitudes and distances and forces,
and to bring the whole splendid chaos under the sway of
the one simple law that reigns supreme throughout all
space. So, in the region of what is spiritual and divine,
the faculty of seeing things in their true relations is not
elsewhere or otherwise to be acquired, than in the school
and under the teaching of the Holy Ghost. It is his
anointing of the eye with eye-salve that gives spiritual discernment, not only to understand separately, as distinct
objects of contemplation and thought, many of the truths
proclaimed and the objects exhibited in revelation, but to
perceive how, under the leading and guiding principle of
the free, full, and sovereign grace of the glorious gospel,
they all assume their fitting places and proportions, and
form together one consistent whole. Mere human study
might master all that has been ever said or written about
God and his works and ways. But still knowledge thus
got always runs the risk of being prejudiced and partial.
All the articles of all the creeds may be thoroughly sifted,
in all their doctrinal, controversial, and historical bearings.
The all-knowing theologian may be able to discuss them all,
and all about them. But left to himself, and without
"unction from the Holy One," how apt is he to let some
peculiar leaning, some personal bias or idiosyncrasy of his
own, prevail ; exaggerating some one portion, or aspect, or
feature of the divine plan, and raising many a cloud of
lettered dust, such as may cause endless perplexity and
doubt, and sadly mar "the simplicity which is in Christ."
It is not, therefore, any such knowledge of all things that is
here commended. Rather, it is that of which our Lord himself speaks when he says : " I thank thee, O Father, Lord

of heaven and earth, because thou hast hid these things
from the wise and prudent, and hast revealed them unto
babes. Even so, Father: for so it seemed good in thy
sight" (Matt. xi. 25, 26).

For how does that Holy One, the Son, reveal to these
babes the Father, and "all things delivered unto him of his
Father?" How but by imparting to them that anointing
which he has himself? It is as the Holy One, the Christ, the
Anointed, that the Son has all things delivered unto him
of his Father, and knows the Father so as to reveal him to
us. And it is by making us partakers with himself in his
own anointing; by making us christs, the Lord's anointed,
as he himself is the Christ, the Lord's anointed; by causing
us to have the same unction with himself;—that he reveals
to us the Father.

How wonderfully, in this view of it, does this unction
which we have from the Holy One unite and identify
us with the Holy One himself, in respect of our knowing all things! It is indeed a marvellous way of grace
and condescension in which the great Teacher teaches
us. He does not stand on an elevated platform apart hand-
ing down to us the lessons we have to learn, and reporting,
as it were, the observations and discoveries he makes. He
lifts us up to be beside himself. He puts his own glass into
our hand: he puts his own eye into our head: he puts his
own intensity of loving gaze into our heart; and bids us
look for ourselves; and see the Father as he sees him, and
know all things as he knows them; "all things delivered
to him of his Father." Well might Paul say of the spiritual man, thus—by such a spiritual discernment as this—
judging all things; himself judged of none: "Who hath
known the mind of the Lord that he may instruct him?
But we have the mind of Christ." For the unction of the
Spirit which we thus share with him,—or rather he with

us,—gives us the same knowledge of the Father—of all things—that Christ the Son had when he himself received the unction of the Spirit; the same, I mean, in kind, not in degree ;—not yet the same in measure, though gradually coming more and more nearly to be so ; meanwhile, the same in manner.

What was his manner of knowing the Father and all things about the Father's will and purpose, when he was here, as the Holy One anointed by the Spirit? Ah ! how practical it was ! how experimental ! how thoroughly a learning of it all by obedience ; by suffering ; by unreserved submission and acquiescence ; by patience ; by waiting; by faith, and love, and hope ! Therefore, and only therefore, it was in his case a knowledge thoroughly simple, and in its simplicity thoroughly complete. " Little children," let it be so in our case too. Let us remember his own saying : " If any man will do his will, he shall know of the doctrine, whether it be of God." It was as a doer of God's will that he, in his human experience, having the Spirit's unction, knew all things. Let it be as doers of God's will that we learn to know them too.

And let us remember, " This is the work of God, that ye believe in him whom he has sent." Believing in Jesus we attain to his clear knowledge of the Father and of all things. Clouds of guilt and wrath, of misconception and suspicion, of doubt and fear, are driven away before the rising of the Sun of Righteousness with healing in his wings. We walk no more benighted and befooled ; stumbling in the dark, amid unseen stones and pitfalls, and dire visionary phantoms. We walk safely and at liberty, knowing all things, seeing all things in the light of God ; in the light of his reconciled countenance ; in the light of that love wherewith he " loveth us even as he loveth Christ." It is by the love with which the Father loves him that the

Son knows the Father, and all things which the Father has, and which also are his. It is by the love with which the Father loves us as he loves him, that we, having unction from him who is the Holy One, know all things; "the love with which the Father hath loved him being in us, and he in us" (John xvii. 17–26).

IV. The security which our "having an unction from the Holy One and knowing all things" affords, in trying times, must now surely be seen to be very ample and firm. Others may "go out from us;" it being thus "made manifest that they were not of us;" and may become anti-christs, or the prey of antichrist. But "will ye also go away?"—ye who share the very unction and the very knowledge which the Holy One himself has? Is not this your preservative against all error and apostasy? Is it not a sufficient preservative? "To whom will ye go? He has the words of eternal life; and you believe and are sure that he is the Christ, the Son of the living God." And you are joint-christs with him; and joint-sons with him; and joint-heirs with him. What have you to do any more with idols?—or with the husks of the swine-trough, to which citizens of the far country may be for sending you?—or with seducing lies and doctrines of devils to which you may be tempted to give heed?—or, in a word, with any of the modifications of the way of grace and salvation,—any of the readjustments of the terms of acceptance,—any of the devices for pacifying conscience,—any of the new lights, mystical or rationalistic, sacramental or sentimental,—by which men would fain seek to be wiser than God, and even holier than God, and better than God? Ye who have found Christ, or whom Christ has found; ye who have the same anointing that Christ had; ye who taste and see how good his Father and yours is,—loving you even as he loveth him,—"will ye also go away?"

And be sure that this is the only preservative ; the one specific. Much learning, great enlightenment, the intelligence of an age of progress in all that relates to high mental culture and social improvement ; intense earnestness, profound study, patient inquiry ; anxious searching of the heart and of all that has been proposed for meeting the heart's wants ; devotional feeling ; self-renouncing and self-sacrificing humility ;—these, and other equally promising means and tokens of good, are found to be no effectual safeguards. Nay, at any season when men's minds are stirred, their consciences moved, and their souls melted ; when the deadness of an age of formalism is giving place to a time of inquiry, of awakening, of thought and sensibility, of speculation and discourse, on things spiritual and divine ; the very shaking of the dry bones caused by the wind of heaven may only make you more susceptible of influences, and more open to suggestions, carrying you away from the old paths and the footsteps of the flock, into wanderings in search of rest or of revival,—of peace or of perfection,—that may issue in your being fain at last to believe any prophet and follow any guide, even if he lead you into the arms of an infallible church, or down the steep bank that ends in the dreary void of scepticism and unbelief.

At such an era ;—when "it is now the last time, of which ye have heard that antichrist shall come ; when even now already there are many antichrists ; whereby ye may know that it is the last time ; " when, on all hands, too many who seemed to be of us—as serious and as safe as ourselves—are going out from us ; "Little children," see that ye have indeed "unction from the Holy One and know all things." Be very sure that no ignorance, no emptiness, no vacancy ; no unhealed sore and unanointed eye ; no halting or hesitating belief ; no "vague and doubtsome faith;" will stand in the midst of such peril. Nothing will stand but what is real, positive, satisfying, in your personal acquaintance with God, and your saving knowledge of the things of God; nothing but your having yourselves found the Messiah, the Christ, and your bringing others to find him: that they and you may really become partakers with him in all that he is to the Father as his Holy One, and all that as his beloved Son he knows of the things of the Father delivered to him for us.

15

THE GUILELESS SPIRIT, AMID ANTICHRISTIAN DENIAL OF THE SON, ACKNOWLEDGING THE SON SO AS TO HAVE THE FATHER ALSO

"I have not written unto you because ye know not the truth, but because ye know it, and that no lie is of the truth. Who is a liar but he that denieth that Jesus is the Christ? He is antichrist, that denieth the Father and the Son. Whosoever denieth the Son, the same hath not the Father [*but he that acknowledgeth the Son hath the Father also.*"] 1 John 2:21-23

THE last part of the 23d verse, although considered doubtful by our translators, and therefore put by them in italics and within brackets, is now admitted to be genuine. It completes the sense of the passage. To deny the Son is not to have the Father; to acknowledge the Son is to have the Father. And this is the ultimate difference between an antichrist and a joint-christ; between those who are against the Anointed One, and you who share his anointing; "having unction from the Holy One and knowing all things." By that unction or anointing, which passes to you from the anointed Holy One, you know all things; all the truth; the truth in all its bearings; and therefore you can discriminate between the truth and every lie. If it were not so, it would be needless for me to write to you (ver. 21). I cannot expect you to detect a liar unless you know the truth yourselves. For the test by which you detect a liar, or the liar, is the truth which you know. He contradicts the truth; he denies that Jesus is the Christ;

and that denial is enough to mark the liar. It marks him also as an antichrist, or, in spirit, the antichrist. For it amounts to what is the criterion or characteristic of antichrist, a denial of the Father and the Son (ver. 22). The denial, indeed, so far at least as the Father is concerned, is not express and avowed, but virtual rather and by implication. The lie touches immediately the Son alone; and reaches the Father only through the Son. It is not, however, on that account, less really a denial of the Father as well as of the Son. For the Father and the Son are one; and therefore, he that "denieth the Son, the same hath not the Father," while "he that acknowledgeth the Son hath the Father also."

Two questions naturally occur here. I. How is a denial that Jesus is the Christ equivalent to a denial of the Son? And II. How is a denial of the Son a denial of the Father, so that to deny the Son is not to have the Father; and how, on the other hand, does the acknowledgment of the Son secure our having the Father?

I. Plainly, in John's view, to deny that Jesus is the Christ is to deny the Son; the two denials are declared to be one and the same. And yet there is a difference. The object of the one denial is a proposition; the object of the other is a person. Nor is the difference accidental or unimportant; on the contrary, it is very significant.

One thing, at least, is very clear. If the denial of a proposition concerning any person is to be viewed as identical with the denial of the person himself, the proposition must be one that vitally affects his nature and character. Take any illustrious personage who may be supposed to occupy my thoughts; the heir-apparent to the throne, for instance. If I choose to deny that he is what you believe, or even know him to be, as to his height, or complexion, or turn of mind, or habit of body, you may charge me with falsehood, or even say that I lie. But you would scarcely allege that in denying any affirmation of that sort about him, I deny the prince. It must be something far more deeply touching his birth, or his birthright, or his worthiness of either, that I deny, before you can construe my denial of it, into a disloyal and traitorous denial of himself. So here, if to deny the proposition that "Jesus is the Christ" is to deny the Son; the proposition itself must mean more than at first appears.

1. It cannot mean simply that he is the person foretold in the Old Testament under the name of the Messiah; there is more in it than a mere identification of the individual. The official designation, Christ, or Messiah, or Anointed, marks not only a certain relation to the Jewish Scriptures, but also and still more a certain relation to God, whose Christ he is.

In the dreamy and misty theosophy of the Gnostic antichrists, any Christ whom they would acknowledge at all could be nothing else than a sort of efflux or emanation of Deity, a detached portion of the divine nature, or a mysterious outgoing of the divine power, or wisdom, or love; altogether visionary and unsubstantial; but withal very sublime. The idea of such a transcendental Christ being identical with the historical man, the man of "flesh and bones," Jesus, was an outrage on their philosophy. They might admit an occasional and temporary illapse. Now and then, or perhaps generally, all through his life and ministry, Jesus might be in a certain spiritual relation to this Christ. There might be upon him, and in him, moving and inspiring him, what of God they thought proper to call the Christ. But that he was truly and personally himself the Christ,—in his manhood and in his manhood's history and experience,—especially in his birth and in his death, their subtle notions of spirit and matter compelled them strenuously to deny. This denial necessarily reduced Jesus to the level of a mere man ; a representative man perhaps, the ground and type and head of restored or perfected humanity ; a divine man too, in some vague use of the phrase ; but still really not more than a man ; his birth no real incarnation ; his death no real propitiation. It is this which stamps value on the confession that "Jesus is the Christ ; " that from his being born of the Virgin to his expiring on Calvary, he is the Christ. And it is this which makes the denial of the proposition so serious. It is the denial of his vicarious character and position ; his being in any fair sense, or to any substantial effect, the substitute of men ; of men viewed as guilty, condemned, and lost.

I have said that he might be owned, after a fashion, as a representative man, or the representative man. Humanity in its best state, whether of development or of recovery,— perfect humanity, if you will,—might have its culminating grace and glory in him. And as the model man, or some-thing more, as the man in whom human nature and the human race, as such, are elevated, he might be so visited by the overshadowing of a divine energy as to be in some sense partaker of the divine nature. But as to what he is himself personally, he differs in no material or essential re-spect from other men. Born like them, like them he dies. Not only has he all in common with them ; but he has no-thing in him or about him but what is in common. He is not " separate from sinners." * For there the stress of this

---

* So Jesus is described in the Epistle to the Hebrews : "For such an High Priest became us, who is holy, harmless, undefiled, separate from sinners, and made higher than the heavens " (vii. 26). Here the three epithets, "holy, harmless, undefiled," exhaust the account of his pure and perfect moral character. The phrases that follow, "separate from sinners," and "made higher than the heavens," must refer, I think, the former to the manner of his birth, the latter to his exaltation after his death.

great controversy lies, in our own day, as well as in that of John.

Jesus must be acknowledged as not only one with us, but "separate from us." Not otherwise can he save us by being our substitute ; redeem us by being our ransom ! reconcile us to God by the sacrifice of himself in our stead. He must be "separate from us" in his birth ; exempt, by special miracle, from all participation in the sin of humanity, whose guilt he is to expiate. He must be "separate from us" in his death ; his death being what no other death ever was, or ever can be, a real satisfaction to offended justice ; a valid atonement for the offence ; an actual enduring and exhausting of what the penal severity of law requires ; a true and literal "suffering, the just for the unjust, that he might bring us to God."

The denial of the proposition that "Jesus is the Christ," according to the notions then current, precluded all such views of the way in which he saves sinners. Under a different form, a similar mysticism precludes them now.

There has always indeed been a school in the church tending in that direction ; willing to exalt Jesus as high as any one would wish, in one aspect of his mediatorship, his being one with us, and so qualified to represent us; but ever stopping short of that other aspect of it, his being "separate from us," and so qualified to atone for us. Of Jesus personally much appears to be made. Not too much certainly ; for that is impossible. Jesus, personally, the real, living Jesus, cannot be too much thought of. His very name is as ointment poured forth. He is the chiefest among ten thousand and altogether lovely. The church, the spouse,—every soul that as a chaste virgin is espoused to Jesus,—is ravished with the beauty of his person and the endearments of his fellowship. But it is a snare to forget, it is a sin to deny, that he is the Christ ; or, in other words, to overlook or set aside that real and actual work of substitution and satisfaction, of vicarious suffering and obedience, in respect of which he is the Christ. Ah! will not every true lover of Jesus feel that, apart from his being thus the Christ, he has in fact no Jesus at all to love? "Dear, dying Lamb!" is his adoring and grateful invocation; "Worthy the Lamb, for he was slain for us," is his song; "Thou hast redeemed us with thy blood," is his worship. He, therefore, is at no loss to see how the denial of the proposition that "Jesus is the Christ," thus viewed in its bearing on his work, is substantially and most sadly a denial of the person.

2. This will appear still more clearly when we consider that the person is the Son. As the Son he stands in a distinct and definite relation to the Father. He must be owned in that relation if he is to be owned at all; otherwise he is to all intents and purposes denied.

The Gnostic dreamers fancied that they could get a notion of a Son of God from a mere contemplation of the divine nature in the abstract. By a sort of effort of imagination they personified a divine attribute or emanation, calling it the Son; sometimes distinguishing that idea from the idea of the Christ, sometimes identifying them. Nor did they hesitate to allow the title Son of God to Jesus, considered as the representative man, or type of perfect humanity, who, as such, enjoyed the presence of somewhat of the Divinity with him and in him. Between these two conceptions of a Son of God they may be said to have oscillated; the one high, but indistinct; the other, more distinct perhaps, and intelligible, but comparatively low. They are the two conceptions, on this great theme of the Sonship, between which, as opposite extremes, I am apt to be tossed to and fro.

I fix my thoughts on the everlasting God considered

abstractly as he is in himself. I try to body forth in my imagination the idea of there being in the essence of the Divine nature, from all eternity, a Son of the Father; "God of God; light of light; very God of very God; begotten, not made; of one substance with the Father;" his only begotten. Abstracting my mind from earth and time, I gaze on the Eternal Three in One; Father, Son, and Holy Ghost. I would pierce the mystery of high heaven; how "the Son is of the Father;" and "the Holy Ghost is of the Father and the Son." Alas! it is impenetrable. The distinction of persons in the Godhead I may believe, though I cannot comprehend. The second person I may be taught to call the Word, or the Son. But the name tells me nothing. I am lost in the dark sublimity of the infinite unknown. Coming down from heaven to earth and time, I see Jesus, "a man approved of God, who went about doing good;" and I can understand why, as a good and holy man, the perfect model of human goodness, the restorer and perfecter of all humanity's excellence, after the divine ideal,—he should be specially and above all others honoured with the title of Son of God. Such a view of sonship, however, scarcely rises above what is matter of mere figure or sentiment. Thus, on the one hand, considering the nature of God apart, in the deep, dark wonder of the eternal generation, the Son being eternally begotten of the Father; or, on the other hand, considering the nature of man apart, in the clear light of the history of Jesus, and his being found pre-eminently and exclusively worthy to be called God's Son; I am either soaring up to what is too high for me, or I am apt to acquiesce in what is too low for him.

But let me fully realise the fact that Jesus is the Christ. And let me fully enter into the great transaction between the Father and the Son, of which that fact is the expression.

Then a new and blessed sight of this divine sonship breaks upon my soul. For now, as I am carried back, in rapt musing, to the remotest point of possible retrospection, along the vista of the ages of a past eternity, before all worlds, the Father and the Son are seen, not in repose, but in counsel at least, if not in action. A momentous consultation is going on. A great covenant is negotiated. The Father and the Son, with the Spirit, are, if one may dare to say so, in solemn conference together. From the bosom of the Father, in which he is dwelling evermore, the Son receives a commission to come forth. He is appointed heir of all things. Creation is assigned to him as his proper work. All providence is to be his care; and above all the providence of this spot of earth. Here, on this earth, from among a fallen race, he is to purchase for himself, and for his Father, at a great price, a seed given him by the Father, to share with him in the blessedness of his being the Son. So it is arranged between the Father and the Son from everlasting; the Holy Spirit being a party to the arrangement, as he is to have a large share in carrying it out. And so, accordingly, in the fulness of time, the Son appears among men. He appears as the Son ; on his Father's behalf; entrusted with his Father's commission ; to be about his Father's business. Thus Jesus is seen as the Son. And it is in the character of the Christ that he is seen to be the Son. He is the Son, not merely in respect of his being the holy Jesus, receiving proofs and tokens of God's fatherly presence and approval, as any holy being might. He is the Son also, and chiefly, in respect of the work or office with a view to which he is the Christ. He is the Son consenting to be the Father's servant, and as such anointed of the Father for the accomplishment of the Father's purpose. Only, therefore, in so far as you acknowledge Jesus as the Christ do you really receive him as the

Son.   Any denial, whether practical or doctrinal, of the proposition that Jesus is the Christ, is tantamount to a disowning of him personally as the Son.   It is only when you recognise him as anointed to do his Father's will in the sacrifice of himself that you really own him, in any distinct sense, as the Son.

Such, then, is the import and significancy of the proposition that Jesus is the Christ, considered in itself; and such its bearing on the owning of him personally as the Saviour and as the Son.   It is a proposition which so vitally affects the essential character of him to whom it relates, that the denial of it is virtually a denial of himself.   For the completeness of this illustrious personage depends on a full and adequate recognition of his double relation; to us sinners, as our Jesus, and to God the Father, as his Son. And neither of these relations can be fully and adequately recognised, unless his being the Christ is recognised, with all that his being the Christ must be held fairly to imply. Neither what he is to us as our Jesus, nor what he is to God as his Son, can be otherwise known than by what he is anointed to do, and actually does, as the Christ.   Set aside his being the Christ; the anointed sacrificer and anointed sacrifice; the anointed priest and anointed victim; set aside his actual work for which he is anointed, the work of redeeming us by his obedience, and the shedding of his blood, or the giving of his life, in our stead; and we have neither any Jesus fit to be our saviour, nor any Son of God worth the owning.   The stress must always, for practical purposes, be laid upon his office and ministry as the Christ.*

Hence he that denieth that Jesus is the Christ is not only a liar; he is antichrist.   And being antichrist, setting himself against the Christ, thrusting him aside from his blessed office and ministry of real and effectual reconcilia-

* See note at the end of this Lecture.

tion for which he is anointed,—he, as antichrist, denies the Father and the Son.

II. This raises the second question : How is it that to deny the Son is to deny the Father, so that "whosoever denieth the Son the same hath not the Father; but he that acknowledgeth the Son hath the Father also ? "

I. "Whosoever denieth the Son, the same hath not," and cannot have, "the Father." This may be regarded in one view as matter of positive appointment. In the exercise of his absolute sovereignty, God is entitled to say upon what terms and in what way any of his creatures shall have him ;—have him, that is, as theirs ; have him so as to have an interest in him, a hold upon him, and a bond of union with him. He may set forth any one he pleases, and say, If you deny him you cannot have me. In this case however he sets forth his Son, and therefore the appointment must be allowed to be in the highest degree reasonable and fair. One would say even, it is natural that this law should be in force ;—You cannot have the Father otherwise than through your owning the Son. The disowning or denial of the Son cannot but be an offence to the Father ; deeply wounding and grieving his heart. It will be so all the more if the Son is disowned or denied, not merely in a personal, but, if one may so say, in an official capacity ; not merely in respect of something connected with his own manner of being with the Father, but in respect of his exercising a great ministry, as bearing the Father's commission and executing the Father's purpose.

If the Son remained at home with the Father, in the inscrutable privacy of inaccessible light, which to us is impenetrable darkness,—so that beyond the fact of the Father having a Son of his own nature, dwelling in his bosom for ever, nothing of what they are to one another was ever to be known,—then to deny, or not to acknowledge the Son, might not be so culpable in us, or so justly displeasing to the Father. In that case we might possibly have the Father irrespectively of our knowing and owning the Son. It is otherwise when the Father "bringeth in the first-begotten into the world," with the proclamation, "Let all the angels of God worship him." It is otherwise still when to you, perishing in your sins, the Father sends the Son on a mission of richest grace. Now it must be very palpable that if you deny the Son you cannot have the Father; especially if your denial of the Son take the form of a denial that Jesus is the Christ. For that is a denial of the Son in the very character in which he comes to you from the Father, sent, sealed, and anointed, to save you from your sins, by his being "separate from sinners;" separate in the manner of his holy birth, in the merit of his vicarious obedience, and in the efficacy of his atoning death and justifying resurrection.

Here it becomes especially important to observe that the object of your denial is not a proposition merely, but a person. It is not with a statement about Jesus that you deal; but with himself personally. And he with whom you deal is the Son. And he is the Son in the very act of coming, as he says, " to do the Father's will;" which will is " your being sanctified or cleansed by the offering of himself, once for all, a sacrifice to take away your sins" (Heb. x. 10).

Yes! it is a living person who is now before you; showing himself to you; addressing you. You see him as he was when Pilate brought him out, his head all bleeding from the crown of thorns, and exclaimed, Behold the man! or when John saw his side pierced, and blood and water coming forth; or when the Roman soldier gazed on his meek pale face of agony, and murmured, "Truly this was the Son of God;" or when the dying thief prayed, "Lord, remember me when thou comest into thy kingdom." The same now as then, he draws near to you; bleeding still; his freshly-pierced side still giving forth fresh blood and water; his face as woful as when he cried, My God, My God, why hast thou forsaken me? his voice as calm as when he bowed his head and gave up the ghost, and said, It is finished. He draws near, " wounded for our transgressions, bruised for our iniquities." And you deny him. He tells you he is the Son in all this, doing the Father's will, carrying out the Father's purpose of infinite compassion and benignity toward you a miserable sinner. And you deny him ; you deny the Son. He stands still beside you, knocking at the door of your conscience, of your heart; assuring you that he is the Son ; that at the Father's bidding he takes your place, and bears your sin ; that for the Father's love to you he is with you to take you home with him to the Father; now ; immediately ; this very instant ; as you are ; altogether vile and polluted, and helpless in your guilty state. He pledges himself to you that you have nothing now to fear ; that a full pardon is freely yours ; and a perfect peace ; and a new heart; and a right spirit. And you deny him ; you deny the Son. How can you have the Father? Is it not in the very nature of things an mpossibility? It is no abstract truth that you deny ; but the true and living Son ; and that too in the very execution of his commission from the Father on your behalf. It cannot be that so denying the Son you can have, or ever hope to have, the Father.

2. "But he that acknowledgeth the Son hath the Father also." He hath the Father; how surely, how fully, may partly appear, if we consider, not only what Jesus is to us, as our anointed Saviour, but also what he is to the Father as his beloved Son.

For whatever is implied in his being the Son, in so far

as it is compatible with human nature and a human condition,—whatever of grace, whatever of glory there is in
the relation in which he who is the Christ stands as the
Son to the Father,—he shares with you who acknowledge
him. The Father makes you partakers of it all with the
Son. You therefore have the Father as he has the Father;
after the same manner, and largely after the same measure
too.

How would you say that Jesus, as the Son, when he was
as you are now, had the Father? All through his humiliation, how has he the Father? On what footing is he with
the Father? What is his habit of intercourse with the
Father? The Father's love he has; his love of boundless
complacency, approval, delight. He is sure of it. The assurance of it is never lost or interrupted; not even when
he is made to taste the bitterness of the cup of wrath, and
know the doom of a God-forsaken soul. He has the Father's
gracious presence with him always. He has the Father's
consolation and support, in the ministry of angels sent to
comfort him, and in the constant abiding of the Spirit with
him. He has the Father; having right of access and appeal
to him always; and using that right always. "Abba Father"
is on his lips always, and in his heart always. It is "Abba
Father when there is work to do; when there is contradiction of sinners against himself to bear; when there is resisting unto death in the strife against sin; when the voice is
heard, Awake, O sword, against my Shepherd; it is "Abba
Father" still always. It is "Abba Father" when he for
once rejoices in spirit,—"I thank thee, O Father." It is
"Abba Father" when he soothes the sisters and gives
them back their brother,—"Father! I thank thee." It is
"Abba Father" when he takes leave of his sorrowing
followers, and commends them to the Father. It is "Abba
Father" when hanging on the cross he prays for his mur-

derers,—"Father, forgive them,"—and for himself, "Father, into thy hands I commend my spirit."

So he, as the Son, had the Father, when he was as you are. So he would have you, acknowledging him, to have the Father also. You own him as Jesus, the Christ of God, the Son of the Father; the Christ of God, washing you in his blood, clothing you with his righteousness, and presenting you with acceptance to God whose Christ he is; the Son of the Father; your own elder brother; come out to seek you in the far country, and to bring you home to his Father and yours. Nor will he be satisfied unless you have the Father even as he has the Father. He shows you what it is to have the Father in the state in which you now are; amid the trials of earth, the enmity of the world, the very pains of hell. He shows you how even here you can have the Father as, in a work and warfare infinitely harder than yours, he had the Father; how you, in all your toil and tribulation, can rest in the consciousness of the Father's favour; and rejoice in the doing of the Father's will; and resign yourself contentedly to the Father's disposal; and quietly wait the Father's pleasure to call you hence when the time comes.

And what shall I say of your having the Father then? —not as the Son on earth had, but as the Son in heaven now has, the Father? Even now he says, "If a man love me, he will keep my words, and my Father will love him, and we will come unto him, and make our abode with him." So you have the Father now. But more, far more, is yours. "Father, I will that they also, whom thou hast given me, be with me where I am; that they may behold my glory, which thou hast given me : for thou lovedst me before the foundation of the world." He comes to receive you to himself; to take you to be with him where he is, that you may have the Father as he has the Father.

O glorious day! O blessed consummation! Is this indeed the end of your not denying but acknowledging that Jesus is the Christ, and so not denying but acknowledging the Son?

Low he stoops,—how low none but a holy God and lost souls can tell,—as Jesus who is the Christ. Down into the depths of sin's guilt and doom he goes. Over the head of the anointed righteous One, the obedient servant, the billows of wrath roll. And you deny him not, but acknowledge him, as thus redeeming you. You confess that "Jesus is the Christ." You are not ashamed of his cross. It is your glory. And well it may be. For what fruit is yours through your not denying, but acknowledging, the Son, in his coming forth from the Father as his Christ to such humiliation for you? Is it that you escape punishment merely, and are saved from hell? That would be no mean boon. But what privilege is yours now,—what hope hereafter? It is the Son whom you acknowledge. He has the Father. He has the Father's kingdom; the Father's riches; the Father's joys. He has the Father's heart. He has the Father himself. And nothing will content him but that you, who acknowledge him, shall have the Father as he has the Father. Surely of the future, as well as of the present fruit of your acknowledging the Son, it may be said: "Eye hath not seen, nor ear heard, neither have entered into the heart of man, the things which God hath prepared for them that love him." And surely, beyond question, the whole plan and system of saving mercy is surpassingly gracious and glorious,—according to which, "when the fulness of the time was come, God sent forth his Son, made of a woman, made under the law, to redeem them that were under the law, that we might receive the adoption of sons."

NOTE REFERRED TO AT PAGE 186

I have always had an impression that neither the doctrine of the Trinity nor that of the Incarnation, with its correlative, the Resurrection, can long continue to be really held by those who deny that of the Atonement, in the ordinary orthodox sense of it. If the Second Person in the Godhead has not an office to execute, and a work to do, effecting a real change in the relation of fallen man to God, and bringing him, upon his consenting to be brought, out of a state of condemnation and estrangement, into a state of acceptance and reconciliation,—and if the Third Person has not an office to execute, and a work to do, for obtaining the consent needed; in other words, if Father, Son, and Holy Ghost are not to be regarded as sustaining different, and distinctly defined, parts in the economy of grace ;—I see not how distinct personality, in respect of being or essence, can well be conceived as either necessary or even possible. If they present themselves to me as acting differently and distinctly, each doing some specific thing which neither of the others does, or, according to the Divine arrangement, is competent to do,—then, with all its mystery, the Trinity becomes so far intelligible as a reality, if not in its nature, at least in its manner of actual working or doing. Otherwise, if the whole process of man's restoration or education is to be resolved into discovery and influence—the discovery of what he already is in relation to God, and the influence of that discovery—the distinction of the Divine Persons is to me merely nominal ; I am driven into virtual Sabellianism. So also, if Jesus, when on earth, had no special work of redemption to accomplish,—special, I mean, in the sense of its being what none but a real Divine Person, having a real human nature, could do,—the work, in short, of the actual substitution of himself in the room and stead of the guilty, to meet legal demands on them, and answer for them judicially,—I confess myself unable to form any idea of the propriety or meaning of the hypostatical union of the two distinct natures in one person. It becomes to me quite notional or nominal, not real ; I am apt to resolve it into a sort of figure of speech ; or to substitute a mystical "divine man," for the real Son of God become the real son of man, or "the Word made flesh." This has always appeared to me to be the dangerous tendency of the speculations of that school which some broad-church divines of our day represent. Giving them all credit for sincerity in holding, or thinking that they hold, the old orthodox doctrines of the Trinity and the Incarnation, I am persuaded that their view of the Atonement and kindred subjects must evacuate these doctrines of their sense and significancy, and land its adherents in some modification of the Sabellian and the Gnostic heresies, if not ultimately in Socinianism itself. It is on that account that, having given some attention formerly to the subject in an examination of certain essays, I attach much importance now to the *Formula* employed by John here and elsewhere—"Jesus is the Christ"—"Jesus Christ is come in the flesh," as I understand and have ventured to expound it.

16

THE GUILELESS SPIRIT ABIDING THROUGH THE WORD IN THE SON AND IN THE FATHER, SO AS TO RECEIVE THE PROMISE OF ETERNAL LIFE

"Let that therefore abide in you which ye have heard from the beginning. If that which ye have heard from the beginning shall remain [abide] in you, ye also shall continue [abide] in the Son, and in the Father. And this is the promise that he hath promised us, even eternal life." 1 John 2:24,25 *

THIS practical appeal, concluding the previous argument, has a singularly close resemblance to the opening statement of the epistle. The same remarkable phraseology prevails. There is a " hearing from the beginning," and a "declaration " or promise connected with it. "That which was from the beginning," " that which we have seen and heard declare we unto you ; " so the apostle speaks of the apostolic position and commission (i. 1-3). "That which ye have heard from the beginning"—"the promise which he hath promised ; "—so he speaks here of the standing of those to whom he writes. And as, in the former passage, it is the Word of life that is seen and heard and handled ; it is " the life," " the eternal life," that is " manifested " and " declared ; " so here, "this is the promise that he hath promised us, even eternal life." The appeal runs exactly thus : " You, therefore, what ye have heard from

---

* It is the same word in the original that is differently rendered in our version,—"abide," "remain," "continue" (ver. 24). This is an instance of the sacrifice of exactness to variety, not to be justified.

the beginning, let it abide in you." For you must now perceive that "if what ye have heard from the beginning shall abide in you," then, and only then, shall ye "abide in the Son and in the Father." And this is the secret of your having fellowship with us in what is common to both of us : "the promise of eternal life" (ver. 25).

I. "Let that therefore which ye have heard from the beginning abide in you." The phrase "from the beginning" must here refer to the first preaching of the gospel. It cannot be understood in the same absolute sense in which it is used in the opening of the epistle. And yet John, I am persuaded, has that great thought in his mind. His object is to identify your position with that of himself and his fellow-apostles. You are to "have fellowship with us" (i. 3). We would have you to be upon the same footing with us; in the same boat, as it were; the boat tossed on the Galilean sea, to whose troubled crew no phantom ghost but the living Jesus appears and says—"It is I; be not afraid." It was given to us to see, to hear, to touch and handle, "that which was from the beginning"— "of the Word of life." And this is that which we have declared unto you, and which "ye have heard from the beginning." Let it abide in you.

For this end, that it may abide in you, let "that which ye have heard from the beginning" be not only known but felt; not only known as a matter of fact or doctrine, but felt as a matter of experience. Let it so lay hold of you, that it shall be the nature of God becoming in a sense part and parcel of your nature ; the great heart of the Father entering in a measure into union with your heart.

The nature of God is light; the heart of the Father is love. Light, pure and unsullied, is the essence of God, and his dwelling-place. He is light and he dwells in light. It is light which no darkness can invade. It is light, moreover, in which nothing but love can be at home. It is light before which,—the true light shining,—the darkness of the world, and all that is in it, must be passing away, and only he that doeth the will of God can abide for ever. It is in Christ that this true light now shines. Without him you cannot come to the light, or dwell in the light, or walk in the light ; without his blood which cleanseth from all sin, without himself as your advocate with the Father, the righteous one, the propitiation for your sins.

This is what " you have heard from the beginning ;" and have believed; and have found experimentally to be true. Let it so " abide in you ; " let it be " Christ dwelling in your hearts by faith" (Eph. iii. 17).

For otherwise you cannot face the light; you cannot meet with clear and open eye the light of that clear and open eye of God ; you quail beneath its truth and love. If at any moment you in any measure lose Christ, you so far lose both truth and love, the truth and love which alone can bear the light. You fall into darkness again, and come under its power, the power of its untrue and unloving ways. The old dark doubts and fears of guilt beset you : the old dark refuges of lies tempt you ; the old dark devices of self-justification return upon you ; the old dark habit of tampering with the world's lusts, and listening to the world's palliations of them, seduces you ; and the old dark disquietudes of a peevish and angry discontent with yourselves, with your God, and with your fellow-men, begin again to rankle in your bosom. Instead of the light of truth, there is dark guile in your spirits. Instead of the light of love, there is dark suspicion and enmity and alienation.

Ah! if you would have all to be always clear and bright in the spiritual atmosphere around you; all open between your God and you; open truth and open love;

"let that which ye have heard from the beginning abide in you." Let all of Christ you have ever known, seen, heard, handled, tasted, "abide in you." Let all you have learned of Christ,—as being with the Father, from everlasting, in his bosom,—as coming forth from the Father to reveal and reconcile,—as purging your sin with blood, and bringing you to be all to the Father that he is himself to the Father,—let it all "abide in you ; " always, everywhere.

II. So "ye also shall abide in the Son and in the Father."

First, "Ye shall abide in the Son." What the Lord elsewhere enjoins as in itself a duty, "Abide in me" (John xv. 4), the apostle describes as the consequence of another duty being rightly discharged. He points out the condition or the means of our abiding in the Son ; as indeed Jesus also may be held to do when he says, "If ye abide in me, and my words abide in you, ye shall ask what ye will" (John xv. 7). The meaning clearly is :—"Ye abide in me through my words abiding in you ;"—the Lord's expression, "my words," being equivalent to the apostle's, "that which ye have heard" of the word of life "from the beginning."

Thus it is by faith that we " abide in the Son ; " for it is by faith that what we have heard of him from the beginning abides in us. The manner, therefore, of our abiding in the Son is neither sacramental on the one hand, nor mystical on the other ;—neither physically ritual, nor metaphysically transcendental.

We do not "abide in the Son" by any sacramental act on our part, or any sacramental grace or virtue on his. The Lord's Supper may be a help to our abiding in the Son ; but only indirectly, through its being a help to our having " that which we have heard of him from the beginning abiding in us." It is the expressive sign and sure seal of it, and therefore may contribute to its abiding in us, and so to our abiding in the Son. But that is all. There is no charm or efficacy in the rite itself to secure our abiding in the Son. The relation described by our abiding in the Son is not of such a sort as can be kept up by any act or process apart from intelligence, consciousness, and volition.

And therefore this abiding in the Son cannot be mystical or transcendental, any more than it can be ritual or sacramental. It cannot be such as the visionaries of John's day imagined in their splendid dreams; in which abiding in the Christ, or in the Son, considered as an emanation or efflux of Deity, was a kind of absorption; a height of self-identification with some portion or manifestation of the Divine essence, or self-annihilation in it, to be reached by a long course of abstract musing on the first principles of things, or deep but vague contemplation of the eternal, infinite Being.

John's idea of abiding in the Son is much humbler and more practical. We abide in the Son, as we may be said to abide in any one when his words abide in us,—or when that which we have heard of him, or from him, from the beginning, abides in us; when we understand and know him, by what he says and what we hear; when what we thus understand and know of him takes hold of us, carries our conviction, commands our confidence and love, fastens and rivets itself in our mind and heart, and so abides in us. Thus we abide in the Son precisely as we abide in a friend whom we know, and trust, and love.

Doubtless the Son in whom we abide transcends infinitely any such friend. In him are excellencies which are to be found in no other. In himself personally, and in his relation as the Son to the Father, there are riches of wisdom, knowledge, goodness, grace, and glory, which our " abiding in him" through eternity will not enable us thoroughly to search or ransack. Not when myriads of blessed ages in yonder realms of light have rolled over our heads will one tithe of all the wonders of him whose "name is Wonderful" have been discovered ; no, not though our abiding in him there will be without a break and without a cloud. And what shall I say of the raptures of that personal intercourse and interchange of thought, feeling, and affection, in which our abiding in the Son then must mainly consist ? Can any limit be set to the ravishing joy of our walking with him and his walking with us in Paradise,—when we go in and out together,—we seeing him without a vail,—and he, as he talks with us without reserve, causing our hearts to burn within us ? And what comparison can there be, even now, between our abiding in him and our abiding in any other, even the best of friends ?

Still it is important to remember, that we do abide in the Son very much as we abide in any other friend ; it is important now, as well as in the apostle's time. For there is a fancy abroad of a sort of abiding in the Son that may be to a large extent independent of his words, or words about him, abiding in us. There is a tendency to put a sort of sentimental pietism, itself undefined and hating definition, gazing with rapt and fascinated eye on a soul-melting "Agnus Dei" or "Ecce Homo," seen in dim religious light, in the place of intelligent faith, or the engagement of mind and heart in personal converse with one who speaks and would be spoken to ; of whom and from whom and about whom we hear and read, in the teaching of his own apostles, in the Scriptures of his own Spirit's inspiration. These are practically set aside ; or, at least, any attempt to make their statements yield precise information concerning Christ and his work is disparaged. A Son of God and Son of man, rising out of some deep soundings of divinity and humanity, is substituted for the Son of whom apostles spoke and disciples heard from the beginning. And abiding in him is not a plain, practical, personal dealing with him about that for which he came into the world, and has been manifested to us, to us as individuals one by one; but an attempt somehow to grasp the notion of abstract divinity and universal humanity being in him mysteriously at one. Let no such speculations beguile us. Rather "let that which we have heard from the beginning abide in us;" and let us thereby " abide in the Son; " using as the means of our abiding in him the Scriptures which we search, and which testify of him. Let us thus turn all that we learn into the materials of that personal communing of him with us and us with him, which is indeed the essence of our abiding in the Son.

All the rather let us do so because, secondly, this abiding in the Son is abiding in the Father; for the Father and the Son are one. Abiding in the Son, we enter into his relation to the Father, into the whole of it and into all its fruits. We enter into all that the Son is to the Father, as his chosen servant, as the man of his right hand, as his anointed, as his lamb, the Lamb of God that taketh away the sin of the world, as his fellow, against whom his sword of justice awakes, as his smitten shepherd, as his victorious king set on his holy hill of Zion, as his beloved Son in whom he is well pleased, declared to be the Son of God with power by his resurrection from the dead. Into all that the Son is to the Father, in these and other similar views of his mediatorial character and ministry as the Son, we enter, when we abide in the Son. And so we come to be to the Father all that the Son is to the Father. We abide in the Father as the Son abides in the Father. So we abide in the Son and in the Father.

And still all this depends on our letting "that which we have heard from the beginning abide in us." It depends on that faith which cometh by hearing, as hearing cometh by the word of God. In vain we look for any other mode of indwelling in God than that which is through the Spirit giving us a sympathising insight into what we have heard and may always hear in the gospel,—into what we have read and may always read in the Scriptures,—of the great transaction between the Father and the Son on which depend the expiation of our guilt, the forgiveness of our sin, the ending of our long estrangement, and the ratifying of our reconciliation and peace. By study, meditation and prayer, let us get more and more,—the Spirit helping us in our musings,—into the very heart of all "that we have heard from the beginning," from the Father, of the Son; from the Son, of the Father. So we abide, more and more intelligently, more and more consciously, more and more believingly, lovingly, rejoicingly, "in the Son and in the Father."

III. Of all this "the fruit is unto holiness, and the end everlasting life." For "this is the promise that he hath promised us, even eternal life."

The meaning here may be that "the promise of eternal life" is superadded to the privilege or condition of our "abiding in the Son and in the Father," that it is something over and above that, held out to us in prospect; or it may be that our "abiding in the Son and in the Father" is itself the very "life eternal" that is promised. The difference is not material; the two thoughts, or rather the two modifications of the same thought, run into one. "The promise that he hath promised us is eternal life." And "this is life eternal, that they might know thee the only true God, and Jesus Christ whom thou hast sent" (John xvii. 3).

Hence we need inquire no farther at present into the nature of eternal life; nor need we conceive of it as an un- known boon held out in dim and distant prospect before us. We have only to work out what is implied in our " knowing the Father, the only true God, and Jesus Christ whom he has sent." We have only to prove and realise more and more, in our experience, what it is to " abide in the Son and in the Father." And that is the promise already fulfilled. That is " eternal life." It is in a real and valid sense, the very life of God himself made ours.

For the life of God alone can be truly said to be life at all; it alone can be " life eternal." All other life is but death; either death possibly impending, or death actually inflicted. At the very best, the life of an intelligent and responsible creature is, as it was in unfallen Adam, precarious ; and if not doomed, at least liable, to death. In fallen Adam and his race, it is simply death; "the wages of sin is death," " in the day thou eatest thou diest." " But the gift of God is eternal life through Jesus Christ our Lord ; " " God hath given unto us eternal life, and this life is in his Son." For the Son liveth. It is " given to the Son to have life in himself, even as the Father hath life in himself." This is a gift even to the Son, in our nature and in our stead. It is given to him, as one with us, our kinsman-redeemer ; for he says, "Because I live ye shall live also." Let us enter then into the life which the Son has by the gift of the Father ; his past life of obedience to the Father and acceptance with the Father, on earth, his present life of fellowship with the Father in heaven. Let us apprehend that life as a reality. Let us apprehend the essence of it, which is really intercourse, blessed intercourse, between the Father and the Son ; converse, communion conversation.

We have materials for this in " that which we have heard from the beginning," if we let it " abide in us." We have the Father speaking of and to the Son, and the Son speaking of and to the Father. That is the life of the Father and the Son ; that is " life eternal." And it is that which he has promised to us, even that very "life eternal;" the Father so speaking of and to us as he speaks of and to the Son; and we speaking of and to the Father as the Son speaks of and to the Father. It is that very life that is promised to us when we, "letting that which we have heard from the beginning abide in us, ourselves abide in the Father and the Son." *

Hence the Lord says (John xv. 7) : "If ye abide in me, and my words abide in you, ye shall ask what ye will and it shall be done unto you." To ask ; to be ever asking, and asking freely, confidently, boldly ; is one way in which "eternal life," or "abiding in the Son," acts itself out. The very breath of that life is prayer. Hence also the Lord says (ver. 5) : "He that abideth in me, and I in him, the same bringeth forth much fruit ;" for he partakes of my life ; and my life is fruitful, abundantly, richly fruitful. The life which I have with God my Father is fruitful in all good works, to the praise of his glory. And if that very life is yours, through your abiding in me and in my Father ; if your life is hid with me in God ; then it must now be fruitful in you, as it was in me when I was as you now are ; fruitful in all the fruit of the Spirit, which is "love, joy, peace, long-suffering, gentleness, goodness, faith, meekness, temperance."

---

* See Lectures xl. and xli. for a fuller discussion as to the nature of "eternal life."

17

THE GUILELESS SPIRIT, THROUGH THE ABIDING MESSIANIC UNCTION AND ILLUMINATION OF THE HOLY GHOST, ABIDING IN CHRIST, SO AS TO HAVE CONFIDENCE AT HIS COMING

"These things have I written unto you concerning them that seduce you. But the anointing which ye have received of him abideth in you ; and ye need not that any man teach you ; but as the same anointing teacheth you of all things, and is truth, and is no lie, and even as it hath taught you, ye shall abide in him. And now, little children, abide in him ; that when he shall appear, we may have confidence, and not be ashamed before him at his coming." 1 John 2:26-28

THE discourse is still about abiding in God, in the Son and in the Father. And the special lesson taught is, that the security for our thus abiding in God is to be found, not in our resisting outward solicitations drawing us away from him, but in our having in ourselves an inward principle to keep us near and close to him. If we have not that, no warning, however faithful, against seducers will avail. If we have that, no such warning should be needed.

And what is that? It is what has been already indicated in the twentieth verse ; the "unction" or anointing which we "have from the Holy One." Of that unction or anointing it is here testified, that its teaching is both thoroughly comprehensive and infallibly true ; "It teacheth you of all things, and is truth, and is no lie." The effect of its teaching is our abiding in him ; "Even as it has taught you, ye shall abide in him ;" or it may be put imperatively, "abide in him" "having this unction, and being taught by it, abide in him" with whom you share it. And you have the strongest inducement to abide in him; you and we alike. For we all look for his appearing; and must surely wish that, "when he shall appear, we may have confidence, and not be ashamed before him at his coming."

Two topics here occur for consideration—I. The provision made for our abiding in him; II. The motive urged for our abiding in him.

I. The provision made for our abiding in him is the "anointing which we receive of him abiding in us." That anointing, as we have seen, is our sharing with him in the gift of the Holy Ghost. And it is an anointing which abideth in us. "I will pray the Father, and he shall give you another Comforter, that he may abide with you for ever." So the Lord gives the promise of which John here attests the fulfilment. And it is with special reference to his teaching, illuminating, and enlightening grace, that both the Lord and the apostle speak of the Holy Ghost and his unction abiding in us. "He shall teach you all things and bring all things to your remembrance, whatsoever I have said unto you;"—"he shall guide you into all truth;" —"he shall take of mine and show it unto you." That is the Lord's way of describing the Spirit's abiding presence and its use. And to that the apostle agrees. This anointing "teacheth you" and "hath taught you," so that you need no further teaching; for "it teacheth you of all things, and is truth, and is no lie." There is a fulness in its teaching that admits of no supplement, and an assurance that excludes all doubt.

Observe the manifold worth and value of this anointing.

1. It is in us; it is an inward anointing. Not with oil on the head, but with the Holy Ghost in the heart, we are anointed; as he from whom we receive the anointing was

himself anointed. It is not an application or appeal from without; it is a gracious influence, a gracious movement or experience, in the inner man. It is beyond the world's cognisance; "the world cannot receive the Comforter, the Spirit of truth, because it seeth him not, neither knoweth him;" and it is only what it sees and knows by the palpable evidence of sense that the world can take in. But the inward work and witness of the Holy Ghost is apprehended by faith as real; as being really the indwelling in us of the Spirit that dwelt in Christ.

2. This anointing is permanent; "it abideth in you." It is not a fitful emotion or wayward impulse, a rapture of excitement, alternating perhaps with deep depression. It partakes more of the nature of a calm, constant, settled conviction. Frames, feelings, fancies, are all fluctuating; they are like the surface waters of the ocean, agitated by every wind. But this inward anointing is far down in the still depths beneath. It "abideth in us;" the same always in its own inherent stillness and strength, amid whatever tossings its contact with the upper air may cause. Through tears and cries, as well as smiles and laughter, it abides in us the same; as it did in him who "rejoiced in the Spirit," and who also "groaned in the Spirit." "With our groanings which cannot be uttered," the anointing Spirit, abiding in us, "maketh intercession for us;" and our joy, like Christ's, is "in the Holy Ghost." This unction then is not to be confounded with our own varying moods of mind, or the varying impressions made on us by things without. It is something far more stable. It gives a certain firm and fixed apprehension of divine things and persons, which these vicissitudes can scarcely interrupt or weaken, and cannot destroy. There may be more or less of the vivid sense of this anointing, at different seasons and in different circumstances; the signs of it may be more or less clearly discer-

nible, and the hold we have of it in our consciousness may
be more or less strong. But it "abideth in us;" keeping
God and eternity still before us as realities, in our sorest
trials and darkest hours; causing us, as we fall back upon
it, like David in his recovery from doubting despondency,
to exclaim :—"I said, This is my infirmity : but I will remember the years of the right hand of the most High"
(Ps. lxxvii. 10).

3. This anointing is sufficient in and of itself; its teaching needs no corroboration from any one; it has a divine
self-evidencing power of its own that makes him who receives it independent of human testimony : "ye need not
that any man teach you." The gospel is its own witness;
it carries in itself, as apprehended by this anointing, its own
credentials. Like its author, it speaks as having authority,
and approves itself experimentally to all who make trial of
it. All this is through the anointing Spirit. It is by the
Spirit that we are moved to make trial of the gospel; it is
by the Spirit that the gospel is so applied and brought home
to us,—in its sovereignty, as God speaking, and in its
special and pointed adaptation to our case, as God speaking
to us,—that we cannot but say in our hearts, "Speak, Lord,
for thy servant heareth." This is "the anointing which we
have received of him;" it is the Holy Ghost causing us to
"taste and see how good he is." And this is the real
ground and evidence of our faith; that faith which realises
the fulfilment of the great covenant promise, "They shall
not teach every man his neighbour, and every man his
brother, saying, Know the Lord : for all shall know me,
from the least to the greatest. For I will be merciful to
their unrighteousness, and their sins and their iniquities
will I remember no more."

4. The teaching of this anointing is complete and
thorough, all-embracing, all-comprehensive; "it teacheth

you of all things." It is not partial, or one-sided, as human teaching on divine subjects is apt to be ; but full-orbed, well-rounded, like a perfect circle. It is not, of course, all things absolutely that this anointing teaches ; but all things about the theme or subject of the teaching : about him from whom you receive it, and whose it is. Of the very best of human systems, I suppose that every spiritual man will feel and confess, that it is not on all points satisfying ; it cannot but bear the marks of man's confined standing-ground and restricted range of vision. This is no disparagement of such human systems, when used as helps to the orderly understanding and right arrangement of the several parts of the truth of God. But it indicates the limit to their use. They cannot come in place of the Holy Spirit's teaching us the words of Christ. Even at the best, when the intellect is most pleased with the symmetry and beauty of a finished theological scheme, the spiritual mind, or rather the spiritual heart, feels that all is not there ; that there is something wanting of what passes between the living God and the living soul when peace is made between them ; that there are more things in heaven and earth than are dreamed of in man's best divinity. " The secret of the Lord is with them that fear him, and he will shew them his covenant." It needs the divine anointing of which we speak to teach, to unfold, to exhaust, all that is in the song of the angels, " Glory to God in the highest, and on earth peace, good will toward men."

5. Finally, this anointing " is truth, and is no lie." It carries with it, and in it, an assurance not to be called in question or shaken ; an assurance, one may say, infallibly sure.

But you ask, Though I may be assured of the anointing itself that " it is truth and no lie ;" how may I be assured that my having it is truth and no lie ? And without this last assurance what will the other avail? Nay, it avails much. Even apart from the question of your assured personal interest in it, and your assured personal experience of it, is it not much to know and believe assuredly that in itself, in its own proper nature and working, this anointing is very truth, and'verily is no lie? Is it not something to be told that there is such an oil of gladness, such a precious ointment, poured out upon the High-Priest's head, and running over upon all his members; the oil, the ointment of the Spirit, teaching of all things, and teaching of them with absolute certainty? You know what the things are of which his anointing teaches; they are the things which belong to God's glory and your peace. But you will not be content with knowing them merely as discoveries of your own, or as communicated by others. Know them as taught to you and attested to you; above all, as wrought out and acted out in you; by the anointing of the Holy Ghost. Proceed upon the faith of your thus knowing them, in the expectation of your thus knowing them, more and more. And do so, not doubting, but believing assuredly, that "the anointing which teacheth you of them is truth and is no lie."

Yes! "There is truth and no lie" in what the Spirit shows you of the love of God in Christ, and sheds abroad in your heart of that love; be sure of that, and be not afraid to act upon the assurance of it. "There is truth and no lie" in what the Spirit opens up to you of the freeness and fulness of the Father's overtures of mercy in the Son; be sure of that, and be not afraid to act upon the assurance of it. "There is truth and no lie" in what the Spirit would have you to grasp of "the peace which passeth understanding, the hope that maketh not ashamed, and the joy that is unspeakable and full of glory;" be sure of that, and be not afraid to act upon the assurance of it. "There

is truth and no lie" in "that which ye have heard from
the beginning so abiding in you that you abide in the Son
and in the Father. That really is "the anointing which is
truth and is no lie." Be sure of that, and be not afraid to
act out and out upon the assurance of it.

Thus receiving of the Lord Christ this anointing, you
may well be proof against all seducing antichrists (ver. 26).
And not otherwise can you be proof against them; for not
otherwise can you abide in him. "Abide in me," he says,
"and I in you." Abide in me; and that you may abide in
me, let me abide in you. Let my word dwell in you richly;
and my Spirit, giving to my word fragrance to fill the whole
heart with the sweet savour of my name, as well as also
penetrating power to reach every hard corner of the heart
with the softening influence of my grace. Yes; let Christ
dwell in your hearts by faith. Let the anointing Spirit
infuse into your whole inner man the holy beauty, the
meekness, the gentleness of Christ. Let his anointing
mould and mellow your whole moral nature into a real
identity with that of Christ. Thus becoming assimilated
to him, growing up into him, you more and more closely
and surely abide in him, and so are safe from "all them
that would seduce you." No other security, in fact, will
suffice; not your utmost vigilance against their lies, but
the full indwelling in you of the truth, and the Spirit of
the truth.

II. The motive urged for your abiding in Christ is the
hope or prospect of "his appearing," "his coming." It is
urged very earnestly and affectionately. There is a tender
emphasis in the appeal "And now, little children!" Nor
is the change of person, from the second to the first,
insignificant—"that we—"

John might have kept to the mode of address which
he has been using, and to which in the next verse he re-

turns; as an apostle exhorting his disciples; a teacher
instructing his scholars; speaking authoritatively or *ex
cathedra*. But when the end of all comes in view, he cannot
separate himself from them. We are to be together with
the Lord, you and we; you disciples and we apostles; you
scholars and we teachers. And for this end we would have
you to abide in him, that we may have confidence together
when he appears.

John had said at the outset, "That which we," who are
apostles, "have seen and heard declare we unto you, that
ye also may have fellowship with us," the same fellowship
that we have, "with the Father and with his Son Jesus
Christ." Our object is to make you joint partakers with
us in what might seem to be our distinctive privilege as
apostles, our having seen the Lord. That is our aim in all
that we write to you. With a view to that we tell you of
the light in which we may jointly walk together, and of the
blood of Jesus Christ, the Son of God, which cleanseth us
all alike from all sin. With a view to that we warn you
against having any fellowship with the unfruitful works of
darkness. With a view to that we remind you of the
anointing which you as well as we have received of Christ,
the Holy One. With a view to that we counsel you to
abide in him; that as there is no real difference now
between you and us, there may be none hereafter, when it
would be final and fatal; that when he shall appear, we
may altogether appear with him in glory; that you and we
alike "may have confidence and not be ashamed before
him at his coming." For we all alike need to be admonished of this risk.

And what a thought! what a contingency or possibility
to be imagined! "To be ashamed before him at his coming!" It is a very strong expression. It carries us back
to that old scene in Paradise when it was lost. The guilty

pair " hear the voice of the Lord God walking in the garden, in the cool of the day." And they shrink with shame from him " at his coming." Is it thus that we should shrink at his coming now ? Were he at this moment to appear, how would we feel ? What would be our first impulse, our instinct ? To run to meet him, or to shrink from him in shame ? There are those who at the coming of the Lord shall " hide themselves in the dens and in the rocks of the mountains, and say to the mountains and rocks, Fall on us, and hide us from the face of him that sitteth on the throne and from the wrath of the Lamb ; for the great day of his wrath is come ; and who shall be able to stand ? " Would we be among that terrified multitude, that woful crowd ? It is to have in it not a little of the pomp and fashion of the world ; " kings of the earth, great men, rich men, chief captains, mighty men, as well as bond and free men, without number." They may know no shame or fear now ; unused to blush, or be abashed, or tremble in any presence, however they may force others to blush, and be abashed, and tremble before them. But at the Lord's appearing, their brave, bold looks are gone. Ashamed, alarmed, despairing, they shrink from him. Surely we would not be of that miserable crew. Nay, fear apart, we who believe and love him would not wish to be found by him, at his coming, in any mood of mind, in any attitude of body, in any company, at any work, in any pleasure, over any book, that would cause even a momentary shrinking from him in shame. We would not choose to be so caught by him and taken by surprise ; when we were not thinking of him, or serving him ; when perhaps we were tempted to be ashamed of him, or of one of his saints, or of some things about his cause and kingdom, before those who happened to be our associates at the time ;—so caught, I say, and taken by surprise, as to wish for a moment's delay, that we might get over our nervous flutter and confusion, and summon courage to bid him welcome.

Who is he who comes? And for what? Is it not "he whom our soul loveth," our Saviour, friend, brother, who has gone to prepare a place for us among the many mansions of his Father's house? And for what does he come? To take us to himself, that where he is we may be also. Can we tolerate the idea of being ashamed before him when he comes, and comes on such an errand? Ah! if we would be safe from any such risk then, let us " abide in him" now ; " abide in him" always. So, " when he shall appear, we may have confidence."

Let me be ever asking myself, at every moment, If he were to appear now, would I have confidence? If he were to come into my house, my room, and show himself, and speak to me face to face ; would I have confidence? Could I meet his look of love without embarrassment? Only if he found me " abiding in him ;" doing whatever I might be doing " in his name, giving thanks unto God even the Father by him ; " only if he found me keeping him in my heart.

Let us then be always abiding in him ; every day, every hour, every instant ; even as we would wish to be found abiding in him, were he to appear this very day, this very hour, this very instant. He is about to appear ; to appear suddenly ; to come quickly. Oh let us see to it, that as we would not wish him to come when we were in such a state as to cause shrinking from him in shame ; as we would rather that when he appears we were in a position to spring forward with keen eye and outstretched arm, to welcome in all confidence him whom we love ; let us see to it that we " abide in him." Let us be always in the posture in which he who gives his " little children " this counsel was himself when he closed the book of the Revelation. " He which testifieth these things saith, Surely I come quickly, Amen. Even so, come, Lord Jesus."

PART TWO

DIVINE FELLOWSHIP—INTERMEDIATE CONDITION—RIGHTEOUSNESS
1 John 2:28-4:6

18

GROUND OR REASON OF THIS CONDITION IN THE RIGHTEOUS NATURE OF GOD—THE NEW BIRTH UNTO RIGHTEOUSNESS

"If ye know that he is righteous, ye know that every one that doeth righteousness is born of him. Behold, what manner of love the Father hath bestowed on us, that we should be called the sons of God."
1 John 2:29; 3:1

THE apostle passes to a new thought or theme; a new view of the fellowship in which he would have us to be partakers with himself and all the apostles. It is "fellowship with the Father and with his Son Jesus Christ." He has viewed it as a fellowship of light. He now views it as a fellowship of righteousness. "God is light,"—that is the key-note to the former view. "God is righteous,"—that is the key-note to the present view. It is introductory to the third, —"God is love."

For it is an indispensable condition of this fellowship with God that we realise in ourselves, and in our doings, what is in accordance with his nature. If therefore it is his nature to be righteous, it must be our nature to do righteousness. But that to us is a new nature. It implies that we are born of him to whose nature ours is to be conformed ; that we are " born of God." *

" Born of God !" The idea seems to strike John's mind with fresh astonishment. Familiar as it is, he sees in it, as it here occurs to him, new cause of wonder ; "Behold, what manner of love the Father hath bestowed upon us, that we should be called the sons of God !" For this rapturous exclamation in the beginning of the third chapter is based on the principle of sonship brought out in the last verse of the second ; "If ye know that he is righteous, ye know that every one that doeth righteousness is born of him."

The starting-point in this new line of argument is the statement that "God is righteous." It is analogous to that given before, that "God is light." And as there, so here, the inference is obvious. Only the doer of righteousness can be really born of him, and the doer of righteousness certainly is so.

---

* It is thus that the last verse of the second chapter is connected with what goes before ; and thus also the abrupt change, as regards the person spoken of, between that last verse and the preceding one, may be explained. In the one (28th) it is Christ the Son ; in the other (29th) it is God the Father. There could be no misunderstanding among John's readers, as if it was Christ that was meant in the latter verse as well as in the former ; for not only would it be contrary to all gospel usage, and to the very gospel itself, to speak of believers as being born of Christ ; but the very next verse (iii. 1) makes all plain. Besides, the verse in question (29th) is to be read in the light of one farther back (24th). Our abiding in the Son is there represented as carrying with it our abiding in the Father ; it is our abiding in the Father as manifested in the Son. And the condition of this abiding in the Father is being born of him ; that our righteous doing may be in harmony with his righteous nature. The doer of righteousness alone can abide in the righteous God. And the doer of righteousness is " born of God."

For to be born of God implies community of nature between him and us. I cannot be really his child unless I am possessed of the same nature with him. So the Lord Jesus himself teaches in two remarkable passages (Matt. v. 43–45, John viii. 38–44). In both of these passages, but especially in the last, there is a general principle involved. A family likeness, in features of character as well as of countenance, will betray an evil paternity, and must prove a good one; "I speak that which I have seen with my Father; and ye do that which ye have seen with your father." You say that you are Abraham's children. If that were true, you would do the works of Abraham. He would not like you have sought to kill me, for telling the truth which I have heard of God. But I will tell you whose children you are, and who is your father. It is he whose deeds you do. You reply, We have one Father, even God. Nay; if God were your Father, you would do the work of your Father, which is "loving me;" for he loveth me. But you reject me, and so prove that, in spite of your claim to be God's children, your actual paternity is very different; "Ye are of your father the devil."

John may have had these words of his Master in his mind when he wrote down the brief and pithy maxim, "God is righteous, and every one that doeth righteousness is born of him." His object is to supply a searching test by which our abiding in God may be surely tried. For our abiding in God is our abiding in the Son; and through our abiding in the Son, abiding in the Father, as the Son abides in the Father. But that implies our being "born of God." It is as "born of God" that the Son abides in the Father. And it must be as "born of God" that we, abiding in the Son, abide in the Father as he does.

The practical way of proving so high and holy a filiation is very simple : "If ye know that he is righteous, ye know that every one that doeth righteousness is born of him."

It is a mode of proof which may, without irreverence, be applied in the first instance to the Son himself. We have his own warrant for so applying it (1 John xv. 9, 10). It is by keeping his Father's commandments that he, as the Son, born of the Father, abides in the Father's love. As the Father is known by him as righteous, so he, doing righteousness, is proved to be born of him. He doeth the works of his Father, and so evinces his sonship.

All through, the stress is laid on righteousness. That is the distinguishing characteristic which identifies him that is born of God ; the common quality connecting what he does as born of God with the nature of him of whom he is born. Already this attribute of righteousness has been brought prominently forward in this epistle. God is righteous in forgiving sin (i. 9). Jesus Christ is righteous as our advocate with the Father (ii. 1). But it is in the section on which we are now entering that righteousness bulks most largely.

"God is righteous ;" that is his perfection. We are to "know that he is righteous." His Son, born of him, knew this ; " O righteous Father, the world hath not known thee, but I have known thee." I have known that thou art righteous. It is a great matter to know that, in the midst of a world that knows it not.

For does the world know that God is righteous ? Have "the workers of iniquity" that knowledge, when "they eat up God's people like bread, and say God seeth not" ? when they call not upon the name of the Lord ? when they do deeds of darkness, and, because he keeps silence, think that he is altogether such an one as themselves ? Do we know that God is righteous ? That God is kind, compas-

sionate, merciful, bountiful,—all that we can easily know.
Such knowledge is not too wonderful for us; it is not high
or unattainable. But that he is righteous! Have we a fixed
and firm knowledge of that? Do we understand what it
means? Do we grasp the meaning of it and hold it fast?

Ah! it is not natural for us to do so. That God is
righteous, absolutely and perfectly righteous;—that he
thinks and feels and purposes and acts, always according to
what ought to be, and never in accommodation to what is;
that he makes uncompromising rectitude the rule of all his
judgments and proceedings in all his dealings with men;—
that he is not facile and bending, open to appeals and appliances from without, but inherently and unalterably
righteous;—to know that; really to know it as a fact, and
a great fact; true now and true for eternity; ah! such
knowledge is not easy for me, a guilty and fallen man. It
is not possible, unless I am "born of God."

Jesus knew it; he knew the righteous Father. Born of
God, he knew that God is righteous; and he did righteousness accordingly. How thoroughly he did so, let some
cases in which he might have been tempted to do otherwise
attest.

1. I cite an instance already referred to in a somewhat
different connection. A young man comes to him asking
the way to eternal life. He is rich, amiable, good; a keeper
of the commandments from his youth; ingenuous, attractive, sincere; so that Jesus beholding him loveth him.
May he not stretch a point in this goodly youth's favour?
May he not accept his goodness as being, if not all that
strict law requires, yet on the whole sufficient? No. He
knows that God is righteous. And, knowing that, he doeth
righteousness, though his doing it drives the youth away,
with what issue who can tell?

2. He draws near Jerusalem, and beholds the city. It

is inexpressibly dear to him. If other Israelites hailed it
as beautiful for situation, and boasted of it as the joy of
the whole earth, the city of the great king; the great king
himself may well have a favour for it. The anguish of his
human soul, as he contemplates its present security and
coming desolation, must be all but intolerable. Can there
be no help? Is no indulgence possible for his own chosen
city's sin? May no miracle be wrought sufficient to rouse
it to repentance? He knows that God is righteous; and he
doeth righteousness. He weeps in the doing of it. The
city's fate rings his heart. But what can he say? What
but "O Jerusalem, Jerusalem!"

3. He is in the garden; praying the prayer of agony;
sweating great drops of blood. The cup is handed to him;
the cup of woe; the cup of wrath; the cup of his Father's
judicial reckoning with him as answerable for all his
people's sins. "Father, if it be possible!" May it not be
possible? Is there no way of salvation but through the
shedding of my blood? No. He knows that God is
righteous; and he doeth righteousness. "Father, thy will
be done!"

Thus it is plainly seen that he is born of God. He
knows the righteous Father. And knowing him as the
righteous Father, he doeth righteousness as his only begotten Son.

You who believe are born of God as he is. I speak of
his human birth; in which you, in your new birth, are
partakers with him; the same Spirit of God being the
agent in both, and originating in both the same new life.
His birth was humiliation to him, though it was of God:
your new birth is exaltation to you, because it is of God.
His being born of God by the Spirit made him partaker of
your human nature;—your being born again of God by
the Spirit makes you partakers of his "divine nature."

You, thus born of God, come to be of the same mind with him who is the first begotten of the Father; especially as regards your knowing that God is righteous, and that it is, therefore, and must be, the impulse and characteristic of every one that is born of him to do righteousness. For if you are thus born of God, must you not be as thoroughly on his side, as unreservedly in his interest, in the great outstanding controversy between his righteousness and man's sin, as is his well-beloved Son himself?

Is it really so? Was he ever seen as infirm and irresolute, as weak and wavering, in his moral judgments, as you too frequently are in yours? Was he ever equivocal or feeble in his utterances about God's claims, and man's duty, and man's guilt? Did he ever hesitate to act upon the principle: "Let God be true and every man a liar?"

Nor will it do to say that he had not so much inducement as you have to tamper with God's righteousness, and be disloyal to his throne. Personally, it is true that he had no need to have recourse to any expedient of accommodation or compromise. God's judicial righteousness and his acceptance in God's sight never could come into collision. Never could he have occasion to desire that God were less righteous than he is, in order that there might be hope for him. But when I think of him as taking my place, bearing my sin, receiving in his bosom the sword that should have smitten me; can I say that he had no cause to wish, had it been possible, that God might be less inflexibly and inexorably righteous than he there and then found him to be? And when I think of the exquisite tenderness of his sensibility; how he could not witness human suffering unmoved, or see a human soul perish, or run the hazard of perishing, without a tear;—I can scarcely fancy it less difficult for him than for me to acquiesce com-

placently in God's righteousness reigning, as it must reign,
not only "through grace unto eternal life," but through
wrath unto everlasting death. But that is what is implied
in knowing that God is righteous. And to do righteousness, is to think and speak and act accordingly. It is to
be unflinching and unfaltering in preferring God's righteousness to man's sin. It is to justify God's righteousness
and condemn man's sin, with an entire and utter abandonment of all attempts, and even of all desire, to make terms
between them. It is to proclaim internecine war between
them; yes, even though the issue should be the triumph
of God's righteousness in the sinner's inevitable ruin.

A hard saying this! who can hear it? A heavy burden!
who can bear it? Who that is not born of God? Who
but one who reaches, by the new birth, the position which
the Son, in his birth, took as his? Who but one who,
born again of the Spirit as he was born of the Spirit, comes
to occupy the same point of view that he did; to see
righteousness and sin, God's righteousness and man's sin,
as he saw them; and to deal with them as he dealt
with them in all his ministry, and especially on the
cross?

First, in him, and with him,—born of God into fellowship with him in his birth,—you enter into that doing of
righteousness on his part, which was the main design of
his being born; which brings into perfect harmony, not
God's righteousness and man's sin, but God's righteousness
and man's salvation from sin. This is your first step, as
born of God; and it is all-important for yourselves, and for
your fellow-men. It places you on the very vantage-ground
on which the Son himself stood, when, coming into the
world, he surveyed its sad, sinful case, in the light of the
will of God which he came to do, and the righteousness of
God which he came to vindicate and fulfil. It enables you

to draw the line sharp and clear, as he did, between that loving embrace of him and his cross which wins salvation for the chief of sinners from a righteous God, and in a way of perfect righteousness,—and that rejection of him which seals the fate of the very best of those who, refusing his righteous justifying mercy, brave his righteous retributive wrath. Thus, knowing for yourselves, in and with Christ, that God is righteous, you do righteousness, as he did.

And thus also, in your customary intercourse with other men, you act upon the deep conviction that God is righteous; that his righteousness admits of no relaxation; that there is between it and all manner of iniquity a terrible incompatibility; that there is one only way in which the workers of iniquity can be righteously delivered; and that all who are not found in that way, be they ever so respectable, ever so amiable, are righteously condemned.

Fully to realise that assurance, and to act upon it, without any wavering;—as if you still regarded being in Christ of little moment or being out of Christ of little peril;—so to live in your closet and in the world, at home and abroad, under the constant urgent sense of there being safety only in Christ, and only ruin out of Christ, for you, for all, for any;—that is to do righteousness, in the knowledge that God is righteous.

Ah! what an insight into the righteous nature and character of God; what a measure of cordial oneness of principle and sentiment with him; entering into his very mind and heart; does all this involve! How far removed is it from that loose, easy-going sort of Christian virtue which would not itself do iniquity, but is very tolerant of those who do it; not, like Lot's righteous soul, vexed with evil; nor, like Lot, preaching righteousness; but rather prone to look on sin with indifference or complacency, and to let the sinner go on, without warning or entreaty, to his doom. If you know that God is righteous, and make conscience of doing righteousness accordingly, you cannot be thus tame and acquiescent; thus cold and callous. To you, righteousness, God's righteousness, is not a name but a reality. To be conformed to it, to submit to it, is life. To be ignorant of it, or opposed to it, or far from it, is death. Do you know that? Do you know it so as to feel it for others as well as for yourselves? Can you look out upon the world that knows not the righteous Father, and not be more in earnest than you are?

"Who is on the Lord's side—who?" Who is in the interest of the "righteous Father"? Who is he whose soul burns within him at the thought of the righteous Father being so little known?—whose bowels of compassion melt at the sight of men perishing in the world that know him not? Truly he is "born of God." None but one born of God can be so like his only-begotten Son.

Is not this a position eminently high and holy? Is it not a position, our occupancy of which may well be matter of surprise even to ourselves? Does it not imply a wondrous manner of love bestowed on us by the Father, that on such a footing, in such a sense, and for such an end, "we should be called the sons of God?"—born of him; so born of him as to do righteousness, even as he is righteous; to uphold practically the very righteousness which is his essential characteristic, the peculiar and consummate glory of his infinitely perfect nature?

I do not speak now, at least not yet, of the amazing love manifested by the Father in the provision made for our being called or constituted his sons, through the giving up of his own dear Son for us, to bear our guilt as criminals, that we may share with him his grace and glory as the Son. What at present we have to consider is, not how we become sons of God, but rather what it is to be sons of God ; what oneness of nature and character, of sentiment and sympathy, of feeling and action, between God and us,—especially in respect of that righteousness of his which we thus come to know,—our being his sons, or being born of him, implies. He would have us to be his sons, as he had Jesus to be his Son, when he was on the earth ; knowing him as the "righteous Father," and doing righteousness as he is righteous.   He would have us, as his sons, to be true and loyal to him, as Jesus his Son was, in the great outstanding controversy of his righteousness with the world's sin ; as faithful ; and as tender too.   He would have us, as his sons, to go on the very errand on which his Son, as his righteous servant, went ; and in his very spirit ; with the law of God in our heart, and rivers of water running down our eyes because men will not keep that law.

Ah ! to be thus the sons of God ; as thoroughly at one with God as Jesus his Son was ; witnessing everywhere and evermore that God is righteous ; righteous to punish ; righteous to forgive and save !   What an attainment ! What a responsibility !   What a rank !   Well may it prompt the abrupt ejaculation,—"Behold, what manner of love the Father hath bestowed on us, that we should be called the sons of God."

19

THE DIVINE BIRTH—THE FAMILY LIKENESS

"If ye know that he is righteous, ye know that every one that doeth righteousness is born of him. Behold, what manner of love the Father hath bestowed upon us, that we should be called [the] sons" [children] "of God!" [and so we are!] "Therefore the world knoweth us not, because it knew him" [God] "not. Beloved, now are we [the] sons" [children] "of God, and it doth not yet appear what we shall be: but we know that, when he shall appear" [when that shall appear] "we shall be like him" [God]; "for we shall see him as he is." 1 John 2:29-3:2 *

THE first verses of the third chapter are to be viewed as inseparable from the last verse of the second. It is that verse which starts the new line of thought; our "knowing

---

* As explanatory of my exposition, I must advert to one or two points of verbal detail, in regard to the reading and interpretation of these verses. First, in almost all the most authoritative manuscripts of this book,—though not in that which is called the received text, and which was in use when our translation was made,—there is a brief phrase inserted after "that we should be called the sons of God;"—"and so we are." These words are now generally admitted to be genuine. The sense is not really affected, whether they are allowed or excluded; for undoubtedly, according to common usage, "being called the sons of God" means actually becoming the sons of God. But they add to the emphasis of this noble appeal; and they are characteristic of the writer. Secondly, the pronoun "he," "him," is in these verses to be understood always of God the Father. It must be so understood in the first verse of the third chapter; and consistency requires it to be so understood throughout; all the rather since otherwise the sense is broken, instead of being complete. But thirdly, what is most important is the phrase, "when he shall appear." It is that which leads readers of our translation to bring in our Lord Jesus Christ, as if he must be the party referred to; especially as they are apt to connect the phrase with what is said before of "his

that God is righteous, and doing righteousness accordingly," in virtue of our "being born of him." Born of
him! That is what awakens John's grateful surprise, and
occasions his exclamation, "Behold, what manner of love!"
His discourse now is an expansion of that thought.

I. In every view that can be taken of it, our being called
the sons of God is a wonderful instance of the Father's love.
That we—Who? The lost and guilty; who have forfeited
by sin whatever claim we might have on God originally;
who have become rebels against his authority and criminals
under the sentence of his law; who, if left to ourselves,
would rather continue estranged from him for ever than
consent to return and be reconciled to him in peace :—That
such as we should be called the sons of God! And then
how? Through his own Son making common cause with
us, that we may have a common standing with him ; and by
his own Spirit making us willing, almost against our wills,
to acquiesce in that arrangement. And to what effect?
That we may be to him what his own Son is to him ; the
objects of the same love ; sharers of the same rank. Well
may we exclaim, "Behold what manner of love!"

But it is chiefly one element or feature in this high calling that the apostle has before him when he breaks out
into this rapturous exclamation ; our being the sons of God
as "born of him" (ii. 29); our undergoing a divine birth
which, making us partakers of the divine nature, makes us
thereby really and truly children of God ; children, in a
sense, by nature ; and therefore fitly acknowledged as
children.

---

coming" (ii. 28). But there is no pronoun at all here in the original; and
what is supplied should be "it," rather than "he." The connection is
not with the remoter passage, in a previous section, now ended, but with
what goes before in the very same verse : "It doth not yet appear what
we shall be; but we know that when that does appear, we shall be like
him ;" like God whose sons we are ; " for we shall see him as he is."

Observe the peculiar turn of expression. As exactly rendered, it is not that we should be called "the sons," but rather, that we should be called "children," of God. It is not said merely that we are called his sons, as having him standing to us in the relation of a Father; but that we are called his children; his divinely-born children; deriving from a divine birth a divine nature; children of God, in respect of our being born of God.*

Of course this last view does not exclude the other; on the contrary, they virtually coincide. The thought of our being born of God immediately suggests the thought of the Father's love. It is fatherly love that explains our being called children of God in virtue of our being born of God. It is the very glory and perfection of the love which the Father bestows on us, that we are thus called or constituted children of God.

For it is conceivable that in some other way, and on some other footing, we might be called children of God.

In point of fact, men dream of their being God's children altogether irrespectively of any new divine birth,—anything like "being born of God." Paul, at Athens, quoted a Greek poet as saying, "We are also his offspring." From him we have our origin, and "in him we live, and move, and have our being." Simply as his dependent offspring, we may think that we are entitled to be called his children, and to call him Father. We may speak of his love in creating us and caring for us as fatherly love. It is not however really so, in any valid scriptural sense. At any rate it is not the "manner of love" which John thinks it so amazing

---

* A reference to the original will confirm this criticism. Τέκνα Θεοῦ is the phrase; not υἱοὶ Πατρός. And there is no definite article, as in the English. The expression suggests something more than mere legal and relational filiation; it points to communication of nature.

a wonder that the Father should have "bestowed upon us
in our being called children of God."

Again, our being "called children of God" may be considered simply as an act of adoption, very much analogous
to what is practised among men. Viewed in that light, it
is unquestionably an instance of fatherly love ; and fatherly
love of no ordinary kind. It is as if a judge were not only
to procure a pardon for the criminal he has doomed to death,
and hand it to him on the scaffold as he is awaiting execution ; but were to take him home, and, by a legal deed, constitute him his son and heir; or as if the monarch were to
admit into the royal household a vanquished and forgiven
rebel, to be on the same filial terms with him, and enjoy the
same filial privileges, as his own first-begotten.

Or take the better example of the reception of the prodigal son. The sympathising witnesses of that scene of reconciliation might well utter the ejaculation, Behold, what
manner of love the father has bestowed on him ! He himself could never cease to feel the wonder of it. And yet
even this is not the manner of love that awakens John's
admiring rapture ; or at least not the whole of it. The parable, for its purpose, is complete, although it takes no express
notice of anything on the father's part but his welcoming
his son, "once dead but now alive,—once lost but now
found ; " or anything on the son's part but his "coming to
himself and going to his father." But he who uttered the
parable spoke of our being "born again;" "born of the
Spirit ; " as explicitly as his beloved disciple speaks here of
our being "born of God." And we cannot know what
manner of love the Father hath bestowed on us in our being
called the children of God, unless we realise our being so in
virtue of this new divine birth. Here the parable does not
help ; it may even, if taken alone, mislead. It teaches its
own lesson ; but it does not teach the whole truth of God

on the subject of our being "called children of God." The prodigal's mind underwent a mighty revolution with reference to his father and his father's house. It must have done so before he could be willing, either to accept the father's terms of pardon and peace, or to accommodate himself afterwards to the father's character and way of life; and without such willingness he could not have been really his son. That surely implied a great change of mind, which the parable, however, does not fully, or indeed at all explain.

But we know well, as spiritual men, how the corresponding change in our nature must be wrought. We must be born of God; so born of God that it shall be as truly our nature to do righteousness as it is his nature to be righteous. It is not merely that we need to be made willing to embrace his righteous overtures of mercy, in order to our personal acceptance in his sight. That doubtless requires that we should be born of God; for no man ever yet was found willing to know and submit to the righteousness of God, or unreservedly to consent to be "justified freely by God's grace through the redemption that is in Christ," without so thorough a revolution in his whole inner man, so complete an abandonment of his own way of peace, and such entire acquiescence in that of God, as could only come from his being indeed born of God. To be born of God to this effect, to the effect of our coming to be of the same mind with him, in the great and vital matter of a sinner's justification, and our justification as sinners;—that is much. It is the proof or manifestation of a fatherly love bestowed on us that is of a very wonderful sort indeed. But that is not all. Not only are we to be of one mind with the righteous Father as to the manner of our return and reconciliation to him; we are so born of God as to be ever after of the same mind with him, as to the whole of his righteous

laws, and his righteous administration of them; "doing
righteousness as we know that he is righteous." That is
what his heart is set upon; that is his fatherly love. It
goes far beyond his simply consenting to regard us, in spite
of all our estrangement, as still his children, if we consent
to be so regarded. It is very different from his merely
passing an act of indemnity, and by a summary and sovereign process of will, executing, as it were, a deed whereby
we are declared to be in law his children. That is all the
love which a father can bestow in adopting a child, according to the usages of earth. But it is not all that our Father
in heaven bestows upon us, when we are called children of
God. He contemplates a far more thorough filiation, a
more intensely real sonship, than what can result from any
such transaction outside of us;—any agreement between
him and us, however generous and gracious. He "begets
us" to himself (James i. 18); "we are born of God," by an
inward communication of his nature to us. He must have
us to be, not titular, but real and actual children; children
by participation of nature as well as by deed of adoption;
by a new creation as well as a new covenant; of one mind
and heart, of one character and moral frame with himself;
"doing righteousness," as we "know that he is righteous;"
—so, and no otherwise, "born of him."

"Behold what manner of love" is this that "the Father
hath bestowed upon us!" That in such a sense, and to
such an effect, the righteous God should be bent on our
"being called his children;" his very children; his children in respect of our being made partakers of his righteous
nature as God! Truly it is a love which it would never
have entered into man's heart to conceive, that in this
marvellous way of such a new birth, "we should be called
children of God."

II. And we are his children; "Beloved, now are we

children of God." Our being called children of God is a reality; our being born of God makes it so. The world may not know us in that character, for "it knows not God," and has never known him. We "know that God is righteous;" but the world does not so know him, has not so known him, will not and cannot so know him. How then should it know us, when, born of God, we do righteousness as he is righteous? On the contrary, for this very reason, because we are called children of God, and indeed are so, —therefore "the world knoweth us not."

In this respect our position in the world is identical with that of Christ himself. He was called the Son of God, and was so; therefore the world did not own him any more than it owns us; because "it knew not him whose Son he was." * The world could not understand his thorough sympathy with God; his burning zeal for God; his holy anger kindled at the sight of whatever outraged the righteous character and claims of God; his lofty, uncompromising loyalty to God's righteous government and law; his tender concern for the little ones given to him by God, that they might be shielded from man's wrong and led in God's righteous way. His being the Son of God, not in name only but in nature also;—his being so constantly and consistently true, in all his life, and in his death, to what his sonship involved;—was the very thing which made him incomprehensible to the world. Even his own chosen ones, when he was in the crisis and agony of doing righteousness, knew him not. The three who should have watched with

---

* Here especially the reference of the pronoun, in the last clause of the first verse, to the Father, is to be noted. I introduce the thought of the world's disowning of the Son, not under that clause, but rather under the previous "us," in virtue of the filial oneness of Christ and his people. The clause in question explains the world's ignorance of both, as arising out of its ignorance of the righteous God whose sons or children he, and in him we, are.

him in the garden, slept. When he was on his way to trial
and death, they all forsook him and fled. They knew him
not as the Father's "righteous servant, by his righteousness
justifying many, through bearing their iniquities;" because
they knew not the righteous Father himself, laying upon
him their iniquities. He was left alone with the Father in
that last scene of all (John xvi. 32). All throughout he
was constrained painfully to realise the fact that his mission
from the righteous Father, and the righteous meaning of it,
were but dimly apprehended by his closest friends, and
were wholly set at nought by a world "that by wisdom
knew not God."

That same world has not known God since, any more
than it did before; his children have still to live in the
midst of a world that knows not him, and therefore will
not know them. This is their trial, as it was Christ's.
And in one respect it is to them, if not a sorer or more
painful, yet a more perilous trial, than it was to him. If
the world knew not him, he in a corresponding sense knew
not it. If the world had no sympathy with him in what
he knew of the righteous Father, he had no sympathy with
the world in what it thought of the righteous Father. If
men, not knowing God whose only begotten and well beloved Son he was, could not enter into his deep views of
God's righteous character and claims, he had no leaning
toward their loose notion of all in God's government being
made to bend and give way to them, that they might not
die. That never could be his infirmity. But it is ours;
it is our temptation. Children of God as we are called,
and really are; "born of God," so as to be partakers of his
nature, and to "do righteousness as he is righteous;" we
are not so thoroughly rid of the old nature but that still
we have too strong an inclination to think as the world

thinks, and feel as the world feels, about the righteous God and his righteousness.

Especially when there comes to be a heavy strain upon us as God's children; and a strong case is made out for some concession; and we begin to doubt if we have not been too stiff and strict in refusing this or that compliance, or condemning this or that liberty; and ask if we might not perhaps do more good, and better serve the cause of righteousness and a righteous God, by being a little less precise and more accommodating. Yes; we might in that way disarm somewhat the world's hostility, and win a character for amiable courtesy and a liberal spirit. The world might come to know us, so as to like us better than it does now; better than it likes our more scrupulous brethren. But would not its knowing us in that way be just in proportion to our ceasing so far practically to be God's children, " doing righteousness as he is righteous ? " Let us be upon our guard against so great a danger. Let us lay our account with having to judge and act on principles which the world cannot understand. Let us be God's children indeed; though on that very account the world that has not known God should not know us.

III. For, whatever the world may think or say, " we are the children of God," his dear children; sharers of his divine nature; the objects of his fatherly love. It concerns us to bear this in mind; to apprehend and feel it to be true. It is our safety to do so. It is what is due to ourselves; it is what God expects, and has a right to expect, from us.

And it is especially on our community of nature with God, as being " born of him " and so " called his children," that we are to dwell. It is not so much with a view to heighten our sense of privilege, as to deepen our sense of obligation, that John so emphatically repeats this assertion;

—" Now are we the children of God." It is our nature, as such, being born of God, to " do righteousness, as we know him to be righteous." That is a new nature in us, and it is to be cultivated, exercised, developed, ripened. The field in which it is to grow and be matured is not at all congenial or favourable. It is the world, which not knowing him who begets, cannot be expected to know us who are begotten of him. It is the world, whose influences are all hostile to what is the great characteristic of the new nature in us which our being born of God creates, our " doing righteousness as we know that God is righteous." Still that is our nature; our new nature: " Now are we the children of God." And be the world ever so unpropitious in its atmosphere and soil, we are here in it as " trees of righteousness, the planting of the Lord," to grow as his children, " that he may be glorified."

That is what is John's chief design, in reminding us, in this connection, that we are the children of God. Other views are not to be excluded. The high rank in God's kingdom; the intimate, familiar footing in his house; the warm place in his heart; which that wondrous manner of love bestowed upon us in our being called his children implies;—these all are animating and spirit-stirring motives to face the worst the world can do to us, through its not knowing us any more than it knows him whose children we are. It is a legitimate source of comfort and encouragement when, disallowed of men, we have to fall back upon " the witness of the Spirit, witnessing with our spirits that we are the children of God; and if children then heirs; heirs of God, and joint-heirs with Christ." It is, moreover, a strong and telling appeal that is made to our sense of honour, to every noble and generous impulse of the new nature in us, when we are reminded that we are sent as God's children into the very midst of a world that knows

neither our Father nor ourselves; and sent for this very
end, that we may approve ourselves to be his children indeed; and may "let our light so shine before men, that
they may see our good works, and glorify our Father which
is in heaven." In the face of the world's ignorance of us
and of our Father, and its ignorant opposition to us and to
our Father; though the world may refuse to acknowledge
us as God's children, and give us credit for being what we
profess to be; still let us not lose our own sense of the
reality of what we are. Let us stay ourselves on the conviction that our being God's children is not a matter of
opinion, dependent on the world's vote, but a matter of
fact, flowing from the amazing manner of love which the
Father hath bestowed upon us. And let us be put, as the
saying is, upon our mettle, to make good our claim to be
God's children, by such a manifestation of our oneness of
nature with him of whom we are born, as may, by God's
blessing, overcome some of the world's ignorant unbelief,
and lead some of the world's children to try that manner
of love for themselves, to taste and see how good the Lord
is.

These are important and relevant practical considerations, to which we do well to give heed.

But they must not thrust aside the apostle's main
design, which is that our own personal holiness may be
preserved and may grow. We are the children of God, as
born of him; so born of him as to have the great fundamental principle of his righteous nature wrought and implanted in us. And our task, our trial, our probation, is,
to give that principle fair play and full scope, in opposition
to the world which disowns it; to act out all that is implied
in our being God's children, in the very heart of the world
which knows neither him nor us; to grow in filial likeness
and filial love to God amid all the adverse influences of the

world's ignorant ungodliness. " Now are we the children of God," as being " born of him ; " having his moral image stamped upon us ; his moral nature formed in us. That is what we are ever more and more to realise ourselves to be, amid all the drawbacks and disadvantages of our present state.

IV. And we are to do so all the rather, because these drawbacks and disadvantages will not last long. We are only at the beginning of our life as God's children. What we are, in that character, we grasp, or try to grasp, by faith ; " what we shall be does not yet appear." But it is to appear soon. And one thing we know about it is, that our participation in God's nature, as his children, must then be perfect, for our knowledge of him will be perfect : " We shall be like him, for we shall see him as he is." This suggests two thoughts.

In the first place, what is set before us, as matter of hope in the future life, is not something different from what is to be attained, enjoyed, and improved by us, as matter of faith, and of the experience of faith, in the present life. It is not that now we are the children of God, and that hereafter we are to be something else, or something more. No. The sole and simple contrast is between what we are now, as children of God, and what we shall be hereafter as such. " Now we are the children of God ; " " born of him ; " partakers of his nature ; " doing righteousness, as he is righteous," in the midst of a world that knows us not as doing righteousness, any more than it knows him, the righteous Father, whose righteousness we do. But " the world passes away, and the lust thereof ; " and, lo ! " new heavens and a new earth, wherein dwelleth righteousness ! " What shall we then be as children of God, in a new world, that knows both him and us, all whose arrangements and ongoings are in sympathy with him and us ? " It doth not yet appear." There is a veil hiding that glory from our eyes; and John does not lift it.

But, secondly, one thing he tells us plainly enough. When it does appear what we are to be; when that is no more hidden but disclosed; we shall be like God whose children we are as being born of him; "for we shall see him as he is."

We shall be like him; we shall be such as he is, not almost but altogether. We are like him now. We are of his mind and on his side in all that pertains to his righteous character and government; his righteous condemnation of all iniquity; his righteous way of saving sinners. But the likeness is broken and imperfect. It is a real family likeness so far as it goes, a real oneness of nature; it identifies us as his children. But the features of resemblance are faint at the best, and marred by traces ever reappearing of our old likeness to the world and its prince, whose children we once were. It will be otherwise when "what we shall be" is made manifest or appears. Then our likeness to God will be complete; for then "we shall see him as he is."

"We shall see him as he is;" for "the pure in heart shall see God." The full light of all his perfection as the righteous God will open upon our view; we shall know the righteous Father as the Son knows him.

The Son knows him;—"O righteous Father, the world hath not known thee: but I have known thee; and these have known that thou hast sent me." Here are the two extremes:—"The world hath not known thee; but I have known thee." And here also is, as it were, the intermediate position occupied by us:—"these have known that thou hast sent me." They do not know thee yet, as I, O righteous Father, know thee. But they are in the way of learning thus to know thee; for they know me as sent by thee. I am educating and training them in that knowledge of thee which I would have them to possess as perfectly as I possess it myself;—" I have declared unto them thy name, and will declare it." Nor will I desist until they know thee, as I know thee, by experience of thy love; "the love wherewith thou hast loved me dwelling in them and I in them" (John xvii. 25, 26).

So Jesus, the first-begotten among many brethren, is teaching us now to know, as he knows, the righteous Father, through the love wherewith the Father loveth him dwelling in us, and himself dwelling in us. The school is ill-suited, in many respects, to the teaching; and the scholars are not so apt as might be wished. The school is but dimly lighted and badly aired; the atmosphere is too full of dust and smoke; the learners also are often drowsy; and the lesson-object is seen through a glass darkly. But lo! the hour comes when the benign master, the loving elder brother, leads us into the spacious, lofty, bright hall of his Father's many-mansioned house, and presents us to the Father, face to face, saying, "Behold I and the little ones whom thou hast given me." Then there is clear sight; unclouded vision; a full and perfect understanding of the righteous Father; a full and perfect understanding between him and us; as full and perfect an understanding as there is in the case of his own beloved Son himself. All that is dark or doubtful about his character and ways is cleared up. There is nothing anywhere to awaken a suspicion or suggest a question; nothing to give a partial or distorted view of what he is or what he does. We see him as he is; and so seeing him, we approve, and love, and are like him evermore!

Is not this a hope "full of glory"? And is it not a

hope full of holiness too? Surely it must be true that " every man that hath this hope in God," the righteous Father,—the hope of being like him through seeing him as he is,—" purifieth himself even as Jesus, the Son, is pure."

20

THE DIVINE HOPE PERFECTING THE SINLESS FAMILY LIKENESS

"Beloved, now are we the sons [children] of God; and it doth not yet appear what we shall be; but when he shall appear" [when that shall appear] "we shall be like him [God], for we shall see him as he is. And every man that hath this hope in him [God], purifieth himself, even as he [Christ] is pure. Whosoever committeth sin transgresseth also the law; for sin is the transgression of the law."
1 John 3:2,4

THE crowning glory and joy of sonship is to be like him whose sons we are; and that glory, that joy, is set before us. What we are to be, as sons of God, does not now appear. But it is to appear. And when it does appear, we know that we shall be like him. That one element or feature of our future state as children of God, hidden as that state is, we know. What more, or what besides, there may be in it to make it blessed, we cannot know; for "what we are to be does not yet appear." Only we do know that when it does appear, it will be found to have this blessedness in it; that "we shall be like God."

It must be so; for "we shall see God as he is." Other things about our future state as children of God we cannot know until what we are to be, which does not now appear, shall appear. But one thing we do know, that we are to "see God as he is," and therefore to "be like him." That is our hope; a divine hope; "hope in God;" tending towards the perfecting, even here, of the family likeness that

attests our divine filiation, or our being "born of God."
For "every man that hath this hope in him, (that is, in
God,) purifieth himself, even as he, (that is, Christ,) is
pure" (ver. 3).

There is, as usual, some difficulty here as to the pronouns "him" and "he." The first "him" evidently points
to God the Father, whose children we are. The hope
which we have of being like God, because we shall see him
as he is, is a hope "in him," or upon him, having him as
its object and its ground. It is the last "he" that may
seem uncertain. It is a different word in the original from
the previous word "him;" which again is the same as that
used in the previous verse about God. The "he" in the
close of the verse,—"even as he is pure,"—is emphatically
demonstrative. It means "that one," "that child of God,"
"that Son." So clear is the identification of the person.
Both pronouns, it is to be noticed,—the "him" and the
"he,"—are expressed in the original, and not left to be
supplied. The first naturally refers to the person previously
spoken of, God the Father, whose children we are. The
second as naturally refers to some other person, already
distinctly enough indicated, in whom the ideal of our ultimate perfection in respect of likeness to God is realised,
and in whom, therefore, the model and standard of our
duty, as aiming at that likeness, is to be found. That
person is evidently Christ the Son. The verse, accordingly, interpreted in strict consistency with the exact
grammatical construction, may and must run thus :—Every
man, every one, every one of God's children, every child
of God,—having this hope in God, the hope of seeing him
as he is and being like him,—purifieth himself, even as that
child of God, that Son of God, that Christ, is pure.

Thus the apostle, having set before us the high ideal,
brings in the model of its actual realisation. The ideal is

our being therefore like God whose children we are; our being like him, because we shall see him as he is. This ideal as to what we shall be implies a striving after it as we now are. For "every one who hath this hope in God purifieth himself." And we strive all the better because we have a model of its realisation; "even as the Son is pure."

I. We must look then here, as always, to Christ. He had a hope in God, or upon God; a hope having God for its object, and God for its ground and warrant. "Thou didst make me hope when I was upon my mother's breast" (Ps. xxii. 9). "My flesh shall rest in hope" (Ps. xvi. 9). It was hope for himself as the Son; and it was hope in and upon God his Father. And it was substantially the same hope that we have as children that he had as the Son. True; he could not say, with reference to himself, and his own knowledge or consciousness,—It doth not yet appear what I shall be; at least not exactly as we say it. He knew better what he was to be, than we can know what we are to be. But even he, in his human nature and human experience, did not adequately know this; for even he walked by faith and not by sight. It really did not yet appear what he was to be. There was much, very much, of the joy set before him, that his human soul, in its earthly condition, could not comprehend. The Father had in store for him as his beloved Son such a recompense, such a fulness of consummated joy and glory; that, Son as he was, he could not beforehand comprehend or imagine it. One thing, however, he did know, that whatever the future discovery or development, to himself or others, of his sonship was to be, it would be all in the line of his being like the Father; and being like the Father through seeing him as he is.

I would speak with reverence and diffidence here. I

try to put myself in the position of him who, as regards this very matter, is held up before me as my pattern; I mean, as regards my purifying myself now, in virtue of my having this hope in or upon God my Father, that I am to be like him hereafter, when I shall see him as he is. Christ was as I am; else the reference to him here is vain. He had the same hope in or upon God that I have; the hope of seeing him as he is, and being therefore like him. Is it wrong to say that he did not always see God as he is, while he was on earth? I speak of him as man; and it is as man that he is here set before me. Was he not in circumstances in which what he actually saw of God was to a large extent identical with what we see of God? Did he always see him as he is, any more than we do? He saw him in his actings; and in whatever explanation of his actings he was pleased by revelation to give. He saw him, in that way, more clearly than we see him. But did he see him otherwise, any more than we see him otherwise? Did he see him as he is? Were there not to him the same clouds and darkness around the throne of God his Father that there are to us? Was not God's way to him, as to us, in the deep, and his path in the mighty waters? The medium of vision, at all events, was the same to him that it is to us. It was through the dim and hazy atmosphere of things as they are, with what light revelation sheds on them, that he, like us, had to see God; not as he is in himself, but as he is in his dealings with a world whose fall has made his providence of forbearance, grace, and judgment, a strange and awful mystery to all intelligences; a mystery which the last day alone is to unfold. Jesus lived under that providence, as we do; and saw God, through it, as we do. That is not quite seeing him as he is.

To see God as he is, when the present strange problem —a dispensation of long-suffering patience, subservient to

a dispensation of present mercy and salvation, and preparatory to a dispensation of retribution and reward,—is
at last solved;—to see God as he is, when the shifting
shadows of time flee away, and the repose of the final
settlement of all things comes;—that was to Christ a
matter of hope; exactly as it is to us. It must have been
so. And if it was so, is it too much to say that this in-
cluded, even in his case, the idea of his hoping to be like
God, when he was thus to see him as he is, in a sense and
to an extent not within the reach and range of his human
experience, when it was among the ordinary conditions of
humanity here on earth that he had to see him? Is there
no trace of a conflict between his natural human will and
the divine will of the Father, in the deep movements of
his soul in its agony? Was it never an effort with him to
bring his own mind into harmony, or to keep his own mind
in harmony, with the mind of the Father? Is he not now
more like the Father,—I speak of his human consciousness,
his human sense and feeling,—now that he fully "sees of
the travail of his soul and is satisfied," and sees therefore
God the Father as he is, in the consummated issue of his
mighty plan,—than he could be when he had to bow his
meek and uncomplaining neck to the untried yoke; to meet
the experimentally-unknown doom; when, "though he
was a Son, he had to learn obedience by the things which
he suffered;" when, "in the days of his flesh he offered up
prayers and supplications unto him that was able to save
him from death, and was heard in that he feared?"

That was his trial, as it is ours; to be in a position
in which, seeing God as he is, and being consequently
thoroughly like him, in respect of full and ultimate contentment, complacency, satisfaction, and joy, is "a thing hoped
for." It is in such a position that our purifying of ourselves
is to be wrought out, even as it was in such a position that

his being pure was manifested and approved. We, having this hope in God our Father, are to purify ourselves even as he, having this hope also in God his Father—how shall the sentence run to a close?—purified himself?—nay, that will not do,—was pure?—that might do, but it is not enough,—"is pure?" Yes; that is the way of putting it that pleases the disciple who records the Son's own saying; "Before Abraham was, I am."

"He is pure." It is not enough to say that he was pure; that in the condition and experience in respect of which he is here held out as an encouragement and example to us, he kept himself pure, as we have to make ourselves pure. The use of the present tense is most significant, "he is pure." It is the essential purity of his human nature, as then and now eternally welded into his divine, that is set before us. And the precise lesson is this. The task of purifying ourselves is assigned to us in such circumstances, however unpropitious and unfavourable, as were yet not found to be incompatible or inconsistent with his essential purity. His being pure, in such circumstances, is a motive for our purifying ourselves; his purity, moreover, in these circumstances is the model and measure of what we should wish ours to be. We, having the same hope in God that he had; the hope of being like God because we shall see him as he is; are to purify ourselves as he is pure.

"He is pure." It is with reference to his being a model to us that he is said to be so; we are "to purify ourselves as he is pure." And we are to purify ourselves as he is pure, in the very same world which he, in his perfect purity, defied,—"Which of you convinceth me of sin?" He has really, in this matter, no advantage over us. He, as to his being pure; and we, as to our purifying ourselves; are on the same footing. We have to realise our sonship, as he had to realise his sonship, in a world that knows not God;

and we have to realise it, like him, in hope. So realising it, and having this joint hope with him in God, we purify ourselves as he is pure.

II. With all this, the commission of sin is incompatible. "He that doeth righteousness," and he alone, "is born of God" (ii. 29). For God is righteous; and every one that is born of God must partake of his righteous nature; and be a doer of righteousness, as God his Father is righteous. The doing of sin is inconsistent with so righteous a parentage; for it is the doing of that which is against law; "Whosoever committed sin transgresseth also the law : for sin is the transgression of the law" (ver. 4).

Sin is lawlessness; insubordination to law. It is to be so regarded; especially by us who, on the one hand, being born of God, make conscience of doing righteousness as God is righteous (ii. 29); and who, on the other hand, having this hope in God,—that we are to be like him when we shall see him as he is,—make conscience of purifying ourselves, as our model, his own beloved Son, is pure (iii. 2, 3). We are to look upon sin as a breach of law. That is our security against committing sin, and so compromising the righteousness which we do, and the purity to which we aspire.

There are other views that may be taken of sin; and some that may even seem more spiritual than this, and more in keeping with our character and position as sons of God. For there is a temptation to over-refining here; a temptation to which many in John's day yielded, with most disastrous results to the interests of righteousness and purity; a temptation which may even yet beset us. Am I a child of God, born of him, standing to him in the same relation with his beloved Son? I seem to be raised above the commonplace consideration of sin being wrong because it is against the law. Sin should be offensive to me on higher grounds. Does it not shock the heavenly instincts of my new-born nature ? Do I not feel it now to be beneath me to commit sin ? It is a degradation unworthy of my rank and prospects. There can be no need of law to restrain me. Sin is not to be shunned by me merely because some legal enactment prohibits and condemns it. I loathe its foulness; I despise its baseness; I spurn its ingratitude.

So far, such feelings are gracious, generous, honourable; and they are to be cherished accordingly. But it is dangerous to trust to them, as if they might supersede what may seem the homelier and humbler reason for not committing sin; that it is against the law.

Do I feel or fancy that that is not altogether a filial motive, that it somewhat grates upon my ear and wounds my sensibility, that it scarcely comes up to my notion of what a filial frame of mind should be, and almost subjects me again to the bondage of legal constraint and a legal covenant ? Trust me, I may be inclined to say ; leave me to myself; and you may be very sure that I shall not commit sin. I have no wish for it; no heart for it. I am upon honour not to commit sin. But why bring in again the element of law ? Why be ever reminding me not to break the law ? Let me beware of the insidious entrance of such a thought into my heart. Am I not, in suffering it even for a moment, already committing sin ? Am I not committing the very sin by which Adam fell, the sin by which the angels fell, the sin of counting it an irksome thing to be governed by law as being under authority, and aspiring to a sort of liberty of independence which no created being can ever assume or usurp without just offence to God and inevitable ruin to himself.

And let me look to that Pure One, who is to be my pattern in my life-task of purifying myself. How did he

keep his purity intact when he was in the midst of that
world which has not known God? Was he above law?
Was he not "made under the law?" Was it not "obedience" that "he learned by the things which he suffered?"
Shall I aspire to a more transcendental style of purity than
he exemplified? Shall I adopt a method of self-purification
more refined than that Pure One himself has by his practice sanctioned? Is the disciple to be above his master,
the servant above his lord? Ah! let me remember that if
I have to sustain the character of a child of God here; to
prove myself to be born of God and partaker of his righteous nature; to purify myself as hoping hereafter to be like
God when I shall see him as he is; it is in the midst of a
world that has not known him that I have all this to do.
And what is more, it is in the midst of a world that has
known me, and that I have known, too well. Let me think
of the sympathy that there still is between that world and
me; how far too congenial its ungodly and unholy spirit
still is to my spirit. How am I to keep myself unspotted
from the world, and purify myself in it as Christ is pure?
How but by entering into his mind as he takes upon him
the form of a servant, and becomes obedient? He who is
himself pure; immaculately, incorruptibly, inviolably pure;
essentially pure in his human nature as well as his divine;
manifested and maintained this purity in the attitude of
one saying: "Lo, I come: in the volume of the book it is
written of me, I delight to do thy will, O my God: yea,
thy law is within my heart" (Ps. xl. 7, 8). Much more
must it be in that attitude that I purify myself; I, who am
not by nature "separate from sinners;" I, in whom there
is still always too much of a leaning to their side. How
shall I guard against worldly conformity, against compromises and compliances, against ingenious casuistry or
special pleading, that would try to reconcile with a high

toned spirituality more or less of indifference or indulgence towards the world and its lusts? "To the law and to the testimony" let me be ever subject. Let me be true and loyal to the law. Let me love and fear the law. Let me take my stand on the law of my God; doing righteousness according to the law of the righteous Father; unsparingly and unflinchingly, without equivocation or evasion, condemning, shunning, hating sin as "the transgression of the law."

21

THE SECRET OF SINLESSNESS—ABIDING IN THE SINLESS ONE AS MANIFESTED TO TAKE AWAY OUR SINS

" Whosoever committeth sin transgresseth also the law ; for sin is the transgression of the law. And ye know that he was manifested to take away our sins ; and in him is no sin. Whosoever abideth in him sinneth not : whosoever sinneth hath not seen him, neither known him." 1 John 3:4-6

FOUR arguments against committing sin, or transgressing the law, are here suggested ; all of them connected with him whose essential purity is to be our model in purifying ourselves : I. The end or design of his manifestation,—" to take away our sins ; " II. His own sinlessness,—" in him is no sin ; " III. Our oneness with him,—" whosoever abideth in him sinneth not ; " IV. The incompatibility of sin with any real acquaintance with him,—" whosoever sinneth hath not seen him, neither known him." The four may be reduced to two : the first and second being, as it were, doctrinal ; the third and fourth experimental : the former turning on what he is to us, as our Saviour ; the latter, on what we are in him as his saved ones.

I. " Ye know that he was manifested to take away our sins ; and in him is no sin " (ver. 5).

Let us consider, in the first place, for what end he was manifested ; it was to " take away our sins." Some would understand this phrase as denoting here exclusively the cleansing of our nature from its sinful lusts and habits ;

and as having no distinct reference at all to the removal of contracted guilt. It is admitted that when the phrase occurs elsewhere it is the taking away of guilt by means of atoning blood that is meant ; as in the Baptist's testimony, " Behold the Lamb of God, which taketh away the sin of the world " (John i. 29). But it is contended that here that thought is somewhat irrelevant, since it is moral purification, and not legal satisfaction or legal purging, sanctification in a moral, and not in a legal or sacrificial sense, that John is speaking of; and since, moreover, he seems to make that depend rather on what the Son is manifested to be, than on what he is manifested to do ; on his person rather than on his work. There is no doubt truth in these remarks. But I cannot help thinking that they have led to an unnecessary and undue limitation of the force and fulness of this pregnant phrase. I would not, in that other passage, restrict it to the mere legal removal of the guilt of the world's sin, without including in it also the removal of the sin itself, in its moral pollution and power. Nor am I inclined here to shut out the idea of the expiation of the guilt of our sins, though the other idea of moral purification from them is confessedly the uppermost or leading one. In fact, the two are inseparable : they are really one. I can scarcely conceive of John pointing to the manifestation of him in whom is no sin, as a source of moral purity, as taking away our sins out of our nature, without having in his mind, and wishing us to have in our mind, as a material part of the process by which that object is attained, his taking away our sins out of the record of their guilt, " the book of God's remembrance."

It confirms this view to remember that John has just described sin as " the transgression of the law " (ver. 4). He has fastened upon this as constituting the essence of sin, that it is against law. He is of the same mind with

Paul, in that saying of his,—" The carnal mind is enmity against God; for it is not subject to the law of God, neither indeed can be" (Rom. viii. 7). He, like Paul, knows that as our sins are against the law, so the law is against our sins. It is against our sins, in such a sense and to such an effect as to keep us, on account of them, helplessly under condemnation. We are under the law's just sentence of death. Nay, more, the law, of which our sins are the transgression, is so against our sins as by a natural reaction to stir up in us more and more, the more closely it is brought to bear upon us, that very opposition to itself, and rebellion against itself, in which the sinfulness of our sins consists. In the grasp and under the power of the law, as condemned criminals, we are fettered; and can no more get rid of our sins than a doomed felon can shake off his irons.

If we are spiritual men at all, we know this well. We know and have felt, that the more the law approves itself to us, as "holy, and just, and good;" the more it comes home to us, by the power of the Holy Ghost, in its high excellency and deep spirituality; the more our conscience and our heart are on its side; the more we see and apprehend of its just authority and holy beauty; the more we strive after complete conformity to it; the more we "would do good:" so much the more, while we are thus under the law, is "evil present with us" (Rom. vii.) An impotent sense of failure deadens and depresses us, while the feeling of our prostrate bondage in our sins irritates our natural enmity against God. And if we do not relapse into indifference, or take refuge in formality, or sink into sullen gloom, we are shut up to the one only effectual way of ending this miserable struggle between the law and our sinful nature; the way of free grace and sovereign mercy; the way of embracing him whom "God hath set forth to be a propitiation through faith in his blood;" "in whom we have redemption through his blood, even the forgiveness of sins." Then indeed "sin shall no more have dominion over us, when we are not under the law but under grace;" when "there is now to us no condemnation because we are in Christ Jesus;" when we know him as "his own self bearing our sins in his own body on the cross, that we being dead to sin might live unto righteousness."

All this, I think, must be held to be comprehended in the fact stated;—"he was manifested to take away our sins." And it is all consistent with the object for which John reminds us of it; our purifying ourselves, as he is pure. He was manifested to take away our sins, root and branch. The very completeness of that work of atonement by which he takes them away, in respect of the condemnation and punishment which as transgressions of the law they bind upon us, secures also his completely taking them away, in respect of the carnal mind in us, of whose enmity against God and insubordination to his law they are the fruits. His purging our conscience from the guilt of them, is the very means of his purging our hearts from the pollution of them. Their power to condemn us he takes away; and so he takes away also their power to rule over us. They can never again subject us to the law's curse; and therefore they can never again provoke in us resistance or resentment of the law's authority.

Nor is this all. In virtue of his being manifested to take away our sins, we receive the Holy Ghost. The obstacle which our sin, as a breach of the law, interposed to his being graciously present with us and in us is taken away. The Divine Spirit dwells and works in us; causing us to love the law which is now magnified, not in our destruction but in our salvation, not in our death but in

our life ; and to hate the thought of transgressing it any
more. A new nature, a new heart, a new spirit, as respects
the law of God and God the lawgiver, a new character as
well as a new state, is the result of Christ being manifested
to take away our sins. We know that, personally, practically, experimentally; and our knowledge of it is what
enables as well as moves us to purify ourselves as Christ
is pure.

It is so all the rather because, secondly, we are to consider that he is manifested as himself the sinless one : " In
him is no sin." Here again let us remember that sin is
viewed in the light of the law : it is the transgression of
the law : it is against law. The precise point of this declaration concerning the sinless one lies in that declaration
concerning sin. In him is no sin, because in him is no lawlessness; nothing that is against the law. It is his being
manifested as in that sense without sin, that makes his
manifestation to us,—or our looking to what he is, as well
as our looking to what he does,—effectual towards the taking away of our sins out of our heart and nature. In him,
as " manifested to take away our sins," " there is no sin ; "
nothing of what needs to be taken away from us ; nothing
of that sin which is the transgression of the law.

I do not ask you now to dwell on the thought that this
sinlessness of his, his being himself free from all liability
to the law as a transgressor, was an essential condition of
his taking upon himself our liabilities, so as to take them
away from us. I ask you rather to consider the mighty
moral power which his being manifested as the sinless one
has, in itself and of itself, to take away our sins ; not
merely to take away their guilt lying upon us, but to take
them bodily, as it were, as to their very substance and
spirit, from within us. In that view, it is all-important

that we look at his sinlessness in strict and definite connection with the law.

How do we conceive of him as without sin ? He is before us as one in whom there is no sympathy with what is vile and polluting; or with what is mean and base; or with what is unfair and untrue; or with what is dishonourable and unhandsome; or with what is unkind, ungenerous, unloving. Not a thought, not a feeling, not an affection is in him that could offend the purest taste, the most fastidious delicacy. Benevolence without the slightest alloy of selfishness; integrity such as the breath of suspicion cannot touch; seraphic mildness, sweetness, calmness, that no storm of passion has ever ruffled; a soul attuned to all the melodies of heaven, on which no jarring note of earth's discord can ever strike; a divine dignity; a divine gracefulness in look and mein, in air and carriage, infinitely removed from man's uncertain temper and the rude strife of tongues;—some such ideal, some such picture, rises before our eye. And the contemplation of it may be profitable as well as pleasant; for all these representations of the one only perfectly sinless man are true; and contemplating them, we may to some extent be moved to imitate as well as admire. But we do not thus, " with open face, behold as in a glass the glory of the Lord," so as to be really " changed into the same image, from glory to glory." For the glory of the Lord, manifested in and by him as the sinless one, is his never " transgressing the law." In him is no sin; nothing of what is against the law; against the law under which he was made when he was made of a woman. It is into the image of that glory that we, beholding it, are to be changed " by the Spirit of the Lord."

Does this seem to be a lowering of our high ideal of perfect sinlessness, as exemplified in him ? Does it sound strange to hear it spoken of as his glory ? Do we feel it

to be almost a sort of outrage and offence to speak of this
as his moral glory, that he never broke the law, and never
wished to break it? What glory, what moral grandeur,
is there in that? Much, I answer; much every way. It
is man's highest glory. It is the highest glory of angels.
It is the highest glory of the Son himself, manifested to
take away our sins, that in him, in this sense, is no sin.
"He learned obedience," I repeat, "by the things which
he suffered." And he learned it perfectly; for in him is
no sin; no possibility of any thought adverse to the learning of obedience, entering into, or rising up in, his mind.
That is his essential impeccability; his being incapable of
even the faintest surmise of impatience under the law of
his God and Father, or the most remote approach to a
desire that it were anything else than obedience, anything
less or anything more, that he had to learn. Is not that
"a glory which excels"? Is it not worth while to behold
it,—and to aim at being changed into the same image with
it, from one degree of it to another, from glory to glory,
by the Spirit of the Lord? Behold it! See! It is no
mere negation; no mere abstinence from evil, or absence
of evil. Nor is it any mere spontaneous development of
native, innate good. It is positive, practical, perfect obedience to God's holy law. It is the doing of his will with
the whole heart. It is to live for no other end but that
his will be done. So in his life did he manifest his sinlessness who said, "I must be about my Father's business:"
"The cup which my Father giveth me, shall I not drink
it?" Thus it is seen that "in him is no sin." *

II. With this sinless person we are one; "abiding in
him as the sinless one manifested to take away our sins."

---

* See "Cunningham Lectures on the Fatherhood of God," appendix,
expositions of Rev. xx. 3, and Heb. v. 8, 9.

And that is our security against sinning;—" Whosoever abideth in him sinneth not."

This is the statement of a fact. It is not the enforcing of a duty, as if it were said,—whosoever abideth in him should not sin, and must not sin; let him not sin. It is not even the drawing of an inference or the announcement of what will probably be, and may be expected to be, the issue of oneness with the Lord, as if it ran thus,—whosoever abideth in him will not sin, or is not likely to sin. It is the broad statement of a present fact,—" Whosoever abideth in him sinneth not; " as is also the converse— " Whosoever sinneth hath not seen him, neither known him." Between abiding in Christ and sinning there is such an absolute incompatibility, that whosoever sinneth is for the time not merely in the position of not abiding in Christ, but in the position of not having seen or known him. In so far as he is sinning, his is virtually the very same case with that of the man who has never either seen or known Christ. The statement is very emphatic and very categorical. It is more than a mere assertion of a sort of moral inconsistency or incongruity, a certain manifest unsuitableness, in the view of common-sense and right feeling. It is an assertion of absolute incompatibility, in the nature of things; and it is a very strong assertion of that, put in two forms, positively and negatively, to make it all the stronger. Let us see how it must be so.

I. We abide in Christ by faith; by that faith, wrought in us by the Spirit, which unites us to Christ. Our abiding in him by this faith implies oneness; real and actual oneness; not oneness only in the eye of the law, so that we are regarded and treated as one, in the Judge's dealings with him for us, and with us in him; not oneness merely in the sense of an ordinary alliance or partnership, with a community of goods and interests, of lives and fortunes;

but real and actual oneness of nature. As the husband and the wife are made of twain one flesh; so Christ and we are one spirit. "He that is joined unto the Lord is one spirit." Our abiding in him is our realising this oneness. It is our apprehending ourselves to be consciously one with him, of the same nature, of the same mind, with him, of the same way of thinking and feeling with him. It implies our taking the same view that he does of all things, of God and his law, of righteousness and sin, of guilt and judgment, of holiness and grace and love; our entertaining the same sentiments with reference to them all. It is this which secures our closing with him at first as our Saviour, and carries our consent to his saving us in his own way and on his own terms, so glorifying to the Father, so costly to him, so gracious to us. It is this also which ever after secures our not sinning. We cannot be thus abiding in Christ, realising our oneness of mind and nature with him, and at the same time sinning. The thought or feeling of opposition to the law, or of impatience under it; the wish that we were more free to act as we choose; is no thought or feeling or wish of his: for "in him is no sin." When we sin, when we suffer any such thought or feeling or wish to find harbour in our breasts; we cease for the time to be abiding in him. Between him and us, not then and there abiding in him, there is really as entire a separation as if we had never seen or known him: as wide and deep a gulph as that which lay between the rich man in hell and Lazarus in Abraham's bosom. It is not fixed like that gulph; not yet. But let us beware lest it become fixed. Let us be thankful that it may still be made to disappear. And let us remember that this can only be through our repenting again, as at the beginning,—believing again, as if we had never believed before,—embracing the Lord Jesus, as if now for the first time we saw and knew him,—

"doing the first works,"—becoming anew and afresh, by the grace of the Spirit, "members of Christ's body, of his flesh and of his bones,"—getting shut up into him anew and afresh, so as to be again of one mind and heart with him, abiding once more in him in whom is no sin. For we may be very sure that when we sin, we are none the better for all that we have seen or known of Christ; none the safer. It is the same thing to us as if we had never seen him, neither known him at all.*

2. We abide in Christ by his Spirit abiding in us. That is a filial spirit;—the Spirit of God's Son in us crying Abba Father;—the Spirit of adoption whereby we cry Abba Father. A servile frame of mind grieves and vexes the Holy Spirit, and hinders his continuing to dwell in us. He dwells in us only when we cry Abba Father, and therefore sin not. Sin is ever the fruit of that servile frame of mind which is characteristic of one that has not seen or known the Son. Abiding in him, through his Spirit abiding in us, we have a filial heart towards God. And a filial heart "sinneth not." For a filial heart has no temptation and no desire to go against the will, or the law, of the righteous Father.

From all this we may see how the stress of practical exhortations against sin is to be brought to bear upon a child of God; upon us, who are children in the Son. For it is very important that there should be exhortation, direct and pointed. It is not enough to put the matter in the form of doctrinal statement or anticipated consequence; as if we said: Being God's children in Christ you do not sin; or you will not sin. It is good for you to hear a voice of authority and command: Sin not. And yet that is not the way in which the matter is put here. It is not an

* Compare the exposition in Lecture vi.

order issued, but a fact announced ; " whosoever abideth in him sinneth not." What then ? Is the hortatory method to be given up ? Nay ; it is only necessary to shift a little, as it were, the point of its application. I state it as a fact that whosoever abideth in him sinneth not. And therefore I issue the command : Abide in him. It is his own command : " Abide in me." And that is the right position for the hortatory or commanding mode of appeal. If you would not sin ; that you may not sin ; that it may be impossible for you to sin ;—" abide in him who was manifested to take away your sins, and in whom is no sin." Cleave to him ; grow up into him ; get into his mind ; drink into his spirit. Enter into the design of his being manifested, and into the way in which, being manifested, he accomplishes that design. Enter into the secret of his sinlessness. Keep close to him, abide in him, and sin not.

And forget not the positive, any more than the negative, result of your abiding in him ; your " bringing forth much fruit " (John xv. 5). For it is only in the line of the positive, in the line of bearing fruit, that you can be sure even of the negative,—not sinning. Nay, if your negatively not sinning is the effect of your abiding in Christ, it really resolves itself into your actually and positively bearing fruit, and becomes identical with it. " In him is no sin;" no rebellion against that will of God which he comes to do; no insubordination to that law of God which is within his heart; nothing that hinders, or possibly can hinder, his doing that will and keeping that law always and thoroughly. You " abide in him and sin not." You have in you now nothing more than he had, in so far as you abide in him, of that sullen, slavish, selfish frame of mind; bent on getting its own way, and doing its own pleasure ; grudging God and men their due ; which hinders all cheerful, loyal obedience. You therefore, abiding in him in whom is no sin, that there may be no sin in you, go about with him doing good. Yours is that "pure religion and undefiled before God and the Father," which is this, "to visit the fatherless and widows in their affliction," as well as to keep "yourselves unspotted from the world."

22

THE SECRET OF SINLESSNESS—OUR ABIDING IN CHRIST—THE SEED OF GOD ABIDING IN US—OUR BEING BORN OF GOD

" Whosoever abideth in him sinneth not : whosoever sinneth hath not seen him, neither known him. . . . Whosoever is born of God doth not commit sin ; for his seed remaineth [abideth] in him : and he cannot sin, because he is born of God." 1 John 3:6,9 *

THESE strong statements ;—that one abiding in Christ does not sin, and that one born of God cannot sin ;—are often perplexing, not to say distressing, to serious minds. How is it ? I am forced to ask. I sin, every day, every hour, every moment, I may say, in thought or word or deed. Must I therefore conclude that I am not in Christ ; not born of God ? It is a real practical difficulty. Let us fairly grapple with it.

I. These texts do not teach, either the doctrine of perfection, or that other doctrine which is apt to usurp its place ; the doctrine that God sees no sin in his people, or that what would be sin in others is not sin in them. When I say that this latter doctrine is apt to supplant the other, I do not mean that all who believe in the perfection or perfectibility of the saints on earth are antinomians. I speak simply of what I hold to be a strong tendency in the

---

* I reserve the exposition of the intermediate verses, because I think they can be best considered after we have as far as possible ascertained the sense in which it is said of believers in Christ that they do not and cannot sin.

nature of things. I am told that it is possible for a Christian to live without sinning; that he may be so sanctified as to be incapable of sinning; that such holiness is attainable; nay, that no one can be long a Christian without attaining it; that no one can be sure of his Christianity unless he has attained it. But I see in the most Christian of men, I feel in myself in my most Christian mood, much that is not easily reconcilable with this immaculate sinlessness, unless I can persuade myself that what looks very like sin is not really sin. I am tempted to do so; to defend, on the ground of Christian character, what otherwise I would give over to just condemnation; to stand up for the harmlessness in a believer of ways that would confessedly hurt or ruin the unconverted. And so I really open the door to those perversions of such texts as, " He that is spiritual is judged of no man," " To the pure all things are pure," which have wrought sad havoc with the plain morality of the Bible.

II. There is another mode of dealing with the statements before us which I cannot feel to be satisfactory. It is to limit or restrict their comprehensiveness; and to understand the apostle as speaking, not of sin absolutely and universally, but of sin more or less voluntary and presumptuous. According to this view, one abiding in Christ and born of God does not and cannot sin deliberately, intentionally, knowingly. He may be overtaken in a fault; he may be compassed about with infirmities; he may have his occasional aberrations and failings. But he does not lay plans and go into evil with his eyes open.

Is that true ? Was it true of David ? Or of the man in Corinth who was excommunicated for incest, and upon repentance restored ? Is it any relief to me, when I am staggered by the hard saying that the true Christian does not

and cannot commit sin, to be told that it may be so modified
as to mean that he does not and cannot sin voluntarily ?
Will that modification meet my case ?   Alas ! no.   For I
dare not persuade myself that I never sin voluntarily.   The
saying excludes me, and tells against me, as much as ever.
And then, is it safe to make such a distinction as this between
two sorts of sin : and to make it for such a purpose as this ?
May it not again let in the notion of some evil being tolerable and venial after all in a child of God ?   Where and how
is the line to be drawn ?

III. It may help us out of the difficulty if we first look
at the statements before us in the light, not of what we are
now by grace, but of what we are to be in the future state
of glory.   It will be true then that we sin not ; it will be
impossible for us then to sin.   What will make it true that
we sin not ?   What will make it impossible for us to sin ?
Simply, our abiding in Christ ; our being born of God ; his
seed abiding in us.

It is most important that we should endeavour to form
some distinct idea of this feature or characteristic of heaven's
holiness ; its absolute inviolability ; its being perfectly
secure against the possibility of sin ever marring it.   Saints
in glory do not and cannot sin.   Wherein consists this impossibility of sinning ?   Of what sort is it ?   Plainly it cannot be a merely physical or natural inability ; it must be of
a moral kind.   It is not outward coercion or prevention ;
it is not enforced sinlessness, which would be no sinlessness
at all.   Neither is it sinlessness dependent on external circumstances ; such as want of opportunity or absence of
temptation.   The impeccability is and must be an attribute
of the inner man ; of the saint himself, as perfectly sanctified
in his whole nature.   If in the heavenly world I am not to
sin ; to be incapable of sinning ; that cannot be in consequence of any mere change in my outward position ; any

mere translation from one locality to another, from one system of things to another. It was not his expulsion from Paradise that made Adam peccable, or capable of committing sin. He was so from the first in Paradise, for there he sinned. It is not his return to Paradise, nor his promotion to a better state than that of Paradise, that will make him impeccable. His impeccability must be otherwise attained and secured.

It is true that change of place and of circumstances may do much; and it is a great change that is before us. "We look for new heavens and a new earth, wherein dwelleth righteousness." It will, indeed, be a very different atmosphere that we breathe in heaven from what so often deadens, stupifies, and paralyses our Christian life on earth. We shall be there under other influences and in the midst of other companionships. No more is there any course of this world for us to walk after; no more any prince of the power of the air to intoxicate us with the poisonous vapour of his ungodliness; no more any children of disobedience, seducing us to have our conversation among them. It will, unquestionably, be a blessed relief. To be rid of Satan and of Satan's wiles; to be for ever quit of those worldly ways and habits around us here that are so apt to draw us into conformity with themselves; to be where there is no more any antagonism between what is and what ought to be; to be where God is all in all;—it may well be imagined to be like "a bird escaping out of the snare of the fowler; the snare is broken; and we are escaped!" "Oh! that I had wings like a dove, that I might flee away and be at rest!" "Woe is me that I sojourn in Mesech, that I dwell in the tents of Kedar!" But let me beware. If I imagine that it is my being in heaven that is to make me pure and sinless, or render it impossible for me to sin, I am under a sad and most unsafe delusion. Let it be granted that then all I come in contact with will be holy, and all conducive to holiness; with "nothing to hurt or to destroy in all God's holy mountain." Still, place me there, continuing simply such as I am here; and not only is it not true of me that I cannot sin; but it is true of me that I cannot but sin. Evidently, therefore, its being impossible for me to sin in the future state, must depend upon something else than mere change of scene. And what follows? It must depend upon something that may be actually realised more or less perfectly here. It must depend upon what may be and must be realised here, in the inner spiritual history and experience of every child of God.

Let me remind you that this impeccability lies in the will; the seat of it is the will. It is because, in the state of glory, my will is made "perfectly and immutably free to do good alone," that my will is, or that I myself am, incapable of doing evil.* And let me also remind you that sin, the sin which it will then be impossible for me to commit, is "the transgression of the law;" of the law of God which is the expression of his will. His will is perfectly and immutably free. His law is its free utterance; the free forthgoing of his free will. Your impeccability,—its being impossible for you to sin,—is its being impossible for you to will otherwise than he wills; to think or feel otherwise than he does, as to that law of his which is his will. And if it is your will that is to be thus free; free, as his will is free, to do good alone; and therefore incapable of an evil choice; then your impeccability must be, if I may say so, itself voluntary; voluntarily accepted and realised. The position in which I

---

* See Westminster Confession of Faith, chapter ix., "Of Free Will." In the state of glory, the will is still free: "neither forced, nor by any absolute necessity of nature determined, to good or evil." But it is so thoroughly renewed as to be incapable of an evil choice, "being made perfectly and immutably free to do good alone."

find it impossible to sin must be attested by my own consciousness as a position that is freely and voluntarily mine.

Let me try to imagine myself as regards this matter in the heavenly state. I cannot sin. Why not? What hinders me? Is it that my hands are tied? Is it that my will is fettered? Am I not free? Yes; I am free as God is free. And therefore I can no more sin than God can sin. In the very same sense in which God cannot sin, I cannot sin. My will can no more go against his law than his own will can go against it. For why is it that God cannot sin?—that his will cannot go against his law? Is it not because the law is his will? Is it not because the law is his nature? Yes. The law is his will, his spontaneous will. And it is his nature; the very essence of his moral character and being is in his law. For the law is love; and God is love. The law is holy; and God is holy. He cannot sin, or transgress the law, because he cannot go against his own will, or against his nature. Sin in him, were the thought admissible, would be self-contradictory; suicidal. "He cannot deny himself." Now in heaven am I in this respect such as he is?—really, literally, absolutely such as he is? Yes, that is my heaven! It is my being thus like him when I see him as he is. When, clear from the darkness in which now he hides himself in a world that knows him not, his glory shines unclouded; then I "see him as he is" so as to be "satisfied when I awake with his likeness." It is the likeness of him who cannot sin.

IV. Let me try to bring out more clearly this principle as one that must connect the future with the present. Why is it that in heaven, my will being free as God's will is free, I can no more sin than he can sin? What answer would John give to that question if you could put it to him now? As thus;—"In whatever sense, and with what-

ever modifications, thou didst, in thy experience when
here, find that to be true which thou hast so emphatically
put,—as the test, apparently, of real Christianity,—it is all
true of thee there, where thou art now! How is it so?
Why is it so?" "Because I abide in the Son of God, and
God's own seed abides in me, as being born of God;"—is
not that his reply? What other reply can he give?

No doubt he may also say, "I am no more in a world
that knows not God; exposed to its flattery or its rage. I
have nothing now to apprehend from Satan's subtilty. I
have laid aside the body of corruption that used to weigh
me down. The lusts of the flesh solicit and trouble me no
more. Evil propensities, the remains of my old original
and inveterate depravity, are all thoroughly put away.
Not a vestige of any root of bitterness remains in me; nor
is there any exposure to trial or temptation from without."
These are great and inestimable advantages. "But," he
would add, "not one of them secures, nor do they altogether
secure, my impeccability; or its being impossible for me to
sin. Excepting only immunity from Satan's subtilty, man
in Paradise enjoyed them all; and yet he was peccable; he
sinned. Without any exception, the unfallen angels enjoyed
them all; and yet they showed themselves peccable; some
of their number fell. My heaven is no heaven at all, if in
respect of this matter of my not sinning, or its being impossible for me to sin, I am no better off than Adam was
in the garden, or the angelic hosts in their first estate.
But I am better off. And what, you ask, makes me better
off? My abiding in the Son of God, and having God's own
seed abiding in me, as being born of him. First, I "abide
in the Son of God" evermore, uninterruptedly; and therefore I see God as his Son sees him; I feel towards God as
his Son feels. Secondly, as born of God, I have "his seed
abiding in me," evermore, uninterruptedly; his seed, con-

veying and imparting to me his nature, as truly as a plant's seed imparts its nature to its successor, or a man's seed imparts his nature to his child."

"These two causes combined," John might say, "ensure my not sinning ; make it impossible for me to sin by transgressing the law. For, in virtue of the first, the law is to me what it is to the Son of God, the God-man ; not merely an enforced rule ; far less a yoke of bondage ; but an inward principle also of free, spontaneous choice. It is within my heart, as it is within his. There can no more spring up in my heart than there can spring up in his, the slightest or faintest feeling of impatience under it, or of a longing to be without it or above it. And then, in virtue of the other, the law is to me what it is to God himself. It is the expression of my nature, as it is of his. Being what I am, as born of him, his seed abiding in me, I can no more go against it than he, being what he is, can go against it himself."

Is this the secret of the saint's impeccability in heaven ? Is it at all a true and fair account of his not sinning, of its being impossible for him to sin ?

Then does it not follow that it is an impeccability that may be realised on earth ? For the causes of it are realised on earth ; first, your abiding in the Son of God ; secondly, your being born of God so as to have his seed abiding in you. And so far as they are realised on earth, they cannot but make it impossible for you to sin here, in the very same way in which, when realised perfectly in heaven, they will make it impossible for you to sin there. For they are causes whose efficacy does not at all depend on time or place or circumstances. They act here and now as they will act then and there. They make God's will be done on earth, even as it is in heaven.

V. Viewed thus in the light of "what we shall be," and

of the bearing of what we shall be on what we are, John's
statements assume a somewhat different aspect from what
they are apt to wear when taken by themselves. They
become not one whit less solemn but greatly more encouraging.

For one thing, you may now regard them as describing
a precious privilege, as well as imposing a searching test.
They show you the way of perfect holiness; how you are
to be righteous, even as Christ is righteous,—even as God
is righteous.

I suppose that it is your desire to be so; if it is not,
you are none of Christ's, and are not children of God.
Your earnest longing is, I assume, that you were placed in
such circumstances, or that there were wrought in you such
a frame of spirit, as would make it impossible for you ever
to sin any more.

Well, if it is so, should it not be matter of satisfaction
to you to be told that you have even now within your
reach, realisable in your experience, the elements or conditions, so to speak, of that very state of things which you
so warmly covet? John takes it for granted, that " having
this hope in God;"—the hope that when " it does appear
what you shall be," it will imply your being " like him
whose children you are, because you shall see him as he
is;"—" you purify yourselves even as his own Son is pure."
And surely in that view he does you a kindness when he
tells you how this purifying of yourselves as Christ is pure
may become possible, even to the extent of its being as
impossible for you as for him to commit sin or to transgress
the law. He does no sin; he can do no sin; he cannot
have a thought or wish to transgress the law. Why?
Because he is the Son of God, his only begotten Son, of
one nature with the Father. Even when he takes your
nature, he is, on that account, sinless and impeccable. And

the good news here is, that you also are becoming impeccable in him. Of course, it is good news to you only if impeccability is really the object of your desire; your hope; your heaven. Is it so? Would it be heaven to you not to sin; to be incapable of sinning; to be so situated and so minded, that for you to sin would be as truly and really an impossibility as for Christ or for God? Then these texts are for you. They let you into the secret of this impeccability; they show you wherein it consists. They set it before you, not as something to be reached some time, somewhere, somehow, in some other world, through some mysterious unknown processes to be gone through at death and the resurrection; but as what you may have experience of, and must have experience of, in this present world, and under this present dispensation of the Holy Ghost. For the Holy Ghost makes you really one with the Son of God, so that, abiding in him, you partake of his sonship; his filial relation to the Father and filial heart towards the Father. And the Holy Ghost also implants in you and puts within you the seed of God, the germ of God's own nature and God's own life, so that you are in very truth born of God. When thus in your adoption, rightly viewed, and in your regeneration, the Holy Ghost unites you to the Son, and assimilates you to the Father;—when thus you abide in the Son, in whose sonship you share, and the seed of God your Father, of whom you are born, abides in you;—you have already, in present possession and for present use, all that is essential to impeccability.

VI. Taking this view, I confess I do not feel so much concern as otherwise I might feel about reconciling such strong statements as that one abiding in Christ sinneth not, or that one born of God cannot sin, with the acknowledged and lamented fact that he does sin. John has dealt with that fact already, and told us how to deal with it. It is not his business here to be making allowance for it. It would be beside his purpose altogether, and indeed against it, to be qualifying his high and bold appeal to honest aspirants after perfection, by concessions to those whose object would seem to be to ascertain, not how, and how far, perfection may be reached, but how far they may stop short of it. John has not any such Christians in his eye. Or if he has, it is to bring to bear upon them the whole artillery of these startling statements, in all their strictest and most literal force. They are to be solemnly warned that sin is absolutely incompatible with abiding in Christ and being born of God—all sin, any sin, every sin; that "whosoever sinneth hath not seen Christ, neither known him." To them John has nothing else to say. He cannot otherwise meet their question as to the extent to which sin, still cleaving to a child of God, may be admitted not to vitiate his title. For indeed it is most dangerous to be considering the matter in that light or on that side at all. It is almost sure to lead, first to calculations, and then to compromises, fatal to singleness of eye and the holy ambition that ought to fire the breast; calculations first, about the quantity and quality of the residuum of old corruption which we must lay our account with finding in the purest God-born soul; and then compromises, under the sort of feeling that, as the proverb says, what cannot be cured must be endured.

I beseech you to turn from that downward, earthward way of looking at this great theme; and to look upward and heavenward. I speak to you as believing you to be in earnest about purifying yourselves even as Christ is pure. I tell you that the gospel makes full provision for holiness; and no provision at all for sin. It contemplates, not your sinning, but your not sinning; nay, its being impossible for you to sin. If it did not, it would be no gospel to you. For you are weary of sinning ; weary of finding it always so possible, so easy to sin. The risings of a rebellious spirit in you against God, and his will, and his law ; your feelings of irksomeness, as if his commandments were grievous, his ways dark, his sayings harsh, his service hard, himself austere ; are a continual grief to you. Well, may it not be some consolation, some encouragement, to know, that you have within you, if you will but stir up the gift that is in you, the elements of a holier and happier life ? For these are indeed, when rightly considered, most precious assurances ; " Whosoever abideth in Christ sinneth not ; " " Whosoever is born of God doth not commit sin ; for God's seed remaineth in him : and he cannot sin, because he is born of God."

Let a few practical inferences be suggested.

1. I think the texts teach, or imply, the doctrine of the final perseverance of the saints ; the impossibility of their either wholly or permanently falling away from a state of grace. I cannot understand statements so strong as " sinneth not," or " cannot sin," especially when taken in connection with the reasons given,—" abiding in Christ ; " " being born of God ; " " the seed of God abiding in him," —in any sense consistent with the idea of one who by faith has been united to Christ, and by adoption and regeneration made a child of God, proving ultimately a castaway. It may be quite true that it is not John's immediate design to dwell on that tenet. But nevertheless he uses words that seem very plainly to assume it. It is not easy to see how any one could be called upon to recognise in himself, as actually his now in possession and experience, the principle, if I may so speak, of impeccability, excepting upon grounds precluding the risk of his losing altogether his character and standing in Christ.

2. The texts teach however, very plainly, that this

doctrine, whatever may be its practical use and value in
its right place, and when turned to legitimate account, cannot give to any man security in sin; cannot make him
safe when he is sinning, when he is committing sin or
transgressing the law. When he is sinning, he can draw
no assurance whatever from his "having seen and known
Christ." Virtually, to all intents and purposes, he is exactly in the same position with one who "has not seen him,
neither known him" (ver. 6). Never, at any moment, may
I reckon on a past act of God towards me,—his calling me,
justifying me, adopting me in his Son; or a past work of
God in me,—his regenerating me by his Spirit;—as giving
me any present confidence, if my present state is one of
sin. Not only is this not right; I believe it to be impossible. I believe that no man ever yet felt himself secure in
sinning now, on the ground of his having been brought to
"see and know" Christ long ago. His feeling of security,
in so far as he has such a feeling, does not really spring
from that belief as to the past, but from ignorance now of
Christ and of God; from present unbelief. For the present, he is an unbeliever, not seeing or knowing Christ; no
better than if he had never seen or known him. The
moment he comes again to believe, and has his eyes opened
to see and know Christ; Christ looking on him when he is
sinning as he looked on Peter;—security there is none;
confidence there is none; only bitter weeping. He re-
pents, and does the first works. He believes, as if he had
never believed before. He realises again, as at the first, his
abiding in Christ and God's seed abiding in him. Our
sinning, therefore; our feeling it to be possible for us to
sin; is in fact, and as a practical matter, absolutely incompatible with our abiding in Christ and being born of God.
We are only really abiding in Christ, and consciously and
influentially, if I may say so, born of God so as to have his

seed abiding in us,—in so far as we do not sin,—in so far as we cannot sin.

3. For this, let me again remind you, is John's true design and purpose; it is to put you in the way of not sinning; of its being impossible for you to sin. It is to let you into the secret of sinlessness, of impeccability; that you may be successful in purifying yourselves as Christ is pure. Realise your abiding in Christ, your being born of God, his seed abiding in you. And realise all that, as you may realise it, not as what is to be in heaven; when it will appear what you shall be; but as what may be, and must be, and is on earth; even when "it doth not yet appear what you shall be." Do not imagine that you must wait till you get to heaven until you can know what it is not to sin; to be beyond the possibility of sinning. No doubt it is only in heaven that you can know that perfectly. But you may know something of it on earth. You need not imagine that if you know nothing of it on earth, you can know anything of it in heaven. For it is not, I repeat, any change of scene that will make you know it. Some have fancied that by getting out of the world into the wilderness they might come not to sin; nay, might get themselves into a state in which they could not sin. Away from society's pomps and vanities, its pleasures and vices, in the solitude of the desert, they have sought for immaculate and impeccable holiness; they have sought for it painfully, with tears and stripes. Alas! they have sought for it in vain. But you may find it, in the midst of all evil, if you seek it aright, in the way of abiding in Christ, and having God's seed abiding in you, as being born of him. And you will find it, if you apprehend the force of the Lord's own words: "As thou, Father, hast sent me into the world, even so have I sent them into the world. And for their sakes I sanctify myself, that they also may be sanctified through the truth."

23

THE SECRET OF SINLESSNESS—THE CONTRASTED
"DOINGS"—DOING RIGHTEOUSNESS AND DOING
SIN—THEIR INCOMPATIBILITY IN RESPECT OF
THEIR OPPOSITE ORIGINS OR PARENTAGES—
GOD AND THE DEVIL

"Little children, let no man deceive you: he that doeth righteousness is
righteous, even as he [Christ] is righteous. He that committeth
[doeth] sin is of the devil; for the devil sinneth from the beginning.
For this purpose the Son of God was manifested, that he might destroy
the works of the devil." 1 John 3:7,8

THESE verses are embedded, as it were, between the two
already considered (6 and 9); which teach what may be
called the secret of sinlessness as a possible attainment, and
one that a child of God must apprehend and realise. They
fit into that theme, placing in marked contrast the two opposite lines of conduct,—"doing righteousness and doing
sin,"—and tracing them up to their respective sources, a
righteous nature on the one hand, indicating a divine birth;
and a sinful nature on the other, betraying a devilish origin.
Thus they shut out the very idea of any mixture of the
two characters, or anything intermediate between the two.
Thus also they connect the argument with the introductory
statement at the beginning of this second part of the
epistle, "If ye know that God is righteous, ye know that
every one that doeth righteousness is born of God" (ii. 29).
For this doing righteousness, which at once implies and
tests our being born of him who is righteous, must evince

a family likeness to him, or a participation of nature with him. It must, therefore, be very thorough and complete, and cannot be compatible with doing sin. For that, evincing an opposite family likeness and participation in an opposite nature, points not to a divine birth or our being born of God, but to a very different parentage, our being of the devil.

The passage before us opens accordingly with a very solemn warning : " Little children, let no man deceive you." It assumes an urgent and serious danger. There are those who will do their utmost to deceive you, and the point on which they will try to deceive you is a very vital one. It is so all the rather because it is one on which your own hearts may be but too willing to be deceived. It turns upon the indissoluble connection that there is between being and doing; between character and conduct; between what a man is and how he acts.

The false teachers of John's day held that one might reach in some mysterious way a height of serene, inviolable, inward purity and peace, such as no things without, not even his own actions, could stain. In a less transcendental form, the same sort of notion practically prevails in the world. It used perhaps to be more common than it is now to give a person credit for having right principles, though his practice might be often wrong; to admit his claim to a good heart, in spite of his habits being to a large extent bad. But the delusion is one against which we still need to be cautioned.

John meets it by bringing out in marked contrast the two opposite natures, one or other of which we must all share ; that of God and that of the devil. As it is the nature of God to be righteous, so it is the nature of every one who is born of God to be righteous also. So he who is pre-eminently the Son of God is righteous ; and we who are children of God in him are righteous as he is righteous. But his being righteous necessitates his doing righteousness ; to imagine otherwise in his case would be a profane calumny. So also to think that we can be righteous as he is righteous, if our being righteous does not necessitate our doing righteousness, must be a gross and grievous delusion. On the other hand, it is the devil's nature to be evil; and being evil, he cannot but be doing evil. If we are doing evil, doing sin ; that proves our identity of nature with the devil; we are of the devil. And being of the devil, the originator of sin,—sinning from the beginning,—we cannot be children of God as Christ is his Son. For he was manifested for this very purpose, that he might destroy the works of the devil.

Let us consider the three steps in this argument, as thus adjusted.

I. "He that doeth righteousness is righteous, even as Christ is righteous." It is clearly moral character that is here in question, not legal standing. There is no reference to Christ's vicarious righteousness ; its imputation to us through our oneness with him by faith, and our consequent justification in the sight of God. That doctrine, so clearly revealed elsewhere underlies, as we have already seen, the whole of John's teaching in this epistle. But to import it into this passage is to destroy the sense. Of course it is equally destructive of the sense to use the passage as a support to the doctrine of justification by works, as if it meant that the doer of righteousness is thereby, on the ground of his personal doing of righteousness, justified or accounted righteous before God. John is not thinking of justification at all, but rather of sanctification ; of holiness of life being inseparable from holiness of nature. The precise lesson taught, the great principle asserted, is that righteousness, moral righteousness, cannot possibly exist in

a quiescent or inactive state ; that it never can be a latent
power or undeveloped quality ; that wherever it is it must
be operative. It must be working, and working according
to its own essential nature. Moreover, it must be working,
not partially but universally ; working everywhere and always ; working in and upon whatever it comes in contact
with, in the mind within and the world without. Otherwise, it is not righteousness at all ; certainly not such as we
see in Jesus ; it is not " being righteous as he is righteous."
Therefore being righteous and doing righteousness are not
twain, but one ; one in the very nature of things, by divine
ordination and arrangement. God has joined them ; and
what God has joined man may not put asunder. The
attempt to separate them on either side, or to confound
them, is a fatal error.

Hence those err who would sink the being in the doing
as if the doing were all in all,—quite as much as those who
would divorce the doing from the being, and leave the
being all alone.

" He can't be wrong whose life is in the right," is a
perilous half-truth. Doing righteousness, in the sense of
merely leading what is called a virtuous life, being irre-
proachable in manners, and performing acts of kindness,
may thus be made to constitute the sum and substance of
religion and morality. Evidently that is not John's teaching. On the contrary, it is with the inward frame of mind
that he is chiefly occupied ; it is about the heart being
right with God that he is concerned. The very righteousness, pure and holy, which is the distinguishing characteristic
or attribute of the moral character of God, is to become the
attribute of ours, as it is of Christ's. Far from under-
valuing, or as it were postponing, the inward, or being
righteous ; he lays on that the whole stress of his appeal
about the outward, or doing righteousness. For the very

reason of his appeal is this, that if there be not the being there cannot be the doing ; and therefore, on the other hand, if there be the doing, it proves and insures the being.

This last is the important practical consideration here. But it is so only when we rightly understand what doing righteousness, in John's notion of it, really is. It is not merely performing righteous actions; doing things that are in themselves, or in their own essential nature, right and good. The abstract form righteousness is significant and all-important. To do a righteous deed is one thing : to be doing righteousness in the doing of it is another. The difference may be immense.

Jesus "went about doing good." And in doing good he was ever doing righteousness. For he did good because he knew that to do good is to do what is righteous in the judgment of the righteous Father. He did good, not as doing himself a pleasure or his fellow-men a service, but as doing the Father's righteous will. To do good thus is to do righteousness indeed. Viewing it in that light, we cannot err, or go too far, in the way of identifying it with being righteous. So to do righteousness is really to be righteous ; in the highest and holiest sense ; according to the most perfect type and model; "even as Christ is righteous." It is a vain dream, a fond imagination, for any of us to aspire to being righteous in any other manner or after any other fashion. The humble path of obedience to the righteous Father,—the consistent doing of righteousness as we know, and because we know, that God is righteous (ii. 29),—is practically being righteous. So Christ, the Son of God, is the Father's righteous servant, doing the Father's righteousness. So let us, as born of God, be the Father's righteous servants in Christ; doing righteousness as Christ does righteousness, and being righteous as Christ is righteous.

II. As "doing righteousness,"—through its being thus associated or identified with "being righteous as the Son is righteous,"—proves our being "born of God;" so "doing sin" proves a very different relationship, a very different paternity. "He that committeth" or doeth "sin is of the devil." That is his genealogy or pedigree. And the reason is plain. The devil is the author of sin; it is he who "sinneth from the beginning." The "doer of sin" cannot, as such, have any other father than the originator of sin. And he cannot repudiate the ancestry. It is fastened upon him by the same law or principle which enables "the doer of righteousness" to claim kindred with the righteous Father, in respect of his "being righteous as his own Son is righteous." The medium of proof is the same. It is this, that what one does is really what one is; the doing being the index or identification of the being. "He that committeth" or doeth "sin is of the devil;" for, by doing sin, he shows his identity of nature with him who is a sinner from the beginning. And it is upon identity of nature, proved practically, that the question of moral and spiritual parentage must ultimately turn.

That is the question which John raises here, and to which he afterwards returns (ver. 10). It is with a view to that question that he lays down the essential moral truth involved in his two contrasted propositions or arguments; first, "He that doeth righteousness is righteous, even as he, the Son, is righteous," and so, as "born of God," may assert a divine paternity; secondly, "He that doeth sin is of the devil," the original and archetypal sinner: he must consent, therefore, to trace his genealogical line from a devilish beginning and in a devilish stream.

And still the test is the consistency or identity of the doing with the being. The doer of righteousness is righteous, as Christ the Son, who is one in nature with the

Father, is righteous. The doer of sin is not so, but on the contrary is of the same nature with the devil, who "sinneth from the beginning." He who is born of God, knowing that God is righteous, can do nothing but righteousness, in so far as he realises his position; being himself righteous as Christ is righteous. He that is of the devil can do nothing but sin, as the devil has been doing all along from the beginning. So far as his nature is allowed full development, that is its working. But that proves a paternity the opposite of divine.

Thus two parentages are here contrasted. Two fathers, as it were, desire to have us as children. They are wide as the poles asunder. Of the one relationship it is the characteristic not to sin; of the other, to be always sinning. The one father never has sinned, never could sin, being the "righteous Father." The other has been always a sinner; sinning from the beginning; his first act being to sin. Each father imparts his own character to his children. The virtue or the vice; the wholesome purity or the poisonous matter; the sweet charm or the sour taint; runs in the blood. The children of the one father have infused into them the seed or germ of his impeccability; his being of such a nature that it is impossible for him to sin. The children of the other inherit his absolute incapacity of not sinning; his being of such a nature that it is morally impossible for him not to sin.

It is a terrible inheritance. It is the devil's nature to sin. When we sin we give proof of its being our nature too. And it is a nature which we derive from him. It was he that communicated it to us. Our relation to him, therefore, in respect of our thus sharing his nature, is very close. It may be true that it is only in a figurative sense that we can be called "children of the devil," or said to be "of the devil." Still the figure has in it a sad reality.

If it is natural for us to sin, he is the father of that nature in us. His seed is in us; the seed of his nature, his natural life, which is to sin, to do nothing but commit sin.

And let us remember John's definition of sin (ver. 4), and Paul's (Rom. viii. 7). The essence of sin is refusing to be subject to law. That is the sin which "the devil sinneth from the beginning;" he sinneth by insubordination. That is his nature, his natural life. And he put the seed of it in us when he said to Eve, "Yea, hath God said, Ye shall not eat of every tree in the garden?"

This phrase, therefore,—"being of the devil,"—as used here and elsewhere in Scripture, does not imply what in human opinion would be accounted great criminality or gross immorality. To call any one a devil, or a child of the devil, is to impute to him, according to ordinary notions, an extreme depravity. We paint the great Apostate Spirit in the blackest colours of foul pollution, rancorous hate, and wanton cruelty; and it is only monsters of vice among ourselves that we characterise as satanic. Thus we extricate ourselves from the shame of so discreditable a lineage as is involved in being of the devil. But neither John nor his Master will let us off so easily. The sin which lost Satan heaven was neither lust nor murder. It was not carnal at all, but merely spiritual. It was not even lying, at least not at first,—though "he is a liar, and the father of it." It was pure and simple insubordination and rebellion; the setting of his will against God's; the proud refusal, at the Father's bidding, to worship the Son. So "the devil sinneth from the beginning." And when you so sin, you are of your father the devil. Peter was sinning in that way when Jesus called him Satan. There was nothing of what we might be inclined to stigmatise as satanic in his very natural wish to arrest his Master's fatal journey. It was an impulse of generous affection which

burst out in the expostulation, "Be it far from thee." But
he was "of the devil" then, notwithstanding. Therefore
Jesus said to him, "Get thee behind me, Satan; thou art
an offence unto me" (Matt. xvi. 23). Not saying it thyself, thou wouldst hinder me from saying to my Father,
"Thy will be done." And that is devil's work.

In order then to enter into the full meaning of John's
solemn testimony, it is not needful to wait till some horrid
access of diabolic fury or frenzy seizes us. It is enough
if "the tongue speaketh proud things," or the heart conceives them. "Our lips are our own; who is lord over
us?" Or, why are they not our own? May they not at
least occasionally be our own,—this once; for singing one
vain song, or uttering one idle word, or joining in an hour's
not very profitable, but yet not very objectionable, talk?
Is there any rising up in us of such a feeling as this, as if
it were hard that we may not occasionally take our own
way and be our own masters? It is the devil's seed abiding in us; the seed of the devil's sin, and of his sinful
nature.

Thus this testimony is of wide range and searching
power, when the Spirit brings it home. The law says—
Thou shalt love God with all thy heart; thou shalt not
covet. Let that commandment come to me, in its real
spiritual force; and how thoroughly, how helplessly, how
miserably, does it make me out to be a very child of the
devil! Many laws I cannot charge myself with breaking;
I do not feel them to be irksome; the laws of my country
and of society, for example; the laws of just dealing between man and man; the laws of kindness, courtesy, good
breeding, good taste and feeling; the law of chivalry; the
law of honour. Of all such laws I can cheerfully acknowledge the authority. But this law,—the law binding me
by peremptory statute to love God supremely, and not to

covet, not to love at all except as he loves,—I feel that I cannot own. There is that in me which makes me rebel against what it enjoins being made matter of law at all. I would have it left to my own discretion. I object to love upon compulsion, or to worship, or to obey. Yes, there it is ! That is it ! I have in me the seed, the root, the germ, of the satanic spirit and the satanic nature. I cannot bring myself to be thoroughly under authority and law, when the authority and law are God's. And why ? Why but " because the carnal mind is enmity against God : for it is not subject to the law of God, neither indeed can be ? "

III. " But for this purpose the Son of God was manifested, that he might destroy the works of the devil."

The expression,—" to destroy the works of the devil," —if it is to meet the previous statement, must be understood as meaning, in substance, that the Son of God was manifested to undo what the devil has done and is doing; to counteract and counterwork him, in respect of all his doings generally ; but especially in respect of his imparting to us, as his children, the germ or seed of his own sin of insubordination to the authority and law of God. The phrase, indeed, might be taken in a wide sense ; and might lead us to consider the many various ways in which the gospel tends to redress, and has actually to a large extent redressed, the manifold wrongs and mischiefs that the devil, by introducing moral evil and turning it to account, has wrought in the earth. But evidently the reference here is rather to the one inherent quality, than to the various effects, of the devil's working. The Son of God was manifested to destroy the works of the devil—to destroy in you that sort of doing, or working, which you have derived from the devil; that sinning, or committing sin, which is his nature, and of which he has implanted in you the seed.

It is a work of destruction which he is manifested to do, or which his being manifested does; for we need not be very particular as to which of these ways of putting the matter is to be preferred : they are virtually the same. Execution is to be done upon what is the essence of all the devil's works, so far as our sharing in them as his children is concerned; the spirit of suspicion, impatience, and rankling discontent, under God's loving rule, which the devil insinuates into our hearts, and fosters, inflames, and irritates there.

In thus destroying the works of the devil, in this sense and to this effect, his being manifested as the Son of God was, in itself alone, a great step. For he was manifested, in the very form, in the very position, which the devil had himself felt, and had persuaded us to feel, to be grievous, irksome, and intolerable. He, being the Son, " took upon him the form of a servant." He was so manifested as to make it plain, beyond all question, that there is no such root of bitterness as the devil would insinuate that there is, in a creature's subjection as a servant to the law of God his Creator, in a Son's subjection as a servant to the law of God his Father. The Son of God is manifested as submitting to that place of subordination to authority which the devil and his angels spurned; giving himself to a service infinitely more humiliating than they were called to when they were commanded to worship him. It was a great blow to the works of the devil; it cut up by the roots the very pith and staple of his power to work at all ; when the Son of God was thus manifested ; when it was made patent to all the universe that it was no degradation or bondage for the Son himself to be the servant of the Father; when it was seen that his being so was not incompatible with sonship, but was in fact its very perfection.*

---

* See the *Fatherhood of God ;* Appendix I. Exposition of Rev. xxii. 3.

This, however, is not all; it is only a small part of what he does in destroying, to me and to all his people, the works of the devil. The Son of God might have been manifested as sustaining the very character of a servant, under authority and law, which the devil found, and which the devil makes me find, so provocative of an inward sense of impatience and spirit of rebellion; and he might have been manifested as sustaining that character in such a way as to win me over to the conviction that it is, if I can but reach it, my highest freedom and joy. But what of that, if I cannot reach it? And I cannot reach it, unless the Son of God, thus manifested, does two things on my behalf.

In the first place, he must make my relation to the Father such as his own is. In order to that, and as an indispensable preliminary to that, he must abolish and destroy the relation in which the devil has got me, along with himself, to stand to God; the relation of a guilty criminal to a righteous and avenging judge. Fain would the devil keep me in that relation to my God; scowling impotent defiance, or writhing under the lashings of despair. Or he would set me to the task of painfully working out for myself deliverance; and all in vain. The Son of God is manifested to make short work of all that. I see him taking my relation to God as his, that I may take his relation to God as mine. And I have literally nothing to do but say Yes! Yes; I allow him to take my relation to God as his, the relation of a condemned criminal, a sentenced transgressor of the law!—to take it, so as to exhaust all the curse of it, and destroy it, as the devil's work, for so it is, utterly and for ever! Wondrous condescension, is it not, on my part! And I accept his relation to God, the relation of a beloved son and faithful servant, as mine! More wondrous condescension still! Ah! let me be ashamed to hesitate here. Let me be willing to be to the Father all that his own Son is, in both views of this wonderful substitution and most blessed union.

But, secondly, that I may be willing, he must put within me his own heart towards God, as well as place me in his own relation to God. For this purpose also the Son of God is manifested; not only that through his entering into my guilty relation to God the righteous judge, and making an end of it for me, I may enter into his relation to God the righteous Father, and make full proof of it, in him ; but also that, through the Spirit dwelling in me, as in him, I may have the same heart that he has to cry, "Abba, Father."

Let me never forget that it is for this double purpose that the Son of God is manifested. Root and branch, the works of the devil must be destroyed. The seed, the germ, the principle of all his works must be eradicated. Suspicion, dislike, servile dread, criminal sullenness, self-justifying pride, must all be scotched and killed. These are the devil's works. They must be all destroyed. Let me look to the Son of God as he has been and is manifested ; and are they not, through my so looking, destroyed ? I cannot think and feel, with reference to God and his authority and law, as the devil does, when I look to the Son of God manifested for this very purpose, that I may think and feel as he does ; that God may be to me what he is to him, and his law to me what it is to him ; that thus in me he may " destroy the works of the devil."

24

CONNECTION OF DOING RIGHTEOUSNESS WITH
BROTHERLY LOVE AS PROVING A DIVINE BIRTH,
IN CONTRAST WITH THE UNRIGHTEOUS AND
UNLOVING SPIRIT INDICATING A DEVILISH
PARENTAGE

" In this the children of God are manifest, and the children of the devil :
whosoever doeth not righteousness is not of God, neither he that
loveth not his brother. For this is the message that ye heard from
the beginning, that we should love one another. Not as Cain, who
was of that wicked one, and slew his brother. And wherefore slew
he him? Because his own works were evil, and his brother's righteous." 1 John 3:10-12

THE antagonism between the righteous Father and the
great adversary, and between their respective seeds or off-
springs, is here announced in such a way as to run it up to
a very precise point. The question to which of the two
you belong; which of the two parentages or fatherhoods,
God's or the devil's, is really yours; is brought to a narrow
issue. It is put negatively; and it is all the more searching
on that account. The want of righteous doing, the absence
of brotherly love, is conclusive against your being of God;
" Whosoever doeth not righteousness is not of God, neither
he that loveth not his brother." These two things are here
virtually identified; or the one is represented as implying
the other. The general is now made particular; what was
general and abstract, "doing righteousness" (ii. 29), is now
reduced to a particular practical test, "loving one's brother."

What sort of love is here meant will appear more clearly as we proceed. It is, at any rate, love whose obligation is not of yesterday; the commandment rendering it obligatory is of old standing, of ancient date : " For this is the message that ye heard from the beginning, that we should love one another." And the question arises—What message or commandment is here referred to ?

The idea is apt to suggest itself, not unnaturally, that it is our Lord's commandment in the beginning of the gospel : " A new commandment I give unto you, that ye love one another; as I have loved you, that ye also love one another;" "This is my commandment, that ye love one another, as I have loved you;" " These things I command you, that ye love one another" (John xiii. 34, and xvi. 12–17).

But may not "the beginning" be held to date, not from Christ's teaching, but from the real beginning of the gospel, immediately after the fall? Does not the mention of Cain indicate as much? Is not the law or message of love in question that which was violated in the beginning, when Cain, being of that wicked one, slew his brother ?

God's commandment, heard from the beginning, is that we should love another. Therefore " he that loveth not his brother doeth not righteousness,"—the righteousness required to make good or verify the fact of his being " born of God." He " committeth or doeth sin ;" the sin which is " the transgression of the law." He is " of the devil ;"— like Cain, who " was of that wicked one, and slew his brother."

We are thus carried back to the earliest manifestation of the distinction between the children of God and the children of the devil in the old familiar history of Cain and Abel.

Of Abel little is recorded in the history. But it is plainly implied, in what is said of him here, that he loved his brother. We read that " Cain talked with Abel his brother." And we read this in immediate connection with what the Lord said to Cain on the subject of his rejected offering :— " But unto Cain, and to his offering, he had not respect. And Cain was very wroth, and his countenance fell. And the Lord said unto Cain, Why art thou wroth ? and why is thy countenance fallen ? If thou doest well, shalt thou not be accepted ? and if thou doest not well, sin "—a sin-offering—" lieth at the door "—at thy disposal, and available for thee. After that " Cain talked with Abel his brother." It is in that connection that we read of his doing so.

It is not needful to suppose that his talk was, at least in the first instance, a deliberate plot to draw his intended victim into his power. It is quite probable, or rather more than probable, that the conversation began in good faith. The walk of the brothers in the field may have been as much without any purpose on the one side, as without any suspicion on the other, of anything like treachery or violence. It is quite natural that Cain should have talked with Abel his brother. And the talk might turn on the recent incident of the two acts of worship ; on the disappointment which Cain had experienced, and the explanation of it which the Lord had been pleased to give him. That " Cain was still wroth, and his countenance still fallen," we may well believe. He has not been able to bring himself to submit to God and his righteousness. He is in no mood for being amiable to one who seems to him to be a favoured rival. But he does not meditate actual wrong. He would startle at the thought of fratricide, when the talk with Abel his brother begins.

As it goes on, we may imagine Abel, warmly and affec-

tionately enforcing the gospel message which Cain has just
got from heaven ; opening up its gracious meaning ; trying
to persuade his misjudging brother that there is really no
respect of persons with God, no partiality for one above the
other ; but that for both alike there is acceptance, as well-
doers, if they can claim to stand on that footing, and for
both alike, if not well-doers, a sin-offering at the door and
at command ;—as near to thee, brother, as to me, as available for thee as for me, as much at thy service as at
mine ;—thine, as freely as it is mine, if thou wilt but have
it to be thine.

Had I, brother, sought acceptance as a well-doer, needing no atoning blood of the slain lamb, coming merely with
a tribute of grateful homage, the Lord would have had as
little respect to me and my offering as he had to thee and
thine. Nay, less. I must have been more decidedly and
justly rejected ; for of sinners I am chief. But, in my sin,
I looked and saw the sin-offering at my door. And,
brother, it lieth at thy door too, if thou wilt but consent,
as a sinner, to make use of it. Has not our God been
telling thee so ? Is not this his gospel to thee as well
as to me ?

Is it too much to conceive of righteous Abel thus manifesting his being of God ; thus doing righteousness and
loving his brother ? Is it at all conceivable that he should
deal otherwise with his brother, or not deal thus with him,
while Cain gave him the opportunity, by talking with him
in the field ? Could anything else be the burden of the
talk than his beseeching his brother to be reconciled to God
by the sacrifice of the slain lamb ?

And is it not just by his manner of requiting such
brotherly dealing with him on the part of Abel that Cain
manifests his being of that wicked one ? Is not that the
explanation of his slaying him ? For " wherefore slew he

him ? Because his own works were evil, and his brother's righteous."

That was the real reason; though of course he did not avow it to himself. Probably he was not conscious of it. He had some plausible plea of self-justification or of self-excuse. His younger brother took too much upon him; affecting to be on a better footing with God than he was, and to be entitled to dictate and prescribe to him. It was bad enough that God should have rejected his plea of well-doing, or of righteousness; and bid him come, not with "God I thank thee " on his proud lips, but with "God be merciful to me a sinner " in his broken heart. That one who is his junior in age, and in strength so completely at his mercy, should press the same humiliating lesson, is more than he can stand. He cannot reach God; else his anger would find vent against him. But the meek and unresisting child of God is in his hands. And therefore he slays him; " because his own works were evil, and his brother's righteous."

Well did our Lord say of the Jews who sought to kill him : " Ye are of your, father the devil ; and the lusts of your father ye will do. He was a murderer from the beginning." And he was so, " because he abode not in the truth, for there is no truth in him." To lie and hate the truth, is his nature; "when he speaketh a lie, he speaketh of his own;" it is his native speech, his vernacular; for " he is a liar, and the father of it" (John viii. 44). And you are of him ; for it is " because I tell you the truth that ye believe me not " (ver. 45); and it is that which provokes you to " seek to kill me " (ver. 40).

Here then are two instances of the children of God being manifested, and the children of the devil : Abel, and his brother Cain who slew him ; Jesus, and the Jews who sought to kill him. It is the first that John cites ; but the second throws light upon it. For Abel is to Cain instead of Jesus; and Cain is to Abel what he would have been to Jesus. The antagonism is clearly and sharply defined. On the one side there is love, brotherly love; love to one who slays his lover, and love to him as still a brother; which is indeed " doing righteousness as God is righteous," and therefore betokens a divine birth. On the other side there is hatred, deadly hatred; hatred of the righteous for his righteousness; which is " a work of the devil," and savours accordingly of a devilish parentage.

For what brings out the antagonism in both cases is truth or righteousness; truth, as the Lord puts it (John viii.); righteousness, as John puts it here; the truth of God; the righteousness of God. Whosoever doeth righteousness is of God; born of God. And such an one will, like Abel, love his brother; not sinning, or transgressing the law which commands love to men as brethren. " Whosoever doeth not righteousness is not of God." And such an one " loveth not his brother," but " doeth the work of the devil;" being like Cain, who " was of that wicked one, and slew his brother, because his own works were evil and his brother's righteous."

Mark how these opposite dispositions towards truth and righteousness, the truth and righteousness of God, operate in producing the opposite dispositions of love and hatred.

i. Consider that old message or commandment, heard from the beginning, that we should love one another. On what is it based? It cannot, since the fall, be based on our joint participation in the ills to which the fall has made us heirs. Companions in guilt, shut up as criminals in the condemned cell, together awaiting execution, can scarcely be expected, need scarcely be exhorted, to love one another. There is not much mutual love lost in a band of outlaws or a community of rebels. "Hateful and hating one another" is apt to be the characteristic of the tribe. They may call one another brothers, sworn brothers; in the riot of a common feast, in the presence of a common foe. But there is little real confidence or cordiality in their fellowship. It is not, it cannot be, to guilty and sinful men, in their natural condition of guilt and sinfulness, estranged from God and at enmity with God, that "the message" or commandment "heard from the beginning," to love one another, is now addressed. At least it is not to such that it can be addressed with any hope of its being complied with and obeyed. It is a message or commandment that plainly, from its very nature, proceeds upon the fact of their being a method of extrication, actual or possible, out of that wretched state. It is redemption, and redemption alone, with the regeneration which is involved in it, that makes mutual brotherly love among men, in its true and deep sense, a practicable duty, an attainable grace. It is only one who, "being born of God, doeth righteousness as knowing God to be righteous," that is capable of really loving his fellow-man as a brother. Only righteous Abel can so love even murderous Cain.

If you are the children of the righteous Father, you can so love even those who "despitefully use you and persecute you." For as his children you are one in sympathy with the righteous Father; you are of one mind with him; you are on his side in the great cause of righteousness, and of a righteous salvation, which lies so near his heart. Submitting yourselves to his righteous and sovereign grace; receiving pardon and peace, a new nature and a new life, on the footing of your oneness with his righteous servant and beloved Son; you are now, as his children, being born of him, altogether for his righteousness and against the world's sin.

What brotherhood then can there be between you and the men who sin; and who harden themselves, or justify themselves, in their sin? Is there not a great gulf between you and them? Are they not cut off from you? Are you not precluded from holding them to be your brethren?

Nay; it is only now, now for the first time, that you are in a position, that you have the heart, to feel anything like a brother's love towards them. And it is the very sharpness of the line that severs you from them that makes your brotherly love towards them burn bright and keen and warm. You love them as brethren now, in a sense and manner in which you never could love them before; however closely you and they might be knit together, as issuing from the same womb, or dwelling in the same house, or associated in the same calling, or walking in the same way.

Yes; though you have " known that man after the flesh;" known him intimately, known him affectionately, known him so as to love him as a very brother when you sat together at the godless festive board, or drained together the cup of sinful pleasure; yet now henceforth you " know him no more." It is after another fashion than that of the flesh that you know him now; and after another fashion that you love him; with an intensity of brotherly longing for his good, unfelt, unimagined before. What sacrifice would you have made for him then? You would "lay down your life" to save his soul now. He was your playmate, your plaything then; you used him; you sported with him; you enjoyed him. And you had a kindly enough feeling towards him. He was profitable to you; or you found him always very pleasant to you. But he is far more to you now. He is precious, oh! how precious, in your eyes; precious, not as the congenial companion of a passing hour, but as one whom you would fain grasp as a brother for eternity.

2. No such brotherly love is possible for him who, not doing righteousness, is not of God. His frame of mind must be that of Cain; a frame of mind that but too unequivocally identifies him as one of the devil's children, and not God's. For there is no room for any intermediate position here. Either you are of God; or you are like Cain, who "was of that wicked one, and slew his brother." It was the contrast between his brother and himself that moved Cain to this act; and before he was moved to it, that contrast must have become very irksome and intolerable. It was not because he was void of natural affection, or because his disposition was one of wanton cruelty and bloodthirstiness; it was not in the heat of sudden passion, or in a quarrel about any earthly good, that Cain slew his brother; but "because his own works were evil, and his brother's righteous."

It is this which chiefly marks the instigation of the devil; and his fatherhood of Cain, and such as Cain.

No doubt he has a hand in every sin or crime that his children commit. He fans the flame of lust, and fires the hot blood of furious passion. He sharpens the wits of wily craft, and helps the plotter in many a stratagem. He infuses fresh bitterness into the malign temper of envious hate, whoever or whatever its object may be. But he has a special grudge and spite against "the seed of the woman who is to bruise his serpent-head." More than anything else on earth;—infinitely more than any remains or remnants of good that the fall has left in human nature and human society;—for these he can turn to his own account and make his own use of;—does that wicked one detest the faintest trace of the footsteps, the slightest breathing of the spirit, of him "whose goings forth have been from of old;" who has been ever in the world, the wisdom and the word of God, the light and the life of men. Wherever his power appears, setting up God's righteousness and its claim to vindication against man's sin and its boast of impunity, there Satan's malice is stirred. And he makes his children fierce even to slaying; as he made Cain.

He does so commonly by fretting and irritating the conscience, while at the same time he fortifies the stronghold of stout-heartedness and pride. For these two in combination, an uneasy conscience and an unbroken heart, are in his hands capable of being wrought mightily to his purpose. Let the truth and righteousness of God be brought so near to a man, by the divine word and Spirit, as to stir and trouble thoroughly his inward moral sense, while his desire and determination to stand his ground and not give in remains unabated, or rather is inflamed and aggravated; let the process go on; and let all attempts towards an accommodation, between the conscience's increasing soreness and the heart's increasing self-righteousness and self-will, be one after another frustrated and foiled; —you have then the making of a Cain, a very child of the devil, who, if need be and opportunity serve, will not scruple to cut short the terrible debate and end the intolerable strife by slaying his brother Abel; by " crucifying the Lord of glory ! " O my fellow-sinner, let us beware ! Let us not be " as Cain, who was of that wicked one, and slew his brother."

I may think that there is no risk of my being as Cain; it will be long before I slay my brother Abel ! But let me give good heed to what John records as the natural history, as it were, of Cain's sin. He "slew his brother; and wherefore slew he him ? because his own works were evil, and his brother's righteous."

Let me ask myself a plain. but pointed question. Is there no child of God, no godly man or woman of my acquaintance, the thought of whom, or the sight of whom,

or his or her talk in the field, troubles me and makes me
feel uncomfortable ? Many professing Christians I know
and like. Many who pass for serious and evangelical I can
meet and converse with, easily and satisfactorily enough.
There were four hundred prophets of the Lord that Ahab
had no sort of objection to have near him and to listen to.
But there was one Micaiah that he did not care to send for.
" I hate him," said the king, " for he doth not prophesy
good concerning me, but evil." Is there any Micaiah who
is thus a sort of eyesore to me ? any Abel who provokes in
me a kind of Cainish spirit ?

It is not, strictly speaking, envy, or mere jealousy of
another's superior excellence. It is the tacit rebuke ad-
ministered to my shortcoming and sin ; the awakening of a
lurking consciousness of something wrong in my state of
heart or way of life, the unsettling of my security, the
begetting in me of—I scarcely know what to call it—dis-
satisfaction, apprehension, an uneasy and unpleasant feeling
of my not being altogether, in some particulars, what I
ought to be, or might be ;—it is that which disturbs me, in
the presence of some child of God, or in the thought of such
an one, as an unquestionable type of godliness.

Ah ! it is a dangerous symptom ; you brother, as well
as I, may give good heed to it. It is the very germ of
Cain's murderous mood. It may not lead you to slay your
Abel ; him or her who is thus obnoxious to you ; whose
eminent nearness to God causes you to be too sensible of
your distance. You have other ways of getting rid of the
troubler of your peace without raising the cry, Crucify him ;
away with him. You can evade his company, keep out of
hearing of his voice, and elude the glance of his eye. You
can shut him out of your mind, and bid him be to you as
if he was not. Or you may try another plan. You may
open your ears to whispers against him ; you may sharpen

your sight to discover faults and follies in him ; you may
" sit and speak against your brother, slandering your own
mother's son," if by any means you can make him out to be
not so very immaculate or so very heavenly, after all, but
that you may stand your ground and pass muster beside
him in the end. What is all that but slaying your brother ;
slaying him virtually if not literally ; slaying him very
cruelly ? And wherefore ? " Because your own works are
evil and your brother's righteous." Be not deceived. Be
very sure that " in this the children of God are manifest,
and the children of the devil : whosoever doeth not
righteousness is not of God, neither he that loveth not
his brother."

I draw an important practical inference from the views
now submitted. They may teach us something of the
nature, and what may be called the *genesis*, or natural
history, of brotherly love.

We are accustomed, when we speak of the particular
affection of brotherly love, as distinguished from the general
affection of love or charity, to rest the distinction chiefly
on the opposite characters of those who are the objects of
the two affections respectively. Charity or love—I speak
of it in its earthward, not its heavenward direction—has
for its objects men, all men, indiscriminately ; men, as such.
Brotherly love has for its objects the children of God ; the
members of the family or brotherhood of Christ's people ;
who have one Father, one Lord and elder Brother, one
Spirit, one hope, one home. We love all men with a love
of benevolence ; we love the brethren with a love of congeniality and delight. So far as it goes, this is of course a
true account.

But does not John's statement here suggest a somewhat different, or at least an additional, explanation ?

May not the root of the distinction lie in the subject of the affection rather than in its objects; in the person loving, rather than in the persons loved? Is not the character of the affection determined by the character of him in whom it dwells, even more than by the character of him to whom it goes forth?

At all events, when my character is changed, the character of all my love,—let who may be its objects, and let it have ever so many objects, differing ever so widely,—is changed in a corresponding manner. There is not one of those I loved before whom I love now as I used to do. My love to every one of them is a quite new love. The wife of my bosom, the child of my house, the servant and stranger within my gates, the beggar at my door, the queen reigning over me, the companion of my leisure, the partner of my business, the holy man of God, the wretched prodigal, the child of misery and vice—there is not one of them whom I love now as I did before. It is a new affection that I feel to every one of them.

And what is it that is new about it? Is it not that it is all now brotherly love? Is it not that one and all of the varieties of natural affection,—not stifled, not lost or merged, but subsisting still, as distinct as ever and stronger than ever,—have infused into them this one common element of brotherhood in the Lord? In me, in my heart, there is brotherly love to every one; equal brotherly love to all.

It does not call forth the same response from all; it has not the same free course with respect to all. In some, alas! it is deeply wounded, meeting with what sorely tries and grieves it, as when the sad cry breaks forth, "Who hath believed our report?"—"All day long have I stretched forth my hands to a perverse and gainsaying generation." In others, again, it finds a blessed, present recompense;

and the fellowship of saints on earth becomes the foretaste of heaven's joy. But is it not the same affection, real, true, deep brotherly love, that is so sorely vexed in the one instance, and so richly gratified in the other? Was it not the same affection in the heart of Jesus that caused him to "rejoice in spirit," as he lifted up his eyes to heaven and said, "I thank thee, O Father, Lord of heaven and earth, because thou hast hid these things from the wise and prudent, and hast revealed them unto babes; even so, Father, for so it seemed good in thy sight"?—was it not, I ask, the very same affection that caused him to exclaim, as he drew near to the city, and wept over it, "O Jerusalem, Jerusalem, how often would I have gathered thy children together, as a hen gathereth her chickens under her wings; and ye would not"?

25

BROTHERLY LOVE THE FRUIT AND TEST OF PASS-
ING FROM DEATH UNTO LIFE—THE WORLD'S
HATRED—THE LOVE OF GOD

"Marvel not, my brethren, if the world hate you. We know that we
have passed from death unto life, because we love the brethren. He
that loveth not his brother abideth in death. Whosoever hateth his
brother is a murderer : and ye know that no murderer hath eternal
life abiding in him. Hereby perceive we the love of God, because he
laid down his life for us : and we ought to lay down our lives for the
brethren." 1 John 3:13-16

THERE is an emphatic meaning in the address (ver. 13),
"my brethren." It prepares the way for the use of the
first person "we" (ver. 14). You are of the company of
the brethren, as I am. I address you as such, when I exhort you "not to marvel if the world hate you."

For why should you not marvel at this? Why should
you not count it strange or take it amiss?

For this, among other reasons : because we know,—you
and I, as brethren, know,—that to love as brethren is a
grace belonging entirely to the new life of which we are
partakers. It is the very mark of our possessing that life.
Why then should we marvel if the dead are incapable of
it? It is the world's nature to hate the godly; it was our
nature once; and if it is not so now, it is because we have
undergone a great change; "we know that we have passed
from death unto life because we love the brethren." It
must be so. The absence of this brotherly love is, and

must be, a fatal sign of death, and of continued death ; " he
that loveth not his brother abideth in death." For not to
love a brother is to hate him ; and to hate him is to murder
him ; and to murder him is to forfeit life : " Whosoever
hateth his brother is a murderer : and ye know that no
murderer hath eternal life abiding in him." Whereas, on
the other hand, the presence of this brotherly love is a
blessed sign of life ; for it marks our oneness with the
Living One ; our insight into the manner of his love and
our sympathy with it : " Hereby perceive we the love of
God, because he laid down his life for us : and we ought to
lay down our lives for the brethren."

Here then we have, in broad contrast, the way of the
world, which is death, and the way of God, which is life.
It is the way of the world to hate, and so to hate as to
murder. It is the way of God to love, and so to love as to
lay down life to save. And it is in virtue of this contrast
that the test holds good : " We know that we have passed
from death unto life, because we love the brethren."

The world's hatred ; God's love ; these are what are
here contrasted. And yet there is one point at least of
partial similarity. The affection, in either case, fastens in
the first instance upon objects opposed to itself. The world
hates the brethren ; God loves the world, " the world lying
in the wicked one." And in a sense too the ends sought
are similar. The world, which hates, would assimilate those
it hates to itself, and so be soothed or sated ; God, who
loves, would assimilate those he loves to himself, and so
have satisfaction in them. This indeed may almost be said
to be a universal characteristic of sentient and intelligent
mind ; be it pure and benevolent or depraved and male-
volent ; be its ruling passion hatred or love. It is, so far,
common to the wicked one and the Holy One. The wicked
one, in whom the world lies, hates ; and his hatred fastens

on the brethren. In his hatred he will not scruple about murdering them outright in cruellest fashion. But he is as well, or even better pleased, if he succeeds in murdering them after a milder method; by getting them to listen to his wily speech. The Holy One loves; and his love fastens on the lost. It is a love in spite of which he must, at the last, acquiesce in the inevitable ruin of multitudes, whom alas! its manifestation fails to touch. But his heart is set on winning them to his embrace, and having them to be of one mind and nature with himself. And his love has this advantage over the opposite affection. Who ever heard of the wicked one laying down his life to secure the accomplishment of his object?—or any Cain who is of the wicked one? "But hereby perceive we the love of God, because he laid down his life for us: and we ought to lay down our lives for the brethren."

I. Of the world's hatred of the brethren two things are said: it is natural, and it is murderous.

In the first place, it is natural; not marvellous, but quite natural. The Lord prepared his disciples beforehand to expect it, warning them not to look for any other treatment at the world's hands than he had met with. It should not, therefore, be matter of surprise to you if the world hate you. And yet it is sometimes apt to be so. Notwithstanding all warnings, and all the experience of others who have gone before him, the recent convert, the young Christian, fresh, buoyant, enthusiastic, may fancy that what he has to tell must pierce all consciences and melt all hearts. He goes among his fellows, eager to appear in his new character, to bear his new testimony, to sing his new song. Alas! he comes in contact with what is like a wet blanket thrown in his face, cold looks and rude gestures of impatience, jeers and jibes, if not harsher usage still. Instead of the welcome he anticipated, as he hastened forth, with face

all radiant from the heavenly fellowship, and lips divinely
touched with a live coal from off the altar, crying,—I have
found him, come and see; he meets with chilling indifference, or contempt, or anger. He is tempted to give up as
hopeless the task of dealing with the dead. But no. Count
it not strange, brother, that you fall into this trial. Why
should you? Is their reception of you very different from
what, but yesterday perhaps, yours would have been of one
coming to you in the same character and on the same
errand? Surely you know that love to the brethren,
brotherly love, true Christian, Christ-like love—willing to
give a cup of cold water to a disciple in the name of a
disciple, and welcome the least of the little ones for the
Master's sake—is no plant of natural growth in the soil of
corrupt humanity; that, on the contrary, it is the fruit of
the great change by means of which a poor sinner " passes
from death unto life." Have you not found it to be so in
your own case? Would anything short of that have made
you love the brethren, and hear them gladly, when speaking
in a brotherly way to you? Would anything else have
overcome your hatred of them? Then " marvel not," nor
be impatient, " if the world hate you."

Again, secondly, the world's hatred of the brethren is
murderous, as regards its objects: "He that loveth not
his brother abideth in death: whosoever hateth his brother
is a murderer."

"Loveth not," "hateth," "murdereth!" There is a
sort of dark climax here! Not loving is intensified into
hating, and hating into murdering. The three, however,
are really one; as the Lord teaches in the sermon on the
mount, to which undoubtedly John here points (Matt. v.
21–24). Not to love is to hate; and to hate is to murder.
If, therefore, you would be safe from the risk of being a
murderer, see that you are not a hater. And if you would

not be in danger of being a hater, see that you are a
lover.

It is a solemn lesson that is thus taught; and it would
seem to be meant for you who are apt to marvel if the
world hate you, as well as for the world that hates you.
In that application, it may suggest some important practical thoughts.

1. When Abel first caught a glimpse of Cain's state of
mind towards him, he might feel as one who painfully
dreamed. He must have been slow to take it in. They
had grown up together in the same home; worked and
played together; prayed together at the same mother's
knee; listened together to the same father's teaching; done
one another many offices of kindness; enjoyed much
pleasant intercourse in house and field. While that strange
conversation about God and his worship goes on, Abel is
startled as he sees Cain's dark frown betokening growing
wrath. Hate gleams more and more from those kindling
eyes. Is it fear that pales the meek martyr's face, or is it
anger that agitates his frame, as that hoarse voice threatens
and that cruel arm is raised? Not so. It is horrible
surprise at first; and then deep concern, tender pity, bitter
grief. That Cain has ceased to love him as a brother;—
that is what chiefly wounds him; wounds him more
keenly than the stroke that fells him to the ground. Has
he lost, can he not win back, a brother's love? Is there
such hatred, so murderous, in one who is still so dear to
him? Will he rather slay me than taste and see how good
our God is who has provided for us both the same sin-
offering of the lamb? It is a bitter sorrow. But it is not
the bitterness of a sense of his own wrong; it is the bitterness of the melancholy insight he has got into his poor
brother's dark and miserable heart.

Ah! think;—when you come in contact with some one

to whom you would fain commend the Saviour and the
sacrifice you have yourself found so precious,—an old
familiar friend perhaps with whom your intercourse has
been wont to be frequent and sweet,—a humble neighbour
who has often been glad to see you under his lowly roof, to
accept your alms in his poverty or your kindly sympathy
in his distress; and when you begin to discover that, as a
child of God, you are not so welcome now as you were
when like himself you were a child of the world; when he
treats you coldly or rudely, and makes it plain that he
would fain in any way get rid of you;—think rather of his
case than of your own. It may be hard for you to bear
with his irritability and incivility; and you may be provoked, if not to retaliate, yet to let him alone and make
your escape. But consider him; and have pity upon him.
This malignant spirit of dislike to righteousness, and to
him whose works are righteous, is far worse for him to
cherish than for you to suffer. Leave him not. Rather
stay by him and plead with him; even though his hatred
rise to murder.

2. For you need, for yourselves, and with special
reference to the world's hatred of you, to be ever on your
guard, lest somewhat of the old dark spirit should creep in
again into your own hearts. And remember it may insinuate itself very insidiously and stealthily.

Consider once more the stages or steps: not loving;
hating; murdering. Ah! how easily may the first of these
begin: not loving. It is a simple negation; no taking of
any positive step; but only, as it were, not taking any
step at all; or not this or that particular step; giving up;
letting alone; using less energy of prayer and pains; feeling less interest.

Who is it that you have ceased, or are ceasing, to love
with a true brotherly love like Christ's?

Is it one still unconverted and unsaved ? You have
been dealing with him, as you think, faithfully and affectionately; pleading with him for Christ, and with Christ
for him. You have had much patience, and have persevered
long. Nor has it been mere taskwork with you; it has
been a work of love. You have felt a real concern for his
soul, a real longing for his salvation. But somehow the
case is not very hopeful; it was not very hopeful at first,
and it is becoming less so, or at least not more so. You
are getting reconciled to the idea of failure and disappointment. You are not at first conscious of a diminished regard
for your poor brother; but you are becoming less sanguine,
and gradually less earnest. The work of love becomes
more like taskwork now. You will do your duty; you
will continue to be kind to him, to warn and exhort him,
to set Christ before him, and urge him to believe and live.
But there is less cordiality in what you do and say; you
bestow less of your heart upon him. This may be natural,
in a sense and measure perhaps unavoidable, and not altogether unreasonable. There may be a limit to your earnest
striving, in love, with an obdurate sinner, as there is a
limit to the striving, in love, of God's own Spirit with him.
But beware. It is not because he ceases to love that the
Spirit ceases to strive. See that it be not otherwise with
you; that it be not your ceasing to love that makes you
cease to strive. If it be Christ's mind that you should
shake off the dust of your feet as a testimony of judgment
against any one whom you have been plying with the
testimony of mercy, he will make that plain enough to you
by unmistakeable indications of his will. And you will see
all the more clearly, and judge all the more fairly, if there
be no ceasing to love; no growing coldness and indifference; no feeling of a sort of apathetic acquiescence in the
inevitableness of that poor soul's fate. No such feeling is

there in the tears of Jesus over Jerusalem. Beware, I repeat, of any such feeling insinuating itself into your bosom. Not to love, with a love that yearns to save, and weeps rivers of waters for the lost, is to hate ; and to hate is to murder. "Deliver me from blood-guiltiness, O God, thou God of my salvation."

Or is it one of Christ's little ones ; one of the fatherless and widows whom you visit in their affliction ; one whose feet you have counted it a privilege to wash ? The service has been a delight ; that suffering saint's chamber has been to you a Bethel. You have got in it far more than you have given of spiritual refreshment and consolation. So you say and feel, under the impulse of your first love for that brother in Christ. But on further acquaintance you find, or think you find, things in him or about him that are fitted to damp and repel your ardent advances. He is not so perfect as you thought ; his person not so pleasant ; his room not so tidy. Infirmities come out ; disagreeable incidents occur ; rude friends interfere. It is not romance now, but reality. You are not quite so enthusiastic as you were in your esteem of him, or quite so frequent and regular in your calls upon him. A sort of weariness comes over you when you knock at his door ; a sort of distasteful recoil arrests you as you enter his chamber. It is plain that your Christian admiration, your brotherly love towards him, is not exactly what it was ; not so glowing and so gushing. It may be as real and genuine ; it may be even more trustworthy, because it is more sober. If so, it is well. But beware. It may be otherwise. There may be an approximation to a state of mind not quite so right or safe ;—"not loving your brother," ceasing to love him as your brother in Christ, allowing natural or accidental causes of estrangement or indifference to cool your brotherly affection. And what then ? May there not come something worse ? A certain half-unconscious dislike ; a certain pleasure, even in hearing him ridiculed or defamed ; a not unwilling participation in the idle talk that, exaggerating defects, and over-looking or misrepresenting excellencies, would take away his fair name and reputation, and play the murderer as regards his Christian character and standing ?

Be on your guard against this spirit of the world finding harbour again in your breasts. I speak to you who have "passed from death unto life," and who know what it is to love the brethren ; to love all men with a true brotherly love in the Lord, a love that looks on them as immortal beings, having near them a Saviour dying for them, having in them a Spirit striving with them, having before them a Father waiting to be gracious. Even you need to be warned against the world's evil temper of dislike and envy. Consider how insidious it is. It begins with what may attract little observation and awaken little alarm ; a change, scarcely noticeable, or if noticed easily explained by altered circumstances, sobering age, sad experience, repeated dis-appointment, or any of the thousand causes that make the heart beat less wildly as time rolls on. Consider also its deadly danger. The "not loving," or not loving so purely and so truly, comes to be "hating, avowed or unavowed, distaste, disinclination, displeasure, dislike ; estrangement, suspicion, envy. And to hate is to "murder ; " one way or other, by neglect or by calumny, by ill thoughts or ill words or ill deeds, it murders. Consider, finally, how natural it is ; so natural that only your "passing from death unto life " can rid you of it, and make you capable of its opposite. You need not marvel if the world thus hate ; for it is its nature. Nor need you marvel that you should still require to be exhorted not thus to hate ; for it is your nature too. Grace may overcome it ; grace alone can do so. And even grace can do so only through continual watchfulness and prayer, continual recognition of the life to which you pass from death, and continual exercise of the love which is the characteristic of that life.

II. Of this love, as of the hatred, two things are said. In the first place, it is natural now to the spiritual mind ; natural as the fruit and sign of the new life ; " We know that we have passed from death unto life because we love the brethren." It is natural to us, in our old state of death, to hate ; it is, or should be, natural to us, in our new state of life, to love. For our life is our participation with Christ in his life ; and his life, like the Father's, is manifested in love ; or is love. Our life, therefore, is also love ; it is our loving as the Father loves, and as the Son loves. And this, secondly, implies that the love in question is the very opposite of the murderous hatred of the devil ; it is self-sacrificing, like the love of God himself : " Hereby perceive we the love of God, because he laid down his life for us : and we ought to lay down our lives for the brethren " (ver. 16).

It is a high ideal of this love to men as brethren that is set before us. It is sympathy with God in his love to us ; and in that love as measured by his laying down his life for us. Whom does he thus love ? Us : and all such as we are ; or as we were, when his love reached us. " Scarcely for a righteous man will one die : yet peradventure for a good man some would even dare to die. But God commendeth his love towards us, in that, while we were yet sinners, Christ died for us." " When we were without strength, in due time Christ died for the ungodly." For us sinners, for us without strength, for us ungodly, he laid down his life. And it was a brotherly love to us that moved him to do so. It was as our brother that he sacrificed himself for us. It is that we may be his brethren that he would have us to perceive his love in sacrificing himself for us, and to believe it.

Oh! to be enabled to enter more and more into this brotherly love of Jesus ; to apprehend its nature ; to imbibe its spirit ! Truly it is the opposite of the hatred of a brother which marks one abiding in death. That hatred prompts to take away another's life ; this love to lay down one's own. " Whosoever hateth his brother is a murderer ;" but here is one so loving his brother, that to save him alive he sacrifices himself. Cain was bent on slaying his brother : Abel, was anxious, at the risk of death, to win Cain. We, in our hatred, because he was righteous and we were evil, slew a greater than Abel. He loved us with more than Abel's love when " he laid down his life for us."

We know that we have passed from death unto life, when we love our fellow-men with a brotherly love like his; when we are so bent on saving and blessing them, that we are willing not only to give our whole lives for their good, but to suffer all loss, even death itself, at their hands. Even when they are still our enemies, because the enemies of our Lord ; even while they hate us, and persecute us, and say all manner of evil against us ; how does it become us still to love them as brethren, with a love that would seek them as brethren, and welcome them as brethren, and live and die for them as brethren ! Can they be more hostile or injurious to us, than we were to Christ when he loved us and laid down his life for us ? Have they wearied us as we have wearied him ? or provoked us as we have provoked him ? or pierced us as we have pierced him ? How shall we not continue to care for them and plead with them, as Christ continued to care for us and plead with us,—oh ! how long, how patiently, how tenderly,—if by any means he might bring us to receive him as laying down his life for us ! And when, by his Spirit, they are moved and melted, and on the foot-

ing of that great propitiation reconciled to God and to us ;
how shall we set bounds to the warmth and cordiality of
our embrace of them as now our brethren indeed ! Can we
grudge any service or sacrifice to show our love, even should
it be the laying down of our lives for them, as he laid down
his life for us ?

This is our security against the evil spirit of Cain coming in again to trouble us. It is to make full proof of the
better spirit of Abel, or of him in whom Abel, like us, believed, even Jesus, who so loved us, even when dead in sins,
that he gave himself for us, the just for the unjust, that he
might bring us to God ; and who so loveth us, as his brethren, for whom he laid down his life, that he would have
us to be sharers as his brethren with him in all the love
with which the Father loveth him and all the glory which
the Father giveth him.

26

RIGHTEOUSNESS OR TRUTH IN BROTHERLY LOVE—
ESSENTIAL TO THE ANSWER OF A GOOD CON-
SCIENCE IN OURSELVES AND BEFORE GOD

"But whoso hath this world's good, and seeth his brother have need, and
shutteth up his bowels of compassion from him, how dwelleth the
love of God in him? My little children, let us not love in word,
neither in tongue ; but in deed and in truth. And hereby we know
that we are of the truth, and shall assure our hearts before him. For
if our heart condemn us, God is greater than our heart, and knoweth
all things. Beloved, if our heart condemn us not, then have we confidence toward God." 1 John 3:17-21

THE lesson here is sincerity. It is with special reference to
the grace or affection of brotherly love, that this lesson is
in the first instance enforced ; and the manner in which the
subject is introduced is noticeable.

The highest possible model or ideal has been presented
for imitation : "Hereby perceive we the love of God, because
he laid down his life for us : and we ought to lay down our
lives for the brethren." Then immediately, by way of contrast, the testing case put is made to turn on one of the
simplest and commonest instances of the exercise of human
pity : "But whoso hath this world's good, and seeth his
brother have need, and shutteth up his bowels of compassion
from him, how dwelleth the love of God in him ? " It looks
almost like irony or sarcasm. Your love to the brethren,
to men as brethren, should reach to your laying down your
lives for them. Yes ! And it would, if that were necessary,

or might do them good.   So you say, and think.   But what
if, having this world's good, and seeing your brother have
need, you shut up your bowels of compassion from him?
How then dwelleth the love of God in you?   Is that loving
as God loves?

Beware of self-deception in this matter.   It is easy to
imagine what you would do to win or help a brother; and
you may please yourselves by carrying the imagination to
any length you choose.   If a great act of self-sacrifice would
avail, you would not shrink from it.   But what if you
grudge some far readier and easier service, a gift to the
needy out of your abundance, or a visit of sympathy to the
widow out of your leisure, or a word in season to the weary
out of the fulness of your own happier experience, or a helping hand to snatch a perishing soul from the pit and set him
on the rock on which the Lord has set you?   You will lay
down your life for one who is, or who may be, a brother!
And yet you cannot lay down for him your love of this
world's good; your love of ease and selfish comfort; your
fastidious taste, that shrinks from contact with squalid
wretchedness and vulgar ways; your proud or shy reserve,
that keeps the humble at a distance; your false shame, that
sends you in upon yourself when you should be sowing
beside all waters.

Thus somewhat sternly John's tender expostulation—
for it is very tender—is introduced: "My little children,
let us not love in word, neither in tongue."   There is enough
in the world of that sort of love.   "Let us love in deed and
in truth."   It is only thus that we can "know ourselves to
be of the truth," or to be true, and so can "assure our hearts
before God."   We can have no such assurance if our consciousness hints that there is guile in our spirit.   "For if
our heart condemn us," how can we face him "who is
greater than our heart and knoweth all things;" all things

about our heart; its secret windings and subtle refuges of lies? It is only "if our heart condemn us not,"—condemn us not, that is, as unrighteous and insincere in the matter on hand,—it is only then that we can "have confidence toward God."

Thus John brings out into prominence a general principle connecting conscience and faith, with immediate reference to his particular topic of brotherly love.

The principle may be briefly stated. There can be no faith where there is not conscience; no more of faith than there is of conscience; no firm faith without a clear conscience. In plain terms, I cannot look my God in the face if I cannot look myself in the face. In a sense, I must be able to justify myself if I would look on God as justifying me; I must be able to acquit myself of guile if I would reckon on his acquitting me of guilt. If my heart condemns me, much more must he condemn me who is greater than my heart, and knoweth all things.

But must not my heart always condemn me? Must I not be always confessing that my heart condemns me, and that therefore the searcher of it must condemn me much more?

No. This is not the language of legitimate confession, although it is often used as such. On the contrary, it is rather a protest against the very sort of confession which it is too commonly employed to express. It rebukes all conventionalism; all formal routine or covert guile; all false dealing with myself and with God. It demands, in worship and fellowship, that I approach him who is greater than my heart and who knoweth all things, as one whose heart does not condemn him.

Reserving the special application of this principle to the grace of brotherly kindness, I ask you for the present to consider it more generally with reference to the divine love; first, as you have to receive it by faith; and, secondly, as you have to retain it and act it out in your loving walk with God and man.

I. I am a receiver of this love. And it concerns me much that my faith, by which I receive it, should be strong and steadfast; which, however, it cannot be unless my conscience, in receiving it, is guileless. David experienced this; and he describes his experience in the thirty-second Psalm. There was a time, he says, when he kept silence; when there was guile in his spirit. Then he had no rest. He was unwilling to be thoroughly searched and tried by God; to have the hurt of his soul otherwise than slightly healed; to have the deadly sore probed to the bottom, that the oil and balm to be poured in might reach the root of the disease. His heart condemned him; and there was one greater than his heart, knowing all things, whose "hand day and night was heavy upon him" (ver. 3, 4). He got enlargement and assurance only when he tried the more excellent way of full and frank confession, apprehending full and free forgiveness (ver. 5-7). Then his heart did not condemn him, and he had confidence towards God; being of the truth, he assured his heart before God.

It must be noticed, however, that the ground of this assurance or confidence is not the consciousness of integrity, thus declared to be indispensable, but that gracious dealing on the part of God for which it makes way. The negative form of John's language is not without its meaning here, —"if our heart condemn us not, then have we confidence toward God." It describes simply the removal of an obstacle; a hindrance or obstruction taken out of the way. A haze or mist of earth is dispelled, that the sun from heaven may give light and warmth. A work of the devil is undone, that the work of God may be wrought. For this inward misgiving, this secret consciousness of insincerity, "our heart condemning us," is of that wicked one. It comes of his lie still heeded, and, as it were, half believed. We must let it go, that the truth may make us free.

The plain question then is, Are you dealing truly with God as he deals truly with you? Are you meeting him, as he meets you, in good faith? Is reserve on your part laid aside, as it is thoroughly laid aside on his part? He makes advances to you in his gospel, advances most generous and free; he gives you assurances most firm and faithful. These are the ground and warrant of your confidence before him; these alone, and not anything in yourselves, in your own consciousness of integrity, or in your conscience acquitting you of deceit. But they can be so only when they have their free course and their perfect work in you. And that they cannot have if there is guile in your spirit, if your heart condemns you.

May not this be the explanation of that want of assurance of which some anxious souls complain? They are not at ease; they have not comfort, peace, liberty: they feel as if they could not win Christ, so as to be sure of being in him. They see how complete he is for them, as well as how complete they would be if once in him; and they would fain win him and be found in him. But they cannot. Why not? What is there between him and them? Guilt it cannot be; for guilt of deepest dye he takes away; but it may be guile. Sin it cannot be; but it may be silence; keeping silence. Let them not lay the blame of their unquiet and unsatisfied state of mind upon God, or Christ, or the Holy Spirit; upon the gospel way of salvation, or upon the gospel call. All the persons of the Godhead are in favour of their assuring their hearts before God. In the Father, they have rich, free, sovereign grace; altogether gratuitous; unbought and unconditional. In the Son, they have an infinitely precious atonement, an infinitely meritorious work of righteousness, meeting all claims in law against them and upon them. In the Spirit, they have an almighty agency, shutting them up into Christ, and taking of what is his to show to them. Then in the gospel, they have all this love of the one God,— Father, Son, and Holy Ghost,—made over to them, if they will but have it, without price and without reserve ; just in order that they may assure their hearts before God. The whole plan of salvation contemplates that result, and makes full and adequate provision for its being realised.

If it is not, why is it not? Look well to this question, my brother. See if there is not in you some double-dealing, for which "your heart condemns you." Is all straight-forward ? Is all real and downright earnest with you ? Or are you toying and playing with spiritual frames as if it were all a mere affair of sentimentalism ? Or are you brooding over your own gloomy thoughts with that sort of morbid self-satisfaction that feeds on doubt and despair ?

Thus, first, is it a real thirsting for God, a genuine and strong desire for his face and favour, that is moving you ; such as will break through obstructions and "take the kingdom by force"? Or is it the old Israelitish temper of peevish and petulant discontent, rather pleased than not to have to complain that you cannot find the living water ? And is all right as regards your perfect willingness to fall in with God's plan ? Is there no disingenuousness here ; no dislike of being indebted wholly to free grace; no hesitancy about letting go your last hold of the prop on which you have been leaning, and casting yourself, as by a leap in the dark, into the arms of the waiting Saviour ? Above all, thirdly, is there a clear understanding as to the terms on which you would choose to be with God ? Is there no shrinking from the footing on which Christ would place you with his Father and your Father, his God and your God? Is there a sort of half-consciousness in you that you would really apprehend and welcome the mediation of Christ better than you do, if it were meant merely to establish a relation between God and you, so far amicable as to secure your being let alone now and let off at last; and that in consideration of certain specified and ascertainable acts of homage; without its being insisted on that God and you should become so completely one? If your heart misgive you and condemn you on such points as these, it is no wonder that you have not peace with him "who is greater than your heart, and knoweth all things."

But, beloved, now your hearts condemn you not! "You are of the truth;" you are true yourselves, and truth is your object; the truth; the truth of God. Then you can have no objection to take in the truth, full and entire, no matter what humiliating discoveries it gives you of your own character and state; or what demands it makes upon you for submission to the sovereignty and grace of God. You have no quarrel with the gospel method of salvation for anything in it that abases you and exalts the Lord alone; if you are "of the truth." Nor can you now be cleaving to any righteousness of your own. You cut the last cord that binds you to the old natural way of making your peace with God, and sink into the embrace of him who is himself your peace. And it is peace, immediate, full, free, unreserved, that you are eager to have. No truce or compromise will content you now. You cannot be too completely reconciled to God, or brought into friendship too intimate, or fellowship too close and confidential, with your Father in heaven.

Is it so? In all this your hearts condemn you not. Then why should you not "have confidence toward God"? Is it not precisely thus that he is willing, in truth and faithfulness, to deal with you? Then taste and see that God is good; suffer the love of God to dwell in you, without obstruction on your part or any partial dealing any more.

II. Not only as receiving God's love does it concern me to see to it that my heart condemns me not; but as retaining it, and acting it out, in my walk and conduct. Otherwise, "how dwelleth the love of God in me"?

The apostle Paul speaks of "holding faith and a good conscience;" "holding the mystery of faith in a good conscience." "Herein," he says, "do I exercise myself, that I have always a conscience void of offence, toward God and tŏward men." This was, in a large measure, the secret, or at least one indispensable condition, of his confident boldness, as a worker and a witness for Christ. His heart did not misgive or condemn him, as to any part of his habitual demeanour and behaviour. If it had, he would have been instantly smitten with a sort of moral or spiritual paralysis. For the absence of conscious, or half-conscious, guile, is not more essential to your standing right with God, as regards your acceptance and peace, than it is to your continuing to stand right with him in the whole work of faith and labour of love by which you have to glorify him.

What a source of imbecility and unhappiness, even for the Lord's own people, is there in this; "their heart condemning them!" Peter's heart must have condemned him, more or less consciously, when he entered the high-priest's hall, and mingled with the servants. What had he to do there at all; getting in as he did; taking the place he did, and the character? Could he fail to have some misgivings, as he stood beside the fire warming himself, like any ordinary onlooker, while false testimony, that he could have contradicted, was swearing away his master's life?

He "kept silence" and slunk away among the menials of the office. He must have felt that either he should not have been there at all, or if there, he should have been at his master's side. He could not "assure his heart before God," or "have confidence toward God." It is all the less surprising, in these circumstances, that he should have fallen when sharper trial came. He was not found "holding faith and a good conscience."

May we not thus account for the want of joy and power that too often characterises your practical Christianity? Your experience is felt to be lacking in life; your influence somehow does not tell. May it not be because "your heart condemns you"? "Happy is he that condemneth not himself in that which he alloweth." Is that happiness yours? Is there nothing in which you allow yourself about which you have a doubt? Have you a latent suspicion that you are not quite acting up to the standard of attainment at which you ought to aim; that you are not following out your convictions to the full extent to which they might lead you; that you are tolerating what may be at least of questionable expediency? You may have your excuses; your reasons why you cannot be expected to be altogether so heavenly as one, or so self-denied as another, or so decided and outspoken as a third, or so emphatic a protester against the world's follies as a fourth. But do these reasons satisfy you? Do they keep your mind at ease? Or have you occasional qualms?

It is a great matter if the eye be single; if your heart do not condemn you. The consciousness of integrity is, of itself, a well-spring of peace and power in the guileless soul. The clear look, the erect gait, the firm step, the ringing voice, of an upright man, are as impressive upon others as they are expressive of himself. But that is not all. The assurance or confidence of which John speaks, is not self-assurance or self-confidence. No. It is "assurance before God;" it is "confidence toward God."

Why does the apostle make "our heart condemning us" so fatal to our "assuring our heart before God"? It is because "God is greater than our heart, and knoweth all things." He assumes that it is with God we have to do; and that we feel this. Our own verdict upon ourselves is comparatively a small affair; we ask the verdict of God. "With me," says Paul, "it is a very small matter that I should be judged of man's judgment; yea I judge not mine own self." I am not consciously self-convicted; "yet am I not thereby justified; but he that judgeth me is the Lord."

If indeed my heart condemns me, there can be little room for question as to what I am. Even then, however, what is fatal to my peace and power, is not my heart condemning me; but God's being greater than my heart, and knowing all things. My own heart is not likely to condemn me without God condemning me also, and still more. But does it follow that, if my heart acquit me, he must do the same? The contrary, rather, might be inferred. My heart not condemning me might be no proof or presumption that God did not condemn me. He may not acquit me as easily as I acquit myself; for he is greater than my heart, and knoweth all things. There is, therefore, not a little grace here; in our being permitted to infer, from our own heart not condemning us, a like acquittal on the part of God.

And yet how should it not be so if we are his children? Does not the Spirit witness with our spirit that we are so? And that, not merely generally, with reference to the general question of our being God's children; but specifically, with reference to our being at each successive moment in our Christian experience, and each successive step in our Christian life, his children; his children, not in right of a past act of adoption and work of regeneration, but in virtue of a present filial heart and filial frame of mind towards him. It is thus that "the Spirit witnesseth with our spirit."

Our spirit witnesses first; faithfully; for we are upon honour. How is it with you, brother, with reference to this present duty; this present trial? What are you thinking and feeling about it? That it is hard, too hard; that too much is asked of you, or laid upon you; but that you must do, or bear, as best you may, simply because you cannot help it? These are servile thoughts and feelings; they breathe the spirit of bondage, not the spirit of adoption. Your heart condemns you; your own spirit witnesses against you; the Divine Spirit therefore cannot witness for you. You cannot lift an honest filial eye to your Father; for "he is greater than your heart, and knoweth all things." But if now, by grace, you get the victory over these risings of the old slavish mind in you, and have again somewhat of the same mind that was in him who was ever saying, "Abba, Father," as to every business, every cup, every cross; ah! then your heart condemns you not of servile guile, and the sullen, dogged sense of bondage is all gone. Your own spirit witnesses, not of past but of present sonship. It is "Abba, Father," with you and in you, here and now; you are here and now crying, "Abba, Father." And another there is who is in you here and now crying, "Abba, Father;" the Spirit of adoption; the Spirit of God's own Son. So he witnesses with your spirit that you are the sons of God; that you are so here and now, at this moment, in the doing of this painful business, in the drinking of this bitter cup, in the bearing of this heavy cross. And thus he gives you great enlargement and assurance, great boldness and confidence, as you walk abroad in the light of God's loving face shining upon you, to manifest his love

everywhere and always among your fellowmen, his love as
"dwelling in you."

For I must advert again to the immediate occasion of
this appeal of John on the subject of sincerity or truthfulness. It is brotherly love of which he is discoursing; the
duty of loving all men as brethren; loving every man as a
brother; with a true and real brotherly love; a love that
has respect to his being, or becoming, a brother in the
Lord. Judge yourselves here, that you may not be judged.
What says your heart, your conscience, as to this matter?
Does it acquit you? Does it absolve you from the blame of
blood-guiltiness? Paul could take the people among whom
he had lived and laboured to record, the day he bade them
farewell, that he was pure from the blood of them all; for
he had not shunned to declare unto them the whole counsel
of God. May I venture to do so? Woe is me! Can you
venture? Have you done what you could? Are you doing
what you can? Or have you misgivings? Here, a stum-
bling-block is put in the way of an inquirer by some sad
inconsistency, or some cold repulse! There, a precious
opportunity of showing a little kindness, or speaking a
word in season, is lost irretrievably? Ah! are these hands
of yours clean which you hold out to some dear friend, or
some well-disposed neighbour, or some stranger at your
gate; clean from the sin of careless dealing with that man,
as regards the welfare of his soul for eternity? Are you
conscious of indifference or insensibility about his spiritual
state being your prevailing temper, in your intercourse with
this or that person in your house, or in your social circle?
Are you conscious of estrangement, alienation, distance,
dislike? Does your conscience tell you that you are not
treating him kindly as regards his own good, or not treating
him faithfully as regards the claims of God? Ah! then,

you cannot face your own heart; and how then can you, with open eye and upward gaze, face your God? If there be even a lurking suspicion of duty possibly neglected, or of wrong possibly done, rest not till all is righted. "If thou bring thy gift to the altar, and there rememberest that thy brother hath ought against thee; leave there thy gift before the altar, and go thy way; first be reconciled to thy brother, and then come and offer thy gift."

And generally I would urge the vast importance of guilelessness and unreservedness, in the whole domain of your spiritual experience. Why is it that we see so many joyless, cheerless, one might almost say useless Christians? Why so many living and walking in such a way as to give the notion of godliness being all gloomy doubt, painful discipline, self-absorbing anxiety, listless musing? Awake! Arise! Shake off the chains that bind you. Go forth in open day, under the open sky, to meet your God and Father, with your heart open to him, as his heart is open to you. Stand fast in the liberty with which Christ makes you free. Be upright. Be honest, frank, and fearless. Be yourselves; out and out yourselves. Dare to avow yourselves what you are, to God, to your own hearts, to all men. Be of the truth, the whole truth, and nothing but the truth; yourselves true; receiving all truth, declaring all truth; everywhere, and always. Be honest, thoroughly honest, in the closet, in the family, in the market-place, in the parlour. Be transparently honest to yourself and to your brother. Be honest to your God and Father in heaven. Do but consent to treat him as he treats you. His whole heart, he himself wholly, is yours; all his love; all his fulness. Let your whole heart be his. Be you yourselves his; with no reserve; be altogether, now and for ever, his.

27

RIGHTEOUSNESS ESSENTIAL TO OUR PLEASING GOD AND TO HIS HEARING US

"And whatsoever we ask, we receive of him, because we keep his commandments, and do those things that are pleasing in his sight. And this is his commandment, That we should believe on the name of his Son Jesus Christ, and love one another, as he gave us commandment." 1 John 3:22,23

THIS is one of the strongest assertions that we have in Scripture of the efficacy of good works, as bearing on our relation to God. It has no reference, however, to the question of our acceptance or justification; it raises an ulterior question. It manifestly connects a certain privilege with a certain practice, in the case of true Christians, considered as already in a state of grace. And it connects them, so as to make the privilege dependent upon the practice.

The privilege is, that "whatsoever we ask, we receive of him." This is partly an explanation of the previous statement (ver. 21), and partly an additional thought. The "confidence which we have toward God" is such as emboldens us to ask what we will. And we ask confidently, because we know that God will not refuse us anything that we ask.

But it is the fact itself here asserted, and not our sense or apprehension of it, that chiefly claims attention. It is certainly a strong assertion, "Whatsoever we ask we receive of him." And it is altogether unqualified; absolute and unrestricted. We are on such terms with God that he will deny us nothing ;—that is the plain unequivocal meaning of what John says. And it is not to be modified or explained away by any supposed exceptions or reservations. It must be taken in all its breadth as literally true, in connection with the practice on which it is dependent.

That practice is obedience, "we keep his commandments;"—or the performance of good works, "we do those things which are pleasing in his sight." For there are not two separate acts or exercises here spoken of; but only one. "Doing things pleasing in God's sight" is not something over and above "keeping his commandments," or something different from it. That cannot be. For it is not merely doing things, any things, that may be pleasing in his sight; but doing "those things;" which must mean doing the things which he has commanded, and none other.

Is, then, this second clause a mere redundancy? Nay, it adds much to the meaning. For one thing, it implies that when "we keep his commandments," or do the things commanded, we do them as "things pleasing in his sight;"—we take that view of them in the doing of them. And further, it implies that God is really pleased with them. They are done in obedience to his commandments, and so done as to be in very truth "pleasing in his sight:" They do please him; and it is because they do please him, that he is so pleased with us who do them, that he can refuse us nothing that we choose to ask. He derives real gratification from what we do for him. What then will he not do for us?

To make this view of the matter clear, let us take our Lord himself as our example, in respect of both of these sayings of his beloved disciple.

I. "We keep his commandments, and do those things that are pleasing in his sight." So John writes; and so also Jesus speaks ; " He that sent me is with me : the Father hath not left me alone ; for I do always those things that please him " (John viii. 29). That was the hold which he had on the Father. It is, in a measure, the same hold that John says we have on the Father. " I do always those things that please him." " We do those things that are pleasing in his sight." The language is the very same; the sense and spirit in which it is used must be the very same also. Let us consider it as used by Jesus ; let us try to enter into his mind and heart in using it.

There is indeed in it, as used by him, a depth of meaning which we dare not hope, or even try, to fathom. It touches what must ever be an inscrutable mystery ; the ineffable mutual complacency of the great Three in One, Father, Son, and Holy Ghost ; and especially the Father's ineffable complacency in the Son of his love, as fulfilling on earth and in time the counsel of the Godhead which dates from everlasting in heaven. But Jesus uttered the words for our sakes ; and as expressing a human feeling which we may understand, and with which he would have us to sympathise. That human feeling in the bosom of Jesus must have been very simple, and intensely filial; realising intensely his filial relation to the Father, and his filial oneness with the Father. There is, if I may venture so to speak, a childlike simplicity, a sort of artless straightforwardness, in his saying so confidingly, so lovingly, so naturally, " I do always those things that please him." It is almost as if the words came out, half-unconsciously, from his lips; as if he were thinking aloud. And certainly it is not of himself and his merit that he is thinking ; but of the Father and the Father's love. I always please him ; what I do always pleases him ; is the quiet comfort he takes in a trying moment. For it is indeed a trying moment. He has the cross in view. Men, displeased with him, are to "lift him up," and leave him to die in his agony alone. Not so the Father. He leaves me not alone; he is with me; "for I do always those things that please him."

Somewhat similar are the circumstances in which John would have us to say; " we do those things that are pleasing in his sight." We are not to marvel if the world hate us; the source of its hatred we know (ver. 13). And we know also the source of that better spirit of brotherly love with which it is to be met (ver. 14-16). Only let there be, on our part, open, guileless, unreserved sincerity (ver. 17-21). Let our heart, as in the sight of God, acquit us of all secret dishonesty. Let there be truth in the inner man; the truth in love. Then we have the confidence of little children toward God. And, as little children, we join with John, and with Jesus, in saying,—Whatever the world may do to us, we are not alone; the Father is with us, and heareth us, for " we do those things that are pleasing in his sight."

There is nothing then here of a legal spirit; nothing of the Pharisee's self-righteous gratitude : " God, I thank thee that I am not as other men are." It is not thus that John asks us to join with him in saying "we do those things that are pleasing in God's sight." Rather, he makes our saying this the very test of our entire freedom from all guile in our spirits; all that sort of guile which such prayer as the Pharisee's implies. For the Pharisee's prayer represents him as keeping God's commandments, in so far as he does keep them, merely to gain a selfish end and serve a selfish purpose. If he cares about doing what pleases God at all, it is merely with that view. He may be in earnest, ever so much. It is the earnestness of one seeking to make terms with an adversary, and win his favour or forbearance by a measure of forced submission. It is the earnestness of one striving to effect a truce or compromise, on conditions ever so severe, for a boon ever so far off, and apt to be lost after

all. Take the man who is serving God most anxiously, and
with most painstaking observance of the letter of the
commandments, on that footing ; on the footing of his having thus to win his way to such kind and measure of God's
countenance as he thinks he needs, or cares to have. Ask
that man, as before God, and in the eye of his own conscience, Is all clear and open, free and forthflowing, between
you and him whom you so painfully serve ? Is there not,
on the contrary, reserve and restraint; a holding back, as
it were, of confidence on both sides ; something still outstanding between him and you which makes you feel that
all is hollow and unsatisfying ?

Oh ! to be converted, and become as little children !
First, to be made willing as little children, that all this
misunderstanding should be ended, and this breach
thoroughly healed at once, and once for all, as the Father
would have it to be, in the Son. And then, as little children, to know something of a little child's touching and
artless simplicity, as we look with loving eye into the loving eye of the Father, and lovingly lisp out the touching
words : " We keep his commandments and do those things
that are pleasing in his sight."

Therefore now, O humble and simple child of God, if,
in saying this, you feel yourself to be identified with the
holy child Jesus ; if your saying it is really his saying it in
you by his Spirit; if it is as one with him that you say it,
or in all honesty would fain say it ; do not hesitate, or have
any scruple, from any apprehension of its being presumptuous, or any misgiving lest it should savour of self-righteousness. There can be no risk of that, if you say it in and
with Christ. There was no self-righteousness in him ;
there could not be. For he began his work, himself already
personally accepted as righteous; and it was as a Son that he
learned obedience. He makes you one with himself in his

acceptance and in his sonship. He asks you to let him make you thus one with himself; on the ground of his making himself one with you in your sin and death. You are as he is when you join with him in his saying, "I do always those things that please him." There is no self-righteousness here ; scarcely even self-consciousness. It is all direct, outward upward motion of the soul ; the outgoing of filial trust and love and loyalty ; the fond and guileless unreserve, one would say, of an unreflecting child, who would be amazed if any doubt were cast on his father's being always with him, and always hearing him ; for his heart bears him out in saying, with a child's simple and artless love,—I keep his commandments, and do those things that are pleasing in his sight.

Only make sure that with reference to this matter there is no guile in your spirit; that your heart does not condemn you. And there is one plain and practical test or safeguard. Your doing those things that are pleasing in God's sight, is simply your keeping his commandments. If your heart is not right with God, you will be seeking to recommend yourself to him, by services or sacrifices that you think may give you some extra claim upon him, and almost lay him under obligation to you, as if you could benefit or profit him. You will be going about to establish or make good certain meritorious and tangible grounds of confidence, that may avail you when you have to plead with him in the judgment. But does not all that imply deceitful and double-dealing both with him and with yourselves ? If you would really please him, he has told you how to do so. You are not to cast about for ways and means of winning his favour; his favour is freely yours, in his Son. And what now will he have at your hands ? How, on the footing on which he would have you to be with him, are you to please him ? How, but just as his own Son pleased him ? It was his meat to do the will of him that sent him, and to finish his work. He kept the Father's commandments, and so abode in the Father's love.

II. " And whatsoever we ask, we receive of him." In this saying also we have the countenance of Jesus ; for we find him using it : "Father, I thank thee that thou hast heard me. And I knew that thou hearest me always" (John xi. 41, 42). It was beside the grave of Lazarus. What it was that he had been asking, is not said. So far as appears, the prayer for the answer to which he gives thanks consisted not of articulate words but of tears and groans. At all events he was heard ; what he asked, whatever it was, he received of the Father. And while openly acknowledging this, for the sake of the bystanders, he is careful to explain that it is no exceptional case. " Thou hearest me always ;" " whatsoever I ask, I receive of thee always;" thou never refusest me anything. Why Jesus was so anxious, in this instance, publicly to connect the miracle he was intending to do with the Father's hearing his secret prayer, it is perhaps useless to conjecture. It was a signal display of his power to overcome the corruption of the grave that he was about to give; that power which he is to put forth on a wider scale when he comes again. It was fitting, one might say, that in giving it he should, with more than ordinary explicitness and solemnity, carry the Father along with him. But his studied generalisation of his thanksgiving is remarkable. " I knew that thou hearest me always." Never doth the Father leave me alone ; for I do always those things that please him ; and he heareth me always; I have his ear always; and whatsoever I ask I receive of him.

The Lord's manner of asking varies much. He weeps. He groans in the Spirit. He offers up prayers and supplications, with strong crying and tears. He asks, sometimes, as it might seem, almost incoherently (John xii. 27). Once, at least, he asks conditionally, "Father, if it be possible." But, be his manner of asking what it may, always the Father heareth him; always, whatsoever he asks, he receives of him.

"Thou hearest me always!" It is a blessed assurance. And the blessedness of it really lies, not so much in the good he gets from the Father's hearing him, as in the Father's hearing him itself; not so much in what he receives, as in his receiving it from the Father. For this is the charm, the joy, the consolation, of that access to the Father and that influence with the Father which you now have in common with the Son. It is not that you may enrich and gratify yourselves with what you win by asking from him. But it is literally that whatever you ask you receive of him, as his gift; the proof that he is ever with you and heareth you always. Do you not lay the stress on the "him"? Whatsoever you ask you receive of "him." You might have to do with one as to whom your only consideration would be, how much you could get out of him or extract from him. There is a common proverb about quartering upon an enemy. And there is no little satisfaction in the idea that you have a powerful and wealthy patron at your command, on whose resources you may draw at pleasure. But it is not thus that you stand with God. In these other instances, the chief, if not the whole value of any influence you have, is merely the amount of actual benefit obtained. The asker cares little or nothing for the motive which leads the giver to give, or for the disposition towards himself that the gift implies and indicates. It is all the same to him, whether it be extorted by menace; or wrung reluctantly by importunity; or made matter of cold and cautious stipulation. So as only he gets, any how, and on any terms, a certain amount or quantity of what he wants, he is content. That is not the mind of Christ, when he says, "The Father is with me;" "thou hearest me always." The support which this thought gives to him is not that it warrants him in demanding any personal benefit he may choose to specify, that would be pleasing to flesh and blood. No. It is its imparting to his inmost consciousness the sense of his being such a Son to the Father, so dear in the Father's sight, that the Father can refuse him nothing. He may ask what he will; and he is sure to receive it of the Father.

Ah! how then shall I ask anything at all? If such is my position, in and with Christ, how shall I have the heart or the hardihood to ask anything at all of the Father, except only that he may deal with me according to his good pleasure? If I am really on such a footing with the Father that "he heareth me always," and "whatsoever I ask I receive of him;" if I have such influence with him; if, as his dear child, pleasing him, and doing what pleases him, I can so prevail with him that he can refuse me nothing; what can I say? What can I do? I can but cast myself into his arms and cry, Thou knowest better than I, O my Father! Father, thy will be done!

Yes. And under that blessed committal of all to him, what freedom may I not use? When told that I and my doings are so pleasing to him that I may ask what I will and it shall be done; the very abundance of the grace silences me. It is enough for me, Father, that such is my acceptance in thy sight. But can I wield the sceptre? Can I use so tremendous a power as this, that whatever I ask thee to do thou doest? Nay. I am thy servant. Undertake thou for me. Enough for me to be assured that I so find grace and favour in thy sight that I have but to ask thee to do anything and it is done. Enough! Nay, more than enough! I can ask nothing on these terms, I must leave all to thee. But leaving all to thee, I pour out all the more freely my whole soul to thee, I spread out my whole case to thee. I speak to thee of all that is upon my mind and heart. I tell thee all my desire. My groaning is not hid from thee.

Let us look in closing at the two specimen commandments, if one may so call them, or the two parts of the one specimen commandment, which John expressly mentions in this connection.

1. "That we should believe on the name of his Son Jesus Christ." The keeping of this commandment is the doing of what is pleasing in the Father's sight. It is so in proportion to the love with which he loveth the Son, and loveth us in the Son. We can do nothing that will please the Father more. It is what his heart is set on ; that the Son of his love should be the object of our faith.

Is there not here a word in season for you, O sinner, whoever you are, however guilty and however helpless, poor and needy, lost and undone ? You, as it might seem, are in no condition to keep God's commandments so as to please him ; and you cannot venture to ask anything, or to hope that you will receive anything, at his hands. Nay ; but here is something that you may do, and that will be very pleasing to him. "Believe on the name of his Son Jesus Christ." It is true that he will not be pleased with your keeping any other commandment ; but he will be pleased with your keeping that one. You may not be in circumstances to do anything else that will be pleasing in his sight ; but you are in the very circumstances to do that which will please him best. He asks you if you will not do him this pleasure, "to believe on the name of his Son Jesus Christ." Be it that you cannot receive anything you ask otherwise than on the footing of your keeping his commandments and doing those things that are pleasing in his sight. Here is the commandment for you, here and now, to keep; here is the thing pleasing in his sight for you, here and now, to do. Without faith it is impossible to please God; but faith pleases him; it pleases him well. Then believe now.

And take a right view of the duty of believing. It is not using a great liberty to believe on the name of Jesus; it is simply "keeping the commandment of God." The liberty is all the other way. You use a great liberty when you refuse to believe. Be not disobedient; displease not God by unbelief; rather please him by believing. And believing, ask what you will, and it shall be given you.

Keep on believing. Continue to believe more and more, simply because you see and feel it more and more to be "his commandment that you should believe on the name of his Son Jesus Christ." Unbelief, in you who have believed, is aggravated disobedience. And, as such, it is and must be especially displeasing to God. It is his pleasure that his Son should be known, trusted, worshipped, loved; honoured as he himself would be honoured. You cannot displease the Father more than by dishonouring the Son; refusing to receive him, and rest upon him, and embrace him, and hold him fast, and place full reliance upon him as redeemer, brother, friend. Do not deceive yourselves by imagining that there may be something rather gracious in your doubts and fears; your unsettled and unassured frame of mind; as if it betokened humility, and a low esteem of yourselves. Beware lest God see in it only a low esteem of his Son Jesus Christ. Beware of guile. May not your staggering, hesitating faith be but half-faith after all? May it not be that you are unwilling to be wholly Christ's, and to have Christ wholly yours?

Can that be pleasing to God? "What shall we do that we might work the works of God?" asked the Jews, and the Lord replied: "This is the work of God, that ye believe on him whom he has sent." Therefore let us believe; and let us be "strong in faith, giving glory to God."

2. "And love one another as he gave us commandment." The keeping of this commandment of love, as well as the keeping of the former commandment of faith, is the doing of that which is very pleasing in God's sight; and, therefore, in the keeping of it we may with much confidence reckon and rely on the assurance that "whatsoever we ask we shall receive of him;" that "he will hear us always."

I do not know—who can tell me?—what connection there was between the silent prayer of Jesus at the grave of Lazarus, and the utterance of that voice of power, "Lazarus, come forth!" Evidently the Lord wished it to be seen and known that in some very special manner the Father was with him, and went along with him, in that great work. "Father, I thank thee that thou hast heard me. And I know that thou hearest me always; but because of the people that stand by I said it, that they may believe that thou hast sent me." He would have it understood that he did the work as one whom the Father had on this occasion heard; as one whom "the Father heareth always," and whom "the Father hath sent." For he was to do it, not as a thing that might please himself, but as a thing that would please the Father. He "loved Martha and her sister and Lazarus," and he was about to manifest and gratify his love by a very signal proof and token. But he would have all men to observe that it was not merely on the impulse of a spontaneous burst of affection that he acted, but as doing what the Father com-

manded, and what would be pleasing in the Father's sight.
Loving, in that way, Martha and her sister and Lazarus, he
knew that in the practical outgoing of his love towards
them; in whatever loving words he was to say, and whatever loving works he was to do; he might be sure of the
Father being with him. For "he pleased the Father;"
he sought to please the Father, and did please the Father.
Therefore he was sure of receiving what he asked; sure of
the Father hearing him then and hearing him always.

Go ye and do likewise. Love one another; love your
brother; love as a brother every one with whom you have
anything to do; love him with the love that would fain
have him for a brother. And let your love still always be
" the keeping of God's commandment," and " the doing of
what is pleasing in his sight." Let it not be, as it were, at
your own hand that you love, but in obedience to the commandment of God. This may, in one view, be felt by you
to be a sort of damper; a drawback upon the warm spontaneous flow of your affections. It may seem to detract
from the generous enthusiasm of your good will and your
good offices. It takes away the chivalry and romance of
this virtue. It makes Christian philanthropy a very humble
and homely duty. You are to go among your fellows,—not
loving them of your own accord, and at your own discretion
showing your love,—but loving them in obedience to " the
commandment of God ;" and in all the expressions and acts
of your love, simply bent on doing what is " pleasing in his
sight." But after all, if this is a lowlier, it is a far more
becoming and safer position for you to occupy. And it is
one in which, if you honestly occupy it, you may with all
the greater confidence rely on his hearing you now, and
always. You do good and communicate; you are fruitful
in every good work; you wash the feet of saints; you visit
the fatherless and widows; you speak a word in season to

the weary ; you stretch out a helping hand to all that need ; not merely as indulging your own loving impulses, but rather as carrying out God's loving purposes. You do these things because they are " well pleasing in his sight." Doing them thus, in singleness of eye, what encouragement have you to expect that he will be with you in the doing of them ; that he will hear your prayer for those to whom you do them ; and that whatsoever you ask on their behalf you will receive of him !

But in all this, let us see to it that we are " of the truth ; " simple, guileless, upright ; as regards our whole life and walk of faith and love. Only then can we have confidence before God that whatsoever we ask we shall receive of him. Let us lay to heart the Psalmist's acknowledgment, —" If I regard iniquity in my heart, the Lord will not hear me ; " and his thanksgiving,—" But verily God hath heard me ; he hath attended to the voice of my prayer. Blessed be God, which hath not turned away my prayer, nor his mercy from me." Let us lay this to heart, not in any spirit of self-righteousness or vain-glory ; but in simple sincerity, as little children, honouring our Father ; according to the quaint thought of an old writer :—" I find David making a complete syllogism, perfect in mood and figure. The first premiss being, ' If I regard iniquity in my heart, the Lord will not hear me ; ' and the second, ' But verily God hath heard me ; he hath attended to the voice of my prayer ; ' I look for his drawing the conclusion : Therefore I regard not iniquity in my heart. But no. When I expected him to put the crown on his own head, he places it on God's ;—' Blessed be God, which hath not turned away my prayer, nor his mercy from me.' I like David's logic better than Aristotle's ; that whatever be the premiss God's glory is the conclusion." *

* Fuller's *Good Thoughts in Bad Times.*

28

OUR RIGHTEOUSNESS ATTESTED BY OBEDIENCE,
AS IMPLYING OUR ABIDING IN GOD, AND HIS
ABIDING IN US BY THE SPIRIT GIVEN BY HIM
TO US

"And he that keepeth his commandments dwelleth [abideth] in him, and
he in him. And hereby we know that he abideth in us, by the Spirit
which he hath given us. Beloved, believe not every spirit, but try
the spirits whether they are of God : because many false prophets are
gone out into the world." 1 John 3:24-4:1

THIS is another fruit of the keeping of God's commandments; or another view of the blessedness of doing so.
It ensures our abiding in God, and his abiding in us; and
that in a manner that may be ascertained and verified.
Two practical questions are thus virtually put and answered. I. How may we abide in God?—so abide in him
as to have him abiding in us? By keeping his commandments. How may we know that he abides in us? By the
Spirit which he giveth us,—and giveth us in a way that
admits of the gift being verified by trial.

I. In the keeping of God's commandments there is this
great reward, that he that doeth so "dwelleth in God, and
God in him." Negatively, it has been already shown that
there can be no such mutual indwelling if there is on our
part disobedience to God's commandments. Sin, as "the
transgression of the law," is incompatible with such high
and holy communion (iii. 6). It is the positive form of the
statement that is now before us. Obedience, or the keep-

ing of God's commandments, actively promotes this communion. It is more than the condition of it; it is of its
very essence. If this mutual indwelling is not to be mere
absorption, which some dreamers in John's day held it to
be;—if it is not to be the swallowing up of our conscious
individual personality in the infinite mind or intelligence of
God;—if it is to conserve the distinct relationship of God
to man, the Creator to the creature, the Ruler to the subject,
the Father to the child;—it must be realised and must
develop itself, or act itself out, through the means of
authority or law on the one side, and obedience or the keeping of the commandments on the other. It is, in fact, the
very consummation and crown of man's old, original relation
to God; as that relation is not only restored, but perfected
and gloriously fulfilled, in the new economy of grace.

For consider the divine ideal, if I may so speak, involved
in the creation of man after the image of God, and in the
footing on which it pleased God to place man towards himself. Evidently God contemplated obedience, or the keeping of his commandments, as the normal state or character
of man. While that state or character continued, there
was the best understanding between the parties; between
God and man; they were on the best of terms with one
another. There was entire complacency on both sides;
each resting and dwelling in the other with full and un-
alloyed satisfaction. You would not say, in these circumstances, that this mutual indwelling of man in God and
God in man was, in any proper sense, procured or obtained
by man's obedience, by his keeping the commandments of
God. You would rather say that it had in that way its
proper outgoing or forthgoing, its conscious realisation. It
is man's method of intercourse with God; the only competent, the only conceivable method, if God and man
respectively are to keep their relative positions as distinct

intelligences. It is only along the line of God ruling and man obeying, that the two, as separate persons or individuals, can so walk together as to get into one another's minds and hearts, and thus abide in one another. Such mutual indwelling of God in man and of man in God, becoming day by day more close, confidential, loving; through man's increasing insight into the exceeding excellency of the commandments he is keeping, or rather of him whose nature and will they discover, and through God's increasing delight in the growing intelligence and sympathy with which man keeps them; might seem to be complete; having in it all the elements of perfection, as regards both the holiness and the happiness of man. Can God and man be more to one another?

Alas! the drawback of a conditional standing, and a possible fall, is fatal. It leaves an opening for suspicion creeping in, upon the hint of a seeming friend, who would insinuate that restraint is irksome and independence sweet. Then all mutual indwelling is over. God and man must dwell apart. There may indeed be some sort of formal dealing between them; at least man fondly imagines that there may. He thinks that he can so far keep God's commandments as thereby to right himself with God; to the extent at least to which he cares to be righted. He will make certain terms with God, or conceive of God as making certain terms with him; and he will be punctilious in the fulfilment of these terms. But that is not really keeping God's commandments. It is the keeping of a paction, if you will; the doing of his part in a bargain. And if the two parties concerned were equals, or if the relation between them were one of mutual independence, this might lay a foundation for some sort of mutual indwelling, by faith and love, in one another. Even in that case, however, the foundation is too narrow and precarious. If the mutual indwelling is to be real and thorough, there must be something more than the fulfilment of certain stipulated conditions between the parties. They must submit themselves, each to the other, cordially and without reserve; they must study to obey and please one another. Between God and man especially, the introduction of the conditional element, of anything that savours of the striking of a bargain or the making of terms, is and must be destructive of all real fellowship or intercommunion. No obedience rendered on that footing or in that spirit can ever secure your dwelling in God and his dwelling in you. In point of fact, it is apt, —if not from the first to occasion a breach,—yet ever afterwards, when a breach occurs, to widen, deepen, and perpetuate it, however it may be meant, and may seem to bridge it over.

The practical value of a free gospel is, that it places your " keeping of God's commandments " on a different footing, and breathes into it a different spirit. You look to Jesus, and are one with him. You are in the same position of advantage for keeping God's commandments in which he was. You start, as he did, on the walk and work of obedience, not as seeking acceptance, but as already accepted; not as a servant on trial, but as a son abiding in the house evermore. You are not only what unfallen Adam was when the task of keeping God's commandments was set before him; you are as Christ was when the same task was set before him.

Consider then what sort of keeping of God's commandments his was; and how it must have conduced to his abiding in the Father, and the Father's abiding in him. Of course that mutual indwelling never could, through all his keeping of the Father's commandments, become more full and complete, in principle and essence, than it was before he began to keep them. But we may well imagine that to his human consciousness, and in his human experience, the sense of it must have been growing more intense, and more intensely soothing and beatific, as his keeping of them went on, and on, to its terrible and triumphant close. Among the things about obedience which he learned by suffering, surely this was one, that it has a mighty power to promote, enhance, and intensify the indwelling of man in God, and of God in man. He learned the grief and pain which such obedience as he had undertaken to render involved. Did he not learn something of its joy and pleasure too, the joy and pleasure of apprehending and feeling, more and more, in his human soul, his dwelling in the Father and the Father's dwelling in him throughout it all?

I dare not venture upon particular illustration here. But I ask you, in any hour of deep and private meditation, and after you have prayed, or while you are praying, for the help of the Spirit, to put yourself alongside of Christ, in the sorest and hardest of the experiences which his keeping the Father's commandments entailed upon him. Try to enter into what his soul was feeling when it was "exceeding sorrowful, even unto death." There was anguish, agony; the anguish and agony of having guilt to answer for, and a penal death to die. But was he not then and there, in his keeping of the Father's most dread and awful commandments, and through his keeping of them, dwelling in the Father and the Father in him, in a sense and with a depth and force of meaning, of which that human soul of his could not otherwise have had any experience? What insight, what sympathy, what rest, repose, and peace,—the rest, repose, and peace of unutterable complacency, on his part, in the Father and on the Father's part in him, must there have been in his utterance of these simple words, "It is finished;" "Father, into thy hands I commend my spirit!"

Let our keeping of God's commandments be like his. Let us seek grace that it may be so. In our case, as in his, this may imply a bitter cup to be drunk; a heavy cross to be borne. Like him, we have to learn obedience by suffering. Let the obedience we thus learn be of the same sort as his. Let it be the giving up of our own will, always, everywhere, that God's will may be done. We shall then prove how good and acceptable and perfect that will of God is. We dwell thus in God when our will is merged in his will; we have rest and repose in him; our will in his will; our thoughts in his thoughts; our ways in his ways. And he dwells in us; his will in our will; his thoughts in our thoughts; his ways in our ways. We enter into his mind and heart; and he enters into ours.

II. The manner of God's abiding in us, or at least the way in which we may know that he abides in us, is specified:—"Hereby we know that he abideth in us, by the Spirit which he hath given us." We are to distinguish here between our dwelling in God and his dwelling in us. Both are to be known as facts of our own consciousness; not as revealed truths merely, but as realised experiences. The one, however, our dwelling in God, is to be thus known by our "keeping his commandments;" the other, God's dwelling in us, by "the spirit which he giveth us." The one we know by what we do to God;—the other, by what God does in us. And yet, the two means of knowledge are not far apart. They are not only strictly consistent with one another; they really come together in one point.

For the Spirit is here said to be given to us;—not in order to our knowing that God abideth in us, in the sense of his opening our spiritual eye and quickening our spiritual apprehension;—but rather, as the medium of our knowing it, the evidence or proof by which we know it. He giveth us the Spirit; and by that token, his giving us the Spirit, we are taught by the Spirit to know that God dwelleth in us. The question therefore as to what this gift of the Spirit may be, is thus narrowed to a precise point.

Is it the gift of the Spirit enabling men to perform supernatural works that is meant? That can scarcely be; the gift of the Spirit for such works was never a sure sign of God's really and savingly dwelling in those who did them. Surely it must be the gift of the Spirit for the ordinary purposes of the Christian life and walk that John has in view; the gift of the Spirit common to all believers in all ages. God giveth us the Spirit in order that, by the Spirit being given, we may know that he dwelleth in us. He means us, therefore, to recognise this gift as a sure evidence of that fact. And how are we to recognise the Spirit as given to us? How otherwise than by recognising the fruit of the gift? The Spirit given to us is, as to his movement or operation, unseen and unfelt. But the fruit of the Spirit is palpable and patent. "It is love, joy, peace, long-suffering, gentleness, goodness, faith, meekness, temperance." For "against such there is no law" (Gal. v. 22, 23).

"Against such there is no law." That is an important addition or explanation here. There is nothing in the gift of the Spirit, or in the fruit of the Spirit as given, that is contrary to law; nothing, therefore, that can again bring us under the risks and liabilities of law. On the contrary, the Spirit being given, with such fruit, is precisely what secures that kind of keeping of the commandments on our part, by which we "dwell in him." For, I must repeat, it is as the Spirit of adoption that he is given; "God sendeth forth the Spirit of his Son into our hearts, crying, Abba, Father."

Thus the two elements and conditions, the two means

and evidences, of this mutual indwelling of us in God and of God in us meet together. We dwell in God by keeping his commandments; he dwells in us by giving us his Spirit. But our keeping his commandments and his giving us his Spirit are really one; one and the same fact viewed on opposite sides. It is not any sort of keeping his commandments on our part that will ensure or attest our dwelling in him. It is not any way of giving us his Spirit on his part that will ensure or attest his dwelling in us. Our keeping his commandments in the spirit of bondage; in a legal, self-righteous, formal, and servile frame of mind; is not our dwelling in God. God's enabling us, by the power of his Spirit, to work miracles, would not be his dwelling in us. Our dwelling in him is our keeping his commandments, as his Son did, on the same filial footing and with the same filial heart. His dwelling in us is his " sending forth the Spirit of his Son into our hearts, crying, Abba, Father."

III. From all this it follows that the counsel or warning, " Believe not every spirit, but try the spirits whether they be of God" (iv. 1), is as needful for us as it was for those to whom John wrote. We may think that it is the Spirit of God whom we are receiving into our hearts and cherishing there, when it may really be another spirit altogether : one of the many spirits inspiring the " many false prophets that are gone out into the world." Therefore we must " try the spirits."

Do you ask how, or by what test?—" Hereby know ye the Spirit of God : Every spirit that confesseth that Jesus Christ is come in the flesh is of God : and every spirit that confesseth not that Jesus Christ is come in the flesh is not of God."

The full meaning of this pregnant and searching test will be afterwards considered. Meanwhile, as bearing on the subject now in hand, it admits of at least one obvious application.

The Spirit that is of God will ever honour Christ; and especially Christ come in the flesh; which means not only Christ incarnate, but also and emphatically Christ crucified. The person and work of Christ, as the outward object of our faith, the ground of our confidence before God outside of us and apart from us, the true Spirit of God will ever magnify and glorify. He will not consent to substitute for that any inward experience, however heavenly, as superseding it or setting it aside. That is what false prophets, moved by an antichristian spirit, are apt to do. It was a very marked characteristic of their teaching in John's own day. An inward light, an inward sense, something, or much of a Christ in them; an inward revelation, or rapture, or elevation, a sort of mystical indwelling of God or of Christ in them, they extolled and cried up; making it the sum and substance of all Christianity, the whole gospel of the grace of God. Now any spirit that fosters such a tendency is not of God. Any spirit that would encourage us to look in upon ourselves and not out to Christ for peace or holiness is not of God. Inward experience is very precious; it is indispensable. A growing inward consciousness of our "keeping God's commandments," or, in other words, of our conformity of mind and heart and will to God's character and law,—a growing inward consciousness of the fruit of the Spirit, love, joy, peace—we must have; and we must seek to have it more and more, if we would have real communion with God. But if we are rightly exercised, how will this affect our views of "Christ come in the flesh," our feeling of our need of him and of his exclusive sufficiency for us? Will it make us at all the less inclined to be ever looking to Christ, ever leaning on Christ, ever laying hold of Christ, ever having recourse to Christ, and that blood of Christ which cleanseth from all sin ? Nay, on the contrary, our growing aquaintance with God, our growing delight in his law, our growing apprehension of the blessedness of perfect oneness, in nature and in will, with him, will only give us deeper convictions of sin, and open up to us new and fresh discoveries of our corruption and our guilt, and lead us to be ever saying, with reference not to past but to present evil in us : " O wretched man that I am ! who shall deliver me from the body of this death ? "—and to be ever taking refuge in Paul's last stronghold—" This is a faithful saying, and worthy of all acceptation, that Christ Jesus came into the world to save sinners ; of whom I am chief."

Let us then, acting upon the belief that " whatsoever we ask, we receive of him," be ever asking God to give us the Holy Spirit, that we may know experimentally his dwelling in us. We cannot have too much of this gift of the Spirit, if it is indeed the Spirit " confessing Christ " that we ask God to give. We need not be afraid of having too much of the inward fruit of the Spirit ; nor need we shrink from recognising the Spirit given to us by God as the spirit of assurance ; " the spirit of power, and of love, and of a sound mind." If indeed we find ourselves leaning to the imagination that we have got past the stage at which we need to be living, as sinners, upon Christ the Saviour, and are tempted to live upon inward frames and feelings ; putting the Spirit's work in us instead of Christ's work for us ; then we do well to beware. But there is really no incompatibility between the two ; our coveting, asking and obtaining more and more of the inward testimony of the Spirit, and our being by that very testimony—as it unfolds to us more and more God's high ideal and our sad coming short of it— shut up more and more into Christ as the Lamb of God ; with whose atoning blood and justifying righteousness we feel more and more that we can never for a single moment dispense.

Finally, let us remember that it is in the actual "keeping of God's commandments" that we find all this great mystery of "our dwelling in God and his dwelling in us," practically cleared up. In the onward path of the just, which is as the shining light, shining more and more unto the perfect day, we come to know the Spirit given to us, by his "confessing Jesus Christ as come in the flesh." Let us therefore so keep God's commandments as not to vex or grieve the Holy Spirit. For we do vex and grieve him when our keeping them is either ungracious on the one hand; or, on the other hand, becomes to us a ground of confidence before God. As the Spirit of God, he is vexed by our submission to God being any other than a submission of the whole heart; filial altogether, and not servile at all. And as "the Spirit confessing Jesus Christ come in the flesh," he cannot but be vexed if we unduly lean even on his own work in us, to the disparagement of what is the one only ground of a sinner's hope, from first to last, "Christ and him crucified." But let us keep the commandments of God simply, humbly, lovingly; not as doing any great thing, but only as doing his will, and content that his will be done. So keeping his commandments, we abide in God, and so also we know that he abideth in us, by the Spirit which he hath given us.

29

OUR RIGHTEOUSNESS EXERCISED IN TRYING THE
SPIRITS; THE TEST, CONFESSING THAT JESUS
CHRIST IS COME IN THE FLESH

"Hereby we know that he abideth in us, by the Spirit which he hath
given us. Beloved, believe not every spirit, but try the spirits
whether they are of God; because many false prophets are gone out
into the world. Hereby know ye the Spirit of God: Every spirit
that confesseth that Jesus Christ is come in the flesh is of God: and
every spirit that confesseth not that Jesus Christ is come in the flesh
is not of God: and this is that spirit of antichrist, whereof ye have
heard that it should come; and even now already is it in the world.
Ye are of God, little children, and have overcome them: because
greater is he that is in you, than he that is in the world." 1 John
3:24-4:4

THE appeal in the beginning of the fourth chapter springs
out of the closing statement in the third: "Hereby we
know that God abideth in us, by the Spirit which he hath
given us." This evidently throws us back into ourselves;
into some consciousness on our part of his having given us
the Spirit. It is an inward or subjective test. Have we
in us the Spirit as given to us by God? If so, we have the
Spirit in us "confessing that Jesus Christ is come in the
flesh." And by his confessing that truth, we may distinguish his indwelling in us from all attempts of any antichristian spirit, or any false prophets or teachers inspired
by an antichristian spirit, to effect a lodgment in our
hearts. For this is their characteristic; they refuse to
"confess that Jesus Christ is come in the flesh."

The meaning of that confession, objectively considered, has been already brought out in what John says of Antichrist as "denying that Jesus is the Christ;"—and so virtually "denying the Father and the Son" (ii. 21-25). I am inclined to think that we have now to deal with it more subjectively; as a matter of inward experience rather than of doctrinal statement. For the starting-point is our "knowing that God abideth in us, by the Spirit which he hath given us." It is the fact of the Spirit confessing in us, and not merely to us, that we have to ascertain and verify; and therefore the test must apply inwardly:— Have we in us "the Spirit that confesseth that Jesus Christ is come in the flesh?" As it stands here, therefore, I think we are called to deal with that formula rather experimentally than dogmatically; and so to make it all the more available for the searching of our hearts.

Taking that view, I shall consider, in the first place, what the inward confession of the Spirit in us that Jesus Christ is come in the flesh may be held to imply; and then, secondly, how our realising this in our experience secures our personal and practical victory over all antichristian spirits or prophets who deny that great and blessed fact.

I. It properly belongs to the Spirit to "confess that Jesus Christ is come in the flesh." He had much to do with the flesh in which Jesus Christ came. He prepared for him a body in the Virgin's womb, so as to secure that he came into the world pure and sinless. And all throughout his sojourn on earth the Spirit ministered to him as "Jesus Christ come in the flesh;" he could not minister to him otherwise. It is the flesh, or humanity, of Jesus Christ that brings him within the range of the Spirit's gracious care. It was his human experience that the Spirit animated and sustained; and it is with his human experience also that the Spirit deals when he "takes of what is Christ's and shows it unto us." His object is to make us one with "Jesus Christ as come in the flesh." That practically is his confession to us and in us. Let us see what it implies.

1. He identifies us with Jesus Christ in his humiliation. There is no real humiliation on the part of the Son if his coming in the flesh is denied. He might be conceived of as coming gloriously, graciously, condescendingly, in his own original and eternal nature alone; taking the mere semblance of a body, or a real body now and then, as the Gnostic dreamers taught. But there would have been no humbling of himself in that, and no room for any concurrent humbling testimony or work of the Spirit in us. It is Jesus Christ as come in the flesh, "made of a woman, made under the law," that the Spirit owns and seals. And he confesses or witnesses this in us by making us one, and keeping us one, with our Lord in that character, as "Jesus Christ come in the flesh." In our divine regeneration he brings us to be,—what, through his interposition, Jesus Christ in his miraculous human generation became,—servants under the yoke; subject to the authority and commandment of God; willingly subject; our nature being renewed into the likeness of his.

2. The Spirit identifies us with Jesus Christ, not only in his humiliation but in its conditions and liabilities. For "to confess Jesus Christ come in the flesh," is not merely to admit the fact of his incarnation, but to admit it with whatever consequences necessarily, in terms of law, flow from it. His coming in the flesh is not simply an incident or event in history; it has a special meaning in the moral government of God. It brought him, not merely into the position of one made under the law, but into the position, under the law, of those whose place he took.

The old deniers of his coming in the flesh saw this ; and it was their chief objection to the doctrine. They might have allowed that the mysterious efflux or emanation of Deity that they seemed to own as a sort of Saviour did somehow identify himself with us, by making common cause with us, and even temporarily assuming our nature with a view to purge and elevate it. But they perceived that the literal incarnation of the Son of God, truly and fairly admitted, carried in its train the vicarious substitution and atonement. Modern teachers in the same line think that they may hold the first without the last. But I am mistaken if any incarnation they may thus hold does not slip insensibly, in their handling of it, into some modification, suited to modern turns of thought, of the old vague notion of a certain divinity being in every man ; and in some one man perhaps pre-eminently as the type and model of perfect manhood. That, however, is not to " confess Jesus Christ come in the flesh ; " for his coming in the flesh, accepted as a reality, implies his really putting himself alongside of those in whose flesh he comes, and serving himself heir to all the ills to which their flesh is heir.

Let us look, then, at "Jesus Christ coming in the flesh," the Son of God taking our nature into oneness with himself. He takes it pure and sinless, so far as he is personally concerned ; but he takes it with all the liabilities which our sin has entailed upon it. And the Spirit, confessing in us that he is come in the flesh, makes us one with him in this view of his coming ; our guilt and condemnation being now his, and his taking our guilt and bearing our condemnation being ours. His coming in the flesh is his consenting to be crucified for us ; the Spirit in us confessing him as come in the flesh makes us willing to be crucified with him. And so, by means of this confession, the true Spirit of God and of Christ opens to us a prospect of glory and joy such as no lying spirit of antichrist can hold out. If it was not really in the flesh that he came; or if, coming in the flesh, he failed to redeem by substitution those whose flesh he shared; then flesh, or human nature, can have little hope of reaching the blessedness of heaven. But having really come in the flesh, and in the flesh suffered for sin, he raises the flesh in which he suffered to the highest capacity of holy and happy being. "In my flesh I shall see God," was the hope of the patriarch Job. It is made sure by Jesus Christ come in the flesh, and by the Spirit confessing in us that he is come.

II. This accordingly is the secret of our present victory over antichristian spirits and men: "Ye are of God, little children, and have overcome them" (ver. 4). The intimation (ver. 3) that the spirit of antichrist is already, even now, in the world, is fitted to make this assurance very welcome. For war is proclaimed; war that is to last as long as the world lasts. It is the old war, proclaimed long ago, between the serpent's seed and the woman's. But it has taken a new form; and that its final one. From the first manifestation of it,—from the day when Cain slew his brother,—it might be seen to turn upon the question of the worship of God by atoning sacrifice. Is there, or is there not, to be the shedding of blood for the remission of sins? That, more or less clearly, with variations suited to the varied aspect of the church and the world, has ever since continued to be in substance the point at issue. Now that Christ has come in the flesh, it is so more than ever. "Jesus Christ come in the flesh" is its ultimate expression and embodiment. In the contest about this high theme, "you, little children, have overcome them." The victory is already yours: for "you are of God."

Two questions here occur:—1. What is the nature of

the victory ? 2. How is it connected with your being of God ?

1. The victory is a real victory got over the false prophets or teachers, who are not of God, whom the spirit of antichrist inspires. And it is a victory over them personally ; not over their doctrines and principles merely ; but over themselves : "Ye have overcome them." True, it is, in a sense, a war of doctrines or of principles that is waged ; its field of battle is the field of argument and controversy. You and they meet in discussion and debate ; and when you succeed in refuting their reasonings, you may feel the complacency of a personal triumph over them as, vanquished, they seem to quit the field. But even though vanquished they may argue still. They are silenced, merely, and not subdued ; and their silence is only for a time. You may soon have the battle to fight over again ; and in the incessant fighting of it, you may be doomed to suffer wounds, in your temper at least, if not in your faith ; in your equanimity of spirit towards men, if not in your peace of mind within yourselves, or even your peace with God. I cannot think that that is the victory on which John congratulates his " little children " so affectionately.

No doubt such victory is valuable, as the sort of war in which it is won is inevitable. It is idle to effect to run down controversy, as long as there is error abroad among men. It is mere prudery to be always groaning over the symptoms of irritability which controversialists have exhibited, and bemoaning evermore their lack of a smooth and oily tongue. All honour to the champions of God's holy word and blessed gospel, who have waxed valiant in fight against the adversaries of both ! All sympathy with them in their indignant sense of what touches the glory and insults the majesty of him whose battles they fight ;

with large allowance for the heats into which, being but men, they may suffer their zeal to hurry them! And all thankful joy in the success with which they wield the weapons of their keen logic, their learned study, their burning eloquence, in baffling the sophistries of heresy and infidelity, and rearing an impregnable defence around the battlements on which the banner is planted which God " has given to them that fear him, that it may be displayed because of the truth ! "

But that is not exactly the victory which is here meant when it is said, " ye have overcome them." For what really is your contest with them ? It is not about an abstract proposition, a mere article in a creed. It is not whether you can prove that Jesus of Nazareth was man as well as God, or God as well as man ; or they can prove the reverse. No. " Jesus Christ come in the flesh " is not with you a mere matter of disputation. It is a pregnant and significant fact in God's government of the universe, grasped by you as such, and apprehended as such in your experience. By faith you know and feel what it means. You identify yourself with him in his coming in the flesh ; consciously and with entire community of mind and heart ; and in the very doing of this you " have already overcome them."

For it is the fact that they dislike ; not argument about the fact. It is the actual " coming of Jesus Christ in the flesh," and his actual accomplishment, in the flesh, of all that in the flesh he came for, that they resent and resist. It is that which Satan, the original spirit of antichrist, would fain have set himself to hinder ; moving Herod to slay Jesus in his childhood, and Judas to betray him in his manhood ; tempting Jesus himself to make shipwreck of his integrity. And it is your actual personal participation with him, as " Jesus Christ come in the flesh ; " your being

really one with him in that wondrous humiliation, in its
spirit and its fruit ; that, so far as you are concerned, they
seek to frustrate. In realising that, you get the better of
them ; confessing thus Jesus Christ come in the flesh, you
have overcome them. It is not that you are able to discuss
with them, as debatable questions in argument, the reality
and the meaning of Jesus Christ having come in the flesh.
You may have to do so, and if you do so on a clear call of
duty, you are sure of divine support and help ; perhaps
even of success and triumph. But that is not your having
already overcome them. Very gladly would they often
drag you into this snare ; making you mistake the chance of
overcoming them in a discussion about Jesus Christ come
in the flesh, for the certainty of your having overcome them
through your simply confessing him in that character. But
be not drawn down to lower ground. Stand upon your
position of oneness with him whom you confess as Jesus
Christ come in the flesh. Meet thus any and all antichrists ;
antichristian spirits, antichristian prophets. They are not
to be overcome. You have already overcome them.

2. Your having overcome them is connected with your
" being of God " (ver. 4) ; which again is intimately connected with your " confessing that Jesus Christ is come in
the flesh " (ver. 2). Your being of God is the intermediate
link between your confessing that Jesus Christ is come in
the flesh (ver. 2), and your having overcome them who
reject that truth (ver. 4).

" Ye are of God " (ver. 4). This, let it be observed, is
what has previously been asserted of the Spirit that " confesseth that Jesus Christ is come in the flesh." He " is of
God " (ver. 3). And it is denied concerning any spirit
refusing to confess that. Such a spirit " is not of God."

Now what, as applied to the Holy Spirit, does this
mean ? How,—in what sense and to what effect,—is the

Spirit that confesses that Jesus Christ is come in the flesh said to be " of God " ?

He is of God essentially, being himself God ; proceeding from the Father and the Son ; one with them in the undivided essence of the Godhead. He is of God, if I may so say, officially ; condescending in infinite love, to be the gift of the Father and the Son to guilty and sinful men. But here more particularly, he is of God as confessing, or in virtue of his confessing, that Jesus Christ is come in the flesh. He is on the side of God, or in the interest of God; he consults and acts for God; he takes God's part and is true to God. It is as being thus of God that the Spirit confesses that Jesus Christ is come in the flesh. He contemplates, if I may so say, that great fact with all its issues from the divine point of view ; in its bearing on the divine character and nature, the divine government and law. He is " of God " in it; in that fact and in all its issues.

Do I take too great a liberty in speaking thus of the Holy Ghost ? I scarcely think so when I call to mind how this phrase describes Christ's own position in the world with reference to the Father. He was " of God ; " he was so in a very emphatic and significant sense ; not only as regards his origin and mission ; his coming from God and being authorised by God ; but also, and specially, as regards his end and aim all through his humiliation, obedience, and sacrifice. He was " of God ; " on the side and in the interest of God. It was the zeal of God's house that ate him up. It was the doing of God's will, and the finishing of God's work, that was his meat. It was the glorifying of his Father, and the finishing of the work which his Father gave him to do, that ministered to his satisfaction in his last farewell prayer. Of him pre-eminently it might be said : " He is of God." And in his being thus " of God," as to the whole mind and meaning of the phrase, the Holy

Ghost is with him and in him. Jesus Christ come in the flesh is, in this sense emphatically, confessed by the Spirit. The Spirit is with him, and in him, as the Spirit that is of God; and as being to him the Spirit that is of God. He and the Spirit are at one in being both " of God." And you, in the Son and by the Spirit are "of God;" as truly of God as is the Spirit, or as the Son was when God " gave not the Spirit by measure to him."

The essential characteristic of the spirit of antichrist is that it is, in the sense now explained, "not of God." It does not look at the Saviour and the salvation as on the side of God; rather it takes an opposite view, and subjects God to man. It subordinates everything to human interests and human claims; looks at everything from a human and mundane point of view; measures everything by a human standard; submits everything to human opinion; in a word, conceives and judges of God after the manner of man. This, indeed, may be said to be the distinctive feature of all false religions, as well as of all corruptions of the true religion. They exalt man. They consider what man requires, what he would like, what is due to him. Even when they take the form of the most abject and degrading superstition, that is still their spirit. They aim at getting God, by whatever means of persuasion and prostration, to do the bidding of man. For it is the essence of our corrupt human nature, of which these corrupt worships are the expression, to care and consult for self, and not for God. This is the essence of the spirit of antichrist; the spirit that breathes and moves in the false notions that have gained currency in the church respecting " Jesus Christ come in the flesh." Their advocates give man the first place in their scheme. Their real objection lies against those views of gospel truth which assert the absolute sovereignty of God, and put forward pre-eminently what he is entitled to demand,—what, with a due regard to his own character, government, and law, he cannot but demand. They dislike such representations as bring in the element of God's holy name and righteous authority, and lay much stress upon that element, as one of primary consideration in the plan of saving mercy. Hence they naturally shrink from owning explicitly Jesus Christ as come in the flesh to make atonement by satisfying divine justice. They prefer some loose and vague way of putting the fact of his interposition, and the manner of it. Admitting in a sense its necessity, they are unwilling to define very precisely, either the nature of the necessity, or the way in which it is met. He came in the flesh, to redeem the flesh, to sanctify, elevate, and purify it. He came in the flesh, to be one with us, and to make us, in the flesh, one with him. So they speak and think of his coming in the flesh. Any higher aim, any prior and paramount design involved in this great fact, viewed in its relation to the nature and supremacy of God, his holiness and justice, as lawgiver and judge, they are slow to acknowledge. Hence their gospel is apt to be partial and one-sided ; looking rather like an accommodation of heaven and heaven's rights to earth and earth's wishes and ways, than that perfect reconciliation and perfect assimilation of earth to heaven for which we hold it to have made provision ;—our heavenly Father's name being hallowed, his kingdom coming, his will being done, in earth as it is in heaven. Their system is not " of God " as the primary object of consideration ; for they themselves are not out and out, in this sense, " of God."

But "ye are of God, little children," in this matter ; in the view that you take, and the conception that you form of Jesus Christ come in the flesh ; of the end of his coming, and the manner in which that end is attained. You look at that great fact, first and chiefly in its relation to God, and as on the side of God. It is from God and for God that Jesus Christ is come in the flesh. So he always taught; and so you firmly believe. He placed God always first; the glory of God, the sovereignty of God, the will of God, always took precedency. Man's concerns and interests were subordinate to that. Nothing is more conspicuous in "Jesus Christ come in the flesh," throughout his whole ministry, in all his life and in his death, than this loyalty to God his Father, prevailing even over his amazing tenderness and pity for men. He was truly of God, even when his being so might tell against men; tell to their destruction rather than their salvation. He does not shrink from the darkest issues which, in that view, his coming in the flesh carries in its bosom. He did not shrink from them when realised in his own person, and in his personal experience, as the suffering substitute of the guilty. He does not shrink from them as they are to be realised in the persons, and in the personal experience, of those who " will not come unto him that they may have life."

If you are " of God," you are of his mind. You approve of this principle; you recognise the propriety of what is due to God being first attended to and provided for, in preference even to what may be needed by man. What God, being such as he is, must require, since "he cannot deny himself," that is the first question; then, and in subordination to that, what can be done for men. It is a great matter for you to view the whole plan of salvation, as being yourselves, in this sense, "of God." It is your doing so that secures your having overcome all spirits of antichrist. If thus "you are of God," you are already raised to a higher platform than they can occupy, so as to have a loftier and wider range of vision. Your profound reverence for the majesty of God; your loyal, loving recognition of his holy and righteous sovereignty; your deep, admiring esteem of his government and law; your calm conviction that the Lord reigneth; your intense desire that the Lord should reign; your determination, may I say, that the Lord shall reign; lifts you out of the region of human questionings and all doubtful disputations. It is your very humility that lifts you up. You sit at the feet of Jesus Christ come in the flesh. You stand beside his cross. You do not now stumble at the mystery of its bloody expiation; or quarrel with the great propitiation-sacrifice through unbelief of its necessity. The ideas of justice needing to be satisfied; punishment inevitably to be inflicted; one willing to bear it in your stead being found; that one being "Jesus Christ come in the flesh;" do not now offend you. Nay, being "of God," on his side and in his interest in the whole of this great transaction, you can meekly, in faith, commit to him and leave in his hands even the most terrible of those ultimate and eternal consequences, involving the aggravated guilt and final ruin of many, that you cannot but see to be inseparably mixed up with the confession that "Jesus Christ is come in the flesh."

30

THE SPIRIT OF CHRIST IN US GREATER THAN THE SPIRIT OF ANTICHRIST IN THE WORLD

"Ye are of God, little children, and have overcome them: because
greater is he that is in you, than he that is in the world. They are
of the world: therefore speak they of the world, and the world
heareth them. We are of God: he that knoweth God heareth us;
he that is not of God heareth not us. Hereby know we the spirit of
truth, and the spirit of error." 1 John 4:4-6

THE security for our full and final victory over antichrist
and his spirit lies in the emphatic declaration: "Greater is
he that is in you, than he that is in the world." He that
is in you is the Spirit of God; for "hereby we know that
God abideth in us, by the Spirit which he hath given us;"
the Spirit that, being of God, "confesseth that Jesus Christ
is come in the flesh" (iii. 24; iv. 2). He that is in the
world is the spirit of antichrist, "whereof ye have heard
that it should come, and even now already is it in the
world" (iv. 3). Therefore you who "are of God have
overcome them,"—"the spirits," the false prophets, "that
are gone out into the world" (iv. 1). They are of the
world; what they speak is of the world and meets with
the world's acceptance (ver. 5). We, the true teachers, are
of God; what we speak is of God; and meets with the
acceptance, not of him who is not of God, but of him who,
being of God, knows God (ver. 6). By this test the spirit
of truth which is in us is to be distinguished from the spirit
of error that is in them (ver. 6). From whom do we obtain
a hearing?

" Ye are of God ; " and your being of God raises you above the risk of being "seduced by false prophets ; " for it enables you to " try the spirits." " We too are of God." And this is the proof of it,—that our teaching commends itself, not to the world, but to you who know God and are of God. Between you and us there is a blessed harmony ; between your state of mind as you try the spirits, and our teaching as we stand the trial. You who are hearers, are secure in trying the spirits against all false prophets ; for you have overcome them, being yourselves of God. We who are preachers, being of God as you are, have assurance that our spirit, the spirit of our teaching, is the Spirit of truth, when we see the world hearing them, and only you who are of God and know God hearing us. Thus you and we are both safe ; you who try and we who are tried ; you safe from being misled by false prophets, we safe from being confounded with them. And our joint safety lies in both you and us being " of God."

Taken thus, this passage bears closely on a deeply interesting subject ; the self-evidencing power of the gospel of Christ in the hands of the Spirit of God. There is a wonderfully gracious correspondence between the spiritual intelligence of the man who is of God and knows God ; and the spiritual intelligibility and acceptability of the teaching which is of God. The two fit into one another ; the state of mind and heart in the receiver who tests, and the character of what is submitted to him to be tested. You who test, and we who are tested, are in a close and intimate relation to one another. A common quality unites us ; or a common agency ; opening your eyes to try, and fashioning our doctrine for being tried. The same spirit is in you and in us; the Spirit that is " of God " the Spirit of truth.

There is something like this on the other side. There

is the world; and there are the false prophets who are of the world. They are mutually related to one another, precisely as you and we are. What you are to us, that the world is to the false prophets. What we are to you, that they are to it. The world knows its own. The teaching which is of the world commends itself to the world. That teaching, therefore, must be antichristian; for the world is antichristian.

Here, then, are the opposite workings of two opposite powers; and here is the secret of their greatness. For both are great; and both are great, not only in themselves, but in their adaptation to those with whom they have to deal.

I. " He that is in the world is great." And his greatness lies in this, that he operates in a twofold way. He forms and fashions the world spiritually; and he finds for it, or makes for it, appropriate and congenial spiritual food. He creates or moulds the world's appetite for some sort of religious teaching; and he inspires for his own ends the religious teaching that is to suit his world and be accepted by it. Hence his false prophets are sure of their own measure of success; "they are of the world: therefore speak they of the world, and the world heareth them " (ver. 5).

But he cannot succeed with you who are " of God;" for there is one in you who, great as he is, is greater still. And he also operates in a double way. He gives you inwardly spiritual intelligence, spiritual insight and sympathy, to try; and he gives you outwardly spiritual truth to be tried. You are yourselves of God, and therefore competent to judge what we speak. And we too, being of God, speak what cannot be acceptable to the world, but only to him who is of God, and knows God. Thus what you are prepared to apprehend and appreciate, and what we are moved to speak, harmonise and are at one. It is all the doing of "him who dwelleth in you," and of whom "we know," through your acceptance of our teaching, "that he is not the spirit of error, but the Spirit of truth."

Look for a little at the world, and him that is in the world. He is great, undeniably great ; great in power and wisdom ; in command of resources and subtlety in the use of them. He has largely, as to its moral and spiritual tastes and tendencies, the making of the world in which he is, and of which he is the moving soul. The world, in a sense, lives, and moves, and has its being, in him. He is in it as the spring of its activities, the dictator of its laws, the guider of its pursuits and pleasures ; in a word, "the ruler of its darkness." The darkness of its deep alienation from God, he rules. And he rules it very specially for the purpose of getting the world to be contented with an image, instead of the reality, of godliness. For he knows well enough that the world is, and must be, in a sense and after a fashion, religious. He cannot put it off with the "no God" which the fool would fain say in his heart. He is far too sagacious and shrewd to attempt that. What he does attempt is a much more plausible device. He takes advantage of whatever may be the world's mood at the time, as regards God and his worship ; throws himself into it ; controlling or inflaming it, as he may see cause, so as to turn it to his own account. And then he contrives to bring under his sway prophets or teachers ; not always consciously false ; often meaning to be true ; able men ; holy men ; men of God and of prayer ; pre-eminently so it may be. And bringing into contact the world which he has doctored and the doctors whom he has tutored, he adjusts them skilfully to one another. He causes his teachers, perhaps insensibly, to draw much of their inspiration from the particular world which, as to its religious bias, he has influenced with an eye to their teaching. And so "they are of the world ; therefore speak they of the world, and the world heareth them."

Numberless instances and illustrations might be brought forward here ; reaching from the grossest corruptions that have ever disgraced the name of religion, to the most refined forms of ingenious speculation that have ever imposed on the fancy of the most devout enthusiast, or the feelings of the most amiable. They might all, I believe, be explained on the principle now suggested. There is one in the world who is great ; great in a religious point of view ; great in his power and skill to master and manage, from age to age, the world's ever-changing fits and fashions of religiousness ; great in the strange and terrible command he often wields over the most gifted, and even the most godly, of the prophets or teachers who have to deal with them.

Thus, if the world, at his instigation, wants a golden calf, there is an Aaron, under his influence, ready to provide one. If the people, moved by him, will have smooth things spoken to them, he has prophets of smooth things prepared for them. If men are growing weary of the old wine ; and he will be but too glad to make them more weary of it, and help them also to excuses for their weariness ; it shall go hard but he will mix plenty of new wine for their use. It is not he who has to take up the complaint ; nor his agents either ;—" We have piped unto you, and ye have not danced ; we have mourned unto you, and ye have not lamented." He is in and among the crowd of those to whom the children in the market-place are to cry. And the children who are to cry are his ministers. He can prepare the crowd to hear, and move the children to cry, according to his good pleasure ; so that there shall be flock for pastor and pastor for flock; people for priest and priest for people; the times for the teaching and the teaching for the times; all in perfect harmony. Yes; he that is in the world is great; great in his ability to make the world,— the world in the church,—what he would have it to be; great in his ability to find and fit and fashion ministers and agents, who, being of the world, as regards its religious tastes and tendencies, will " speak of the world," and whom, therefore, the " world will hear."

There is, indeed, a power or law of action and reaction between the world and its prophets—the world in the church and its false prophets,—which, as indicating the greatness of him who is in the world, deserves very careful notice. The world in the church, I repeat. For I have nothing to do now,—John here takes nothing to do,—with the world outside of the church, the world of those who do not even profess to be religious; his sole concern is with the church, and the spirits in the church that are to be tried, and the parties that are to try them. Satan, the spirit of antichrist, has within the church a world of his own, a world in which he is, and is great. And he is great in it, very much through his making skilful and sagacious use of this law of action and reaction, between what the world craves and what its false prophets give.

Do you suppose that if you have " itching ears," there will not be found preachers who, catching perhaps unconsciously the contagion from you, will feed and foster the disease? If you incline to a gospel explaining away the atonement, and reducing the incarnation to a mere glorifying of humanity in the mass, instead of its being the redemption, by substitution, of individual men; a gospel of that vague sort will soon be forthcoming. If, in any church or congregation, there springs up a craving for excitement, a demand for novelty, which the old preaching of the cross fails to satisfy; if a certain restless prurience of spiritual taste begins to manifest itself; if a cry or a sigh for gifts and miracles, for signs and wonders, is heard; all experience, all history, proves that it will not be long before men appear who, carried away themselves and led off their feet by the strong tide, will prove apt and able agents in encouraging others to try the virtue of its flowing waves. It is not that they purposely or dishonestly accommodate their teaching and prophesying to the spirit that may be abroad in their world. They drink it in themselves; it intoxicates their own souls. "They are of the world: therefore speak they of the world, and the world heareth them." Truly great is he that is in the world; great in adapting the world and its prophets very perfectly to one another.

II. But "greater is he that is in you, little children," for he is the Lord God Almighty. He is strong; and he "strengthens you with might by his Spirit in the inner man; Christ dwelling in your heart by faith; and you being rooted and grounded in love." He is strong; and he makes you strong; strong in holding fast the form of sound words, and contending earnestly for the faith once delivered unto the saints; strong in cleaving to the truth as it is in Jesus; strong in your real, personal, close, and loving acquaintance with him, "whom to know is life eternal." He who is in you is God; God abiding in you; giving you the Spirit. He is in you; not merely on your side, at your right hand, around you; but within you. He is working in you; so working in you as to secure your safe triumph, in this great fight of truth against error, over the world and him who is in it. And his working in you is of the same sort as is the working of his great antagonist in and among those with whom he is so busy.

He makes you, who are of God, to be men of quick

understanding in the fear of the Lord ; quick to apprehend what they who are of God are moved by him to speak. He takes these two things : the mind or heart of the learner or inquirer who is of God, and what is spoken by the apostle or teacher who also is of God. He adapts them to one another, brings them together, welds them into one. So he insures that what we who are of God speak, however it may be received by the world, shall prove acceptable to you who know God and are of God. He imparts to you, in whom he is, a certain spiritual tact or taste,—call it spiritual intelligence, spiritual insight, spiritual discernment,—by means of which he enables you to recognise, in what you hear or read or remember, the very truth of the true and living God, sanctifying and saving to your own souls. He brings out in you, palpably to your own consciousness, the marvellous correspondence that there is between the heart with which he is inwardly dealing and the word or doctrine which, through the teaching of men of God, he is outwardly presenting. He is in you ; breaking your heart in deep conviction of sin, and then healing the broken heart, oh ! how tenderly, by the sprinkling of atoning blood. He is in you ; causing the commandment so to come home to you that you die, helplessly condemned, under the righteous sentence of the law, and then bringing near to you, oh ! how lovingly, the life-giving assurance that " there is now no condemnation to them that are in Christ Jesus." He is in you ; causing you to see and feel that instead of " being rich and having need of nothing, you are poor, and wretched, and miserable, and blind, and naked," and then pressing upon you, oh ! how graciously, the Lord's affectionate counsel to buy of him " freely," without money and without price, " gold tried in the fire, that you may be rich ; and white raiment, that you may be clothed, and that the shame of your nakedness do not appear ; and to anoint your eyes with eye-salve, that you may see." He is in you; forming you for Christ and forming Christ in you. He is in you; fitting your whole inner man for Christ, and fitting Christ into your whole inner man. He is in you; so as to cause to spring up from the very depths of your spirit a sense of intimate oneness, not to be broken, between you and Christ,—between your highest faculty of belief and thought, and his doctrine, which now "you know to be of God." What precisely the bond of this oneness may be,—in what exactly it consists,—you may not be able to define. Probably, at bottom, it is the recognition in your heart now, as in Christ's doctrine always, of the high and holy sovereignty of God; his just supremacy. It is the joint owning, in your heart and in Christ's doctrine, of the great truth—"The Lord reigneth." But be it what it may, you feel it. And the feeling of it is your assured confidence and satisfying rest.

I cannot now pursue the subject further. Let me simply, in closing, exhort you to consider well in what it is that your security lies, when you are called to try the spirits—what it is that alone can give you certain and decisive victory over the false prophets. It is God being in you; abiding in you; giving you the Spirit. The spirit of antichrist is in the world; in the church's world; in the worldly materials of which, in too large a measure, the church is composed. "Many false prophets are gone out into the world." The spirit of error, as well as the spirit of truth, is abroad; and it may be that sifting, trying, critical days are at hand. What is to be your protection? How are you to be prepared? Let me warn you that it is not head knowledge that will do; not logic, or rhetoric, or philosophy, or theology; not creeds, or catechisms, or confessions; not early training in the soundest manual; not familiarity with the ablest and most orthodox writings; not skill in argument and debate ;—no ; nothing will do but God being in you ; in your heart, your heart of hearts ; God in Christ dwelling in you ; God giving you the Spirit. An experimental assurance alone will keep you safe. But that will keep you safe. For as he that is not of God will not hear us who speak as being of God ; so he that knoweth God will not hear the false prophets. So the Good Shepherd himself assures us. He " goeth before the sheep, and they follow him, for they know his voice ; and a stranger will they not follow, but will flee from him, for they know not the voice of strangers." " My sheep hear my voice, and I know them, and they follow me : and I give unto them eternal life ; and they shall never perish, neither shall any pluck them out of my hand. My Father, which gave them me, is greater than all ; and none is able to pluck them out of my Father's hand. I and my Father are one."

PART THREE

DIVINE FELLOWSHIP—ULTIMATE CONDITION—LOVE
1 John 4:7-5:1

31

LOVE IS OF GOD—GOD IS LOVE

"Beloved, let us love one another : for love is of God ; and every one that loveth is born of God, and knoweth God. He that loveth not knoweth not God ; for God is love. In this was manifested the love of God towards us, because that God sent his only begotten Son into the world, that we might live through him. Herein is love, not that we loved God, but that he loved us, and sent his Son to be the propitiation for our sins." 1 John 4:7-10

LIGHT, Righteousness, Love;—these are the three conditions or elements of that fellowship with the Father and with his Son Jesus Christ in which John would have us to be joint partakers with himself and the other apostles (i. 3). Of the three, Light and Righteousness have been the heads, or leading thoughts, of the two previous parts of this Exposition (iii.–xvii. and xviii.–xxx.) Love is the ruling idea in the third part (xxxi.–xxxiv.) ; love being the end to which the others are means ; the consummation of the fellowship being in love. Hence there has been some anticipation of this last theme, Love, in the two preceding ones, Light and Righteousness ; especially in the latter. For the righteousness meant being chiefly subjective, denoting singleness of eye; uprightness, honesty of purpose, a guileless spirit, truth in the inward parts, necessarily refers to the matters about which it is objectively exercised, the manner of dealing with God in light, and with our fellow-men in love, which it prompts and regulates. Hence that second part, having Righteousness for its key-note, carries on the line of thought begun in the first part under the idea of Light, and encroaches on the line of thought in the third, which brings out the crowning aspect of the whole in Love. Still it is manifestly Love that is now purely and simply the reigning principle.

"Beloved, let us love one another." The distinction of the personal pronouns is here dropped. It was proper when the trying of the spirits by a sort of doctrinal test was the matter in hand. John must then speak of himself and his fellow-teachers in the first person, and to us in the second. Now, however, when love is the test, all are one. It is the trial of the spirits that still is on hand, in pursuance of the intimation formerly given (iii. 24) :—"Hereby we know that God abideth in us, by the spirit which he hath given us." That intimation is connected with the double commandment in the previous verse (23), "that we should believe on the name of his Son Jesus Christ, and love one another, as he has given us commandment." The question is about assurance ; our "assuring our hearts before God ;" our "having confidence toward God ;" our "having boldness in the day of judgment" (iii. 19, 21; and iv. 17). The indispensable condition of this confidence is righteousness, or "our own hearts not condemning us" of insincerity or guile (iii. 20, 21). But though that is an essential preliminary, it is not itself the ground or warrant of the confidence. The real ground or warrant is "our abiding in God and his abiding in us" (iii. 24). But how is this mutual abiding of us in God and of God in us to be ascer-

tained and verified, to the satisfaction of our own consciousness, as a trustworthy ground and warrant of assured
confidence before God? On our part there is "the keeping
of his commandments;" his double "commandment," to
believe on the name of his Son Jesus Christ, and love one
another in obedience to him." On his part, there is "his
giving us the Spirit." And the last is tested by the first.
His giving us the Spirit is not to be lightly taken for
granted. There must be a trial; and the trial is in accordance with the twofold commandment, to believe and to love.
It is first a trial turning upon the confession or denial that
Jesus Christ is come in the flesh (iv. 1-6). It is next a trial
turning on the possession or the want of love (iv. 7-12).
And the result of the trial is announced: "Hereby know
we that we dwell in him, and he in us, because he hath
given us of his Spirit" (iv. 13);—almost in the same terms
in which the trial is, as it were, instituted: "Hereby we
know that he abideth in us, by the Spirit which he hath
given us" (iii. 24).

Thus it plainly appears that these two things,—righteousness in owning the true doctrine concerning Christ and
righteousness in mutual brotherly love,—are closely bound
together. And thus, by a natural and simple transition, the
discourse passes from the first of these topics to the second:
" Beloved, let us love one another."

This exhortation is here enforced both positively and
negatively;—positively, by the statement that "love is of
God," and therefore "every one that loveth is born of God,
and knoweth God" (ver. 7);—negatively, by the opposite
statement: "he that loveth not knoweth not God; for God
is love" (ver. 8).

I. "Love is of God." This does not mean merely that
love comes from God, and has its source in God; that he is

the author or creator of it. All created things are of God, for by him all things were made, and on him they all depend. But love is not a created thing. No doubt, in the heart even of an unfallen intelligence, it may be said to be created, inasmuch as the being in whose heart it dwells is himself created. And in the heart of a fallen man it is in that sense a new creation; for he himself must be created anew or born again if he is to love. Still, the love to which he is created anew or born again is not itself created. It is not of God, as made by him; as a new thing called into existence by the fiat of his word.

In this respect love differs from light. It is not asserted of love as of light : And God said, Let there be love, and there was love. In a higher sense than that, I apprehend, it is true that love, wherever it exists, is of God. It is communicated, not created ; begotten, one might say, not made. It is a divine property, a divine affection. And it is of its essence to be communicative and begetting ; to communicate itself, and, as it were, beget its own likeness. "Love is of God." It is not merely of God, as every good gift is of God. It is of God, as being his own property, his own affection, his own love. It is, wherever it is found, the very love wherewith God loveth. If it is found in me, it is my loving with the very love with which God loves; it is my loving with a divine love, a love that is thus emphatically of God. Hence the sufficiency and certainty of the test : "Every one that loveth is born of God, and knoweth God."

1. None but one born of God can thus love, with the love which, in this sense, is of God ; therefore one who so loves must needs be one who is born of God. This is almost self-evident. If the love in question is not, like any of the constituent parts of the created universe, whether of matter or of mind, a thing made, called into being out of nothing,

or a thing made over again, formed out of chaos into order ;
but part and parcel of the Divine Being himself, of his very
essence : then its existence in me cannot be explained on
any other supposition than that of my being born of him ;
born of him too in a very close and intimate manner ; in a
manner implying that I become "partaker of his nature ; "
" his seed abiding in me." I doubt, therefore, if this love
formed an element in that image of God in which man was
originally created. I take it to be something more. It is
communicated,—it is of God in such a sense that it can be
communicated,—not by creation, but only by generation.
It is not as a creature that I can have it, in virtue of any
mere creative *fiat* or let it be. I can have it only as a Son,
—adopted ?—nay, not adopted only, but begotten. Many
excellent endowments I may have as a mere creature ; endowments reflecting the likeness of God's own attributes ;
intelligence resembling his ; a sense of right and wrong
resembling his ; benevolence and kindliness resembling his.
As to these, God has merely, in creating me, or creating me
anew, to speak and it is done. But this love is something
quite peculiar. It is something, as I take it, different from
the love enjoined in the "royal law,"—"Thou shalt love thy
neighbour as thyself." It is the very love with which the
Father loves, the love manifested in his not sparing his
beloved Son. It is the very love with which the Son loves,
the love proved by his laying down his life for us. That
is the love, the love of the "new commandment," which is
here in question. Respecting that love I think it may be
said that God alone is originally capable of it. Others are
capable of it, only in so far as God communicates himself
to them ; not by a process of mere creative power ; but by
begetting them into participation with himself in his own
very life.

There is one thus eternally begotten ; begotten before all

worlds; the eternal Son of the everlasting Father. He is "God of God; very God of very God; light of light;" nay, rather, love of love. He is the manifestation of this love which is of God;—"In this was manifested the love of God toward us, because that God sent his only begotten Son into the world, that we might live through him." It shines forth in him; not through him, or by him, merely; but in him. God sent his Son to manifest this love. How? Evidently by his showing that he shared it; approving himself to be born of God by himself loving with the love which is of God. God sent his only begotten Son into the world to give us a specimen, an illustration, perhaps the only possible perfect specimen, the only possible perfect illlustration, of "the love which is of God." None but his only begotten Son could be sent to manifest it; for none but he could fully feel it. No created being, not the highest of the elect and unfallen angels, even when perfected by their trial, could adequately feel it. And therefore none of them could manifest it. But the only begotten Son, dwelling from everlasting in the Father's bosom, of one nature with the Father, loves with "the love which is of God." Therefore he is sent to manifest that love. He is sent to manifest a love essentially different from any love of which we are naturally capable, or of which we can naturally form any conception, a love peculiarly and distinctively divine.

Now, as it is his being the only begotten Son of the Father that qualifies him for being sent to manifest the love which is thus "of God," inasmuch as it is that which ensures his feeling it, it is that alone which makes him capable of it; so it is only your being in the Son, being born of God by the Spirit, that can make you capable of this love which is of God, and can ensure your feeling it. None can love with that love which is of God, none can

love as God loves, save only first his only begotten Son,
whom on that very account he sends to manifest this love,
and then you who in him receive the adoption of sons, and
are begotten by the Spirit into participation with the Son
in his filial oneness and sympathy with the Father. Therefore, if we love one another with that love which is of God,
if we love as God loves, we must be born of God. We
must have become his children, his sons; begotten of him
in time, through believing union with the Son who is
begotten of him from eternity; the Spirit making us, as
thus born of God, in the only begotten Son, really "partakers," in respect of this love, "of the divine nature."

2. Being born of God implies knowing God. This consideration still further explains and illustrates the point
before us :—"Every one that loveth is born of God, and
knoweth God." He loves with God's own love, because,
being born of God, he knows God. He knows God, as
none but one born of God can know him. It is a knowledge of God altogether peculiar; belonging exclusively to
the relation constituted by, and realised in, your being
born of God. It is a kind of knowledge of God of which,
as I think, one who is simply a creature of God's hand, a
subject of his moral administration, however intelligent and
however informed, is not really capable. He is not in a
condition, he lacks the capacity, to take it in. He must be
a child, a son, born of God, if he is to have it. For, in a
word, it is the very knowledge of God which his Son has ;
his only begotten Son, whom he sent into the world to
manifest his love. He, being of God, as his only begotten
Son, knows God ; he, and he alone. "No man hath seen
God at any time ; the only begotten Son, which is in the
bosom of the Father, he hath declared him" (John i. 18).
"No man knoweth the Father save the Son, and he to
whomsoever the Son shall reveal him" (Matt. xi. 27). It

is as his only begotten Son that Jesus knows God. And it is as born of God that you know God ; know him even as his only begotten Son knows him. He, as the only begotten Son, knows God ; he knows the love which is of God, of what sort it is ; he has himself, from everlasting, been the object of it ; he has been ever experiencing it. All that is in the great heart of God the Father, the only begotten Son knows intimately, and experimentally, if I may dare to say so. With a filial knowledge he knows God. With filial insight and filial sympathy, he knows all the overflowing of that love which is of God as it gushes forth in deep, full flood, from everlasting, first towards himself, and then through him towards the family of man ; according to his own glorious word, " The Lord possessed me in the beginning of his ways. When he appointed the foundations of the earth, then I was with him as one brought up with him ; and I was daily his delight, rejoicing always before him ; rejoicing in the habitable parts of his earth ; and my delights were with the sons of men " (Prov. viii. 22-31).

Now it is with the same knowledge with which he, as the only begotten Son, knows God, that you, as born of God, know him ; with a knowledge the same in kind, however far short it may come in measure or degree. Yours, like his, is a filial knowledge ; implying filial insight and filial sympathy. Your being born of God makes you capable of this knowledge, and places you in the only position in which you can have it. Born of God, you occupy the very filial position that he who is the only begotten Son occupies ; you have the very filial heart that he has. You are born of the very Spirit of which he, in your nature, was born. You have in you the very Spirit that dwelt, not by measure, in him. Thus, born of God, you are one with him who is his only begotten Son. To you

as to him, to you in him, God is known,—and the love
which is of God is known,—by close personal acquaintance ;
by blessed personal experience. How God loves ; how it
is the manner of God to love ; what sort of love his is ; love
going out of self ; love sacrificing self ; love imparting and
communicating self ; love unsought and unbought ; unconditional and unreserved ;—what kind of being, in respect
of love, God is ; you who are born of God know, even as
the only begotten Son knows. Therefore you can love with
that "love which is of God," even as he loves with that
love which is of God. He and you alone can so love ; for
he that loves as God loves must needs be one who " is born
of God and knoweth God."

II. The opposite statement follows as a matter of
course :—" He that loveth not knoweth not God ; for God
is love." The connecting link here is all-important ; it is
" knowing God ; " all turns on that. Every one that loveth
knoweth God : he that loveth not knoweth not God ; these
are the antagonist statements. The stress of the contrast
is made to rest on knowing or not knowing God ; he who
loveth knoweth God, being born of him ; " he who loveth
not, knoweth not God ; for God is love."

" God is love ; " therefore, not to love is not to know
God. That is a very clear and simple inference. But why
this change ? Why is it said, on the first or positive side
of the dilemma, " Love is of God ; " and on the second or
negative side of it, " God is love " ? Simply because the
question now turns on knowing God ; not anything of God,
but God himself. To love with the love which is of God,
is to know God ; not to love thus, is not to know God ; for
God is love. In this view, the proposition, " God is love,"
really applies to both of the alternative ways of putting the
case ; the positive and the negative alike. It assigns the
reason why it may be said, on the one hand, " Every one

that loveth is born of God, and knoweth God;" and why it may also be said, on the other hand, "He that loveth not knoweth not God."

"God is love." It is a necessity of his nature, it is his very nature, to love. He cannot exist without loving. He cannot but love. He is, he has ever been, love. From all eternity, from before all worlds, God is love. Love never is or can be, never was or could be, absent from his being. He never is or can be God,—he never was or could be God,—without being also love; without loving. I say without loving; actually loving.

For this love, which is thus identified with his very being, is not dormant or quiescent, potential merely, *in posse*, and not *in esse*. Love in God never is, never has been, like a latent germ, needing outward influences to make it spring up; or like a slumbering power, waiting for occasions to call it forth. If it were so, it could not truly be said that in himself, in his very manner of being, "God is love." It is, it has ever been, active, forthgoing, self-manifesting, self-communicating. It is, it has ever been, in exercise. Before creation it is so. In the bosom of the everlasting Father is his eternal, only begotten Son; and with the Father and the Son is the Holy Ghost. So "God is love" before all creation; love in exercise; love not possible merely but actual; love forthgoing and communicative of itself; from the Father, the fountain of deity, to the Son; from the Father and the Son to the Holy Ghost. In creation, this love is seen forthgoing and communicative in a new way towards new objects. The love which from everlasting has been in exercise evermore within the mysterious circle of the Three-One God; which especially has been evermore passing from the Father to his only-begotten Son; now seeks and finds new means of manifesting itself among created beings. It is still really

the same love. For all creation is the manifestation of
God's love to his only begotten Son. He "made all things
by him and for him." He has "appointed him to be heir
of all things." Specially when that wondrous council was
held in heaven from whence issued the decree, "Let us
make man in our image, after our likeness," this love was
manifested. The only begotten Son is to be the first born
among many brethren. Not, however, by creation merely
is that end to be reached; another manifestation of this
same love must intervene. Created innocence is not enough
to secure the issue on which God's heart of love is set; for
created innocence may and does give way. Sin enters, and
death by sin; all sin, and all are doomed. Still "God is
love;" the same love as ever. And "in this now is manifested the love of God towards us, because that God sent
his only begotten Son into the world, that we might live
through him. Herein is love, not that we loved God, but
that he loved us, and sent his Son to be the propitiation for
our sins."

It is, I say, the same love still; the love which from
everlasting goes forth from God to his only begotten Son
dwelling in his bosom, the love which in the beginning of
creation goes forth in God's making all things by and for
his only begotten Son, and especially making godlike men
to be his brethren; it is the very same love that goes forth
in God's sending his only begotten Son into the world that
we might live through him; sending his Son to be the
propitiation for our sins. It is wondrous love; love passing
knowledge; love of which God alone is capable; love
proper to his great heart alone. It is not such love as we
may feel to him; for "herein is love, not that we have
loved him, but that he has loved us." He has loved us
with the very love which is his own essential nature; which
has been going forth from everlasting, self-manifesting, self-

communicating, from the Father to his only begotten Son, by the Spirit; and has been going forth in time, through his only begotten Son, by the same Spirit, to the world of creation at first, and now also to the world that is to be saved.

This is its crowning glory; the saving mission from God of his only begotten Son. It is consummated in our " living through him," through his " being the propitiation for our sins." For now, effectual atonement being made for our guilt, our redemption and reconciliation being righteously and therefore surely effected by his being the propitiation for our sins; we, living through him, are his brethren indeed. The love wherewith God loves him dwells in us. God loves us even as he loves him. And so at last the love which, from all eternity, it is of the very nature of God's essential being to feel and exercise, finds its full fruition in the " mighty multitude of all kindreds, and peoples, and nations, and tongues, who stand before the throne and give glory to him who sitteth thereon and to the Lamb for ever and ever."

If this is anything like a true account of the sense in which, and the effect to which, it is said that " God is love," the statement becomes almost axiomatic,—" He that loveth not knoweth not God." The fact of his not loving plainly proves that he knows not God; and his not knowing God explains and accounts for the fact of his not loving. How indeed can he know God; know him as being love? To know God thus, as being love, implies some measure of congeniality, sympathy, and fellowship. I cannot so know him if there is still a great gulf between him and me; between his heart and my heart; his nature and my nature. There must be community of heart and nature between him and me; I must be " born of God."

We thus come back to the previous positive declaration:

" Love is of God ; and he that loveth is born of God and knoweth God." And we see what manner of love it is that must be the test of our being born of God, how it is that we are to love one another. We are to love with the love which is of God, the love which is his nature. We are to love as he loves; to love all whom he loves ; and to love them with his own love.

First and chiefly, we are to love, as he loves his only begotten Son. Our thus loving him is one primary criterion and touchstone of our being born of God. So he himself intimates when he says to the Jews,—" If God were your Father ye would love me " (John viii. 42). There would be this feature of family resemblance, this community of heart and nature, between him whom you claim as your Father and you who say you are his children, that you would love me because he loves me, and love me as he loves me ;—love me as sent by him to be the Saviour of the world. Hence the force of that awful apostolic denunciation ; " If any man love not the Lord Jesus Christ, let him be anathema maranatha."

Then we are to love, as God loves it, and because God loves it, the world which he sent his Son to save. We are to love thus one another ; with what intensity of longing, like God's own longing and yearning, for one another's salvation, that all may turn and live ; and with what intensity of delight in all who are really in Christ, who "live through him," and live so as to be indeed our brethren and his, ours because they are his !

32

LOVE GOING FORTH TOWARDS WHAT IS SEEN

" Herein is love, not that we loved God, but that he loved us, and sent
his Son to be the propitiation for our sins. Beloved, if God so loved
us, we ought also to love one another. No man hath seen God at
any time. If we love one another, God dwelleth in us, and his love
is perfected in us."   1 John 4:10-12

THERE is very close and compressed reasoning here. The
steps in the process, the links in the chain, are not all
patent or obvious on the surface; some intermediate bonds
of connection need to be supplied. Thus, the assertion
(ver. 12), " No man hath seen God at any time," seems
intended to answer by anticipation a question that might
be put, as to the omission of love to God in the preceding
verse (ver. 11). Otherwise it is, so far as one can see,
irrelevant. " Beloved, if God so loved us, we ought also
to love "—God;—that is what we might naturally expect
to be the logical inference ; but it is not so; it is " we
ought also to love one another." And why ? " Because
no man hath seen God at any time." Therefore, love to
one another is made the test of " God dwelling in us."
And it is so, all the rather, because it is " the perfecting of
his love in us " (ver. 12).

Two general principles are here indicated as regards
this divine love ; I. It must have a visible object ; or, in
other words, it must be real and practical, and not merely
ideal and sentimental.   II. It is thus not only proved but
perfected ; it has its free course and is consummated.

I. Love, if it is to be a sufficient and satisfactory test of our "knowing God and being born of God," must have a visible object; it cannot otherwise be verified to our own consciousness as real. In a sense, it may be said even of God's own love, the love which is his nature, that it thus verifies as well as manifests itself. It goes forth towards created beings; it seeks created beings towards whom it may go forth. A visible created universe is its object: and so also, in a peculiar manner and degree, is a visible new created church. Only in its exercise toward such objects can its true character, its communicative and self-sacrificing character, be thoroughly brought out.

It exists, no doubt, and is in exercise, before all creation, the first creation as well as the new. In the mystery of the Trinity, in the ineffable fellowship of the three persons in the one divine essence, from everlasting, "God is love." There is love; felt love; inconceivable mutual complacency; love in exercise, mutually interchanging and reciprocating endearments;—there is such love implied in the very nature of God as Father, Son, and Holy Ghost. In particular, from before all worlds, the Father thus, in the Spirit, loves the Son, "dwelling in his bosom." But it is love, however exercised, that is resting and not giving; it is the repose rather than the activity of love. If it is to be manifested as a love that gives, that is active, that actually magnifies or benefits its object, it would seem that there must be creation.

Indeed it is only in creation that the Son himself can become practically the object of this love. If God, because of his love to him, has "appointed him to be heir of all things," the "all things" of which he is to be "heir" must be made; made by him and for him. There must be "goings forth" on his part from the Father; there must be, on the Father's part, "the bringing in of the first

begotten into the world." Then, and only then, when he
appears as " the beginning of the creation of God," " the
first born of every creature," is the Son in a position in
which he can receive gifts from the Father, or in which he
can have bestowed on him the inheritance of all things.
The Father's love to him may now take the form of bountifulness, liberality, lavish giving; it may now express itself
in deeds. And, overflowing from him to the creatures
called into being by his hand and for his sake, especially
to those who, being made in God's image, can know his
nature, this divine love finds vent in those tender mercies
which are over all his works. So, in the beginning of the
creation, God in his Son loved the goodly universe of which
his Son had become the head; with a love to him and to
it that could never weary of bestowing favours. So, when
this earth was made, in whose habitable parts the Son as
the eternal Wisdom rejoiced; and when this race of ours
was formed, the sons of men, with whom were his delights :
" God saw everything that he had made, and behold it was
very good." His love then filled our cup of innocent and
pure happiness to the brim, if only we had been content to
hold it straight.

Thus, for a season, one quality of the love which is
God's nature, which God is,—its simple bountifulness, its
being " ready to distribute, willing to communicate,"—had
room to expatiate, and if I may dare to say so, to indulge
and enjoy itself, in the teeming earth, and in man, its godlike proprietor and lord, for whom he bade it bring forth
all its fulness.

But there is a quality of this love for which that first
creation provided no outlet; a quality more wonderful than
all its bountifulness; the quality for whose exercise the fall
gave occasion. To creatures innocent and pure, God, for
the love he has to his Son, by whom and for whom they

are made, may give all sorts of good things, the good things
with which earth is stored, and better things still if they
will but obey his word. To guilty creatures alone can he
" give his Son to be the propitiation for their sins."

Still, however, it is now as always to the visible creation,
to what he sees and whom he sees, that God's love goes
forth in exercise. The objects of it are seen.

Seen! And how seen? Can it be said now, "God
saw everything that he had made, and behold it was very
good"? To bless and benefit a world and a race seen by
him in that light, might be almost said to be self-gratifica-
tion, rather than self-sacrifice. But it comes to be self-
sacrifice when its objects are seen to be corrupt and vile;
guilty and deserving only of wrath; polluted and unclean;
with nothing to attract, but everything to repel; alike
unloving and unlovely. To continue to love creatures thus
seen;—not only so, but to love them with a love that does
not spare his own Son,—a love that, when law and justice
demand a victim, will rather that he should be the victim
than they;—that is a manner of love implying something
else and something more than bountifulness. And that is
God's manner of love to those whom he now sees, to " the
world lying in wickedness."

Now our "loving him whom we have not seen," never
could be a test of our having in us this " love which is of
God." If the thing to be proved is the identity, in kind or
nature, of our love and God's love :—its being with the very
same love with which he loves that we also love;—that
never can be proved by an appeal to our love to him. It
must turn upon the consideration of his love to the world,
and the likeness of our love to that.

Mark here only one point of difference between God's
love to us and any love we may have to him; look at the
object in either case. On our part, when we love God, the

object is the all-good, the all-amiable. Nay, more. It is the God who "first loved us." When he loves us, he loves the evil, the unamiable. And he loves us with a love which does not grudge the surrender of his own beloved Son to our state and our doom, that we in his Son may become acceptable and well-pleasing in his eyes. Even if, therefore, our love to God were all that could be desired, all that could be looked for, all that our knowledge of his glorious excellency and our experience of the riches of his grace might well be expected to call forth; still it would not suffice for proof that our love is God's love; that we love with the love which is of God; that we love as he loves.

This accordingly seems to me to be the true sense and import of that statement of the apostle, often misunderstood, which, however, when rightly apprehended is very suggestive: "Herein is love, not that we loved God, but that he loved us, and sent his Son to be the propitiation for our sins." One is apt to think that there is here a disavowal or denial of our love to God altogether; in which case the reference must be to our unconverted state. Or else it must be such a disparagement of our love to God, even in our converted state, as would represent it to be nothing in comparison with his love to us. Both of these thoughts are no doubt true. But I am persuaded that there is a deeper meaning in the statement; more appropriate to the context; more to the purpose of the argument. It is assumed that we love God. And much is made of that, as we may soon see, in what follows. But it is not our loving God, however sincerely and warmly, that can prove our love to be the same with his. Were we loving him even as the angels love him, were we loving him even as the Son loves him, that would not suffice. It would still be love on our part of a very different sort from that love of his;

having a very different kind of object, and acting in a very different way. The Son himself proved his oneness with the Father, in respect of the love now in question, by his voluntarily coming to seek and to save the lost. The angels prove theirs by the " joy that there is among them over one sinner that repenteth," and by their being " all ministering spirits, sent forth to minister for them who shall be heirs of salvation."

" Herein then is love," " the love which is of God," the love whose reproduction in us is to be tested ;—" not that we have loved God,"—which, thanks to his grace, we do ; not by that, even though it were all that it ought to be, which, alas ! it is far from being ;—" but that he loved us ;" that he loved us when we were yet sinners ; that he saw us then, and pitied us, and " sent his Son to be the propitiation for our sins." That is the model, the exemplar, the pattern, of the love which is to test our being "born of God."

Two things are thus apparent. In the first place, this love in us, if it is to verify itself as being God's very love, must be love, not to the unseen but to the seen ; to a world that is seen ; to men and women in it that are seen ; to one another, to our brethren, to our fellow-men, as seen. And, moreover, it must be love to them, seen by us as God sees them. The objects of love must be the same to us as to God ; and seen to be the same ; seen in the same light ; from the same point of view. " No man hath seen God at any time ; " but God has always seen, and always sees, every man ; he has seen, and sees you. And, seeing you such as you are, he has loved you. Do you love your brother, your neighbour ; seeing him, I do not say as God sees him, but as God has seen and sees you when he loves you ? There must be identity in the object of this common love, God's and yours ; you and he must love the same object, the same person. But that is not all. He is, both to God and to you, visible ; he is seen. And as seen by God and by you he must be the same ; the same in your eyes, in your judgment, in your esteem, as he is in God's. Or, as I have hinted, it may serve the same purpose, and be more profitable, to put the matter thus : he must be seen by you as you are seen by God when he loveth you. He must be the same in your eyes, in your judgment, in your esteem, as you are in God's. That will do as well.

Who is it who is the object of your love? One seen, of course. But is he seen by you with God's eye, or with the world's eye ; or with the eye of your own natural prepossession, your own natural liking? I am far from saying that this last kind of love is always necessarily wrong. But it is not " the love which is of God ; " which identifies you as " born of God, and knowing God." Is he to you what he is to God? He must be either one whom God with most intense compassion pities, and yearns in his inmost bowels to save ; or one whom God welcomes and embraces, not because he is naturally amiable, but because in him the Son of his love sees of the travail of his soul and is satisfied. In either view, is he the same to you that he is to God?

But I must press the question further. Does what you see in your fellow-men cool or quench your love to them, more than what God sees in them cools or quenches his love to them? All that is unattractive, all that is unamiable, all that is repelling in them is seen by him as well as by you ; seen by him infinitely better than by you. Does it affect him as it affects you? Does it hinder him from loving them, as it seems to hinder you? Still further I must press the question. Is it the same thing, or the same sort of thing, seen in them, which draws God's love to them, that commends them also to your love? What is that? Either it is the misery, be it splendid or squalid, of a doomed soul, or it is the broken heart of a child of God. These call forth the love of God ; these alone ; these always. Do they always call forth yours ? Wherever a sinner still in his sin is seen, does your heart go forth towards him in earnest longing and striving for his salvation, as does the heart of God ? When the poor prodigal returns, and is clasped in forgiving arms, is your sympathy with the loving father or with the jealous brother ? Or, to bring the question home again to your personal experience, is it because you see other men as God sees you that you love them ? You see them, too many of them, alas ! in the same state and of the same character that were yours when God seeing you loved you ; polluted, as you were polluted ; perishing, as you were perishing. Do you love them on that account, as on that account God loved you, when he had pity upon you ? Again, you see them, some of them, like yourselves now, by his grace, dear in God's sight as his ransomed and saved ones. Do you love them on that account, as on that account God loves you ?

For, secondly, this love in us must be the same with God's love, in respect of its character, as well as in respect of its objects. It must be what we have seen that that love is, communicative and self-sacrificing. Our love to God cannot be of that nature. We cannot impart anything of ours to him ; we cannot sacrifice anything of ours for him ; he is beyond the reach of any loving offices of that sort from us. "He is our Lord ; our goodness reacheth not to him." If our love is his love, it must be proved to be so by its going forth in active service, not to him whom we cannot see, but to those whom we do see ; God's creatures, to whom his own love goes forth ; the love manifested in creation's bounties, the love manifested in redemption's grace,—in his "sending his Son to be the propitiation for our sins."

And here, in point of fact, is the real practical test. Love, when its exclusive object is unseen, is sometimes apt to become ideal, shadowy, and merely sentimental. Even when God himself is, or is imagined to be, its object, it has not unfrequently taken that form and aspect. Meditative musing on the nature of God, the rapt gaze of solitary contemplation, the fixed eye of secluded devotion filling itself with great thoughts of the divine majesty, excellency, and beauty, has had the effect of begetting in the soul a certain mingled emotion of solemn awe and melting tenderness, which is apt to pass for divine love. It is akin to the feeling which the hero or the victim of an affecting tale may call forth ; though deeper far and more intense. In real life, in church history, this kinship has been but too terribly exemplified. Love to God has been spiritualised and sublimated, as it were, into a passion ; such a passion as may, and must, end in one of two ways ; either in a sort of mystical and rapturous absorption of the human in the divine, or in a still more dangerous substitution of the human for the divine.

But, short of that extreme, there are tendencies against which sensitive natures, of an emotional and impulsive character, must be on their guard. There is the tendency to put imagination in the room of reality. For instance, it is far easier to smile or weep over a narrative that must consist of the sayings and doings of unseen, because imaginary, actors and sufferers, than to go out among the real parties in life's drama, and meet in close contact their actual cases. Hence the meaning, in another view of it, of this solemn intimation, brought in at this stage, and in this connection : " No man hath seen God at any time." There is, there can be, no safe way of proving that we are born of God and know God, except our loving what is seen. No love to the unseen can suffice ; nay, love to the unseen alone may almost be made too much of; it may become deceptive and delusive, or unwholesome and unsafe. Our love, if it is to be God's very love in us, must be love like his, to what is seen by both alike; to real, actual, living men, seen by us as by him. In that channel, our love to the unseen may always safely run. For—

II. In this human love, in our thus loving one another, the divine love has its consummation or perfection. "If we love one another, God dwelleth in us, and his love is perfected in us."

It is a very solemn position which we are thus called to occupy. In us God's love is to be perfected. We are to be the means of its being perfected; the instruments and agents in effecting that result. Not only so. In us it takes end; in us it is finished. Nothing beyond us remains; no chance, no opportunity, of any manifestation of God's love, that can be at all available for the world lying in wickedness. That love has reached us, and it should, through us, reach the whole world. If not, it cannot otherwise avail. "His love is perfected in us."

There is indeed another sense in which these words may be understood. They may mean that God's love, the love which is of God, the love which is his very nature, reproduces itself in us perfectly, only when, with his own very love, we love one another. That is true. But the inspired meaning here is, I think, somewhat deeper. It seems to indicate that our love to one another, if it is indeed of the same sort with his love to us, the love manifested in his sending his Son to save us, is really on his part the last act, the crowning or final exercise, of his love. It is as if he told us that his love was exhausted in begetting or reproducing itself in us. And it may well be so. No higher instance of love is possible than his sending his Son; no stronger sort of love can be imagined. And if that very love passes from him to us; having the same objects and cherishing towards them the same affection; if we love one another as God loves us; is not his love perfected in us? What more can be done to let it have "its perfect work"?

Ah, then, what responsibility is ours! What an office or duty is laid upon us! To perfect, to complete, the manifestation of God's love for the saving of the world! Through us, his love, the very love manifested in his sending his Son to be the propitiation for our sins, is to pass on to our fellow-men. We are, as it were, in his stead. Nay, he is himself in us. He who is love dwelleth in us; he who dwelleth in us is love. It is not so much we who love, as God who loveth in us. It is his own very love that has now in us its full expression, if we love as he is love. It is ours to see to it that it is and shall be so.

The subject is not ended; but I pause, and offer some practical inferences that may well be pondered.

1. Very plainly the love to one another here enjoined is of such a sort that none but a child of God can be capable of it, or can feel it. None other, in fact, can comprehend what it is. We must first be ourselves the receivers of it, before we can be the dispensers or transmitters of it; before it can have its perfect work in us towards others. We must be taught by the Spirit to know what we are, as seen by God, when we are the objects of his love; what we are, in his sight, when he loves us with a saving love. We must be made by the Spirit experimentally to feel what manner of love it is that, instead of being repelled, is attracted, by our unloveliness; that instead of smiting us, lays the stroke on his own beloved Son; that now, in him, lavishes on us all saving benefits and blessings. This then clearly is our first concern; to

see to it that this love of God is really ours ; embraced by us ; apprehended and appropriated by us ; enjoyed by us richly.

2. This love which is of God, when perfected in us, must contemplate its objects in the same light in which they are seen by God. It is comparatively easy to love the lovable, to love them that love us. If we look only at men's amiable qualities, if we surround ourselves with a circle of friends, all decent, worthy, and upright ; if, shutting our eyes to what they are before him who searches the heart, and judging according to the outward appearance, we perceive only what is fair and charming in their winning ways ; if, in a word, keeping out of view their spiritual state and character, we dwell exclusively on their natural gifts and graces ;—if it is thus that we love them, our love is not God's love perfected in us. For to be God's love perfected in us, our love must see its objects as God's love sees its objects. What we see in them of guilt and sin, of enmity against God and insubordination to his law, must be offensive to us as it is to him. Men estranged from God, whatever may be their other excellencies, must be to us what they are to God. Then, and only then, can we test the identity of our love with God's love. Then, and only then, can we have some idea of what it is to love those whom God loves, with his own very love ; his love, not of indifference to evil or complacency in evil, but of deep compassion to the evil-doer and earnest longing that he may be saved.

Hence the Lord says, " Love your enemies, do good to them that hate you, pray for them that despitefully use you and persecute you." In that way, and only in that way, can we prove ourselves, by our family likeness, to be the children of our heavenly Father. So are we perfect, in this way of loving ; according to the command : " Be ye therefore perfect, even as your Father which is in heaven is perfect."

For it is not absolute or general perfection that is here meant ; perfection in the wide and universal sense of that term. The command, so understood, would be irrelevant as well as impracticable. It is perfection or completeness, thorough simplicity and uprightness, as regards the particular grace referred to ; according to a use of the word very common in the Old Testament Scriptures. The perfection indicated is the perfection of honesty or righteousness in loving our "seen," as God loves his "seen;" loving our enemies with the very love with which our Heavenly Father loved us when we were his.

33

LOVE THE MEANS OF MUTUAL INDWELLING; GOD IN US AND WE IN GOD

"Hereby know we that we dwell in him, and he in us, because he hath given us of his Spirit. And we have seen and do testify that the Father sent the Son to be the Saviour of the world. Whosoever shall confess that Jesus is the Son of God, God dwelleth in him, and he in God. And we have known and believed the love that God hath to us. God is love; and he that dwelleth in love dwelleth in God, and God in him." 1 John 4:13-16

THE statement, "Hereby know we that we dwell in him, and he in us, because he hath given us of his Spirit," carries us back to a previous statement (iii. 24), "Hereby we know that he abideth in us, by the Spirit which he hath given us." We are thus reminded of the scope and design of the whole passage. The question is about the mutual indwelling of God in us and of us in God; and more particularly about his abiding in us. How are we to know this? By the Spirit which he hath given us, is the answer. But that raises another question. Every spirit is not to be believed; there must be a trial of the spirits. By what test or tests are they to be tried? How is the Spirit that is of God to be distinguished from the spirit of antichrist? First, by his confessing in us that Jesus Christ is come in the flesh (ver. 2–6); and secondly, by our loving, with the love which is of God (ver. 7–12). And now, connecting the two, John brings us back substantially to the original statement, as to our knowing that we dwell in God, and

God in us, because he has given us of his Spirit. For the two tests are now brought closely together, and shown to be not so much two as one; or at least not two independent tests, each separately valid in itself, but so intimately related to one another that they mutually involve one another, and thus combine together to make up one cogent and irrefragable proof. It is this virtual unity of the two tests that forms the theme or subject of the verses now before us.

I. The first of the two tests is recapitulated : " We have seen and do testify that the Father sent the Son to be the Saviour of the world ; whosoever shall confess that Jesus is the Son of God, God dwelleth in him, and he in God" (ver. 14, 15). There is a slight difference here from the language of the second verse ; and the difference is evidently designed. It is intended to impregnate, if I may so speak, and vivify the truth confessed, with the love whose origin and nature John has been unfolding. The two ideas,—his being " sent" to be " the Saviour of the world," and "his being the Son,"—are evidently suggested by what has been said of that divine love in the intermediate verses (ver. 9, 10).

It is interesting in this view, to trace the growth and development of the thought. The confession which is to be the sign of its being the Spirit that is of God, or the Spirit of truth, that we receive, is first put as if it were the mere acknowledgment of a bare historical fact. It is much more by implication ; but, so far as the actual expression goes, it is not anything more. But see to what fulness of warm gushing life it has now attained. And how? It has been passing through an atmosphere of love, and has thus got to be impressed with a certain teeming warmth and quickening power. What is to be confessed, when we first look at it and lay it aside, might seem to be, so far as the mere wording of it is concerned, scarcely more significant and affecting than the notice of a birth, or any other common fact, of which we read in old annals, or in the current news of the day. Now, when we take it up to look at it again, after it has been steeped in the rich dew of heaven's love, it glows and is instinct with meaning. "Jesus Christ is come in the flesh;" come to be "the Saviour of the world;" come as "the Son, whom the Father hath sent;"—that is the full confession now.

Hence the real reason of that first test, and of its being so closely interwoven with the other. How should the confession of a mere matter of fact be so certain a token of God's "giving us of his Spirit," and of his "dwelling in us"? For it is a simple matter of fact, to be known and ascertained like other ordinary facts in history; to be received on the very same ground and warrant of historical evidence and testimony. The apostle admits as much, both before (i. 1-3) and now (iv. 14). You have our testimony for it; and our testimony may be relied on; "That which we have seen and heard declare we unto you;" "We have seen and do testify" what we ask you to confess. The question therefore recurs: How should my confessing a mere and simple matter of fact, especially considering that, however wonderful it may be, I have it attested to me by sufficient evidence, prove that "God giveth me of his Spirit," and so "dwelleth in me"?

The answer must be found in the character of the fact or truth confessed; or in the aspect in which it is presented, or presents itself to me. What is it in itself? What is it to me? If it is a fact or truth of a merely historical sort, and is so apprehended by me, my admission and avowal of it will be no proof or presumption of God's having "given me of his Spirit, and dwelling in me," any more than my admission and avowal of any well-attested event that ever happened in the world. That may be my case; if so, it is a sad one. It may be to me a mere fact or truth of history; not only in its original form, naked and bald, " Jesus Christ is come in the flesh;" but even in the more warm and living substance which it takes, when it is, as it were, clothed upon with the love which is from heaven. For whatever can be stated in words about that love, and the measure and the manifestation of it, can all be comprehended by the natural understanding. I can put it all in propositions intelligible enough to myself and others; and I can honestly accept these propositions, and confess my acceptance of them. But it may be head-work and not heart-work with me after all. So long as it is so, it is my work merely; the work of my own mind, not of the Spirit. For his work is mainly in the heart. It is spirit dealing with spirit; not mere intellect dealing with intellect. It is God's Spirit dealing intimately and lovingly with my spirit, and that too upon a special theme; a specific subject; " Jesus Christ come in the flesh," as " the very Son of God, sent by the Father to be the Saviour of the world."

Now if God thus communes with me, his Spirit with my spirit, not mind with mind merely, but heart with heart, upon this special theme or subject; if the fact of Jesus Christ having come in the flesh thus starts from the page of history, and fixes and rivets itself in my inner man, becoming part and parcel of my most inward experience; if, in short, the truth comes home to me, as not simply, a historical event, but, as it were, a honey-filled bee, full fraught with all the love that is in the Father's heart of hearts and is poured out in the saving mission of his Son; —if I take this in, and let this heaven-laden bee pierce me, and fill the wound it makes with what itself is full of;— love, this love of God;—then I have something to confess,

which may well be an evidence of " God's having given me
of his Spirit, and so dwelling in me." Yes ! I may humbly
appropriate the Lord's words to Peter ; " Blessed art thou,
Simon Barjona ; for flesh and blood has not revealed this
to thee, but my Father which is in heaven."

II. The second test is thus in large measure anticipated,
and all but swallowed up, in the first. The confession of
truth is now seen to be identical with the sense and experience of love : " We have known and believed the love that
God hath to us. God is love ; and he that dwelleth in love
dwelleth in God, and God in him " (ver. 16.) " We have
known and believed." This is quite John's manner ; to
unite in one knowledge and faith ; we have intelligently
believed ; we have believingly understood. We have thus
known and believed " the love that God hath to us ;"—or
rather, " the love which God hath in us."* For the expression is very peculiar and emphatical; and, as used here,
can scarcely mean anything else than that his love to us
has become his love in us ; and that we have known and
believed it as such. Of course it is his love to us ; but it
is his love to us, transferred, as it were, or transplanted,
from the gospel, where it is a matter of revelation from
without, to our own hearts, where it becomes a moving
principle and power from within. There, in the gospel, it
is his love manifested to us : here, in our hearts, it is his
love actually existing in us ;—not merely felt by us as his
love to us ; but felt by us as his love in us ;—in us, so truly

---

* This is the literal rendering in the verse before us (16), as it is also
in a previous verse (9). There perhaps it can be more easily explained
than here as meaning merely God's love to us ; though even there more
may be implied. In both verses an indefinite mode of rendering the
phrase may be adopted—" his love in regard to us," or " with respect to
us." But that is not satisfactory in either case; certainly not in that
now in question. What we are said to have known and believed is God's
love ; his manner of loving. And we know and believe it as having it, in
some real sense, in us.

and literally in us, that we become the conscious store-
keepers or depositories of it, as it were, and the dispensers
of it to others who are as much its objects as we are ourselves. The love of God, having us for its objects, passes
from God's outer record into our inner life. It enters into
us; it finds access to the innermost recesses of our moral
and spiritual being; it is therefore now "the love which
God has in us." He pours into us, he puts and plants in
us, his own love. He has it in us; his own very love;
reproduced by himself in us; communicated, if one may
dare to say so, by himself, from his own heart to ours. It
is the love of which we ourselves, in the first instance, are
the objects; of which it was our first relief and joy, when
we were convinced of sin, to find ourselves the objects. It
is the love of which, when all but despairing, we laid
trembling hold, and of which we are still fain to lay hold
continually;—not love to the holy, the pure, the penitent,
the believing, the chosen; but love to the world as such,
of which we are part; love to men as sinners, "of whom I
am chief." But that love is in us now. "God has it in
us." It is not merely that we have it in us, as a ground of
confidence for ourselves; God has it in us as on his behalf
a treasury of love available for others. It is in us,—not
merely as what we ourselves grasp and count to be all our
salvation, but as what springs up in us, and is outgoing
towards others; being thus God's own very love, dwelling
and working in our whole inner man. That, I am persuaded, and nothing short of that, is the great thought
involved in these wondrous words, "we have known and
believed the love that God hath in us." Not only have we
known and believed his love, so as to apprehend and
appropriate it, as it comes from without and from above;
—not only so as to take it and make it available for our
own spiritual life and comfort; but also, and especially, so

as to imbibe it;—to drink it into the very essence of our renovated nature, our renewed selves. In us who know it and believe it, God has his own love in actual existence and in active exercise.

Herein lies that community of nature between God and us which the Spirit works or effects. Love is God's nature; "God is love" (ver. 16). Again that great truth is here proclaimed. And, as it would seem, it is now proclaimed again for the purpose of bringing out what it is of God that we can share with him; that he can "have in us." Much there is about God that must continue always altogether incommunicable to us; much that must remain for ever outward and objective to us, and never can become inward and subjective in us. All that pertains to him as lawgiver, ruler, judge,—all that he is as, seated on the throne of his high majesty and universal empire, he carries on the government of the universe,—is and must be exclusively his own; it is only in a very secondary sense, and in a very subordinate capacity, that we can have any of his authority delegated to us when, besides dealing with us as his subjects, he uses us as his ministers. But it would seem to be otherwise with his holiness and his love. Paul speaks of our being made "partakers of his holiness;"— John speaks of "the love he has in us." The two indeed are one, for his holiness is loving and his love is holy. His holy love therefore is not incommunicable; it passes from him to us. Not only are we its objects; more than that; it begets itself anew, if one may say so, in us. It is God's very love, his holy love, in us, and it is to be known and believed, to be felt and manifested, by us accordingly.

What is this but our "dwelling in love" (ver. 16), in God's own love? Love; the holy love of God; of the Father sending the Son to be the Saviour of the world; is now the habitual home of our hearts. We remain, we abide, we stay in it. We would not quit it, or let it go; we cannot, for it alone is our peace. Away from that love; that holy love; that love with all its holiness; reaching us and saving us, the most worldly of the world, the very chief of sinners; what hope, what health, can we have? Neither can we quit it, or let it go, as a principle of life and activity, going out from ourselves to others. If it is to be God's love to us, known and believed by us, for our own peace and comfort and holy spiritual quickening; it must be God's love in us, his own love, which "he has in us," known and believed by us for outward use, as well as for inward assurance and rest. Only in so far as we constantly realise this love of God, both as the love he has to us and as the love he has in us, do we really dwell in love. But dwelling thus in this love, we do indeed dwell in God. For God is this love; and as such he dwelleth in us. In respect of this love, of which we are now both the grateful receivers and the glad transmitters, there is a blessed oneness between God and us. He dwells in this love; for he is love; and we now dwell in this love also. It becomes our nature, as it is his, thus to love. Therefore this love is the bond of union between him and us;—the meeting-place, the habitation, the home, in which we dwell together; he in us and we in him. This love, this holy love, is that which God and we may have in common. And therefore it is the element or quality in respect of which there may be mutual indwelling of us in God and of God in us.

Hence the two tests of God's "giving us of his Spirit and dwelling in us," coalesce, as it were, and become essentially one. To confess, on the testimony of the apostles as eye-witnesses, that the Father sent the Son to be the Saviour of the world (ver. 14); that Jesus is the Son of God (ver. 15); and to know and believe the love that God has to us and in us (ver. 16); is really one and the same thing. For the confession is not the cold assent of the understanding to a formal article in a creed. It is the warm and cordial embracing of the Father's love, incarnate in the Son whom he sends to be the Saviour of the world. It is the letting into our hearts of the love which is God's nature ; for God is love. It is our dwelling with him in love. For, as Paul teaches, in entire and perfect harmony with John ;—"In Christ Jesus neither circumcision availeth anything, nor uncircumcision availeth anything, but faith which worketh by love ;" faith confessing Christ ; faith knowing and believing the love that God has in us ; faith loving as it sees and feels that God himself loves.

34

THE BOLDNESS OF PERFECTED LOVE

" Herein is our love made perfect, that we may have boldness in the day
of judgment : because as he is, so are we in this world.   There is no
fear in love ; but perfect love casteth out fear : because fear hath
torment.   He that feareth is not made perfect in love.   We love
[him], because he first loved us."   1 John 4:17-19

THE leading idea here is " boldness in the day of judgment ; not boldness prospectively when the day comes, but
present boldness in the view of it now.   It is much the
same thing as we have in a previous section of the epistle
(iii. 19–21), our assuring our hearts before God ; our having
confidence toward God.   This boldness is connected with
the perfecting of love ; " Herein is our love made perfect ; "
or as in the margin, "Herein is love with us made perfect, * that we may have boldness in the day of judgment."

---

* The exact literal rendering is, "Herein is perfected the love with us."
In the twelfth verse, the expression is different, "His love is perfected
in us."   There, I think, it must be the perfection or completeness of his
love to us, as realised by us in our consciousness and experience, that is
meant.   In that verse (12) the participle is used : " His love is in us as a
perfected thing, a consummated fact."   Here (ver. 17) it is the verb that
is used, and so used as to denote a work or process brought to a full or
final issue ; the perfecting of the love with us, as a treaty or transaction
of some sort.

The textual rendering, indeed, of the 17th verse : " Herein is our love
made perfect," is apt to mislead in another way, by suggesting the idea
that we have here the counterpart of the statement in the 12th verse :
" This love is perfected in us."   There it is God's love that is said to be
perfected, his love to us ; here we are apt to suppose that it is our love
that is made perfect, our love to God.   But the subject of our love to God
has not yet come up for consideration ; it does not really come up till the

Love then, or the love before indicated, is perfected with us; and the perfecting of this love with us is bound up with our having boldness in the day of judgment. The bond or connecting link is our oneness with Christ; our being in this world as he is now.

What is perfected is love; not love indefinitely; but the love which is God's nature, and which comes out in the saving gift of his Son. It is to be perfected as "love with us." It is not merely, as in the twelfth verse, to be perfected in us, as love to us; it is to be perfected in us, as "love with us." It is God's love so shared by him with us as to constitute a love relationship, or love-fellowship, between him and us. This is indispensable to our having boldness in the prospect of the day of judgment. And it is realised through oneness with Christ, through our "being as he is;" not as he was before he came into the world; nor merely as he was in the world; but as he is now. It is our "being as he is," that connects in us, in our consciousness and experience, the perfecting of God's love with us, and our having boldness to face the final account (ver. 17).

The boldness must be very complete; for it must exclude whatever is incompatible with the ground on which

20th verse. For, by consent of the best critics, the pronoun "him" is to be omitted in the 19th verse, as not having been in the original; so that the assertion is there quite general: "We love, because he first loved us." How much better this suits the scope of the apostle's reasoning, my exposition of the verse may partly show. Again, if we adopt the textual rendering of the 17th verse: "Herein is our love made perfect," we miss the emphatic article "the," or "this;" "the love," or "this love;" referring to a love previously spoken of. And "our love" is an awkward and unwarrantable substitute for "love with us," or "the love with us," —"this love with us." On every ground the marginal translation is to be preferred, or the still more literal one which I have suggested above: "Herein is perfected this love with us." And let it be borne in mind, as I have stated, that the preposition is not the same in the two verses, the 12th and the 17th. In the 12th it is ἐν ἡμῖν; in the 17th μεθ' ἡμῶν.

it rests. Now it rests on love ; on God's love shared with us. But love shared between the lover and the loved, in a mutual fellowship of love, excludes or " casts out fear." It must do so, for " fear hath torment." A relationship or fellowship based on fear is of course quite conceivable ; but it has torment. It cannot therefore consist with a relationship or fellowship of love. " He that feareth is not made perfect in love ;" in this love ; the love, or covenant of love, here spoken of or referred to (ver. 18). But " we love." We may not be made perfect in love,—the love or loving treaty in question. But we do love ; and our love is a reality ; it may be relied on as a reality ; for it is love springing out of his love to us ; it is his own very love in us. " We love, because he first loved us."

Having offered these exegetical explanations, I now take up the topics suggested in their order.

I. (ver. 17.) " Herein is our love "—God's love with us —" made perfect, that we may have boldness in the day of judgment : because as he is, so are we in this world." The perfecting of " God's love with us," so that we may have boldness in the day of judgment, depends on our being as Christ is,—and that too " in this world." We are in this world, not as he was when he was in it, but as he is now.

In a very eminent and emphatic sense, God's love with him is now made perfect ; in a sense in which that could not be said of him as he was when in this world. The Father's covenant of love with him, as " Jesus Christ come in the flesh "—" the Son sent by him to be the propitiation for our sins "—is now perfectly ratified, so that he may have boldness in the view of any day of judgment.

That, I repeat, could scarcely be said of him as he was when in this world. Personally, no doubt, he was then the object of the Father's love ; and that divine love, as communicated and shared with him, in his human nature and earthly condition, was absolutely perfect. Personally, therefore, he might have boldness,—he had nothing to fear,—in any judicial reckoning. But consider him as "sent to be the propitiation for our sins."

Oh, what a cloud comes in between him and his Father's love ! What a cloud, charged with fiery wrath, about to burst on his devoted head ! And what trembling is there in the prospect of that judicial reckoning with him for our transgression of the law which he has to stand ! It was not then altogether a fellowship of love with him on the part of God. The things that passed between God and him, as he hung on the accursed tree, were not all love-tokens and love-caresses ! Love was with him still, divine love, even then and there; love, if possible, more than ever, for the very death he was dying, in fulfilment of the divine purpose of salvation. But something else was with him too ; something that for a season terribly shaded that love. Divine justice was with him ; justice inexorably demanding, in the interests of law and government, the stern execution of the penal sentence. And that must first be perfected ; that must have its perfect work ; before the love can be made perfect. He feels, he affects, no boldness in meeting that day of judgment. He knows its terror ; he shrinks ; he cries ; he "is crucified through weakness." For us to be as he then was, would give us little boldness in view of the day of judgment awaiting us.

But to be as he is now ! Ah, that is a very different matter ! Now that his dark agony is over, and all his groans are past; now that there is no more present with him, on the part of God, any wrath at all, but only perfect love ; now that, no longer bearing condemnation, but accepted for his righteousness' sake, he has boldness to set any day of judgment at defiance ; now that the Father

need have no other dealings with him any more for ever
but only dealings of perfect love; now that, being raised
from the dead, he dieth no more; death, judicial death,
having no more dominion over him! May this privilege
indeed be ours? Nay, it is; "we are as he is." When
and where? Now, "in this world." It is not the blessedness of the future state; it is blessedness to be got here
and now. Do you ask how? Look to Jesus; to "Jesus
Christ come in the flesh;" "the Son sent by the Father to
be the propitiation for your sins." How was it possible
for him, when he took that position, to be as he now is?
On one only condition. He must consent first to be as you
are, in the full sense and to the full extent of enduring and
exhausting all the pains and penalties which your being as
you are entails on you. Not otherwise could he come to
be as he is now. And not otherwise can you come to be as
he is now; not otherwise than by first consenting to be as
he was then; to die as he died; to be "crucified with
him." Is this a hard preliminary? Nay, it is altogether
reasonable as well as necessary; it is eminently gracious.
It is his own free gift of himself to you; of himself as the
propitiation for your sins.

I take your death as mine, he cries; the death which
as sinners you deserve to die. I die that death in your
stead. You cannot die that death yourselves and ever live
again. But I can. "I am he that liveth and was dead,
and behold I am alive for evermore." How much better is
it for you to make my death yours than to die eternally
yourselves!

Can you refuse to be as he then was, in the exercise of
realising, appropriating, uniting faith; "knowing the fellowship of his sufferings?"—especially when you consider how
this not only secures your never again being, as you naturally are, under condemnation; but secures also your being

as he now is. God's love is with you ; as truly " perfected with you," as it is with him. You may have the same boldness that he might have in facing any day of judgment. To you, as to him, death as the wages of sin is really past. There is no more any judicial reckoning with you on God's part, no more with you than with him ; but only dealings of love, of love made perfect, love having free course, love unfettered and unrestrained. So you have boldness as regards the day of judgment.

II. This love with us, thus perfected, is inconsistent with fear. It founds or establishes a love-relationship, a love-fellowship, with which fear cannot co-exist :—" There is no fear in love ; but perfect love casteth out fear : because fear hath torment ; he that feareth is not made perfect in love."

The love here meant is not our love to God ; neither is it, strictly speaking, God's love to us, or our apprehension of it. In a sense, it may be said to be the mutual love that subsists between God and us, when, " as Christ is, so are we, in this world." Or, still more exactly, it may be understood as denoting the terms of loving agreement, of good understanding and endearment, on which God would have us to be with him, in virtue of " his love with us being made perfect." The great practical truth taught is that our faith, when we " confess that Jesus is the Son of God " (ver. 15), and when " we have known and believed the love that God hath to us " (ver. 16), brings us into a position, as regards God, in which there is not only no occasion, but no room, for fear.

Love and fear are diametrically opposite principles ; and they imply opposite modes of treatment on the part of God towards us, and opposite relations on our part towards him. If God deals with us in the way of strict law and righteous judgment, then the footing on which we are with him is

one simply of fear. His fear is with us; not his love.
And it is so with us that, however it may be lulled for a
time, it will one day be perfected, or have its perfect work,
in "a fearful looking for of judgment, and fiery indignation,
which shall devour the adversary." If, again, God deals
with us in the way of rich and free grace, then the footing
on which we are with him is one of love. He no longer
holds over us the threat of punishment; the fear of it is
not with us any more. It cannot be, for this fear hath
torment.

Mark the reason here assigned for fear being cast out;
it hath torment; the torment of anticipated judgment; for
that is exactly what is meant. It echoes the voice of the
demons :—" Art thou come to torment us before the time ?"
But we with whom " God's love is perfected," have boldness
in reference to the day of judgment; not torment, but boldness. Therefore " there is no fear in that love," thus perfected ; for fear introduces an element the reverse of what
a state of loving fellowship implies. Hence " he that feareth
is not made perfect in that love ;" he does not fully realise
the standing or position which it gives him; he does not
enter completely into the faith and fellowship of "God's
love with us," as a love that " is made perfect."

Here let us consider, first, the evil and danger of
confounding these two opposite footings, of fear and of
love, on which we may be with God; and, secondly, the
careful provision which God has made for keeping them
separate.

1. I take the case of one who is still in the relation to
God in which fear reigns; who yet, at the same time,
assumes that, even in his case, there may be something of
the opposite relation, of which love is the exponent and
expression. He is still under wrath; he has no real boldness as regards the day of judgment; he is subject to the

power of the fear which has torment. But he has a notion
that God's love may yet somehow be with him after all;
he has a dream of mercy; he welcomes the idea of indulgence and impunity; it abates his torment. It does not
really bring him into the region of love, but it mitigates
fear. Is that a good thing for him? Were it not better
far that he should be left, naked and shelterless, to the full
experience of all the torment which fear has? He might
thus be shut up to try "a more excellent way."

But I take, with John, the opposite case. I suppose
that you are within the realm and domain of love. Love;
the love which is God's very nature; the love "manifested
in his sending his only begotten Son into the world that
you might live through him;" that love is the atmosphere
of the region in which you now dwell. You are on loving
terms with God; his love being with you; and being "made
perfect with you." Nay; not quite made perfect. It should
be so, but it is not so. For you let into your heart something of what is proper to the opposite relation; your being
on the old terms with God to which fear belongs. And the
practical effect of this is very disastrous. Not to dwell
upon its sure tendency to mar your peace and joy: it thoroughly cramps your free walk with God in light; it has a
sad bearing on your manner of serving God. For no two
things can be more opposite than service rendered on the
footing of love, and service rendered on the footing of fear.
Not only are the motives different; the kinds of service
which they prompt are different. If I am under the influence of the fear which has torment, and so far as I am under
its influence, I am inevitably inclined to evasion and compromise. I must do some things and leave some things undone; my conscience, moved by fear, will not otherwise let
me alone. But I sail as near the wind as possible, if only I
may keep barely on the safe side of the law. I venture on

occasional omissions of duty and compliances with temptation; stealthily, as it were, "snatching a trembling joy."
The service is all task-work, slave-work. As such I grudge
it always, and get off from it when I can on any plea. That
is my way with God under the torment of fear. It should
be otherwise when I move in the sphere, and breathe the
air, of love; of divine love; "God's love with me made
perfect." There should be no guile in my spirit now; no
inclination to unfair dealing any more. Alas! is it so? Is
it always so with me? Even if I have some sense and
experience of the new and better footing of love on which
it is my privilege to be with my God, am I not too often
visited with questionings and misgivings proper only to the
old footing of fear? Do I not find myself ever and anon
asking, Must I positively renounce this?—may I not, for
once, venture upon that? And does not all such asking
indicate something of the old servile mind? What uneasiness is there in such a way of living with God, and what
unfaithfulness too! What "unsteadfastness and perfidious-
ness in his covenant" of love! Surely it is true that he who
in any measure thus acts from mere fear, under the pressure
of felt necessity, is not "made perfect in love."

2. But why should it be so? God would not have it so.
His will is that there should be a sharp line of separation
between the two incompatible relations; that of love and that
of fear. He would shut you up, completely and exclusively,
into one or other of them.

Are you in that relation to which fear is appropriate?
Then let it be fear alone; fear in the view of the judgment-
day. By all means let fear operate alone; unmitigated,
unrelieved, by any vague notion of mercy; any dream of
love. That is the way in which it should operate. So
operating, let it deter you from crime; let it impel you to
duty. Or, better far, let it drive you to despair; to despair

of yourselves; not, God forbid, of him! You have nothing
to do with love as you are, and continuing as you are;—
you have to do only with fear. Oh that it were, in the first
instance, perfect fear!—fear, pure and simple, casting out,
I say not love, but the idle imagination of love! Yes; it
is yours to fear; and only to fear! Would to God that
your fear had torment enough, not merely to set you on
doing some things and avoiding some things, to soothe it or
set it to sleep; but to set you on crying, with the deep voice
of true conviction : " Who shall deliver me ?" " What must
I do to be saved ?"

Are you, on the other hand, in the relation of which
love, divine love, is the characteristic ? Is it not a relation
of love in which full provision is made, if you will only
realise it, for the entire and absolute casting out of all fear?
I call upon you so to realise it. Have you, in very truth,
"known and believed the love that God hath in you"?
Have you considered this love, its nature, its manifestation,
its effect and issue ? Have you asked yourself, O my
brother! this simple, but very serious, question: On what
footing does this loving God; this God whose very nature
is love, and whose love is with me and in me; mine in
actual possession; mine in all its fulness;—on what footing
does he intend and wish me to be with him ? Ah! is it a
footing that will still admit of the miserable suspicions and
subterfuges of one driven by a tormenting dread of the
lash ? Is it not rather a footing that precludes them all ?
Not a vestige of the old state of liability to judgment remains, if " as Christ is, so you now are in this world."
Not a vestige of the old grudging and guileful frame of
mind, congenial to that state, should remain. Not for your
own comfort merely, but for your single-eyed, and simple-
minded, and honest-hearted walking with God, and serving
of God, I beseech you to let his perfect love cast out your

slavish fear. For fear hath torment; it is torture; and your God and Father is not a torturing inquisitor.

III. That it may be so; that "this love with you" may be so "perfected" as to "cast out fear;" see that you love with a love that springs out of God's love, and is of the same sort. "We love," says the apostle, on behalf of himself and you who believe through his word; passing now from God's love to ours; "we love, because he first loved us."*

"We love." We can take home to ourselves personally and individually what has been said abstractly of love casting out fear. For we love, and do not fear. "He that feareth is not made perfect in love;" he does not perfectly realise the love relationship, the love-fellowship, the love-state, as it were, which God's "love with us made perfect," involves. But that is not our case; "we love."

"We love." It is the first time John has ventured to say so in this passage. Here first he brings in expressly our subjective experience or consciousness, as bearing upon the assured footing of love on which we are to be with God. Hitherto, it has all turned on God's love; manifested by him; known and believed by us; communicated to us; present with us; and as present with us, made perfect; so perfect as to cast out fear. Now, it is our love that is asserted;—"We love." For this must be the issue. It is idle to imagine that anything of the loving relationship and fellowship of which John speaks can be ours, unless we can say with him, humbly, but with some measure of confidence; "We love." And it is no light thing to say so. It is significant of much.

"We love." It is not merely that we have a natural faculty of loving, and exercise it by letting it go forth on things and persons naturally attractive to us. But we

* See note at the beginning of this discourse, page 412.

have now a divine faculty of loving; we love with the love which is of God; which is God's very nature. We love with a love that goes forth towards things and persons, as they are attractive, not to us, but to him. In particular, as regards our life with God, our walk with God, our fellowship with God, our service of God, our obedience to God; as regards all that pertains to the relation that is to subsist between him and us; "we love." Not fear, but love, is now, on our part as well as on his part, the ruling principle and living spirit of it all.

"We love." And in loving, we do but reciprocate God's love; and respond to it. "We love, because he first loved us." For our love would be but a poor and sorry thing unless it were linked on to God's love, as the consequence, or as it were the continuation of it, the reflection or reproduction of it. Always, it must be ultimately, in the last resort, God's love on which we fall back. "God first loved us." This wondrous economy of love, in virtue of which he would have us to be on such a loving footing with him as to have fear utterly cast out, originates in him, and is all his own. If we love at all with the love which is of God, it is only because "we have known and believed the love which he hath to us." For it is "faith alone that worketh by love;"—to that principle we are brought back. If we are to realise, in our experience, the relationship and fellowship of love, as one in which there is no fear, it must be by faith. Therefore I call on you to believe; to believe always; to believe more and more. Believe in God as first loving you;—yes, I say, as first loving you. Be very sure that that must be first; not your loving; but God's loving you. You cannot really know what love is until you believe in God as first loving you. You must first lay open your whole hearts to the free, frank acceptance of the love with which he first loveth you, as the plant opens its bosom

to the rain and sunshine of heaven. Then, from that love
with which God first loveth you,—known, believed, accepted,
embraced,—there will spring up love in you ; such love as
will make your whole intercourse with God an intercourse
altogether loving, and not fearful at all; such love as will
cordially welcome the assurance that God means you to be
to him,—not trembling, disaffected slaves,—but loving,
loyal, and confiding sons.

I close with two practical observations.

1. There is surely much here, in this glorious description of the fellowship of love which God desires to have
with us, and desires us to have with him, that should
encourage earnest though anxious souls. I can conceive
indeed that some may be inclined to question this. They
may feel as if the view now given of the position which God
would have them to occupy places it beyond their reach ;
high above their utmost aspirations. It may seem to them
a perfection quite unattainable ; an ideal that they can
never dream of realising. If something far short of it,—
some far more ordinary and commonplace walk and service,
—will not suffice or be accepted, it is all over, they may be
saying, with them. But let me ask,—In what spirit are
you saying so ? Is it with regret ? Is it with a feeling of
disappointment ? Would you be upon this footing with
God if you could ? I must assume that you would ; that
you see it to be above all things desirable ; that you really
long and pray to be to God all that you now perceive he
would have you to be. Then, if so, I beseech you to remember that this whole business of the adjustment of your
relation to God as one of perfect love, is his and not yours.
It is not you that have to go to him ; he comes to you. It
is not you who have to get up, by a painful process of
inward working, love in yourselves ; it is he who "first
loveth you." It is with his love you have to do, and not

with your own. And his love is not far to seek,—or long
to wait for. It is with you; embodied, enshrined, imper-
sonated, in the Son of his love, sent by him to be the propitiation for your sin. Look to him; believe on him;
consent to be now, in this world, as he is. And remember
that "the righteousness which is of faith speaketh on this
wise, Say not in thine heart, Who shall ascend into heaven?
(that is, to bring Christ down from above:) or, Who shall
descend into the deep? (that is, to bring up Christ again
from the dead). But what saith it? The word is nigh
thee, even in thy mouth, and in thy heart: that is, the word
of faith, which we preach; that if thou shalt confess with
thy mouth the Lord Jesus, and shalt believe in thine heart
that God hath raised him from the dead, thou shalt be
saved."

2. Let sinners be warned against presumptuous confidence with reference to the day of judgment. Whatever
may be our boldness, if "as he is, so are we in this world,"
it does not spring from any questioning of the certainty, or
any abating of the alarm, of that great and dreadful day.
On the contrary, we have reached that boldness in a way
that gives us an insight we never can forget into the reality
and intensity of the pains of hell. "We know the terror
of the Lord;" we know it by our "being crucified with
Christ." What we see of it in the cross,—in Jesus hanging
there, bearing guilt, bearing wrath;—what we feel of it in
ourselves, when we take his death of condemnation as ours;
—deepens our sense of God's love in saving us from it, and
fills us evermore with sensitive apprehension at the very
thought of our being again "castaways." And knowing
thus this terror of the Lord, we would fain "persuade men."
Snatched ourselves as brands from the burning, going softly
all our days in the remembrance of our narrow escape, our
most seasonable deliverance, we cannot contemplate un-

moved their going down into the pit. We beseech them to lay no flattering unction to their souls, as if judgment were not both absolutely certain and inconceivably terrible. We bid them fix their eyes on Jesus suffering judicially on the accursed tree, and hear his voice :—" If these things be done in the green tree, what shall be done in the dry ?"

"Now then we are ambassadors for Christ, as though God did beseech you by us : we pray you in Christ's stead, be ye reconciled to God." For "it is a fearful thing to fall into the hands of the living God." Who shall be able to "stand before the face of him that sitteth on the throne," and brave "the wrath of the Lamb, when the great day of his wrath is come?" "Kiss the Son, lest he be angry, and ye perish from the way, when his wrath is kindled but a little. Blessed are all they that put their trust in him."

35

THE OBJECTS OF OUR LOVE—THE CHILDREN OF GOD AND GOD HIMSELF.

"If a man say, I love God, and hateth his brother, he is a liar: for he that loveth not his brother whom he hath seen, how can he love God whom he hath not seen? And this commandment have we from him, That he who loveth God love his brother also. Whosoever believeth that Jesus is the Christ is born of God : and every one that loveth him that begat, loveth him also that is begotten of him. By this we know that we love the children of God, when we love God, and keep his commandments. For this is the love of God, that we keep his commandments." 1 John 4:20,21; 5:1-3

THE apostle has just announced the law of love : " We love, because he first loved us." He has still in his mind the twofold test of God's giving us his Spirit ;—our " believing on the name of his Son Jesus Christ," and our "loving one another" (iii. 23). The Spirit in us confesses,—we by the Spirit confess,—that Jesus Christ is come in the flesh ; that he is the Son of God. It is a confession implying the believing recognition of all God's love to us in him. It implies therefore also the perfecting of God's love with us, so as to exclude fear, and insure our loving as he has first loved us. We respond to his love and reciprocate it ; it reproduces itself in us. And it does so, as love going forth to the seen, not the unseen ; otherwise it would not be our loving with God's very love to us ; it would not be our loving because God first loved us.

I. " We love, because he first loved us." Whom do we thus love ? " Him who first loved us," we say. And we say well. But let us beware. Our saying so may be deceptive; in saying it we may lie; not perhaps deliberately, but deceiving ourselves. There is less risk when the question is made to turn upon loving our brother; for we cannot so readily say falsely or mistakenly that we love the visible, as we can say falsely or mistakenly that we love the invisible. Hence the reasonableness of this test: "If a man say, I love God, and hateth his brother, he is a liar: for he that loveth not his brother whom he hath seen, how can he love God whom he hath not seen?" (iv. 20).

But it may be asked: Wherein precisely consists the impossibility? Is it merely that it is easier and more natural to love one whom we see than one whom we have not seen; that the first is a lower attainment, more within our reach, while the other is more transcendental, spiritual, and sublime; so that if we cannot acquire the terrestrial virtue of loving our brother whom we have seen, it is vain for us to aspire to the heavenly elevation of loving God whom we have not seen? Nay, to put the matter on that footing is to degrade the grace of brotherly love, and wholly to destroy and overthrow the apostle's noble argument. It is by no means clear that our seeing or not seeing the object of the affection makes any real or serious difference as regards our faculty or capacity of loving. There is no reason why one whom we have never seen, whom we have known only by report and fame, or by his friendly offices towards us, should not draw our hearts out towards him more even than the most familiar friend whom we see every day. Nay, in this very case it must be so. The unseen God, known only through the discoveries of himself which he makes to us in his word, and the communications of himself which he shares with us by his Spirit, must command our affections more than the best of created beings our eyes can ever light on, if the due order of the two great

commandments is to be observed. Nor will it do to hold
that our loving our brother is in the least degree more easy
or more natural than our loving God; as if, beginning with
loving our brother, because he, being nearest us, is the most
palpably manifest object of our regard, we might through
that means hope to find our love rising to the more remote
and less palpably manifest object, even God. No. This
love of our brother is not a natural attainment, but a divine
gift or qualification, and therefore has this testing-place
assigned to it here. Consider again what it is for us to
"love because God first loved us." It is loving as he first
loved us; loving with the very same sort of love. But the
only person whom I can love with that sort of love with
which God has loved me is my brother. It is vain for me
to say, in this view, that I love God. I cannot love God,
in the sense and on the ground required, otherwise than
through the intervention of my brother.

For the unseen God cannot possibly be to me the object
of the kind of love with which he first loved me. That is
surely love, not to the unseen, but to the seen. It was
when he saw me in my original state, like "an unpitied
child, cast out in the open field, to the loathing of its person,
in that day that it was born," that he first loved me.
"When I passed by thee, and saw thee polluted in thine
own blood, I said unto thee, when thou wast in thy blood,
Live; yea I said unto thee, when thou wast in thy blood,
Live." To me, if I am the conscious object of that love, it
must ever seem so marvellous as to be all but incredible,
that, seeing me as I was, he should have so loved me; nay
more, that, seeing me as I am, under all his gracious dealing
with me, he should so love me still. It is because he is
God and not man. Well may I, whom, thus seeing me, he
so loves, love him warmly, gratefully, in return. It appears
almost natural that I should spontaneously love him; I feel

almost as if I could not help it. But how apt is such a frame of mind, especially in a highly sensitive and excitable temperament, to grow into a sort of vague, dreamy, mystical or sentimental pietism, such as may be really little better than a refined form of solitary self-indulgence! At all events, it is not the love wherewith he has first loved me; it is not my loving as he has loved me. If I am so to love, I must love, not the unseen, but the seen. My love must go forth toward those whom I see, as God saw me when he first loved me. And my love must be what his love is; no idle sentiment or barren sympathy, but a love that seeks them, and bears long with them, and knocks, and waits, and longs, and prays, for their salvation; a love that gives freely, and without upbraiding; a love self-sacrificing, self-denying; a love that will lay down life itself to save them. And when they become by grace, what by grace I am, I must love them, as God loves me, for what I see in them ;— yes, and in spite of what I see in them too. I may still see many things about them to offend me. But what does God see about me? Do I not try my loving Father's patience far more than any brother can ever try mine? But still he first loveth me. He is ever first in loving me; notwithstanding my being often last in loving him. And shall I not be loving my brother, first loving him, and that continually? Shall I withhold my love until he is all in my eyes that I would like him to be? How would it be with me if God so postponed his love to me? Surely, "if I say I love God, and thus hate my brother, I am a liar;" what I profess is an impossibility. Let me rather give heed to his own announcement of his will: "This commandment have we from him, that he who loveth God love his brother also" (iv. 21).

II. This commandment of God still further explains the importance attached to our loving our brother, as a

sign of the Spirit being given to us. And it does so in
two ways.

In the first place, I may be apt to think that this setting
of me upon loving my brother, as the test of my "loving,
because God has first loved me," disparages the prior claim
which God has on me, that I should love him. But it is
not so. For I am now told that it is his special good
pleasure that the love I have to him should, as it were,
expend itself upon my brother. I need have no fear therefore of my love to my brother on earth interfering with my
love to my Father in heaven; or being imagined to be a
substitute for it. There is indeed a spurious sort of
brotherly love; a vague philanthropy; which is sometimes
put in the place of what God is entitled to claim. People
substitute a certain easy constitutional good nature, instead
of piety towards God; and even quote the loving apostle
as an authority for doing so. They little know the heart
of the man they quote, or the real spirit of his writings.
Whatever importance he assigns to your loving your
brother, it is to your loving him, because God has first
loved you; loving him with the very love with which God
has first loved you. And more than that. He appeals to
the express commandment of God requiring you in this way
to manifest and prove your love to him.

For, secondly, love to God is not ignored, or set aside.
On the contrary, the very reason why loving your brother
is insisted on so peremptorily is, that it is loving your brother in obedience to God, and out of love to God. In loving your brother, you keep God's commandment; and you
keep it under a very solemn appeal, as it were, from him
to you.

Let us hear his voice. You "say that you love me."
You have good cause to love me, and I give you credit for
loving me. But first, I have to remind you generally, that if

"you love because I have first loved you," your love, like mine, must flow out upon visible objects; on your brethren, such as they are seen in the world and in the church. And next, I tell you that this is my commandment :—If you love me, and as you love me, love your brother. I do not ask that your love to me, which I willingly accept, should manifest itself in any other way than that.

Ah ! what a constant tendency is there in my heart to think that I can love God otherwise, and manifest my love to him otherwise, than in the way of loving my brother, and loving him simply at God's command. I would fain try to lavish upon God directly proofs of my affection, such as, if he were man and not God, might please him. I would fain make him the object of immediate familiar and affectionate acts and offices of endearment; as if I might return and reciprocate his love, as I would that of an equal. But he checks me. "He is my Lord ; my goodness reacheth not to him." It is not thus that you can really act out the very love with which I have first loved you. To do so, you must deal as I do with the seen, not the unseen. Nay more. It is not thus that I would have you to act out the very love with which I have first loved you, assuming that you return and reciprocate it to the full. For this is my commandment to you, that loving me you love your brother also. It is my commandment now, and will be the criterion, the test of my judgment, in the great day. For, hear the words of my beloved Son, who is then to sit on the throne of judgment : "Verily I say unto you, inasmuch as ye have done it unto one of the least of these my brethren, ye have done it unto me ; "—" Verily I say unto you, inasmuch as ye did it not to one of the least of these, ye did it not to me."

III. There is yet another view of the connection between love to the brethren and love to God suggested in the next verse, which seems to bring out the real explanation and ultimate principle of John's teaching as to what we may call the law of divine love:—"Whosoever believeth that Jesus is the Christ is born of God: and every one that loveth him that begat, loveth him also that is begotten of him" (ver. 1).

Let the precise point of the argument be once more observed. It is that God's love to us should work in us love to our brother; and that in fact its working in us love to our brother is a better test of our knowing and believing it, than our professing any amount of love to God himself. It is so, first, because it is only in loving our brother whom we see, not in loving God whom we do not see, that we can exercise the very love wherewith God has first loved us. It is so, secondly, because in loving our brother we are obeying the commandment of him whom we profess to love; and so proving our love. And it is so, thirdly, because in loving our brother we love one who is begotten of God; and we love him as begotten of God; on the ground of his filial relationship to him who first loved us, and on account of whose first love to us we love.

My brother whom I love, let it be noted, is now viewed as a believer, a child of God. He was not always so, when I loved him with a brother's yearning pity and a brother's desire to save him, any more than I was always so, when God loved me with a Father's yearning pity and a Father's desire to save me. But he is so now; and I love him as such. Why? Because he is born or "begotten of God." I, as begotten of God, love him, as begotten of God. The bond of love is our being both of us begotten of God, and it is a bond which God owns and sanctions; for the essence of it is love to himself. It is love to him, but it is love to him in a special aspect or character; as a Father—as one who begets. Is not that, however, the very aspect, the very character, in which he best loves to be loved? Is he not from the beginning bent on being loved as a Father, as one begetting? Is it not in that aspect and character, as a Father, as one begetting, that he would be known and loved, when, "bringing in the first begotten into the world, he says, Let all the angels of God worship him"? Is it otherwise than as a Father, as one begetting, that he would be known and loved, when a voice from heaven proclaims, "This is my beloved Son, in whom I am well pleased"? He cares not to receive honour or worship or affection at our hands, unless it is rendered to him as a Father begetting; as the God and Father of our Lord Jesus Christ. Yes; he cries: if you would love me, as I choose to beloved, you must love me as a Father begetting. And the only sure proof of your so loving me, is your loving him who is begotten of me.

First and primarily that must imply your loving Jesus, the Christ, who alone is my only begotten, well-beloved Son. Hear him;—worship him;—if you would love me; —love me as the eternal Father begetting him from everlasting; love me as sending him to save, and raising him from the dead with this acknowledgment, "Thou art my Son, this day have I begotten thee. But now in him I am begetting others to be my sons; so begetting them by the power of my Spirit, as to make them one with him who is my only begotten Son, that he may be the first-born among many brethren." One after another, I am thus begetting children to myself. And every one of them is to me what my only begotten Son is. Can you say that he is so to you? He will be so, if you love me;—"For every one that loveth him that begat, loveth him also that is begotten of him" (ver. 1).

It is at this point exactly that these two affections, or rather these two modes of the same affection of love,—our loving because God first loved us,—loving God as our

Father and men as our brethren,—come to be welded, as it were, together ; and the mode of reasoning seems to be reversed. For whereas before, our loving our brother is made the proof of our loving God in obedience to his commandment, now the matter is put in the very opposite way : " By this we know that we love the children of God, when we love God " (ver. 2).

It is a seasonable and salutary turn that is here given to the train of thought. It ushers in a new subject. But first, it fitly finishes off the present one. It is a useful closing caution. Much stress has been laid upon your loving your brother ; loving him as you see him ; loving him because God commands you ; loving him as begotten of God. But your love to your brethren needs to be carefully watched. Is it really love to them, as brethren, as children of God ? Is it love to them with a 'view to their being children of God ? Is it love to them because they are children of God ? For it may be on other grounds and for other reasons that you love them. It may be a love of mere natural sentiment and affection ; a love merely human ; having little or nothing in common with the love with which God first loved you. To be trustworthy at all, as a test of God's giving you of his Spirit, and so dwelling in you, it must be love having in it the element of godliness ; love having respect to God ; love to them because God loves them and you love God. " By this we know that we love the children of God," as the children of God, when we love them because " we love God, and keep his commandments " (ver. 2).

PART FOUR

DIVINE FELLOWSHIP—OVERCOMING
THE WORLD
1 John 5:2-21

36

LOVE TO GOD KEEPING HIS COMMANDMENTS AND
NOT FINDING THEM GRIEVOUS.

"By this we know that we love the children of God, when we love God,
and keep his commandments. For this is the love of God, that we
keep his commandments : and his commandments are not grievous."
1 John 5:2-3

THE three elements or conditions of the "fellowship with
the Father and with his Son Jesus Christ," in which John
would have us to be joint partakers with himself and his
fellow apostles;—Light, the primary ; Righteousness, the
intermediate ; Love, the ultimate one;—having been considered ;—we enter, as it seems to me, on a fourth section
of this great treatise, in which the divine fellowship
regarded as complete is viewed in its relation to the conflict
that is ever going on between God and the world, between
the Holy and True One and the father of lies. The position of one enjoying fellowship with the Father and with
his Son Jesus Christ in light, righteousness, and love,

demands on the one hand very thorough loyalty, and on the other hand ensures very thorough victory; loyalty as regards God and his law ; victory as regards the wicked one and the system, or state of society, which he organises and influences, the world lying in him.

Hence the fitness or propriety of the introductory text in this part of the Epistle being one that enforces not only obedience, but obedience so thoroughly loving and loyal as to be divested of all the feeling of irksomeness that is apt to embitter a state of subjection and subordination.

For the assertion,—" his commandments are not grievous,"—is not an incidental remark merely; it is of the essence of the apostle's argument. If the test of God's giving us of his Spirit, and so dwelling in us (iii. 24, and iv. 13), is to be pre-eminently our loving our brother (iv. 7 and 20, etc.), it concerns us much that our love to our brother should be itself thoroughly tried and proved. Is it love to our fellow-men as seen by us in the same light in which God sees them and us when he loveth us? (iv. 20.) Is it, moreover, a love that has respect to God (iv. 21); that loves the begotten for the begetter's sake (v. 1); that loves the children for the relation in which they stand to the Father; out of love to the Father himself, and in obedience to him? (v. 2). This last condition is what really connects our loving them with our loving him. And it does so, in virtue of a general law or principle :—" His commandments are not grievous."

The statement is not absolute but relative. It points out, not what the commandments of God are in themselves, but what they are to us, in our sense and apprehension of them. It may indeed be most truly said of them, considered in themselves, that they are not grievous; on the contrary, they are all most reasonable, equitable and beneficent. Nothing that God orders us to do, nothing that he requires us to suffer, can fairly be called grievous. But to me they are too often very grievous. I feel them to be irksome and heavy. Yes! That is the exact word. They are heavy, weighty, burdensome.

That is my fault, you say. Be it so. Let us ask how it comes to be so; and let us ask also how it may cease to be so.

But first, let us fix it, as a first principle, in our understandings and hearts, that no keeping of God's commandments will suffice to meet the condition or requirement now in question, that is a keeping of them as grievous. They are not kept at all, in the sense of the identification,— " this is the love of God, that we keep his commandments," —if they are kept by us as grievous; if in keeping them we feel them to be grievous. Under this conviction, let us look into this matter of the grievousness of God's commandments, and the way of delivery from any sense or suspicion of their being grievous.

1. Beginning at the lowest stage, it is not difficult to see how God's commandments must be grievous to me, if I am bent on giving full scope to the movements of my inner man which are opposed to them. I cannot shake off the sense of their being binding on me; and binding on me under the sanction of terrible responsibilities. Let me drown conviction as I may in pleasure's bowl, or stifle it in the din and whirl of worldly business, conscience will not let me take my ease; I cannot get rid of God's commandments. They haunt and harass me; they disturb and trouble me; they are grievous; often beyond expression grievous. How shall I ever shake off the feeling of their grievousness?

2. Shall it be by keeping them scrupulously, according to the strictest letter of the law? I become a painstaking Pharisee; a rigid and exact observer of all the commandments. They shall not be grievous to me any more, on

account of my wilful opposition to them. But alas! they
are grievous still. I may reduce them to a minimum of
obligations, and stretch my keeping of them to a maximum
of fulfilment. I may make the least I can of them, by
turning their living spirit into outward formal acts; and I
may make the most of myself and my obedience, in the way
of exaggerating my sacrifices and services. Still God's commandments are grievous to me. My religion, such as it is,
is a mere burden and oppression. I would shake it off if
my conscience would allow me.

3. But my conscience will not allow me. It works in
me deeper and deeper; carrying into the innermost recesses
of my spiritual nature, not the letter only, but the spirit
also of God's commandments. And now, their grievousness
comes out in a new and most distressing experience. For
now, not only is my conscience convinced, but my will is
renewed, with reference to these commandments of God.
Both of these results or effects are of the Spirit. They are
wrought simultaneously, and in harmony with one another;
they act and react on one another. My conscience, quickened by the Spirit, sensitively apprehends a spirituality in
God's commandments,—my heart reconciled by the Spirit,
lovingly owns an excellency and beauty in them,—unper-
ceived and unfelt before. I become alive in my conscience
to the imperative necessity of real spiritual conformity in
my spirit to the holy and loving spirit of the law; and that
precisely when I am smitten in my heart of hearts with love
to it, because it is so spiritually holy and loving. And
what follows? If the work of the Spirit goes on, I sink
deeper and deeper, as under a heavy burden, growing
always heavier. There is an increasingly oppressive sense,
in my conscience, not only of obligation unfulfilled, but of
new guilt contracted. There is an increasingly despairing
feeling, in my heart, of the opposition of my nature to the

commandments of God's law which I love. My very love to the commandments of God, my very "delight in the law after the inner man," brings out now more than ever the feeling of grievousness. Oh, how grievous to me are these commandments of my God, which I so heartily approve and love, but which, alas, I more and more helplessly complain that I cannot satisfy and keep! (Rom. vii. 21–25.)

4. But "there is now no condemnation to them which are in Christ Jesus, who walk not after the flesh but after the Spirit" (Rom. viii. 1). The element of grievousness is extracted from God's commandments, only through my believing consciousness and experience of that great life-giving truth.

How complete is the provision thus made for eradicating every root of bitterness that might make us feel God's commandments to be grievous!

There is, *first*, a removal of the curse, or the condemnation, and a complete restoration of our right standing with God. The element of grievousness arising out of the law's righteous sentence of wrath is removed, in a way that completely divests the very sentence itself of all its grievousness. I cannot rebel against the judgment, however terrible, which the righteous law, with its broken commands, entails on me; I cannot complain of it as grievous when, embracing the cross, I am one with him who there on my behalf endured and exhausted it. Nor can the demand of perfect compliance with the spirit of all the commandments, as the only condition of life, grieve me now, when I see it so fully met on my behalf by the obedience unto death of God's own beloved Son.

Then, *secondly*, there is the renewal of my whole moral nature, bringing it back to its original conformity to the nature of God, as that nature is expressed and manifested in his commandments. This also is essential to the removal of the feeling of grievousness. If I am a spiritual man as regards the commandments of God, then,—apart from the feeling of the utter hopelessness of my ever being justified, in the only way in which I now care to be justified, in terms of the law, fully vindicated and satisfied,—there is the other feeling of the utter hopelessness of my ever being sanctified, after the fashion of the only sort of holiness that can now content me, the holy loving law of the holy loving God. But here too my case is met. In Christ Jesus my Lord I have not only justifying righteousness but renewing grace. The grievousness of a felt discrepancy between my nature and God's commandments, between my spirit and theirs, need not continue. There may still be a vast difference in degree ; but there need be no difference in kind. My moral nature and that of God are now one, if I am renewed after his image. May not the grievousness of his commandments now cease for ever ?

5. An ominous fact here looms out from across the gulf that separates the primeval paradise from our present world. Before the fall, in the garden of Eden, God's commandment was felt to be grievous ; the only commandment which he saw fit formally to give. The reptile insinuation—"Yea, hath God said ye shall not ?"—found entrance into the ear, the mind, the heart of righteous innocence, created after the image of God. To Eve, to Adam, yet unfallen, with the divine likeness in which they were made still entire, the commandment of God came to be grievous. What are we to make of that?

It was the devil's fault. Be it so ; let him bear the blame. But what of his own sin and fall, the sin and fall of himself and all his host ? There was no tempter admitted into their abode. There were no outward circumstances to explain the rise of any feeling of grievousness in their breasts. Yet to them, still unfallen, the commandment of

God was grievous. What shall we say to these things? How do they affect us ?

Ah ! do they not serve to bring out a new and most blessed view of the gospel method of salvation ? John says expressly and absolutely, without qualification or reserve, that "God's commandments are not grievous." He says this with reference to himself and all believers. His meaning must be, that he and they are in such a state, and of such a mind, as to preclude the possibility of God's commandments ever being, or ever becoming, grievous either to him or to them. And what does that imply ?

If the plan of grace made provision only for our being restored, in respect of position and nature, to what our first parents were before they fell,—if we were to be even as the angels were,—however thoroughly that end might be accomplished, it would not afford any adequate security against God's commandments being felt to be grievous. For in fact, the risk to be obviated, the evil to be remedied and guarded against, is not that God's commandments in detail are grievous, some more so and some less, but that his commandments as a whole are grievous. The grievance is that he commands us at all. Even when the thing commanded is most easy and pleasant, most manifestly right and good, its being commanded may make it grievous. That was the case in heaven, when the commandment to "worship the Son," turned out to be grievous to so many of the yet unfallen angels. It was the case also in paradise, when the commandment not to eat of the forbidden tree became grievous to our first parents. It might be the case again, in paradise restored, in heaven gained, if we who are redeemed and renewed were to be merely such, in position and in nature, as the angels were in heaven, and our first parents were in paradise, before they fell.*

* See "Lectures on the Fatherhood of God ;" especially Appendix I.

The real seat of the mischief is not reached unless the very possibility of our ever feeling it grievous to be commanded is thoroughly, conclusively, and effectually precluded and barred. And what potent spell, what resistless charm, is to secure that blessed result? What but the spell, the charm of love? And what love? What but the love which is God's very essence, manifested in a way altogether new and inconceivable beforehand; in a way in which, but for the entrance of sin and evil into his moral creation, it never could have been manifested? Yes. That love of God manifested in his sending his Son to be the propitiation for our sins,—known and believed by us,—bringing us into a perfect love-relationship to him and working in us love of the very same sort with itself,—that love of him who is love, thus manifested to us, apprehended by us, and reproduced in us,—that love it is, and that alone, which puts finally and for ever away out of our hearts every shred and vestige of the old spirit, the old leaven, which, jealous of restraint and aspiring to independence, counts it a grievance to be commanded. This is that new thing under the sun for which sin or moral evil gave occasion, and for which that alone could give occasion. This is God's method of overcoming evil with good; higher good than could ever otherwise have been reached. This is the triumph of love; reconciling man's proud soul to dependence and obedience; expelling the last lingering feeling of soreness because he is under authority; the last lingering feeling of desire to be his own master, or to rule himself.

Ah! if that love has its free course in me; if I know it and believe it; if I enter cordially into that perfect relationship and fellowship of love for which it makes provision, and consent to be on that footing of perfect love with God on which he would have me to be; if now, in consequence, all servile fear is clean gone out of me, and only filial reverence and affection reign within me ; how can it ever, at any time, seem to me grievous that this God should command me ?

Grievous ! O my redeeming God, my loving Father, the loving Father of my Lord ! Grievous that thou shouldst command me ! Grievous that I should be under thee ! Grievous that I am not independent of thee ; left to choose for myself, instead of having thee to choose for me ; left free to do my own will, and not thine ! Nay, I will not, I cannot any more take exception to thy rightful rule over me, O thou loving God and Father who so lovingly makest me thine own ! No, nor to any instance of its exercise, be the instance what it may. Whatever thou commandest, in the line of doing or of suffering, shall please me now, simply because thou commandest it. I dare not promise that there shall be no groans, and tears, and cries, in the doing or the suffering of it. There were groans, and tears, and cries, in the doing and suffering of thy will, when the doer and sufferer of it was thine own beloved Son. But to this I will seek to attain, thy grace helping me, that to me now, as one with him, not one of thy commandments shall ever be more grievous than was that " commandment " to him, in obedience to which " he laid down his life for the sheep."

That was his loving us, with a true brother's love, because " he loved God and kept his commandments." That also was his " overcoming the world," and the world's prince. Thus he proved his love to God, by keeping his commandments ; keeping them as not finding any of them to be grievous. Not grievous to him was the commandment to save his people by dying in their stead. Not grievous to him was the commandment to encounter Satan on their behalf, and win for them the victory over Satan's world.

And now what is his word to you? Is it not a word giving you the assurance that you in him will find God's commandments no more grievous to you than they were to him? Yes! Once more hear his voice: "Come unto me, all ye that labour and are heavy laden, and I will give you rest. Take my yoke upon you, and learn of me; for I am meek and lowly in heart: and ye shall find rest unto your souls. For my yoke is easy, and my burden is light." All ye that labour and are heavy laden; ye who are painfully seeking to fulfil the letter of God's law and finding it very hard; working laboriously at religion as at a weary task; feeling God's service to be a very drudgery and weariness of the flesh;—or ye who, smitten with a sense of the beauty of holiness, the spirituality of the commandment, and the exceeding sinfulness of sin, are desperately striving to get rid of indwelling corruption, and bring your whole inner man into subjection to God and to godliness;—"all ye who labour and are heavy laden," not succeeding, not attaining, not able to rise above the feeling of its being, after all, a heavy load that is imposed upon you in the keeping of God's commandments,—"Come unto me; I will give you rest."

But how? "Take my yoke upon you." "For my yoke is easy, and my burden is light."

Thy yoke, O blessed Jesus, easy! Thy burden light! The yoke thou didst take on thyself when thou didst consent to serve and obey, even to the laying down of thy life for us,—was that easy? The burden thou hadst to bear when, all thy life long and in thy death, thou hadst, in obedience to the Father, and as his servant, to carry our sicknesses, our sorrows, our sins,—was that light? Is it that yoke of thine that thou invitest us to take upon us? Is it that burden of thine that thou callest us to bear? And is it in the taking upon us of that yoke of thine, and in the bearing of that burden of thine, that thou assurest us we shall find rest unto our souls ?

Even so. Thus and not otherwise will I give you rest when you come to me,—"Take my yoke upon you." But that it may be really my yoke that you take upon you,— "Learn of me ; for I am meek and lowly in heart." Learn of me my own meekness and lowliness of heart. Learn of me, coming to me, abiding in me, growing up into me, getting it from me and in me,—learn of me that meek, lowly, hearty love and loyalty to my Father,—having in it no element at all of the servile, for all in it is filial,—which makes the hardest yoke easy, the heaviest burden light. For it is thus that, in the consciousness of unbroken filial oneness with him who lays on me the yoke and the burden, I can lift up to him the eye of quiet resignation and reliance, and say,—"Father, glorify thy name ;" "Father, not my will, but thine be done ;" Father, into thy hands I commend my spirit." Thy commandments are not grievous to me, for "by keeping them I abide in thy love" (John xv. 10).

37

FILIAL FAITH OVERCOMING THE WORLD

" For whatsoever is born of God overcometh the world : and this is the
victory that overcometh the world, even our faith.   Who is he that
overcometh the world, but he that believeth that Jesus is the Son of
God ? "   1 John 5:4,5

HERE again the apostle brings in " the world ; " and he
does so in the very midst of a singularly high estimate of
the believer's standing and character.   He has placed him
in a relation of close intimacy with God, and of serious
responsibility as regards the special duty which that implies.
For what is brotherly love, as John describes it ?   It is our
letting the very love with which God has loved us go forth,
through us, to all men ; and our embracing all who accept
that love as brethren in the Lord.   John has associated
this exercise of love on our part, not only with God's exercise of love to us, but with our obligation of loving obedience to God.   That loving obedience, if it is to be the
obedience of persons accepting and transmitting the love
of God, must be uncomplaining and ungrudging.   It must
be obedience counting none of God's commandments
grievous ; because it owns freely God's absolute right to
command, and therefore confesses that nothing which he
commands can be wrong.

But the world comes in ; and it must be somehow
disposed of, and got rid of.   It must be disposed of, and
got rid of, in its bearing on our position and our duty

as now brought out. In this view I ask you to consider—I. What the world is, and how it is that the
only way of dealing with it is to overcome it. And
II. How the world is to be overcome by the new birth
and through faith.

I. The indefiniteness,—the sort of unsatisfactory vague-
ness,—that is sometimes felt to attach to the scriptural
idea of the world, is here somewhat obviated by the connection or train of thought, in which it occurs. The fact
(ver. 4), that "whatsoever is born of God overcometh the
world," is given apparently as the reason why to such a
one (ver. 3) "the commandments of God are not grievous."
The world, therefore, it might seem, must be characterised
by an impression or feeling to the opposite effect;—that
the commandments of God are grievous. Wherever that
impression or feeling prevails, there is the world. Of
course, there are other characteristic features by which the
world may be recognised and identified; some of which
are brought out elsewhere in this epistle, as well as in other
books of the New Testament. For the most part, indeed,
when the world is spoken of in any passage of scripture as
the antagonist of God, of his kingdom, his cause, his people,
his law, there is, in the passage itself, some clue to guide
or help us to a right apprehension of what particular aspect
of the world is meant. And it might serve to give point
and precision to the teaching of any scriptural text on the
subject of the world,—its relation to us as believers and
our attitude towards it,—if instead of contenting ourselves
with a general notion of it, as a system or society somehow
opposed to godliness, we fastened on the exact sort of
opposition which the text in question may be fitted to
suggest. As to our present text, for instance, we can have
little difficulty. What is the world which faith overcomes?
It is whatever system or way of life, whatever society or

companionship of men, tends to make us feel God's commandments, or any of them, to be grievous.

Here then, at all events, we have no mere vague denunciation of some formidable, but somewhat dim and shadowy enemy; but a definition sufficiently intelligible, and sufficiently precise and practical. Ponder it for a little, and apply it as a test. What is the world to you? It is whatever, it is whoever, is apt to make you feel God's commandments to be grievous. That is a searching test, if faithfully applied by one deeply conscious of that carnal nature in himself, even in his renewed self, which is ever ready to prompt or to welcome the suggestion. That carnal nature in you is not necessarily the world; but all that ministers to it is the world. The natural disposition in you to count the commandments of God grievous is very strong. Do you feel its strength? Are you sensitively alive to its continual and powerful working? Does it vex and distress you? If so, and in proportion as it is so, you are in a position to discern this mark by which the world may be known; whether as an order of things, or as a fellowship of men.

There is an order, or, if you will, a disorder, of things; a way of occupying the mind, amusing the fancy, gratifying the taste, stimulating the passions, warming the imagination, interesting the heart; which, if you are spiritual, and honest in your spirituality, you must feel, when you try it by this touchstone, to be the world. Ask yourself, at the close of an hour or two, or half an hour, spent in reading, or in musing, or in walking abroad, or at table, or at any sort of work, or recreation, or elegant accomplishment that you like:—Has the occupation left you less inclined than you were before to comply with a call of duty, to submit to a sacrifice of inclination, to engage in prayer, to go forth on an errand of pious love? Are you more disposed than otherwise you might have been to feel any such demand upon you to be a sort of interruption, and as such to be somewhat irksome? I am not concerned to maintain that absolutely and always this is of itself proof positive that what you have been occupied about is the world. But this I say; it is at least a very strong presumption. And when you find that upon your being occupied in the same way a second time, or a third, the effect is much the same, the presumption rises into certainty. Whatever it may be as regards others, so far as you are concerned, to all practical intents and purposes, that is the world. So also, in the matter of your intercourse with men, this rule of judgment will often help you to separate the precious from the vile. Who are they from whose company, however otherwise pleasant and profitable, you come, a little, just a very little, more apt than is your wont, to think that God is pressing rather hard upon you, or upon some other child of God whose case you pity? You are tempted slightly to lose patience and temper. You may be at a loss to explain how this comes about; for you cannot perhaps lay your finger on anything particular in what has been going on that may explain it. But you feel it; and that should be enough for you. Do not hesitate to acknowledge that such meetings and companionships are to be regarded and treated by you as the world. Let it be fixed in your minds as a great truth, that the world to be overcome comprehends all that you come in contact with which has any tendency to awaken in you the feeling that "God's commandments are grievous."

If this is a true account of the world, as here presented to us, it must be very evident that it is a world to be "overcome." We cannot deal with it, if we would avoid its deleterious and deadly influence, in any other way. We cannot escape from it, or put it aside. As regards some of its forms and manifestations we may do so. Where we have freedom of choice, we may shun its occupations and companionships. And when these are of such a nature in themselves, or have such influence upon us,—or upon any brother whom we are called to love,—as to foster the impression of God's commandments being grievous, we are bound to shun them. We are under no obligation whatever to frequent the theatre, the ball-room, the race-course; to court the friendship of dissolute hunters after pleasure or frivolous votaries of fashion; to expose ourselves to the contamination of unprofitable reading and discourse. So far we may and must " come out and be separate, and touch not the unclean thing, if we would be the sons and daughters of the Lord God Almighty." But we do not thus get rid of the world. It still presses hard upon us, with its suggestions from every side that the service of God is not perfect freedom. All the ongoings and arrangements of its necessary business, even the customary usages of the home circle itself, are but too ready to convey impressions to that effect. Nay, in the loneliest desert, in the remotest cell hermit ever dwelt in, we cannot shut out airy voices whispering in the ear that something we have to do or bear is hard; we cannot lay an arrest on ideal fascinations shedding a gloom on the cloister's austere devotion, or on the real trials of life. No ; the world cannot be shunned. Neither can it be conciliated. We cannot make any compromise with it. The only effectual, the only possible, way is to overcome it.

And the manner of overcoming it must be peculiar. It must be such as thoroughly to meet and obviate that tendency to minister to a rebellious frame of mind which constitutes the chief characteristic, and indeed the very essence, of what is here called the world.

II. Two explanations accordingly, of this overcoming of

the world are given ; the one having reference to the original source, the other to the continued following out of the victory (ver. 4).

I. " Whatsoever is born of God overcometh the world." So the victory begins ; that is its seed or germ. And as to its seed or germ, it is complete ; potentially complete, though not so in actual result, fully and in detail. Being born or begotten of God implies the overcoming of the world. For whatever is born of God necessarily, *ipso facto*, overcomes the world. The statement is very wide ; and it seems evidently to imply that there is positively no other way of overcoming the world except by our being born or begotten of God : that God himself could not enable us to do this otherwise. There is that in our being born or begotten of God which secures, and which alone can secure, our overcoming the world. And what can that be but the begetting in us of a frame of mind which cuts up by the roots the whole strength of the world's hold over us ;—the idea, namely, of God's commandments being grievous ?

Consider, in this view, what it is to be born or begotten of God. It is more than being created, or even created anew. It is not our being made anew, or made over again ; as if the simple fiat of omnipotence went forth : Let what has made itself corrupt be re-made, pure as at the first. That would not be begetting on God's part, or being begotten on ours. The new birth is indeed a new creation ; but it is something more ; at least it is a new creation of a very special sort. Christ's birth was a creation. In his birth there was created for him a body, a holy humanity, in the Virgin's womb. But the angel said, " That holy thing which shall be born of thee shall be called the Son of God." He was to be called the Son of God in a higher sense than any sense in which the first man might have been so called ; and that with reference even,—nay with reference especially,—to his human nature and condition. He was made man, not by a mere creative act as Adam was, but by generation ; being " conceived by the power of the Holy Ghost." So also in us the new creation is a new birth. When the Holy Ghost makes us new creatures, we are " begotten of God ;" " his seed is in us," the divine germ of a new nature and a new life.

This, let it be noted also, is something more than God's consenting to reckon us his children, by a gracious act of adoption. It is his making us really, in our very nature, his children. It is not merely that he takes us to be on a new footing with him, as I might take a houseless orphan to be to me as a son. Literally and truly he begets us as children to himself. The houseless orphan whom I desire to have for my son may never be really a son to me. I may fail in all my attempts to make him, in any true or valid sense, my son. He will be my servant, because he cannot help it ; he will render to me punctual, and even punctilious, obedience. But alas ! it is not such obedience as I care for. I see too clearly that he often looks on me still as a hard master, and feels my commandments to be grievous. No such disappointment can await the Almighty Father. He begets by his Spirit those whom he adopts in his Son. They are begotten of God ; begotten by the agency of his Spirit, as his incarnate Son was ; begotten, to be to him what he is ; to feel towards him as he feels. That ensures their overcoming whatever might tempt them to count God's commandments grievous ; or, in other words, their overcoming the world.

" Look unto Jesus." Was ever any servant of God,—for such he was,—placed in circumstances more likely to make the commandments of God be felt as grievous, such commandments especially as he had to fulfil ? Go with him through all his experience in the world. The command-

ments of God laid on him; the things he had to do, the
things he had to suffer ; were surely capable of being
represented to him as grievous, and regarded by him as
grievous. They were so represented to him by the world
and its prince. Were they so regarded by him? And if
not, why not? Because he was "begotten of God;"
begotten of God, not merely as to his divine nature, but as
to his human nature also ; as " God manifest in the flesh;"
"Jesus Christ come in the flesh ;" "the man Christ Jesus."
In respect of his manhood, as well as his Godhead, he is the
only begotten Son of God ; occupying a son's place in the
heart of God; having a son's affection towards God in
his own heart. Therefore no commandment of God, whatever tears and groans and cries it might exhort from his
feeble flesh, could ever be grievous to his filial spirit. So,
in virtue of his being born of God, he overcame the world.

And so also we in virtue of our being born of God,
overcome the world ; the world which is ever insinuating
that the commandments of God are grievous; that the
things he requires us to do, and the things he requires us to
suffer, are hard. We never can withstand these insinua-
tions of the world, fitting in so well into our own carnal
disposition, unless we stand in a filial relation to God, and
are possessed of a filial frame of mind, a filial heart, towards
him ; being not only adopted by him, but begotten of him.
But being his children indeed ; standing to him in the relation of sons, and having our whole inner man renewed into
harmony and correspondence with that relation ; being to
him all that his only begotten Son is, and feeling towards
him as his only begotten Son feels ; we have such personal
knowledge of him as our Father, such loving acquaintance
with him, such insight into his character and plans, such
cordial sympathy with him in the great work which he is
carrying on in the earth, as must convince us that nothing

he can demand of us as his ministers and servants, nothing he can lay upon us, can be anything else than what we ought to welcome in the words and in the spirit of Jesus : " I delight to do thy will, O my God ; yea, thy law is within my heart.

2. This implies faith ; and faith in constant and lively exercise. Our overcoming the world is not an achievement completed at once, and once for all, in our being begotten of God. It is a life-long business; a prolonged and continuous triumph in a prolonged and continuous strife. We are to be always anew, all our days, overcoming the world ; " and this is the victory that overcometh the world, even our faith." Our being born of God does indeed give us the victory ; it puts us in the right position, and endows us with the needful power, for overcoming the world. But we have still before us the work of actually, from day to day, all our lifelong, in point of fact, overcoming the world. And it is by faith that we do so. Our being born of God is the source of the victory ; our faith is the realisation of it, or the acting of it out. Our being born of God fits and qualifies us for overcoming the world ; our faith really overcomes it.

Nor is it difficult to harmonise these two things ; our being born of God and so overcoming the world, and the victory which overcometh the world being our faith. For our being born of God, which is the secret of our overcoming the world, is itself intimately connected with faith ; it originates faith and culminates in faith ; its immediate outgoing in activity is faith. And therefore faith, continually exercised, constantly acting, is the instrument of victory. Nor is it merely faith apprehending a past event in our moral history, an accomplished change in our spiritual condition, our being " born of God." It is faith exercised upon a present object ; not looking back or looking in, but looking out; "looking unto Jesus." For "who is he that overcometh the world, but he that believeth that Jesus is the Son of God?" Jesus is the ever-present object of this ever acting faith; Jesus considered as the Son of God. For it is the sonship of Jesus that our faith grasps, embraces, and appropriates. And it is because it does so that it is "the victory which overcometh the world." Who is he who is at any given moment, and with reference to any given trial or temptation, really overcoming the world? Is it not he who, at that very moment, and with special reference to that very trial or temptation, is "believing that Jesus is the Son of God;" so believing as to be one with him in his being so; of one mind and of one heart, then and there, as to the precise matter in hand or the particular question raised; of one mind and heart with Jesus the Son of God; judging the case as he, the Son of God, would have judged it; feeling as he, the Son of God, would have felt; acting as in the circumstances he, the Son of God, would have acted?

Jesus himself had to overcome, and did overcome, the world. How? Was it not by faith? by faith in his own sonship, or rather faith in God as his Father, faith ever intensely and vividly realising it as a truth that God was his Father? It was as the Son of God that he looked out upon the world; from his Father's point of view. It was as the Son of God that he met the world's attractions; the consciousness of his Father's love stripped them in his eyes of all their charms. It was as the Son of God that he was tempted; trust in his Father's faithfulness kept him without sin. It was as the Son of God that he suffered, and suffered willingly, that his Father might be glorified. Into his pure, calm, filial spirit, there never did, there never could, enter the very faintest shadow of a suspicion that anything his Father ordered or ordained could be otherwise

than just, and right, and good. Therefore the world had
no hold over him; "the prince of the world had nothing
in him." There was not in him any latent or lurking element of possible impatience under the yoke, to which the
world might appeal, and by means of which, persuading
him that God's way was harsh, the world might subdue
him. For though he became the servant of the Father, he
was still the Son; and therefore in serving the Father,
being still the Son, he overcame the world. So we also,
believing that Jesus is the Son of God, and being ourselves
sons of God in him, may find that in this way we can
overcome the world. At all events, we may be very sure
that there is no other "victory that overcometh the world"
but only this faith; this filial faith in God our Father;
giving the lie to all the world's aspersions on his character,
and all the world's complaints against his government
and law.

O child of God, wouldest thou overcome the world?
Is it thine earnest, anxious, longing desire so to overcome
the world that it shall never have power any more to make
thee feel any one of thy God's commandments to be
grievous? Is it a distress to thee that such a feeling still
prevails so much and so often in thy secret soul; that thy
walk before God, thy fellowship with God, thy service of
God, are all so marred, tainted, cramped, and hindered, by
the ever-recurring suggestion that this or that thing
required of thee is hard? Yes; it is hard to cut off a right
hand and pluck out a right eye; hard to deny self and
take up the cross; hard to crucify the flesh with its affections and lusts; hard to go forth unto Christ without the
camp bearing his reproach; hard to forego a seemingly
harmless pleasure; hard to part with one dearly beloved;
hard to bear excruciating pain; hard to die by premature
decay; hard to lay down life for a brother! Ah! is it a

grief to thee, a sore mortification and disappointment, that thou art so easily moved by the world ; for it is thy love of the world, or the world's power over thee, that moves thee ; thus to think, thus to feel, if not even thus to speak? Here, and only here, is the remedy. Believe, be always believing, that Jesus, so called because he saves his people from their sins, is the Son of God; that it is as the Son of God that he saves thee ; and that he saves thee so as to make thee a son; being himself the first-born among many brethren. Rise to the full height of that great position. Realise its greatness; the greatness of its freedom ; "the glorious liberty of the sons of God." That is "the victory which overcometh the world," even such faith as that.

38

THE THREE WITNESSES AND THEIR AGREEMENT

"This is he that came by water and blood, even Jesus Christ; not by
water only, but by water and blood. And it is the Spirit that
beareth witness, because the Spirit is truth. . . . And there are
three that bear witness, the Spirit, and the water, and the blood:
and these three agree in one."   1 John 5:6 and 8*

THE faith which is "the victory that overcometh the
world" has for its object Jesus, viewed as the Son of God;
for "who is he that overcometh the world, but he that
believeth that Jesus is the Son of God?" This faith,
however, does not simply contemplate Jesus as the Son of
God; dwelling exclusively either on his original and
eternal sonship, or on that sonship as manifested in his
human nature. It has to deal with his work as well as
with his person. It has to deal with him as "come;"
"come in the flesh;" "come into the world." And in
particular, it has to deal with two accessories or accom-
paniments of his coming; two distinguishing facts or
features characteristic of the manner of his coming and its
design. He came, he is come, through the medium, or in
the element, not of water only, but of blood also. So
coming he is "Jesus the Christ;" the anointed Saviour;
and it is our faith in him as the Son of God so come, as

---

* I acquiesce of course in the rejection of the 7th verse, and of the
words "in earth" in the 8th verse, as not in the original. I need not
argue the point, for it is now all but universally admitted by intelligent
critics.

Jesus Christ coming by or with water and blood, which is the victory that overcometh the world. "He is come by water and blood;" not "by water only," as his forerunner came, "but by water and blood;" himself undergoing a baptism of blood as well as of water, and so having blood and water available for those who are one with him.

This was conclusively indicated when on the cross his side was pierced, and "forthwith came thereout blood and water" (John xix. 34). Then he was seen coming by water and by blood. And the fact was verified on the spot. "He that saw it bare record, and his record is true, and he knoweth that he saith true, that ye might believe" (ver. 35). So John writes in his Gospel, very emphatically giving us his testimony, as an eyewitness, for a ground of our faith.

Here, in his epistle, he points to testimony still higher; not human, but divine; testimony, not to the mere matter of fact which he saw, but to its spiritual significancy and power, that we may so believe as by our faith to overcome the world: "it is the Spirit that beareth witness." And of the Spirit as bearing witness, not only may it be said that "his record is true and he knoweth that he saith true," he is truth itself; "he is himself truth," and he guides into all truth. This is a greater witness than John could be; for the Spirit attests, not the outward historical occurrence merely, but its inward meaning and saving virtue.

But even the Spirit can thus bear witness only by associating with himself two other witnesses. These are "the water and the blood;" the very water and the very blood by which Jesus Christ came. Bearing witness that he so "cometh by water and blood," the Spirit makes the water and the blood themselves witnesses along with him; so that "there are three that bear witness, the Spirit, the

water, and the blood : and these three agree in one"
(ver. 8).

Two topics here suggest themselves for inquiry—I. The
manner of this threefold testimony; and II. Its harmony
and completeness.

I. Let the manner of this threefold testimony be considered. Let the witnesses be, as it were, called in court ;
first the single witness indicated in the sixth verse, the
Spirit ; and then the other two pointed out in the eighth,
the water and the blood.

In the first place, " the Spirit beareth witness." He is
the first and principal witness : pre-eminently, the witness-
bearer. That he is a fitting witness cannot be doubted ;
the only question is, how does he give his testimony ?
For he does not appear visibly ; he does not speak audibly ;
we neither " see his shape at any time, nor hear his voice."
And yet it is to us that he testifies ; and he testifies to us
personally, as the living Spirit to living men, present with
us here and now. How then does he make his presence
known ? And how does he make the purport of his testimony understood ? We are called in this matter to take
evidence and decide a cause ; and, strange to say, the first
and principal witness cited is one whom we neither see
nor hear.

But there may be evidence of his presence as satisfactory
as sight ; and there are modes of conveying testimony as
intelligible and unequivocal as spoken language. The
Spirit may announce his presence by " a rushing mighty
noise," or by his swift descent, like a dove, from on high.
By lambent flames, " cloven tongues as of fire," resting or
flickering over the heads of an assembled company ; by new
and strange languages proceeding from their mouths ; by
some evidently supernatural work wrought ; by some supernatural gift, or endowment, or power imparted ; or by

moral miracles of converting and quickening grace, as indisputable as any of these ; the presence of the Spirit may be ascertained. And if now having him actually with us, we inquire what as a witness he has to say ; then, in the inseparable connection which is to be observed between these signs of his presence and certain facts or statements otherwise known to us, we may obtain a silent indeed, but a sufficiently explicit reply. We have the word spoken at first, and then written, by holy men of old as they were moved by the Holy Ghost. And the Spirit, by whose inspiration that word was originally given, may significantly acknowledge it now as his own, by accompanying tokens of his influence not to be mistaken. He may, as it were, in our presence and to our satisfaction, before whom he is cited as a witness, homologate what he dictated ages ago ; and so expressly signify, by some unquestionable demonstration of his power, his actual concurrence now in what was said or written then, as to make it strictly and directly his testimony to us personally ; and his testimony brought down to the present hour. Thus, in the word, we have the deposition of the Spirit as first and principal witness in this great cause ; we have the precise matter of his testimony. And we have it, not merely as the written report of former evidence, but as evidence emitted anew by him to us now.

This is especially important. The appeal is clearly made, not to the Spirit as having borne witness formerly, and left his testimony on record ; but to the Spirit as bearing witness now. For the witness in this case is not, as in other and ordinary cases, one who dies or goes out of the way. In such cases, we must content ourselves with the notes of the deposition, the report or record of the testimony, as given by him and taken down at the time. Here, the witness is ever living and ever accessible. He is not afar off; he is always at hand; to verify his own evidence. Nor can he be at a loss for ways and means of doing so. He is indeed determined, so to speak, to preserve his· incognito and keep himself concealed. But he is almighty, the Spirit of power, having command over all the moving forces of the world, the world both of matter and of mind. Therefore he can give intimation of his presence by works peculiarly his own. And these works now he may so connect with words spoken or written of old, as to make us feel, not only that he then suggested the words as his, but that he is addressing them to us now as his; not only that he did once bear witness, but that he is now bearing witness, and that this is his testimony. Thus the Spirit bears present witness through his own inspired word.

And now, secondly, in the course of giving this testimony, in his very manner of giving it, the Spirit associates with himself other two witnesses, "the water and the blood." And these, like the first, are present witnesses. The Spirit, in bearing witness, "takes of what is Christ's and shows it unto us." He points to the Son of God, Jesus Christ come in the flesh; and especially to his coming "by water and blood."

But how, it may be asked, can the water and the blood be brought forward as witnesses now? They might bear silent testimony at the time when they flowed from the smitten side of Jesus on the cross, and they to whom the Spirit was then bearing witness might see, through his teaching, as the dying thief did, in the pure water and the precious blood, a confirmation of the truth concerning Christ, that in him there is not only renewal of nature, but redemption also, and remission of sins. But the water and the blood are not accessible to us now. The water was spilt on the ground; and the earth opened her mouth to receive the blood. We would seek in vain, where the cross stood, for any traces of the drops that then fell beside it; and even if some of these drops had been preserved and handed down to us, they would have been but dead relics, such as superstition loves to dote upon, not living witnesses, such as the living Spirit may associate in witness-bearing with himself. The water then and the blood are removed out of the way; we have them no more within our reach. We have indeed sacramental signs and seals of them, in the water of baptism and the wine of communion. But these elements are really as dead as are the water and the blood which they represent. There cannot be more life in the water of baptism, than there is now in the water that came from the Saviour's side; nor in the wine of communion than in the blood. But the water and the blood are, as to the matter of them, irrecoverably lost. Still therefore the question remains, How do they now give present living evidence along with the living Spirit?

The real explanation is to be found in this consideration, that though the event itself, the flowing of water and blood from the pierced side, was of brief duration and soon passed away, the relation in which it stands to heaven and earth is permanent and perpetual. For it is the relation in which it stands to heaven and earth, to the divine government and to our human interests, which alone gives to the event, or to any circumstance connected with the event, its significancy as a testimony. The death of Christ, as a mere fact, occupied but a point of time in the lapse of eternal ages; but in its bearing upon the designs of God and the destinies of man,—and it is that alone which renders it important,—it has properly no date at all. " From before the foundation of the world," Jesus is " the Lamb slain;" he is the Lamb slain, to the close of all things. Whatever therefore took place or was going on at Christ's death, we are to regard as taking place and going on now. Viewed as mere incidents of a historical transaction, the water and the blood flowed once, and have long ceased to flow; but then, viewed merely in that light, they tell us nothing, they bear witness to nothing, beyond the bare fact of a human being having died. It is only when they are viewed in their relation to God and to man, that the water and the blood have a tale to tell, a testimony to give. And considered in that light, they must be held as having flowed from the beginning, and as continuing to the end to flow.

Hence their testimony is inseparable from that of the Spirit. For it is not in or by themselves, but only in and with and by the Spirit, that the water and the blood are or can be witnesses at all. Only through the Spirit have the wounds of Jesus an intelligible voice and utterance to convince and move the soul. For in truth it may be emphatically said of the water and the blood, and of any testimony they may bear, "It is the Spirit that quickeneth, the flesh profiteth nothing." The water and the blood carnally apprehended, regarded and understood after the flesh, are not witnesses at all; at least not witnesses of any heavenly transaction, or of any divine and spiritual truth; and of course not witnesses of the bearing of any such transaction or any such truth on the highest spiritual and heavenly interests of men. But "spiritually discerned," the water and the blood, the water for purification and the blood for atonement, like all the words and works of Jesus, are "spirit and life" (John vi. 63). And thus the whole truth concerning Christ and his death attested by the Spirit, and by the water and the blood associated with the Spirit and rendered significant and saving by him, becomes the source of spiritual life and strength to every one who believes that "Jesus is the Son of God," and enables him therefore "to overcome the world." For "this is the victory that overcometh the world, even our faith;" that faith of ours which grasps the threefold testimony of the Spirit, the water, and the blood. Here is Jesus Christ coming by water and blood; very specially by blood; "not by water only, but by water and blood." And the Spirit, with the water and the blood, and by means of them as joint-witnesses with himself, testifies to him as "coming by water and blood," and as, in virtue of his so coming, giving us the victory over the world. Not otherwise than by taking the water and the blood as joint-witnesses with himself, can the Spirit commend to us Jesus Christ, as triumphing in his own person, and causing us who are one with him to triumph, over sin, and the guilt of sin, and the power of sin; over all that makes God's service a bondage to us and his commandments grievous; over what constitutes the essence of the world which we have to overcome if we would walk as children with our Father in heaven.

II. Such being the nature of this threefold testimony, let us look now at its harmony: "These three agree in one." This may perhaps be best brought out by putting the supposition of a partial reception of the testimony in different aspects; and showing how, in every case, the partial reception, if fairly followed out, requires and demands the acceptance of the whole, and must lead the earnest soul to that result.

1. There are some who seem to acquiesce in the testimony of the Spirit, but without having respect either to the water or to the blood. To this extent at least they may go, that they admit the reality of those supernatural works by which the Spirit of old bore witness to the word, and generally they admit the authority of the word as attested by the Spirit to be the word of God. They acknowledge, in a sort of vague and general way, that the Lord Jesus is the Son of God and the Saviour of the world.

He is declared and proved to be so by the Spirit of truth, and they do not question what the Spirit says. Theirs is a kind of indefinite, blind, stupid reliance on something, one knows not what, that the Spirit says in the Scriptures about Christ. But do they really receive the testimony, even of the Spirit alone, in any sense consistent with fairness or intelligence? What would be thought of such conduct in reference to temporal things? Take a somewhat analogous instance.

I come to you with information to give you, on a point deeply affecting your welfare. I hold in my hands a document which I assure you is of urgent consequence to you, securing you against the hazard of loss, putting you in the way of great gain. And how do you receive me? You take the document out of my hands, with many formal compliments and thanks, and many professions of personal respect for me. You will prize it very highly, pay it all due attention, and seek to profit by it. But I have much to say to you regarding the document and its contents. I seek to prolong the conversation with you upon the document. I wish to press upon your regard certain parts of it which I am willing to open up to you; and in particular I am most anxious to help you in turning its discoveries to good practical account. You listen impatiently; for I weary you. Is it not enough that you take the document as I desire you, and really intend not to neglect it? So, getting rid of me, you retain my paper. You treat it with considerable deference; you duly look into it; you find in it some hints that you may follow, some directions with which you can comply; and if you do stumble at a few dark things in it, this is no more than might have been anticipated beforehand. At all events, you are in possession of the deed, which you have been told is, somehow or other, to secure to you safety and victory.

Is it thus that we are treating the blessed Spirit of God? We receive his testimony; that is, we take the Bible at his hands, and on the whole admit as true what he told the world about Christ when he inspired the Bible. But we do not suffer him to bear witness to us now. If we did, he would not indeed give evidence now by such signs as of old; but he would give evidence by tokens no less satisfactory, because no less divine. In particular, the Spirit would bear witness, not generally and vaguely to Christ coming as a Saviour, but specially to his coming by water and blood. This he would do by his divine agency, appealing to our whole inner man, and working there, with and by the word.

Allow the Holy Ghost to have full scope and free course in testifying to you now. Give the Spirit his own place; let him follow out his own plan. What plan? you ask. Ah! is he not already giving you some hint of his plan? He would have you let him keep hold of you, when he has begun to deal with you, to deal with your conscience in the way of conviction, with your heart in the way of persuasion. Does Felix tremble? Is Agrippa almost persuaded? The Spirit is testifying of Christ. Are you beginning to suspect that there may be more in the gospel than you once thought; that you may require to go deeper into religion; that the vague kind of confidence you have been cherishing, and the loose sort of piety you have been cultivating, will scarcely suffice much longer; that you need something more distinct, a more thorough search into what is the real state of the case as between your God and you, a more thorough settlement of the footing on which you are to be with him, a far more thoroughly decided walk? Have you misgivings now as to those generalities in doctrine and those formalities in duty which used to content you? Do not doubt that the Spirit is testifying to you of Christ, and do not resist or grieve him. Let him carry on his own work in his own way, the way in which he has already begun it. And he will soon make you right glad to welcome Jesus Christ " coming by water and blood ; " having in himself and in his cross precious blood to atone for all guilt, as well as pure water to cleanse from all pollution.

2. You may lean to the water as bearing witness, rather than to the blood. The influence of the gospel in purifying the heart and life may be that feature by which mainly it approves itself to your mind. You recognise the necessity of being renewed to holiness or virtue, and therefore you can apprehend and appreciate the testimony of the water by which Jesus Christ came ; his requiring and providing for that result. But this purifying virtue in Christ, or in the gospel of Christ, you view very much apart from his blood of atonement ; so that the change of heart towards God becomes to you, not only the chief part, but almost the whole of personal religion. You may not set altogether aside the blood ; but practically you may be placing little reliance upon it and feeling little need of it. In that case, you set little value on the testimony of the blood ; to the water and the Spirit you give all the preference.

Then, let me say again, give these two witnesses fair scope ; let their testimony be fully carried out. In other words, follow out your own convictions. You see now in some degree, and feel what alone can satisfy your God ; what he is really entitled to claim and to expect at your hands. The law has come home to you, to your conscience and heart, in the full extent of its obligations, as binding you to perfect love, and making even a sin of thought exceeding sinful. That law approves itself as infinitely excellent ; altogether reasonable ; " holy, and just, and good." You perceive now that to this law you must become willingly subject, that you must be brought into that state in which it shall be your meat to do the will of God, even as it was Christ's. Under these impressions, having now a vivid perception of what holiness really is, you may set about being holy, in right earnest and with all your might. Do you succeed? Nay, the very effort defeats itself; the struggle sinks you deeper in conscious guilt, and helpless subjection to the evil that is in you. The corruption of your nature is provoked and stimulated; you feel yourself paralysed, enchained, imprisoned. And while this new discovery of the " desperate wickedness of the heart," this sad proof that you are so very far from being what God would have you to be, grieves you to the quick, the distress is aggravated by the consciousness of utter inability, the bitter impression that it is almost useless to think of being godly at all. For in this state even the assurance of the Spirit's supernatural aid avails you nothing. It is not help in obeying that you need; the very principle of obedience is wanting, and it seems hopeless to think of ever attaining it.

Hopeless, except only in one direction. Let the Spirit not only undertake to assist you, as with purifying water, in your work of holiness; but let him also, and first of all, bear witness to Christ as coming not by purifying water only, but also by atoning blood. Let the blood itself give testimony; and your case is precisely met. For what is it that lies at the bottom of such experience as Paul describes in the passage of his writings to which I have been alluding? (Rom. vii.) Is it not the unsettled controversy between your God and you? But the precious blood of Jesus, his perfect obedience unto death, meets your case. It furnishes the very element you need; for it furnishes the element of instant and complete reconciliation to your God. It cancels your guilt; it sets you free from condemnation; it seals your peace. And now the heart, so crushed and depressed before, springs up as with elastic rebound, and wings its eagle flight to heaven, while the feet run in the way of God's commandments.

3. In another manner, the reverse of the former, this blessed harmony of the divine testimony may be disturbed. Instead of a preference for the water apart from the blood, there may be a leaning to the blood, to the omission of the water; as if Christ came not both by water and by blood, but by blood only. The idea of an expiation of guilt may commend itself to the minds of conscious offenders, who feel their sin and fear the wrath of God. They may welcome the blood which testifies of sin atoned for, and God pacified and reconciled. They may be inclined to acquiesce in the testimony of the Spirit and the blood, as if the gospel were intended simply to pacify the troubled conscience and set sinful men at their ease.

But here again, I say as before, Give heed fairly to the testimony of the Spirit and the blood; and it will be found to require for its completion the testimony of the water. You are open to the impression of the blood; you see and feel the reasonableness and the reality of the atonement made by blood for your sin. But if the Spirit is at all bearing witness with the blood, it must be a spiritual view of the necessity and the meaning of that atonement that he is causing you to take. You cannot, if the Spirit is witnessing along with it, regard it as an expedient for soothing the personally vindictive feelings of an offended God, and purchasing his indulgence for your frailties; a mere provision for averting judgment and giving you security and quiet. No. You take a spiritual view of the shedding of the blood of Christ, as on the one hand vindicating the righteousness and manifesting the love of God; and on the other hand laying a foundation for a holy and loving walk with him.

The blood, if you rightly receive its testimony along with that of the Spirit, speaks, not of God weakly persuaded to be indulgent and sinners allowed to escape unpunished ; but of God righteously justifying believing men, and on the footing of a righteous justification freely restoring them to his favour. Its very end is to bring men near to God ; and so far from setting them free from the obligation of being washed, this is its highest value, that it secures their being "washed," so as to be "sanctified as well as justified, in the name of the Lord Jesus, and by the Spirit of our God."

Thus in these three instances it may be seen that every attempt to give undue prominence to one of the witnesses, to the comparative slighting of the others, necessarily implies an unfair treatment of the testimony even of the very witness that is preferred. If the Spirit alone is viewed as bearing witness ; then his testimony is frittered down till it is nothing more than a sort of vague intimation of there being a revelation and a plan of salvation, without any distinct reference either to what the revelation contains or to what the plan of salvation is. If again the water is selected, and the sanctifying and purifying virtue of the gospel is chiefly commended ; there is danger lest a low standard of holiness be set up, such as may be consistent with a conscience still unpacified and a heart still unreconciled. And if, once more, the blood is the witness on whose testimony we dwell ; we are led to misconceive altogether both the design and the efficacy of the atonement ; making it a mere scheme of accommodation, instead of a glorious plan for upholding the divine righteousness and more than restoring the primeval dignity of man. "There are three that bear witness ; " and it is only when all the three are received with equal faith, that they are found to "agree in one."

4. But there is one other case to which I must briefly

advert. The water and the blood may be received as bearing witness, without a due regard to the testimony of the living Spirit. The gospel may be understood in its full and comprehensive import, and may approve itself to the conscience and the heart. Christ may be known as coming both by water and by blood ; the minister alike of renewal and of redemption ; of purifying as well as of pardoning grace. But what, you ask, what is all that to me ? Christ is set forth crucified before you, and from him all blessings freely flow. The plan of saving mercy, as it comes from heaven, is complete ; Christ coming both by water and blood is the very Saviour you need. But you have difficulty about his really saving you ; about the application of his complete salvation to you ; about your want of faith to lay hold of him and of it.

Beware here of the temptation of the spirit of evil ; receive rather the testimony of the Spirit of truth. These thoughts and misgivings, so dishonourable to God, whose puṛpose of free love they impede, so injurious to you, whose return to God they arrest, are from the father of lies. Resist them, as of the devil ; for they are false as he is himself. He may give them some air of plausibility, in order that if possible he may confuse more and more the question of your relation to God and the footing on which you are to be with God, so as to make you give up the care of your salvation as hopeless. But you must see that they are contrary to the plain testimony of the water and the blood ; for surely these witnesses, the water and the blood, do most emphatically speak to you of the fulness of God's grace, and the ample foundation he has laid at once for your peace and for your holiness.

And even when you are tempted to yield to the surmises of Satan, are you not conscious of other thoughts ? Is it not sometimes borne in upon your mind that this hesitating and halting unbelief is but an unworthy way of meeting such overtures as God is making, and that you might at least make the trial, and venture your soul on his faithful promises ?

It is the Spirit that thus bears witness; and "the Spirit is truth." Put the matter to an experimental test; commit yourself to Christ, of whom the Spirit testifies, as having water from his smitten side to wash, and blood, precious blood, to take away all guilt. For it is in this way of actual trial that you will have the witness of the Spirit, which is the witness of God. In the peace which flows from the settlement of his controversy with you and your justification in his sight; in the glad relief which a simple acceptance of his mercy imparts; in the sense of his love shed abroad in your hearts; in the growing clearness of your views of his character, and the growing enlargement and elevation of your soul for his service; in the laying aside of all reserve on your part, as all reserve is laid aside on his; in the entrusting of your whole way, in darkness and distress, to him, and the surrender of your whole soul and body and spirit into his hands; you will understand, with increasing clearness, the consenting testimony of the three witnesses, the Spirit, the water, and the blood. And through faith in that testimony you will overcome the world. For no commandment of God will ever be grievous to you, if it comes to you in the power of the Spirit, and through the double channel of the water and the blood.

39

THE WITNESS OR TESTIMONY OF GOD TO AND IN BELIEVERS

"If we receive the witness [testimony] of men, the witness [testimony] of God is greater : for this is the witness [testimony] of God which he hath testified of his Son. He that believeth on the Son of God hath the witness [testimony] in himself : he that believeth not God hath made him a liar ; because he believeth not the record [testimony] that God gave [hath testified] of his Son." 1 John 5:9,10 *

THE question is still about faith; the faith which is the victory that overcometh the world (ver. 4, 5). For that is the particular function here ascribed to faith ; that is the light in which faith is to be regarded. Doubtless, gospel faith is the same, in whatever light, and with reference to whatever function, it is contemplated; it has always the same object, and the same ground or warrant. But the manner of its exercise may not be the same. And therefore it is to be noted that it is not faith as justifying ; nor faith simply as working generally by love; but faith specially as overcoming the world ; that is spoken of in this passage. It is as "the victory that overcometh the world," that faith is commended or extolled.

This faith rests on testimony ; as all faith must do. And the testimony on which it rests is sufficient to

---

* It is much to be regretted that in these verses our Translators should have so unwarrantably, and to the utter obscuring of the sense, sacrificed exactness to variety ; using four different English words for one and the same verb, with its cognate noun, in the original Greek.

sustain it; for it is divine: "If we receive the testimony of men, the testimony of God is greater: for this is the testimony of God which he hath testified of his Son" (ver. 9). Human testimony is a trustworthy ground of faith; we rely on it every day, and act accordingly. That is assumed as admitted. But we have what is far better and stronger than human testimony; we have "the testimony of God." Men are fallible and frail; the Psalmist "said in his haste, All men are 'liars." Still we receive their testimony; and we cannot help it; we must come to a dead-lock or stand-still, if we do not. How much more confidently may we receive the testimony of him who can neither deceive nor be deceived; who knows all things and is truth itself. To reject his testimony, and refuse to proceed on the faith of it, while we receive and act upon the testimony of men, is inconsistency and utter folly.

But what is the testimony of God, and how is it given?

First, What is his testimony? That is not expressly stated in this verse; it is left to be inferred. But it is not difficult to say what it is; whether we look back on the preceding context or forwards to that which follows. Of course, it is the preceding context that must chiefly guide us; but the two very much agree. As it stands in the preceding context, it is that "Jesus Christ is the Son of God, coming by water and blood." As it stands in the following context, it is that "God hath given us eternal life, and this life is in his Son."

Secondly, How is his testimony given? As to that, this ninth verse says nothing. But it plainly connects the preceding and following contexts. John evidently means to say that he has been describing, and that he is going on to describe still further, this testifying, on God's part, of his Son, with special reference to the manner of it.

For he draws at this point a broad line of distinction. In what goes before, he has been speaking of God's testimony from without, or to us; in what follows, he is to speak of God's testimony within, or in us. It is the testimony of God in both cases; his bearing witness of his Son; and it is to be received as such. But whereas it has been put in the former passage as operating on us; it is now to be put as ascertained, apprehended, and felt, by us and in us: " He that believeth on the Son of God hath the testimony in himself : he that believeth not God hath made him a liar; because he believeth not the testimony that God hath testified of," or about, " his Son " (ver. 10).

" He that believeth on the Son of God hath the testimony in himself; " the testimony, that is, of God ; for it is upon the warrant of " the testimony of God which he has testified about his Son," that he believes on the Son of God. But in his so believing, that testimony of God becomes to him a matter of inward consciousness. He has it within him; in himself. It is not now merely God testifying to us of his Son, but God testifying in us of his Son; causing us to know experimentally the truth of what he testifies. We find, by actual trial and experience, that the Son is exactly what the Father has been testifying him to be : "the Son of God, Jesus Christ, coming by water and blood." Thus the inward verifies the outward.

It is as if a friend should introduce to me his son, with a high testimony to his personal excellency and rank, as well as to his power and willingness to assist me in an emergency, and be of service to me all my days. I believe the testimony, and on the faith of it welcome the new-comer to my home and heart. He soon approves himself to me as all that his father said I would find him to be. Then I have the testimony in a sense in me, in myself. So far the analogy may hold and be helpful. But, like all earthly analogies of what is divine, it is imperfect. It is only in a sense somewhat vague and loose that, in the case supposed, I can be said to have the testimony of my friend about his son in me. For it is not really my friend testifying in me, as something distinct from his testifying to me; it is I myself who am proving and verifying his testimony. In this case, also, it is that, no doubt; that at least. But is it not something more? For the testifier is God; and he of whom he testifies is his own Son. Literally, therefore, and in the strictest and fullest sense, I can have God's testimony in me; I can have God himself testifying in me. And I can have him testifying in me, not of his Son offered and given to me, as " coming by water and by blood;" but of his Son, so coming by water and by blood, and now dwelling in my heart; "Christ in me, the hope of glory." This is something quite different from our own consciousness apprehending the truth, and feeling the reality, of what God testifies of his Son. It is rather like what Paul indicates when he says : " The Spirit itself beareth witness," or testifies, " with our Spirit, that we are the children of God : and if children, then heirs; heirs of God, and joint-heirs with Christ : if so be that we suffer with him, that we may be also glorified together."

An indispensable condition of this inward testifying of God in us, our having in us his testimony, is our believing on his Son : " He that believeth on the Son of God," and he alone, " hath the testimony in himself." Evidently it must be so. For it is our believing on his Son that brings God into these hearts of ours, in which he is to testify of his Son in us more and more. And just as evidently, this believing on his Son, which thus leads to our having the testimony within us, must rest on the testimony from without. It is our believing on his Son, on the ground and warrant of his testifying to us of his Son, that opens the way for our having him testifying in us of his Son. And so we are brought back to this, that we are to believe on the Son of God, not because God testifies of him in us, but because he testifies of him to us. Is not that, however, warrant enough? Is it not sufficient of itself to win faith the most confiding, since it is the testimony of him who is the truth? Does it not make unbelief inexcusable? For refusing to believe, on the strength of the outward testimony alone, even without the inward, is simply giving God the lie: "He that believeth not God hath made him a liar; because he believeth not the testimony that God hath testified of his Son."

Thus, I. The ground and reward or fruit of faith; and II. The sin of unbelief; are to be viewed in the light of its being God's testimony and not man's that is to be believed.

I. Faith stands here between two divine testimonies, or two modes of the one divine testimony; it is the effect of the first, and the cause or means of the second.

In the first place, as an effect, faith flows from the three-fold testimony of "the Spirit, the water, and the blood;" which is the primary testimony of God, from without or from above. You who believe on the Son of God believe on him as witnessed or attested by God; you believe on him because it is really God who has testified or testifies of him. And the testimony of God, upon which you believe on him, is substantially of the same sort as the testimony of men, to which you are accustomed to give credit. That is implied in what is said: "If we receive the testimony of men, the testimony of God is greater." For it is indeed the testimony of God that you are to receive, "the testimony which he hath testified of his Son." It is testimony to you; not in you. It may be in some sense and to some extent in you, in so far as it enlists on its behalf, or is fitted to enlist, your inward convictions, tastes, and tendencies But as long as it is testimony, not received and admitted, but claiming to be received and admitted, it is testimony to you. And it is upon that testimony that your faith must lay hold and lean.

I have said that this testimony of God to you may, in some sense and to some extent, be in you ; it may be testimony appealing to certain inward instincts or principles of your nature. It is so in the present instance. For in fact, the testimony of God as to his Son which is here compared with the testimony of men, and preferred to it, is altogether and exclusively of an internal nature ; it is God dealing with your whole inner man, through the threefold testimony of the Spirit, the water, and the blood. There is no reference to what are called the external evidences of Christianity ; the historical proofs of the gospel. The Spirit, the water, and the blood, are not represented as testifying through the medium of outward events or signs ; authenticated, as these usually are, by the evidence, not of mere tradition, transmitting hearsay at secondhand, but of competent witnesses, leaving on record what they actually saw and heard. That would be the testimony of men. We have that, God be praised we have it most abundantly ; and we do well to receive it, and on the strength of it to accept the Bible as a divine revelation and the gospel as a divine message. But the testimony of God is greater ; not only because it is the testimony of God and not of men, but because, being his, it adapts and addresses itself to the inner man in us ; to the whole inner man ; to all our sensibilities and susceptibilities of conscience, emotion, will.

For in this testifying or witness-bearing, the Spirit, having the water and the blood associated with him, makes a direct appeal to the moral sense and feeling within us. He does so altogether apart from all the logical arguments and historical demonstrations which may be brought to confirm our belief in Christianity. These are valuable in their place. But the direct and immediate testimony of God, in the threefold witness-bearing of the Spirit, the water, and the blood, is largely independent and irrespective of them. It is a very straightforward dealing of the Spirit with us ; of the Spirit testifying along with, and by means of, the water and the blood. It is the Spirit pressing home upon us Christ ; making us feel our need of Christ ; showing us Christ's suitableness and sufficiency for us. In particular, it is the Spirit bringing near to us Jesus, as the Son of God, eager to make us one with him in his sonship, and for that very end coming by water and blood ; so that neither sin's defilement nor sin's condemnation may stand in the way of our being partakers of his filial relation to the Father. He is come by water to purify, and by blood to atone, that we may be sons of God in him. That is the testimony of God to us, here and now. Is it not so ? Who is there among us to whom the Spirit is not thus, more or less sensibly, bearing witness along with the water and the blood, here and now ?

Ah ! let me assume that I address some spiritually-awakened and spiritually-exercised soul. Has your sin, brother, found you out ? Is the Spirit convincing you of its exceeding sinfulness ? Are you in earnest longing for purity and peace ? Have you been made to feel that you do really need for your Saviour one who can place you on a very different footing with your God and Father in heaven from that on which you naturally are, and create in you very different dispositions towards him from those which you naturally cherish ? And is there dawning upon you more and more brightly the apprehension that Jesus, as God's own Son, coming by water and by blood, is just such a

Saviour, and that if he were but yours all would be well? Is not this the testimony of God to you, warranting and requiring you to believe on his Son, so coming, as really yours, "loving you and giving himself for you"? Is it not far greater and better than any human testimony? What need have you of my assurance, or any man's assurance, to build your faith on? Here is God's threefold testimony; the Spirit commending to you, all vile and guilty as you are, God's own Son as come by water and by blood, to sanctify and save. Having this testimony, you may well "believe on the Son of God." Yes. Believing because of the Lord's own word, approving itself to your spiritually-quickened soul, you may say, as the Samaritans said to the woman, "Now we believe, not because of thy saying; for we have heard him ourselves, and know that this is indeed the Christ, the Saviour of the world."

And now, secondly, thus believing, you may look for a new and additional testimony of God; not to you, but most truly and fully in you. For this simple honest faith, the effect or fruit of one mode of the divine testimony, becomes the cause or means of another. That other is not outward at all, but altogether inward; not to you, but in you: "He that believeth on the Son of God hath the testimony in himself."

Understand well and keep ever in mind, that having the testimony of God in you is not the preliminary to your believing on the Son of God, but the result or consequence of your doing so. Do not imagine that you are to have any knowledge or experience of this inward testimony of God before you believe on his Son; as if it were to be a ground of your believing, or a help to your believing. It is a sort of knowledge or experience which can never go before faith, but must always follow it. For, in truth, it is nothing more than faith in exercise; faith unfolding and developing its energy; faith acting out its purpose; faith realising more and more its object and itself.

In fact, as to its substance, this testimony of God in you is identically the same as his testimony to you. It is the same threefold testimony of the Spirit, the water, and the blood. Only now the Spirit has won for himself, and for the water and the blood, a place within your consciousness; deep down in your inmost soul, as no longer merely appealed to and assailed by this testimony, but cordially acquiescing in it. That, however, makes a vast difference indeed. It is the difference between Christ "standing at the door and knocking," and Christ, "when you hear his voice and open to him, coming in to sup with you and you with him." The testimony is the same; the testifiers are the same. But your believing acquiescence, I repeat, makes all the difference. The testifiers, the Spirit, the water, and the blood, —are now, all three of them, in you; witnessing not to, but from, the far back recess of your willing mind and consenting heart. Their testimony, which is God's, and therefore far better than man's, is in you now; not as a stream forcing its way, as it were, into the depths of your spiritual experience; but as "a well of water" divinely opened in these depths, and "springing up into everlasting life."

For the real and blessed explanation of the whole matter is simple enough. He to whom the threefold testimony of the Spirit, the water, and the blood relates, is himself in you now; not given to you, with ample warrant for your embracing him; but in you, as embraced by you; in you, as the very Son of God, coming by water and blood. Thus, believing on the Son of God, you have the testimony of God in you. The Spirit is testifying in you, with the water and the blood; not now in order to win your assent and consent, but with your assent and consent

already won. And that being so, there is no limit to the
gracious assurance and enlargement to be looked for from
your thus having the testimony of God in you. For now,
not only your conviction, but your cordial choice also, goes
along with the divine testimony, and is all in the line of it.
You make full proof of it; or rather you suffer the Spirit
himself to make full proof of it in you. He does so by
" taking of what is Christ's and showing it more and more
to you." He gives you an ever-increasing clearness and
intensity of insight into Jesus being the Son of God ; and
into his coming, as the Christ, by water and blood. So
believing, you have the testimony in yourselves ; God
testifying in you by the Spirit, the water, and the blood ;
the Spirit testifying in you of the Son of God coming by
water and by blood.

Let me ask you, in all faithfulness, do you believe in
the Son of God, on God's own testimony to you about him
and not man's ? Then, what do you know of this testimony of God in you ? " It is the Spirit that testifieth."
What do you know of his testifying, not merely in his
striving with you, but in his dwelling in you, and revealing
in you God's own Son, Jesus Christ, coming by water and
blood ? What, first, of the blood by which he comes ? Is
God by his Spirit giving you, not only a sight of your need
of it as a sinner, and its sufficiency for you as for all
sinners, but a sense of its actual efficacy in your case, as
bringing you personally near to God, on the footing of your
personal guilt being atoned for, and yourselves being
personally reconciled ? What, secondly, of the water, by
which, as well as by blood, he comes ? Is God by his
Spirit giving you real personal experience of Christ's being
the purifier and sanctifier, in your being " holy, as he is
holy ? " What, thirdly, of the sonship, of its being God's
own Son who comes by water and by blood ? Is God by

his Spirit giving you an apprehension of your adoption as
sons, and moving you to cry, as sons, Abba, Father?

These, unquestionably, are the three kinds of experience in the line of which your having the testimony of God
in you will make itself known and felt. And if you believe
on the Son of God, you will have some growing practical
acquaintance with all the three. The blood;—does it
really first pierce and then pacify your conscience, pierce
and pacify it evermore, constantly, day by day, more and
more every day? The fountain filled with that blood;—
do you bathe your guilty souls in it every morning, every
night? Do you feel it ever opening your wounds more
painfully, and more sensibly pouring itself, as oil and balm,
into the very wounds it opens? The water;—are you
consciously coming more and more under its power? Is
the holiness of Christ filling your soul, fixing your eye,
drawing your heart? Is your loathing of sin growing
more intense? Do you welcome and value Christ as
the minister of purity, even more than as the minister of
peace, and rejoice in his blood purging your conscience
from dead works, mainly because it thus sets you free to
serve the living God? The sonship of him who comes by
water and blood;—are you entering into that? He is
come by water and by blood, not only to make you one
with himself in his atoning death and in his holy life, but
to make you sons of God in him. Are you realising that?
Are you entering into the position which, as the Son of
God, he occupies; and into his mind and heart, as the Son
of God? Thus, and only thus, "he that believeth on the
Son of God hath the testimony in himself."

II. Over against the power or virtue or efficacy of faith,
turning God's testimony to us into his testimony in us,
John places in very emphatic contrast the exceeding sinfulness of the sin of unbelief: "He that believeth not God

hath made him a liar." The two opposite ways of dealing with the testimony of God are here sharply distinguished. Either you believe his testimony to you, and so honour him that he himself gives you an inward, experimental confirmation of it; you taste and see that God is good; you prove him, and see if he does not open the windows of heaven and pour down on you a blessing; you open your mouth wide and he fills it; giving you peace of conscience, purity of heart, filial liberty, enlargement, assurance, love. Or else, you disbelieve his testimony, and so, by your unbelief, not only hinder him from testifying in you, but dishonour him by virtually giving him the lie when he testifies to you.

And let it be well observed that it is the very same testimony of God to you in both cases, whether you receive it or disbelieve it. You may not shelter your unbelief under the excuse or apology that you have not proof or evidence enough. In particular, you may not plead that you have not the inward testimony. Neither had we, when we believed, may be the reply of those who deal otherwise than you deal with the testimony from without and from above. You have the same ground or warrant for believing that we had; the sure word of the true and faithful God. We were not asked to believe on the ground and warrant of any inward testimony of God in us; any witnessing of the Spirit with our spirits to our being the sons of God. It was not as being the sons of God; it was not as having any title to be the sons of God, or any consciousness of our being the sons of God; that we believed. It was simply as hearing the word or testimony of God, commending to us powerfully and persuasively, by his Spirit, Jesus Christ his Son coming by water and blood; coming to save, with a complete and full salvation, sinners, and of sinners us, the chief. That was all that our faith had to grasp; all that it had to lay hold of and lean on. We found it sufficient; we tested it, and it has stood the test. Why should not you? Why should you wait for anything else, or anything more? We had not any inward sign, we had not any inward experience, on which to build our belief. We had simply God speaking to us; to our understandings, our consciences, our hearts; testifying to us concerning our sin, and the sufficiency for us of his Son, coming by water and by blood to save. You have the same. You have all that we had. You have God, in his Son whom he sent to be the propitiation for your sins; you have God, in his Son coming by water and by blood; you have God, in his Son to whom he points, hanging on the cross, pierced by you, while out of his side come water and blood to wash and heal you; you have God, in his Son thus set forth crucified before your eyes; you have this God thus testifying to you; assuring you; swearing to you; and beseeching you—oh! how importunately and affectionately!—to give him credit when he testifies to you, and assures you, and swears to you : "As I live, saith the Lord God, I have no pleasure in the death of the wicked; but that the wicked turn from his wickedness and live : turn ye, turn ye from your evil ways; for why will ye die, O house of Israel?"

Will you still refuse to give him credit? Will you still dare to question his sincerity, his being in earnest, when he thus pleads with you? Will you not believe that he means what he says, when he tells you that, in his Son coming by water and by blood, he is waiting to be gracious? Do him not so great injustice as to treat him in a way in which you would not venture to treat an honourable man. You receive the testimony of such a man. Is not the testimony of God greater? Is he not entitled to be believed on his simple word, much more on his solemn oath? Is he not one whom you can trust, so far at least as to make trial of his faithfulness? Ah! let there be an end of doubt, hesitancy, halting, delay. All that is most insulting to him; for it is really making him a liar. Do not commit so great a sin; do not shut your eyes to its greatness. Consider well how it is not with mere facts of history or the dead letter of books of evidence that you are dealing, but with the true and living God himself. Alleged facts you might question, books of evidence you might criticise, without offence to the recorders of the facts or the writers of the books. But here is God, the God of truth, commending to you his Son from heaven, and summoning you, on the warrant and assurance of his truth, to believe on his Son. Your refusal to do so is a personal affront; it cannot but be construed as giving him the lie, "making him a liar."

40

THE SUBSTANCE OF THE TESTIMONY — ETERNAL LIFE GOD'S GIFT IN HIS SON

"And this is the record [testimony], that God hath given to us eternal life; and this life is in his Son. He that hath the Son hath life; and he that hath not the Son of God hath not life."
1 John 5:11,12

THESE two verses close what John has to say about the faith which overcometh the world, and they explain and apply the statement, " He that believeth on the Son of God hath the testimony in himself" (ver. 10). It is the testimony of God that the believer has in himself; but he has it as not now God testifying to him, but God testifying in him. It is no longer objective and outward merely; it becomes subjective and inward. When it is believed or received, it enters into, and, as it were, passes through the receiving mind; effects a lodgment for itself behind, far back, deep down, in the innermost soul; and makes itself known and felt there, not as an external fact or proposition, but as an internal power or principle of activity. But what is it that gives this testimony of God its ability so to change its position ? Is it not its having in it, not truth merely, but life ? It is not mere truth-telling, it is life-giving also; for " this is the testimony, that God hath given to us eternal life, and this life is in his Son " (ver. 11). Therefore the receiving of it is not merely being convinced, as by evidence or authority from without or from above, but being quickened by a mighty agency and influence within. It is, in short, not merely truth admitted into the inner man, but life communicated to the inner man. It must therefore be inward; intimately and intensely inward : "He that hath the Son hath life ; and he that hath not the Son of God hath not life " (ver. 12).

The testimony of God is first, that he bestows on us life as a gift ; " he hath given to us eternal life ;" and then secondly, that "this life is in his Son." He gives us therefore this eternal life when he gives us his Son.

Consider in what sense and manner this eternal life is in his Son. It is in him, as being possessed by him as his own ; he has it in himself. In his incarnate state he has it thus; not as God only, but as man also, as " Jesus Christ come in the flesh." Let us hear his own words : " As the Father hath life in himself, so hath he given to the Son to have life in himself" (John v. 26). That cannot surely be the life which, as the Son of God, he has from everlasting. It must be life belonging to him as man; life of which his human nature, as well as his divine nature, is capable. And yet it is strangely identified with the Father's own life. It is connected with it and compared to it. And it is connected with it and compared to it, in respect of what might be thought to be the highest and most peculiar property of the everlasting God, his incommunicable attribute of self-existence.

What can this mean ? Is it really self-existence that our Lord claims for himself as " the man Christ Jesus," for his manhood as well as his Godhead ? That can scarcely be his meaning; for he speaks of this life as derived. It is not his originally, like the life which he has with the Father and the Holy Ghost from everlasting to everlasting. It is his by the Father's gift. It is life having necessarily, in that view, a beginning, though it may know no end. It is not therefore self-existence ; it cannot be. And yet it must be something not quite unlike that manner of life which self-existence implies, and not far from being akin to it.

For the statement respecting the Father himself, that he hath "life in himself," may have reference here, not to the abstract nature of his life as being underived and self-subsistent, but rather to the manner of its exercise. The Father lives, not simply as existing; but as existing ever consciously and actively, realising and enjoying existence, if one may dare to say so; thinking, feeling, doing. His life is thought, feeling, action. And what, under that aspect of it, must be held to be one chief characteristic of his life? What but this, that he does not adapt himself to things without, or draw from things without the grounds and reasons of his procedure; of his thinking, feeling, acting, in any case or instance, thus and not otherwise; that these are always found within his own holy mind and heart; that so he "has his life in himself?" Is not that, in truth, the perfection of the Father's "eternal life?" Is it not thus that it is essentially eternal? It is not moved or moulded by what is seen and temporal. It is determined by his own indwelling purpose, which is unseen and eternal.

But, it may be asked, is any creature capable of a life like that? Can any creature, in that sense, have life in himself? Not certainly as a creature living apart from the Creator, or separate from the Creator. Assuredly fallen man has no such life. He does not live a life that is independent, as to its ongoings, of things without. Is he not, on the contrary, in large measure the creature and the child of circumstances? What, in fact, is his life but a struggle to accommodate himself to the state of matters that he finds pressing upon him, all around him, in the world? Selfish he may be to the heart's core; consulting only for his own ease and pleasure. Or, in his philosophy, he may affect to rise above external influences, to bid defiance to all foreign forces, and consult no will but his own. It is all in vain. With all his selfishness, and all his philosophy, he cannot shake himself free from subjection to things seen and temporal. He cannot be, in that respect, "as God." It would not be good for him if he could; not at least unless he was so united and allied to God as to be really and thoroughly one in mind and heart with God.

But was not that the case with the Son of God on the earth, "the man Christ Jesus"? He was united and allied to God as no other man ever was or could be. In him the human nature was perfectly one in character with the divine. He therefore, while living always as self-moved and self-regulated, altogether independently of things without, never could live otherwise than as the Father liveth. Therefore it was possible for him, as Son of man as well as Son of God, to have "life in himself" by the Father's gift, exactly as "the Father hath life in himself."

Look at Jesus Christ come in the flesh; the Father's own Son given to be the Saviour of the world. What was his life? Was it not all from within? He was not insensible to things without; they deeply and powerfully affected him; he felt them keenly. But his life; his real life; the life he lived by purpose and determination, by ultimate choice of will; was not outwardly dictated, but inwardly originated. He had it in himself. Take a testing instance, his saying, "Not my will, but thine be done." "My will!" That was the effect of an impression from without; it was the outer world and its prince pressing him very closely; it was the horror of the cross brought to bear upon him very vehemently. And he had in him sensibilities and suscepti-bilities that laid his inner man very open to the pressure. His very holiness, his holy love to God and holy hatred of sin, made the thought of his being forsaken of God and enduring the penal curse inconceivably terrible. "Father, let the cup pass," is what his will would be if it were moved from without. But no. Even in his worst straits he will not yield altogether, he will not yield at all, to his will being moved from without. He will give uttterance indeed to what his will as so moved would be, if he were to yield to it. Thanks that for our sakes he does so! But it is not as if he were yielding to it. "If it be possible" is still the qualification. And then he falls back upon his real inmost self; his real inner life: "Nevertheless, Father, not my will, but thine be done."

That is surely something like "having life in himself;" having power to pass over, or pass through, the will which outward circumstances of suffering or temptation would prompt; to get far back, far down, within; and to find and feel there an inward impulse overbearing the impression from without and moving the real inward choice; "Not my will, but thine be done."

Is this "eternal life"? Is it "the eternal life which is in the Son"? Is it the power, or privilege, or prerogative of living from within himself, because it is living from within the Father, in whose bosom he dwells; from within the Father's nature, with which his own is always in harmony; from within the Father's will, to which his own is always thoroughly conformed? It is a life quite compatible with the obligation of subjection to authoritative rule or law; and that too in the utmost severity of penal infliction, as well as in the strictest bond of holy requirement. It was so in Jesus as "made under the law." He still had this life in himself, even when he took our death as his own. If it had not been so; if his life had been not from within but from without; if he had been one who lived according to he stress and strain of the external world; he never would have taken our death as his own. But "having life in himself," as one with the Father, he "finished the work which the Father gave him to do."

Now therefore, in an eminent and blessed sense, this life is in the Son for us. There is in him for us such a life as even the death of criminality and condemnation which for us he takes as his own cannot destroy. It would be ruin to us, that death; but it is not ruin to him. If the sentence takes effect upon us, it is without our choice, and against our consent; we cannot walk up to it as "having life in ourselves," or as moved from within ourselves to bear it, as the Father is necessarily moved from within himself to inflict it. But Jesus can, and does (John x. 17, 18). Even in dying for us he has therefore "life in himself." "Eternal life is thus in the Son" as "sent by the Father to be the propitiation for our sins."

And this life is something more than his surviving the endurance of our death. It is a living apprehension and appropriation for us of the Father's life. For it is as the Father hath life in himself, that he, on our behalf and as our head and representative, has life in himself. In that capacity he shares the Father's life; his manner of living is the same as the Father's. It is not a life of shifts and expedients; a life contingent and conditional on the chances of time and tide; a life of afterthoughts, altering the course to suit every current, setting the sails to every change in the fickle wind. It is a calm serene purpose; working itself out steadily "without variableness or shadow of turning." It is living for that for which God lives; living therefore as God lives. Is not that the eternal life of which God testifies as being in his Son? It is in his Son alone; and in him inalienably. It is in him in such a sense that he cannot part with it or give it away. We do not receive this eternal life of God from his Son; we share it with him. The Father's testimony is that the eternal life which he gives us is in his Son.

Here let me remind you that it is the Spirit who bears this testimony on the Father's behalf; the Spirit, with the water and the blood by which Jesus Christ came. The Father's gift of eternal life to you is in his Son; that is the testimony. And it is the Spirit that bears the testimony; the Spirit who takes of what is Christ's and shows it to you; the Spirit making you Christ's and Christ yours; the Spirit making you partakers of Christ's own very life, "the eternal life which is in the Son." Because he lives, you live; as he lives, you live. In him the Father gave, has given, and is giving you, "eternal life;" life that, in and with Christ, can undergo and survive the death of guilt and wrath; life that, in and with Christ, can in a sense become identical in character with God's own life; sharing, in a measure, its inward, self-moving energy, and its independence of things without. For that, and nothing short of that, is the eternal life that he gives; the life that is in his Son. So he is testifying to us; testifying to us by his Spirit; by his Spirit striving with us, and shutting us up into Christ. This eternal life in his Son is his gift to us; already bestowed; assured to us by his own testimony; awaiting our acceptance; ours if we will but have it to be ours, if we will have him in whom it is ours.

Therefore "he that hath the Son hath life." If only he has the Son, he has the very life which is in the Son. Thus the way is made plain and simple; God the Father has made it so. Very wonderfully has he made it so. The end is very high. It is our living as God lives. It is our living as God lives, from within; not as acted upon, but as acting; and that from some inward motive, or impulse, or principle, common to both, to God and to us. And the common motive or impulse or principle, that which is common to God and to us as regards this eternal life,—what is it? Is it not Christ? Is it not Christ having in him this life? God in Christ; we in Christ; is it not thus that God and we meet in a common life?

1. Hence, in the first place, an essential preliminary or condition of this life, nay one chief part of it so far as we are concerned, is the abolishing of death. No one can have this life; a life self-possessed and self-contained, being a life God-possessed and God-contained; who is not consciously and believingly right with himself, because right with God; right in law and judgment; on a right footing; unimpeached and uncondemned. The conscience must be pacified and the heart reconciled. With a sense of sin upon the conscience and enmity in the heart, it is impossible for me to have anything like that free and independent life, in and with himself, which God means me to have, as his gift to me. If he is to give me that life of his, he must first give me deliverance from this death of mine, from my conscious guilt and felt liability to wrath, and the consequent dread, discomfort, and dislike, with which that life of his is wholly incompatible. And so he does; for if I have the Son, I have life, in the sense and to the effect of complete and final deliverance from death. I pass from death to life.

2. But, secondly, the life to which I pass is something more than the undoing of my death; the reversal of the sentence and destruction of the power of my death. It is a new endowment; it is the imparting to me of a new power, or privilege, or capacity; it is the accession or addition of a new faculty of life, over and above any I ever naturally possessed, or ever could have got for myself, even though the blight of sin's guilt and curse had never come upon me.

For he whom I have is the Son; and I have him, if I

have him at all, as the Son. I have him, not merely as he is set before me in his relation to sinners, and to me, of sinners the chief; himself made sin for me and making me righteous in his righteousness. I must indeed first have him in that character and capacity. But I have him also as the Son, in his filial relation to the Father ; as the Son to whom "the Father hath given to have life in himself." I speak not of what he was to the Father from before all worlds, in the past eternity, ere he came into this world : it is not the life he then had that the Father gives me. I speak of him as he has been since his incarnation, and as he will continue to be all through the eternity that is to come. When I have him, I have him thus ; as he now is and ever will be. I have the Son ; and in him I have the very life which the Father has given him.

And that life is "life eternal;" it is "having life in himself." It is having life in himself because it is having life in God his Father. For he and the Father are one ; and their life is one. Whatever constitutes the Father's life ; whatever the everlasting Father may be said to live in, or to live for; that is the life of the Son. And it is the life which you have, if you have the Son. It is your having life in yourself. It is so most emphatically when it is viewed in contrast with any life you may be supposed, or may suppose yourself, to have when you have not the Son.

What is your life out of Christ ? What is your life in your unconverted state ; when you are unrenewed and unreconciled ? Is it anything like your having life in yourselves ? Is it independent of things without ? Take it in any sense you choose. Take it secularly, as the life you live in the world. What keeps you alive, alert, interested, not dull and drowsy, as you too often are, but lively ? Is it an inherent inward principle of activity ?

Or are you conscious that you depend almost entirely on outward stimulants, outward means of occupation, or excitement, outward events or news of company, for what you can really reckon the life of the day; and that without these you flag and droop, and for the time are as good as dead? You can bestir yourself on occasion. You can be roused to sentimental interest or energetic exertion, bodily or mental, when some appliance from without is brought to bear upon you. But when you are left to yourself and your own inward resources, what stagnation is apt to come upon you! Or take the life you live religiously, in the sense of your trust and hope before God! What is it? What is it that ministers to your quiet and peace? Is it an indwelling and abiding assurance, an outgoing and out-flowing affection? Or is it an observance of formal rites and a compliance with devout customs? Is it as being alone with God, or is it as one of a company, lost in a crowd or admitted into a coterie, that you feel yourself to be safe enough and comfortable enough? Certainly, if you are out of Christ, if you have not the Son; your life, in either view of it, whatever real vitality you have, is contingent upon things without; bound up, more or less, with what passes away and is not eternal. For the world, the religious as well as the secular world, passes away; and any life to which it ministers must be fleeting and not eternal.

But now, if you have the Son, how different is your life! First and chiefly, in a spiritual sense, how is it that you now live? What is the seat, what the source, of your life; your confidence; your fellowship; your worship; your joy in God? Is it not Christ in you? Having him as the Son, you are complete in him. You have his life, the life which he has with God, communicated to you and shared with you. Your life, in the sense of your standing with God and your relation to God, is identical with his. Having the Son, you have the Son's life, as being sons yourselves. And now, therefore, the ruling, active, moving principle of your life is identical with his. You live for that for which he, as the Son, lived and lives. And what was, what is that? Not certainly anything out of himself, save only God. He lived here on earth, not for things external, any more than he lived by things external. He drew no inspiration from without himself. He owned no rule without or outside of himself. He said, "Lo, I come; to do thy will, O God. Yea thy law is within my heart." He, being the Son, walked abroad as the Son on his Father's earth, "having life in himself," because he lived with the Father and for the Father; the Father living in him and giving him without measure the Spirit. That was his life. And you have it as yours, if you have the Son himself as yours. You also walk abroad on this earth, which is your Father's, having your Father's love abiding in you, as it abode in him; receiving, as he did, the Spirit.

If then you realise your position, if really and truly, consciously and constantly, you "have the Son;" if you have him as yours, your own very portion and possession, yours now, to hold, to grasp, to identify with yourself; if you thus have the Son and his sonship, what ought to be your port and bearing towards things without, things seen and temporal? Are you still to be the sport of circumstances, swayed to and fro by accidents, dependent on chances and contingencies, leaning on props that an hour may overthrow, fain to snatch a trembling joy from the brief and troubled sunshine of a wintry noon? Nay rather, having the Son, live as having in you "life eternal;" life that can defy the vicissitudes, as it will outlast the limits, of time; life standing, not in the world's or the church's fleeting forms, but in the favour, love, fellowship ; in the law, commandments, ordinances : of the everlasting Father, "his Father and your Father, his God and your God."

Let a few words of practical application be allowed.

1. "He that hath the Son hath life ; " he has this life, and no other. Hence a searching question : Are you willing upon that condition to have the Son ? You may be willing to have the Son, and along with him, and through him, some sort of life. You would have him as providing for you life, in the sense of mere safety from death ; securing your ultimate impunity in the day of judgment. But you cannot have him thus ; for " he that hath the Son hath life," " eternal life ; " the life meant when it is said, " as the Father hath life in himself, so hath he given to the Son to have in himself." If you have the Son at all, you must have him in all the fulness of his filial oneness with the Father ; for that is his life : that alone is " life eternal."

2. "He that hath not the Son of God hath not life ; " he has not this life. Eternal life, in a sense, he has—life without end ; and after death, life without change. Life also in himself it will then be in a very terrible sense : for then all external accessories and alleviations are gone ; the world is not. But the soul not having the Son is. It continues to exist, and that for ever. It lives, with nothing out of itself to lean on, or look to ! There is no congenial earthly system or sphere around to mitigate its pain ; no Saviour waiting to be gracious; no Holy Spirit striving any more ! For him there is, and that for ever, eternal death, instead of eternal life. It must be so because he has not the Son.

3. Eternal life is the gift of God, his present gift; his present gift to all, to all unreservedly, to all unconditionally. It is the life that is in his Son ; the life which his Son lives now, and lives for evermore. This, and nothing short of

this, is God's gift. It is a gift; a mere gift; a free gratuitous gift. It is not a prize; "the prize of your high calling of God in Christ." That is the consummation of this life; for which you have to wait and work, to wrestle in the fight and run the race that is set before you. But the life itself, in the full sense of its being not only deliverance from the criminal's curse through the Son being made a curse for you, but also oneness with the Son, as in his atoning death and justifying resurrection, so also in his filial oneness with the Father,—this life is God's gift, his gift now; not to be waited for; not to be worked for; not to be paid for; but to be accepted and appropriated by faith alone. He gives freely this eternal life.

4. Still he gives it only as life in his Son. He cannot separate this life from his Son; it is so precious, so divine. It is a filial life, and therefore it is in his Son. And it cannot be otherwise. You must have the Son if you would have it. But is that a painful or an irksome condition? Is it any objection, can you feel it to be any objection, that God insists on giving you his Son? Not a boon, a benefit, a blessing through his Son, but that Son himself, his own very Son, Jesus whom he loveth? Would you indeed have it otherwise? Would you rather not have the Son himself, if only you could get the good of his coming between you and eternal death? Oh, be not so ungrateful! Refuse not to receive and embrace him whom the Father is bringing near to you now. Obey the Father's gracious command and call; "This is my beloved Son, hear him."

41

ETERNAL LIFE CONNECTED WITH CONFIDENCE IN PRAYER

"These things have I written unto you that believe on the name of the Son of God ; that ye may know that ye have eternal life, [and that ye may believe on the name of the Son of God.] And this is the confidence [boldness] that we have in him, that, if we ask anything according to his will, he heareth us : and if we know that he hear us, whatsoever we ask, we know that we have the petitions that we desired of him." 1 John 5:13-15 *

THIS would seem to be the beginning of the end of the epistle. Whether the "these things" which "I have written unto you" are simply the things contained in the immediately preceding context, or must be held to reach further back, is not material. John is evidently summing up ; he is pointing his discourse or argument to its close. And he points it very clearly and cogently. He puts very strongly the final end he has in view. It is that you may "know" certain things. Over and over again he uses that word "know ;" not less than six or seven times in the course of about as many verses. The knowledge meant is evidently of a high order, in a spiritual point of view ; not

---

* I incline to the opinion of those who reject the last clause of the 13th verse, "and that ye may believe on the name of the Son of God." On the whole, the authority of manuscripts seems to be against it. The words come in, moreover, awkwardly, and with no real addition to the sense of the passage. And I can see how the introduction of them into certain manuscripts, through the fault of transcribers, is more easily accounted for than the omission of them from any manuscripts, if they had been genuine. That, as I think, is usually a good test.

speculative and intellectual merely, but experimental and practical. It is not simply faith, although it is connected with faith, as flowing from it, and involved in it. Still it is something more than faith. It is, if one may say so, faith realised; faith proved inwardly or subjectively, by being acted out and acted upon outwardly or objectively; the believer ascertaining, by actual trial and experience, the truth and trustworthiness of his belief. It is not now with us—we think, we are persuaded, we hope; but " we know."

Now one thing which you are thus believingly to know is "that you have eternal life." And you are to know this, not in the way of a mere reflex ascertaining of it, but in the way of a direct acting of it out; for "this is the boldness that we have in him, that, if we ask anything according to his will, he heareth us: and if we know that he hear us, whatsoever we ask, we know that we have the petitions that we desired of him." It is thus, in the actual use of it, that you are to know your having eternal life. In plain terms, the outgoing or forthcoming of our boldness, as having eternal life, is in prayer. Prayer is the exercise or expression of it; as it has been said before to be: " Whatsoever we ask, we receive of him, because we keep his commandments, and do those things that are pleasing in his sight" (iii. 22).

I. There is, however, as it might seem, a qualification here which is not there; " according to his will." What that means it is important to see. It cannot well mean that before asking anything we must know certainly that what we ask is according to his will. This would really preclude us, in ordinary circumstances, from asking anything, or at least from asking anything definite and precise. I say in ordinary circumstances. For we may be situated as Daniel was, when, upon an interpretation of Jeremiah's prophecy, he was infallibly led by inspiration to the conclusion that the period of the Babylonian captivity was expired, or expiring, and that Israel's restoration was certainly due. Without claiming, or having any right to claim, inspiration or infallibility, men have considered themselves entitled, on some extraordinary occasions, to ask certain things to be done by God in his providence, in the full assurance that they were according to his will. That there may be such instances of confidence in asking, upon a clear and certain conviction beforehand that what is asked is according to God's will, confidence, not given by fresh inspiration, but reached by faith in exercise upon inspiration previously recorded, may be admitted. But these exceptionable cases can scarcely be held to meet the apostle's broad and general statement as to the efficacy of all believing prayer. Nor will it do to make this seeming qualification, "according to his will," a mere tag or appendix to all prayer and every prayer; as meaning simply that whatever we ask, we are to ask with this proviso, expressed or understood, "if it be according to thy will." No doubt, when we pray for anything which implies that God should order his providence one way rather than another, thus and not otherwise;— and we can hardly pray for anything specific or definite which does not imply that;—we must, if we would not be guilty of presumption or impiety, virtually attach always the reservation which that formula implies. But this is so evidently indispensable, as a condition of all genuine and reverential prayer, that it could hardly be needful for John to state it. He must surely be pointing to some higher function of the prayer of faith.

"If we ask anything according to his will,"—may not this mean, "If we ask anything as we believe that he wills it"? We ask it as he wills it. In asking it, we put ourselves in the same position with him in willing it. He and we look at it from the same point of view. We who ask identify ourselves with him who wills. Whatever we ask, we ask as from within the circle of his will; we being one in our asking with him in his willing.

This may seem too high a position for us to occupy or aim at; too divine a standpoint; that we in asking, and God in willing, should be at one. And yet is it not the only fair, the only possible, alternative or antithesis to what is the only notion of prayer which the natural man can take in, the notion of bending God's will to his? For that, unquestionably, is what, when he prays, the natural man desires.

The priests of Baal, when, in answer to Elijah's challenge, "they cried aloud and cut themselves after their manner," sought by their fierce and bloody importunity to bend the object of their mad worship to their purpose, and make him subservient to their pleasure. The sailors in the ship with Jonah, when they called every man upon his god, simply thought that they might be "heard for their much speaking." The instinct of physical pain in acute disease, or of natural affection in an anxious crisis, or of blank despair in sudden peril, may wring from unaccustomed lips a defiant or an abject appeal to the Ruler over all. It is an unknown God who is invoked, on the mere chance that he may be got to do their bidding. The heathen view of prayer, like the heathen view of sacrifice, proceeds upon that notion of subjecting God's determination to men's desire; the prayer and the sacrifice being both alike intended to work upon the divine mind so as to change it into accordance with that of the worshipper. The idea is that God needs to be appeased, and that he may be persuaded; that he needs to be appeased by sacrifice, so that wrath may give place to pity; and that he may be persuaded by prayer to act otherwise than his inner nature might prompt, in compliance with solicitations, or in deference to pressure, from without.

But a right spiritual apprehension of God, as "having in himself eternal life," and "giving us that eternal life in his Son," places both sacrifice and prayer in an entirely different light. Eternal life must necessarily, in its nature as well as in its duration, be independent of time, and consequently also of time's changes and contingencies, its influences and motives. As it is in God himself, it is self-moved, self-originated, self-inspired. He has within himself the grounds and reasons of all his proceedings. In so far as it is communicable to us through his Son and in his Son, it must possess substantially the same character of self-containedness, if I may use such a term, or independence of things without. Only, in our case, this life of ours is "hid with Christ in God." It is his life in us.

How then does God himself, having life, this eternal life, in himself, stand related to prayer, or to sacrifice and prayer together? Both must be from within himself. They are alike and equally means of his own appointment or ordination. Sacrifice, the atoning sacrifice of his Son for us, is his own way of opening up communication between himself and us. Prayer, our prayer to him in his Son's name, is his own way of carrying on and carrying out the communication. He, having eternal life in himself, moved from within himself, gives to us this eternal life in his Son. And all the fruit or benefit of it he is pleased to give through prayer. For the eternal life which is now, in a sense, common to him and us, comes out in prayer. We meet in prayer, he and we together. And we meet, be it said with reverence, on the footing of our joint possession, in a measure, of the same eternal life ; life in ourselves ; he and we thus meet together.

Thus prayer, as it is here introduced, becomes a very

solemn, because a very confidential, dealing with God. It is asking. But it is asking upon the ground of a very close union and thorough identity between God and us, as regards the life to which the asking has respect, and of which it is the acting out. In plain terms, it is our asking as one in interest, in sympathy, in character, in end and aim—one, in short, in life or manner of living, with him whom we ask; through his giving us eternal life; that life being in his Son, and being indeed the very life itself of his Son.

This is not, however, to be regarded as of the essence of prayer, so that none may appeal to the throne of grace without it. God forbid that I should restrict the efficacy of prayer, however and whenever it is offered, out of a smitten conscience and broken heart. Not merely as a sinner out of Christ, but as a believer in Christ, I find my need, daily and hourly, of that liberty of access, as it were from without, to my God and Father, which I have in and with him who has taught me so to approach him.

But it is a somewhat different attitude that I am here called to assume; different, and yet after all the same. I pray as having eternal life; the very eternal life which God gives, and which is in his Son Jesus Christ. What sort of prayer does that mean? Are we not, in offering it, brought into the position of offering the prayer from the very same standpoint, if one may say so, on which God himself stands, when he answers the prayer? We offer our prayer as having eternal life; God's own eternal life, made over to us as ours in his Son. And that is the ground of the confidence which we have, "that if we ask anything according to his will, he heareth us."

II. Hence we are to "know that we have eternal life" through our thus asking, in this confidence; for "if we know that he hear us, whatsoever we ask, we know

that we have the petitions that we desired of him." We
are to know our privilege in the using of it; we are to
know our position by taking advantage of it. We receive,
in the Son, as the Father's gift, a new life. In its nature
and manner of acting, it is analogous to the Father's own
life, and indeed, in some sense, identical with it. The
identity manifests itself in this confidence of prayer. In so
far as my prayer is the working out of that identity, it
must be confident, confiding, free, and bold. It must be
real and actual conversation with God within his own holy
place; in his own inmost chamber; upon the matter,
whatever it is, that is the subject of my prayer. I get in
now within the veil. I am a dweller in the secret place of
the Most High. I am, as it were, behind the scenes of his
great providential drama, his great economy of grace and
judgment. I am with him; one with him; one with him
in sympathy of mind and heart as to the eternal principles
and laws upon which the whole plan of his moral administration proceeds. From that point of view I consider the
question at issue; the question to which my prayer relates;
and my prayer regarding it is framed accordingly. It is a
setting forth of the matter, as, in all its aspects, it presents
itself to me. It is a spreading of it out before God, as it
appears to me;—to me, however, as having God's gift to
me of eternal life in his Son. For the case is now under
my eye, not as it might present itself to me, judging after
the flesh, looking at things in the light of merely natural
predilections and opinions;—but as it presents itself to me,
judging spiritually; looking at things in the light of the
eternal life which God gives me in his Son. Whatever I
so ask must be according to his will; and therefore I may
have absolute confidence that I have it.

I may possibly see my way, upon this footing, to ask
altogether unconditionally. I may so realise God's giving

me eternal life in his Son,—and so clearly and unmistak-
ably and assuredly perceive how, in the view of that
eternal life, the event at issue might best be ordered,—as
to have the utmost boldness in preferring a specific request,
absolutely and without qualification. Eminent saints of
God have felt themselves entitled, and have warrantably
felt themselves entitled, especially in critical emergencies,
to be thus precise and peremptory ; all the more if a
brotherhood of them conferred and consulted together,
under the guidance of God's word, as applied by the Spirit's
help to his providence. All of them being led by the
Spirit to the same conclusion, finding that the case presented itself to them all in the same aspect, and being of
one mind as to what would best subserve the ends of the
eternal life which they all have in common as God's gift in
his Son ;—they may have considered themselves at liberty
to condescend with great assurance upon the particular
step which they would have God to take. And therefore
they might unhesitatingly ask him to take it, and fearlessly
reckon on his taking it. I suppose that this is partly the
Lord's meaning in that remarkable promise : "If two of
you shall agree on earth as touching anything that they
shall ask, it shall be done for them of my Father which is
in heaven."

Even in such a case, however, the prayer is not mere
importunate solicitation, as from without ; it partakes more
of the nature of confidential conversation, within the circle
of God's house and family. To adopt a homely phrase, it
is as if, using the liberty of trusted children, we were telling our Father how the case under consideration strikes
us ; how it strikes us when we are looking at it, or trying
to look at it, from his point of view ; looking at it in the
light of that "eternal life which he gives us in his Son."

And what does it really matter, in such intercourse as

this, on such a footing as this, with the only wise God, if we should ordinarily count it safer and more becoming to ask conditionally; under the reservation and with the qualification of deference and submission to his better judgment? Our asking anything thus conditionally, if only we ask in the spirit of the eternal life which we have in his Son, is very eminently "according to his will." He cannot but approve of it. Nor does it in the least detract from our confidence in asking.

There is room indeed here for different degrees, not of our confidence in asking, but of the conditionality or un-conditionality, if I may say so, with which we ask. Our confidence in asking is the same; the only difference is as to our making up our mind what to ask. As to that, we may well have some hesitation for the most part in being very definite and positive. Even when we honestly and truly ask as having eternal life given to us by God in his Son, we may be at a loss. Nay, the more we so ask, the more may we be at a loss. We try to look at the matter at issue as God looks at it; not under the influence of things without, and the considerations which they might suggest; but under the rule, and in the light, of that higher life which he has in himself. We seek to judge as God judges; in the view, not of temporal interests merely, but of eternal issues. Well may we pause and be very cautious; well may there be a certain reserve in any judg-ment we form, and a certain reservation in any prayer we frame upon that judgment; well may there be some dubiety, not as to our having what we ask, but as to what we are to ask; what we would have God to do.

But what then? Is this confidence in prayer a delusion, a sort of juggle? I am told that in virtue of the eternal life which God gives me in his Son, I may have whatever I choose to ask. And in the same breath I am told that this very eternal life, which I thus have, may hinder me, for the most part, from ever asking almost anything definitely and positively. Is this not a kind of double-dealing? Is it not putting me off as with the Barmecide's empty feast, or the visionary mirage of the desert? Nay, it is far otherwise.

Let us consider practically our real position; let us take a specific instance.

Our brother Lazarus is sick; and the sickness seems to be unto death. What are we to ask? What is to be our petition, and what our request? If we have respect simply to life temporal; if we take account merely of such considerations as this present earthly scene suggests; we cannot hesitate a moment. Looking at the case from a human standpoint, we need no time for deliberation. The instinct of natural affection will prompt, and many reasons of Christian expediency will occur to enforce, the loud wailing cry to the Lord to spare so precious and useful a life. But we feel that, as admitted to a participation with the Son in the eternal life of God, we have a higher standing and a weightier responsibility in this matter of prayer. We are lifted up to the very footstool on which the throne of the hearer of prayer itself rests; and from thence we look at the question, as he looks at it. Finding ourselves thus placed, our first impulse may be to shrink and hang back altogether. We refuse even to attempt to form a judgment, and to frame the judgment into a prayer, however guarded. But that is not his will; nor on second thoughts is it our wish. It is indeed a singularly high and holy position, in respect of insight and sympathy, that we are called to occupy in fellowship with God. But we are to occupy it boldly, and with all confidence. And now from that position we apply our mind, as it were, along with him, to the determination of what is best to be done; and we express our mind freely to him all along as we do so. We talk the whole affair over with him; conversing about it without reserve. We reason, we expostulate, we plead. We spread out before him all the views and considerations, of whatever sort, that seem to us to have any bearing on the case; not excluding those suggested by warm natural affection and urgent earthly interests, but not limiting our regard to these. We say whatever occurs to us, whatever it is in our heart to say.

What though in all this close and confidential dealing with God we should not be able to say positively what is best? Is it not a blessed intercourse notwithstanding? We may be reduced to utter straits: "Now is my soul troubled, and what shall I say?" In our anguish of spirit, distracted between conflicting motives; altogether at a loss to decide what we would have God to do; driven out of reasoning and speech; we may be reduced to groaning and weeping; to "strong crying and tears." What then? Is our confidence in prayer gone? Nay, it was when Jesus "in the days of his flesh made supplication with strong crying and tears unto him that was able to save him from death," that he had the most complete assurance of his being "heard in that he feared." And it is when "we know not what to pray for as we ought, that the Spirit, helping our infirmities, maketh intercession for us with groanings that cannot be uttered." Our unutterable groanings the blessed Spirit takes as his own, turning them into prayers; prayers very specially acceptable to the hearer of prayer. For "he who searcheth the heart knoweth what is the mind of the Spirit when he" thus "maketh intercession for the saints." His doing so is "according to the will of God."

Let us look then at the light which John's teaching in these verses casts on the privilege and duty of prayer.

1. In the first place, let us consider what prayer is, as thus viewed, in all the fulness and variety of its confident assurance. It is not simply petitioning; it is not monotonous reiteration; the incessant sending up to heaven again and again of the same appeal, the same demand for some specific deliverance, some precise and definite benefit, that may seem to us indispensable, that we feel as if we could not do without. It is a far more confidential dealing with God than that. It is our becoming " the men of his secret." It is our getting into the inmost chamber of his house, and consulting with him there; seeking to know his mind; ready to make his mind ours. I say it is consulting with God. And the consultation may and must be full and free. It will embrace as its topics whatever can be of interest to him or to us; to him primarily, to us as under him. Hence everywhere and always, and with reference to everything, we must be thus consulting with God; not only upon cases of difficulty or distress, but upon all sorts of cases; common cases, everyday cases; little cases, as well as cases of rare and grave emergency.

Prayer of this kind may be short, like the Lord's strong cry of agony in the garden; it may be silent, like his groaning and weeping at Bethany. But it may be long, ever so long, without falling under the Lord's censure of the long prayers of the Pharisees. In such prayer he himself often spent the whole long night. He was at home then and there with his Father; consulting with him about many things; about all things bearing on his Father's glory and his own work; laying his own views and feelings and wishes unreservedly before his Father; and reverently learning his.

Brethren, pray thus without ceasing. "In everything, by such prayer and supplication, make your requests known to God." Carry everything; literally everything; every-

thing that befalls you, or seems likely to befall you ; every
choice you have to make ; whatever you have to say or do;
every care, every duty, every trial, every glad relief; carry
everything to God. Converse with God about it. Turn it
over, as between God and you, in every possible way.
Look at it from every possible point of view. Do not be
in haste to make up your mind as to what is best; as to
what you should definitely ask. Rather prolong the blessed
interview. The very suspending of your judgment, as the
consultation goes on, may make the interview more blessed.
And the issue will be the clear, calm " peace of God keeping your hearts and minds through Jesus Christ your Lord;"
" the single eye, making the whole body full of light."

2. Then, secondly, let us consider how close and intimate
is the connection between life and prayer; between God's
giving us eternal life in his Son, and our asking thus confidently and confidentially. The two are really one ; the
eternal life is realised and acted out in this asking. The
life is prayer ; and prayer is the life. It is as partakers of
the life which the Father has in himself, and which, by his
gift, the Son also has in himself, that we ask and pray.
The essential characteristic of that life is its self-containedness, if I may repeat the phrase ; its independence of things
without ; its drawing from within itself the motives of all
its voluntary determinations. So the Father lives ; not
moved by impulses and influences of a temporal sort from
without ; but purposing and decreeing, willing and acting,
always from himself and for himself. So the Son also lives,
not as God merely, but as " the man Christ Jesus ;" being,
as to his manhood as well as his Godhead, in an intimate
sense one with the Father ; one in purpose and decree, in
will and action ; one in mind and heart. So also in a
measure we, having the Son, live. Our real life is apart
from the contingencies and accidents of time, being " hid

with Christ in God." It is as so living, living that hidden life, that we ask and pray.

What harmony, what concord and agreement, what entire oneness, between God and us, does this imply! It is oneness of opinion, sentiment, feeling, desire; first, on the great fundamental question, What is life?—life worthy of the name,—life worth the living; and then, in subordination to that, upon every question which can touch that life. We form the same idea of life that God has, and that Christ has; the same idea of what it is worth while to live for. And it is under that idea, fixed and fastened deep in our inmost spirit, that we ask and pray. We settle in the Spirit with ourselves,—as well as with Christ and with God,— what is the only true, the only perfect, the only desirable life, for beings possessed of a divine faculty of intelligence, and destined to a divine immortality. Having that life, we commune with the living One, as our Father in Christ, upon all the great eternal aims and hopes which it contains, and all the small temporal casualties by which, for a season, these aims and hopes may be environed and beset. Such communing about eternity, and about time as related to eternity, is prayer; the prayer which acts out "the eternal life which we have as God's gift in his Son."

3. In the third place, let us consider how very holy this life is, and how very holy therefore must be the prayer which acts it out. It is indeed our being "partakers of God's holiness." For such living fellowship and communion as is implied in the life and the prayer, sensitively shrinks from all unholy handling. Sense may not mar it; sin may not pollute it; the touch of earth's vanity or man's corruption breaks its sacred spell, and dissolves its peaceful charm. For the charm of this life of prayer is peace; the peace of God; the peace of conscious sympathy with the God of peace. But all earthliness, worldliness, and selfishness,—

all diversity of judgment or feeling on any point between us and him whose eternal life we share,—in a word, all unholiness,—disturbs that peace. No unsanctified bosom can be its dwelling-place on earth, for its dwelling-place in heaven is the holy bosom of God. Therefore, "as he who hath called us is holy, let us also be holy."

4. For, in the fourth place, this faculty of praying as having eternal life, is itself to be sought by prayer. The life is God's gift in Christ, to be appropriated by faith; the Spirit shutting us up into Christ, and making us one with Christ. The prayer is in the Spirit and of the Spirit. It is the Spirit making intercession for us, with us, in us. It is the Spirit of his Son sent forth by God into our hearts, crying, Abba, Father. But the Spirit is given in answer to prayer. Therefore let us ask, seek, knock, that we may receive the Spirit; that he may dwell in us; that he may move us, as having eternal life in the Son, to pray, as the Son himself was wont to pray, in the Spirit. So moved, we may be praying confidently, as the Son prayed, in all sorts of ways; not only in prolonged midnight meditations, but in brief ejaculations as occasion calls; in hasty utterances; or when utterance fails, in sighs and tears and groans. For we have all boldness to be ever praying, after whatever sort of prayer may suit the times and seasons of our praying. Let us pray that we may receive the Spirit thus to embolden us always to pray;—to "ask according to his will," even as the Spirit "maketh intercession for the saints, according to the will of God."

42

PRAYER FOR A BROTHER'S SIN, BUT NOT FOR A SIN UNTO DEATH

"If any man see his brother sin a sin which is not unto death, he shall
ask, and he shall give him life for them that sin not unto death.
There is a sin unto death: I do not say that he shall pray for it.
All unrighteousness is sin : and there is a sin [not] unto death."
1 John 5:16,17 *

JOHN assumes that one chief use which you will be disposed
to make of your right and power to pray will be to pray for
others. He puts a case. You see your brother sinning.
He is "your brother." This does not necessarily imply that
he who sins is a true brother in the Lord. It has been
already made manifest more than once in this epistle, that
the relation of brotherhood, in the apostle's sense of the
term, is of much wider reach and range. It arises not so
much out of the character and standing of him whom you
call your brother, as out of the nature of the affection with
which you regard him. True, your brother, in the highest
point of view, is he who, being really to God a son, is really
to you on that account a brother. But whoever he may be
whom you love with a brotherly love ; with a love that
treats him as a brother ; not as a mere instrument to be used

---

* I incline to read this 17th verse without the negative in the last
clause. The sense of the entire passage is not materially affected whether
we keep in or leave out the "not." But the authority of manuscripts is
rather against it. And certainly the omission of it makes the meaning
more plain and pointed. (See page 283.)

or companion to be enjoyed for a day, but as one having an immortal soul to be saved for eternity; every one so loved by you is your brother. When he sins, his sin vexes you as the sin of a brother. You cannot look on and see him sinning with indifference or amusement or contempt, as if he were a stranger, or a helot, or a dog. It is your brother whom you see sinning. And therefore you speak to him as to a brother about his sin; not harshly, with sharp reproach or cutting sarcasm, or cold magisterial severity. With a brother's voice, coming out of the depths of a brother's bosom, you earnestly expostulate and affectionately plead with him. Alas! he turns to you a deaf ear, and you have no power to open it. But another ear is open to you, the ear of your Father in heaven; and he can open your brother's ear. To your Father in heaven you go. You deal with him about your sinning brother's case. You ask that life may be given to him; the " eternal life " which the sin he is committing justly forfeits. You grow importunate in asking; your importunity being in proportion to the truth and warmth of your brotherly love; you feel almost as if you could converse with God about nothing else. And you do converse with God about it,—oh, how pathetically! In all this you do well; using the liberty you have, as receiving " eternal life in his Son," to " ask anything, knowing that he hears you."

But is there no risk of excess or of error? May you not be too one-sided in looking at the case yourself, and in representing it to God? May you not be so concerned about the one terrible aspect of it, its bearing on your brother's doom, as to shut out the other aspect of it, which ought never to be lost sight of, its bearing on the Father's throne; on the holy and righteous sovereignty of his government and law? May not your sympathy with your sinning brother overbear somewhat your sympathy with

him against whom he is sinning? May you not thus be
led to overstep the limits of warrantable confidence, so as
to ask that life may be given to him, on any terms, at any
cost, in any way, irrespectively altogether of what, in your
calmer moments, you would yourself recognise as the paramount claims of the Most High? Thus your prayer for
your sinning brother may slide insensibly into an apologetic
pleading for indulgence to his sin. You may be tempted
to represent as excusable what God regards as inexcusable;
and to feel as if, whatever your brother's criminality may
be, there may still be favour shown to him notwithstanding.
It is to guard you against such a frame of mind that the
solemn warning is given: "If a man see his brother sin a
sin which is not unto death, he shall ask, and he shall give
him life for them that sin not unto death. There is a sin
unto death: I do not say that he shall pray for it."

I am persuaded that it is in the line of this train of
thought that the solution of the difficult problem here
suggested is to be sought. The whole analogy of the faith,
as well as the bearing of the context, favours this view. If
I am right in this persuasion, some important consequences
would seem to follow.

In the first place, there is no warrant in this text for
the doctrine which Rome seeks to draw from it as to the
distinction, in themselves,—in their own nature or in their
accompanying aggravations,—between venial and mortal
sins. Let the distinction be admitted as otherwise proved,
it is nothing to the purpose here. A Romanist, in his
anxious prayer for his sinning brother, may be tempted to
put his sin into the wrong category, and to speak of it to
God as venial, whereas it is really mortal. It is a temptation of the same sort that besets me; I admit it to be so.
He, praying according to his creed which allows the distinction, is admonished, precisely as I who deny it am

admonished. We are both warned against asking God to regard as venial what, in the view of his righteous judgment and holy supremacy, is and must be mortal. But this text itself does not decide between us. And if it appears from all the rest of Scripture that the Romanist's idea is not only unproved but disproved, the circumstance that this text might possibly be interpreted in consistency with his idea avails him nothing ; since it turns out that it can be equally well, or even much better, interpreted in consistency with mine.

Secondly, there is no occasion to be solicitous in attempting to identify any particular sin, or any particular manner of sinning, as what is here said to be " unto death." The attempt, as all experience shows, is as vain as it is presumptuous. And yet, in spite of all experience, the attempt is ever renewed. Morbid minds, or minds in a morbid state, become sensitive on the point ; but without warrant or reason. Even if there were "a sin unto death" that might be ascertainable in a man's own consciousness, the mention of it would not be to the purpose here, unless it were ascertainable also in the judgment of his neighbour or his brother. For the question is as to your praying for me. Even if I myself could know that I had sinned the sin unto death, how could you know that I had? However it might affect my praying for myself, how could it affect your praying for me ? And as you have no right to judge me to that effect, so neither have I any right to judge myself. Let it be settled and fixed as a great truth, according to this and many other passages of Scripture, that there cannot be any such thing as my sinning a sin unto death, in such a sense as might warrant me, from my fear of my having committed it, to cease to pray for myself ;—far less warrant you, from an opinion on your part that I have committed it, to cease to pray for me.

For, thirdly, the real and only object of the apostle is to put in a caveat and lodge a protest against the intrusion into the sacred province of confidential prayer, especially when it is prayer for a sinning brother, of a tendency which is too natural and too apt to prevail, even in one having the eternal life which the Father gives in his Son; the tendency, I mean, to subordinate the divine claims to considerations of human expediency or human pity. It is the same tendency which, when the case is our own, is apt to bias and mislead us. Let us trace its working.

1. It is of course strongest in the unrenewed mind and unreconciled heart. While under their dominion, we cannot be expected to consult for God at all; we consult only for ourselves. In forming a notion as to how God may, and as we think, ought to deal with us, we take little or no account of what may be due to him, to the honour of his holy name and the glorious majesty of his throne and law. We pay little or no regard to what the principles of his righteous moral administration and the interests of his loyal subjects may require. We think only of our own relief and safety; our own convenience and accommodation. And hence we see no difficulty in our slight offences being overlooked and our infirmities indulged, upon our making certain formal submissions, and going through some routine of service. Thus we accept the serpent's lie: "Ye shall not surely die;" no sin of ours being, in our view, if all extenuating circumstances are taken into account, "a sin unto death."

2. It should be otherwise with us now; now that "having the Son we have life." We surely ought to be, as the Son is, on the Father's side; one in interest and sympathy with him; ready to give him the pre-eminence in all things, and to subordinate even what most pertains to our own welfare to the glorifying of his name and the

doing of his will. We may be thankful that this does not entail on us the suffering and sacrifice which it entailed on him, when he, in the matter of the cup given him to drink, submitted his own will to the Father's. Well may we be thankful that, through his taking our death as his and our having his life as ours, we may have the same mind that was in him, without its bringing such pain on us. Nay, for us, our putting God and his claims first, and putting ourselves and our concerns second, is in fact the secret of our safety and our rest.

All the more on that account is it reasonable to expect that in whatever we ask of God for ourselves, in our closest communing with him about our own affairs, whether temporal or spiritual, we should allow this principle to have full scope. But is it so? Alas! the old selfish spirit is ever apt to come back and come out again. It comes out, perhaps almost unconsciously, in our secret pleading that something in us or about us may be spared which God has doomed to destruction; be it some unmortified lust in the heart, or some doubtful practice of worldly conformity in the life. If indeed we are honestly communing with God about it, placing his honour first and our case only second, we can be at no loss what to ask. We can ask but one thing; the grace of instant decision to deal with what offends, as we know that God would have it dealt with. Are we asking that, asking it in faith, and acting accordingly? Or are we still irresolute, putting in a plea for some slight indulgence, some short delay; as if, after all, the evil were not so very serious, nor the danger of tolerating it for a little longer so very great? Brother, let me solemnly and affectionately warn you,—or rather, let the beloved apostle warn you :—"All unrighteousness is sin : and there is a sin unto death."

3. In intercessory prayer, the tendency of which I speak

operates powerfully and painfully. A rude and vulgar notion prevails amongst those who reject the gospel which we embrace, that we who embrace it, hugging ourselves in our own security, have a sort of pleasure in consigning all outside of our circle to inevitable and everlasting ruin. Alas ! they know not, either the weakness of our filial faith, or the strength, if not of our brotherly love, yet of our natural affection. The temptation is all the other way. It is all in the direction of our tampering and taking liberties with the sovereign authority and grace of God, in accommodation to the weakness, and even the wickedness, of men. We do not say, abstractly and absolutely, that there is not a sin unto death ; but we fondly hope that our brother's sin may not be held to be so. It is not hoping that he may repent of it. Such hope cannot well be too strong ; nor can our asking in terms of it be too confident. But here lies the danger. Our asking that he may repent of it, if his repenting of it is delayed, is apt,—oh, how apt !—apt in proportion as we love him, to slide unawares into our virtually asking that, though not repented of, it may be overlooked ; that at least it may not be reckoned to him as " a sin unto death."

It is often a very terrible test of our loyalty to God our Father, and our allegiance to his crown and his commandments, that is in such a case to be applied.

4. Take an extreme instance. One whom you loved with truest brotherly love, with most intense longing to welcome him as a brother in Christ to your heart, has gone without affording you that joy ; he has died, giving no sign. He was lovely, amiable, pleasant. You and he were one in kin ; still more one in kind and in kindness. But he has passed away, continuing to the last in a course of life scarcely, if at all, reconcilable with even the profession of godliness. What is your temptation in such a case ? Ah,

it is a very awful one! It is to prefer his interest to the gospel of God, and the law of God. It is to think that, culpable as he may have been, his culpability may not have proved fatal. It is to cherish the fond imagination that, in spite of the law which he has broken and the gospel which he has rejected, he may still, on the ground of qualities which won your admiration, or sufferings which moved your compassion, find some measure of mercy in the end.

It is very tender ground on which I tread; I know it; experimentally I know it. Far, very far, be it from me, to insist on your judging a departed brother, however he may have sinned, and continued in his sin to the last. He is in the hands of God. Leave him there without questioning. Think of the old rhyming adage—

> "Between the stirrup and the ground,
> Mercy I sought, mercy I found."

Think too of the more authentic instance of the thief on the cross; by all means think of that, and take what comfort you can from that. But beware! Sorely,—oh, how sorely!—are you tempted first to wish that there were some room for such as he was, even continuing still the same, within the holy city of the most high God; and then to hope that there may be. It is, I repeat, a very sore temptation. Many a brokenhearted mourner in Zion has felt it; you and I have felt it; and we have felt that, under the influence of it, we have been beginning to underrate the need of regeneration, and conversion, and a living faith, and a holy walk; to dream of men who gave no evidence here of anything like such grace, being possibly safe without it hereafter. And what next? We become insensibly more tolerant than we were of sin in ourselves; less alive to the necessity of immediate repentance and faith ; more inclined to temporise and compromise ; to look at things not from God's point of view but from our own ; as if he had not " given to us his own eternal life in his Son."

Let us see to it above all things, though it may cost us often many a struggle and many a tear, that we do not suffer our firm faith in God, and our loving loyalty to him, to fall a sacrifice to the fond relentings of our own weak hearts. Whatever may be its bearing on the fate of any brother, let us, for God's sake and our own, for God's honour and our own salvation, accept it as a great and solemn fact, that " all unrighteousness is sin, and that there is a sin unto death."

5. You do not pray for the dead ; you do not think it lawful. It is in the indulgence of a trembling hope concerning them that the temptation of which I speak besets you. But the same temptation besets you also when you pray for the living. It is the temptation to wish that, in its application to the sin which you see your brother sinning, God's holy law were not so very uncompromising, nor his righteous judgment so very unrelenting, as they are declared to be. No doubt you ask that your brother may receive grace to repent of his sin. But what if he should not ? You have a sort of reserved notion that, even in that case and upon that supposition, there may be some chance of safety for him. That is the temptation. And it is often a most severe and stern trial of your faith to resist it ; to ask life for your sinning brother ; but to ask it evermore under the deep conviction that " all unrighteousness is sin, and that there is a sin unto death."

Let us see, once for all, what the apostle's solemn statement really implies.

In the first place, let it be very specially noted that this is the one only limitation which John puts upon the liberty of intercessory prayer. And let us mark well where the limitation applies. It does not really touch our privilege of asking life for our brother, in the true and full sense of life ;—the eternal life which God gives, and which is in his Son. We may not ask for him this life, if we ask it for him as sinning, and contemplated by us as possibly sinning unto death. And for the best of all reasons we may not thus ask; for it is asking what, even with God, is an impossibility. But, short of that impossibility, there is no restriction laid on our asking ; we may ask life for him, to the utmost of our heart's desire. We may use the utmost freedom in asking life for him, provided only we do not ask it for him as sinning, and continuing to sin, unto death. Be his sin ever so heinous, let it be the sin of a whole long lifetime of ungodliness, we may ask life for him, in the line of his repenting and believing the gospel, provided only, I repeat, that we do not ask it as if life could be given him in any other way.

I know that a question may be raised even here, as to the extent to which we may absolutely and unconditionally ask for our sinning brother faith and repentance, and having asked, may positively know that " we have the petition that we have desired of God." I know that there are difficulties in the direction now indicated. They are difficulties connected with that decree of election which alone secures the salvation of any sinner ;—but they are difficulties which we may conceive of as possibly hindering the salvation of some sinner for whom we pray. They are difficulties, however, which do not touch such intercessory prayer more than they touch any other sort of prayer ;—and indeed all prayer, generally and universally. The decree of election can no more hinder my praying confidently for my sinning brother, than it can hinder my praying confidently for my sinning self. In either case, it is one of " the secret things belonging to the Lord our God," not one of " the revealed things belonging to us and to our children." At all events, this text has nothing to do with that. It imposes no restriction on our prayer arising out of God's eternal purpose. The only restriction which it does impose is one rendered necessary by our own infirmity, and the temptation to which it exposes us. We are not to ask, what we are tempted to ask, that our brother, continuing in sin, may yet be saved; that while still sinning unto death, he may nevertheless somehow live. But under that reservation, reasonable surely, and necessary, we have all liberty, so far as this text is concerned;—and it is the only text in all the Bible that can by any possibility be supposed to fetter or abridge our liberty;—we have all liberty, I say, to ask life for our brother. It is a wide charter, altogether broad and free.

But, secondly, there is an obvious practical application suggested by the reservation. If we ask life for our brother, knowing that he cannot have it while sinning unto death; or, in other words, that he cannot have it otherwise than in the way of believing and repenting; our prayer for him, if sincere, must imply our personal dealing with him with a view to his believing and repenting. If what we asked for him were simply life,—life in any sense and on any terms,— we might let him alone. Having asked, we might think that we could do nothing more to help in bringing about the desired result. But it is not so; it is far otherwise. We may take part along with him whom we ask, the hearer of prayer, in what we ask him to do; we must take part along with him, if our asking is real and earnest. To ask God to give life to our sinning brother while we ourselves "suffer sin upon him"—not warning him even with tears; —sin, the very sin that is hurrying him on to death;— what mockery!—how insulting to our God, and oh, how cruel to our poor brother himself!

Finally, in the third place, let our conviction be clear, strong and deep, that "all unrighteousness is sin, and that there is a sin unto death." Let us see that there is no faltering, no hesitancy as to that great fact or truth. Upon both the parts of this solemn declaration let our faith be firm, and let our trumpet give no uncertain sound. It is at this point that a stand is to be resolutely made against all antinomian licence in religion; for it is at this point that the enemy has always pressed the church most hardly, and alas! the church has too often shown herself weak. The knowing ones who corrupted the gospel in John's own day undermined the citadel at this very point. They held and taught that unrighteousness, unholiness, uncleanness, which would be sin in any one else, might be no sin in the spiritual man. It could only defile the body. And what of that, the body being perishable? It could not touch the essence of the living and immortal soul. Sin therefore, even when persevered in to the end, might yet be not unto death. John does not reason with these wicked men; it is not a case for reasoning. He meets their vile, foul, base imagination with the stern assertion of law and appeal to conscience: "All unrighteousness is sin, and there is a sin unto death."

Ever and anon, from age to age, the same abominable devil's creed has troubled and polluted the church of God. Nay, even when the church is undisturbed by it, still, ever and anon, it troubles and pollutes the child of God, in some one or other of its insidious temptations.

For alas! alas! it is but too congenial to the sloth and selfishness and sensuality that still prevail too much within him. Ah me! how apt am I to cherish the secret, half-unconscious notion, that this or that infirmity besetting me, or besetting my much-loved brother,—infirmity which, if I saw it attached to any one else, I would not scruple for a moment to denounce as sin,—may somehow in my case, or in my brother's, be more mildly characterised and more gently dealt with! How apt am I to hope that this or that little secret sin which I feel cleaving still to me, or see cleaving still to my brother, may after all, and in the long run, not prove fatal! Ah, if there be but the faintest taint of this damnable heresy lurking in your inner man, how can you be prosecuting, with anything like earnestness, the work of your own personal sanctification, or seeking, with anything like faithfulness, the sanctification of your brother; —asking God to give you life, or to give him life? Be very sure that if you would be safe yourself, and if you would save him, you need to shun, as you would a pestilential blast, or the very breath of hell, whatever tends, however remotely, to confound the everlasting distinctions of right and wrong, or shake the foundations of truth and virtue which are the very pillars of the universe and of the throne of God. It is a " word which doth eat as a canker." Beware, and again I say beware, of scepticism on the great eternal principles of moral duty—of the moral law. "Be not deceived; God is not mocked." "The unrighteous shall not inherit the kingdom of God." "All unrighteousness is sin : and there is a sin unto death."

43

THE BELIEVER AS BORN OF GOD KEEPING HIM-SELF SO AS NOT TO SIN

" All unrighteousness is sin : and there is a sin [not] unto death. We know that whosoever is born of God sinneth not ; but he that is be-gotten of God keepeth himself, and that wicked one toucheth him not." 1 John 5:17,18

THE last clause of the seventeenth verse may best be read without the negative. There is, I believe, preponderating manuscript authority for so reading it. And, as regards internal evidence, it seems easier to explain,—and this is a good criterion,—how, if not originally in the text, it might creep in, than how, if originally in the text, it could fall out. The insertion of it by copyists, perhaps first as a conjectural marginal reading, can easily be explained by their suppos-ing it necessary to harmonise the statement in the seven-teenth verse with that in the verse before, so as to bring in again the idea of the lawfulness of praying for life for them that sin not unto death. This seventeenth verse, how-ever, rather points the thought, not backwards to the six-teenth, but onwards and forwards to the eighteenth. Do not imagine that in praying for a sinning brother, you may overlook the possibility of his sin being unto death. Do not pray for him as if you thought that in accommodation to his case God's law might be relaxed, and he, though sin-ning so as to deserve to die, and continuing so to sin, might yet not surely die. Beware of that ; for your own sake, as well as for his sake ; for your own sake, even more than for his sake. For you are in danger of being led to tolerate in yourselves what you are inclined to palliate in a brother. You secretly hope that there may be impunity for him, even though he is continuing in sin. Is there no risk of your being tempted to cherish a similar hope for yourselves ; and so to forget the great truth that " all unrighteousness is sin : and there is a sin unto death " ?

But you may be saying within yourselves, " Whosoever is born of God doth not commit sin ; for his seed remaineth in him : and he cannot sin, because he is born of God " (iii. 9). You, therefore, as born of God, may hold your-selves safe in extenuating sin in a brother, and deprecating on his behalf its terrible doom. Still beware ! It is true that, as it has been explained, whosoever is born of God does not and cannot sin. " We know that whosoever is born of God sinneth not." Yes, we know that. But we know also that his not sinning, however it may be connected with his being born of God, and secured by God's seed, the seed of the divine nature and eternal life, remaining in him, —is not so connected with that fact, or so secured by it, as to preclude the necessity of care and watchfulness. He has " to keep himself ; " and that too in the presence of a formi-dable enemy. " We know that whosoever is born of God sinneth not." But why not ? Because " he that is begotten of God keepeth himself, and that wicked one toucheth him not."

He " keepeth himself." The phrase might suggest two ideas : that of keeping, as if restraint were needed ; or that of keeping, as if care and culture were intended. This last is probably to be regarded as the right sense, not however by any means to the exclusion of the other. He has to guard himself against the touch of " that wicked one " from without ; and he has carefully to watch and foster the growth of the divine seed within. His thus keeping himself is the effect of his being born of God; and it is the cause, or means, of his not sinning. Not otherwise than in the way of his keeping himself, can one born of God be safe from sinning. In an important and practical point of view, he must be his own keeper. And his keeping himself will be earnest, sedulous, anxious, in proportion to the sense he has of the value of what is to be kept, on the one hand, and of its liability to sustain damage, or be lost, on the other.

I. What is to be kept, O child of God? Yourself! Not yourself as you are by nature, but yourself as born of God. Consider, first, what is implied in that solemn thought.

Even as regards the life that now is, you have to keep yourself. Self-preservation is both your right and your duty; your right, which you are to vindicate though your doing so may involve an assailant's death; your duty, which, whatever you may think about your own worth or value, you are not at liberty to renounce or to neglect. You are not entitled to throw yourself away; you are bound to keep yourself. And that, not only in the sense of your not literally committing suicide; for you may abstain from suicide and yet be virtually a self-destroyer. You are bound to keep yourself as one,—whatever you are, and wherever you are,—that is too costly to be cast away, being still, as you are, within the reach of divine grace and eternal life. You have no more right, in any circumstances, or in any mood or frame of mind, to give yourself up to despair, than you have to give yourself up to death.

But it is as a child of God that you are here said to keep yourself. Consider, I say again, what that means.

Try for a moment to separate in imagination yourself as the keeper, from yourself as what is to be kept. Look upon yourself objectively; as if you were looking at another person. Or, to make this easier, look first at another person, as if he were yourself. Suppose yourself your brother's keeper; keeping him as if he were yourself. And, to make the analogy a fair one, suppose yourself to be, under God, his only keeper. And suppose also that your are his keeper in the sense of having most intimate access to his inner man, as well as entire control over his outward actions.

Well, you keep him; you, as born of God, keep him, as born of God;—would that we were all thus keeping one another! But what sort of keeping will it be? That will depend on the vividness of the apprehension which you have of your own sonship, and of his; of your being born of God, and his being born of God. He whom you have to keep is no ordinary piece of goods. He may have been once vile; a condemned criminal; and as such, unclean. But "what God has cleansed you cannot call common or unclean." He is very precious now, and very pure. He has the seed of God abiding in him; the germ and principle of an absolutely sinless character and life. It is in that view, and upon that supposition, that you have to "keep" him. Your whole treatment of him must be accommodated to that fact. Need I bid you ask yourself what your treatment of him would, or at any rate should, be if you had to keep him as thus "born of God"?

Now if your keeping yourself is to be at all such as you feel that your keeping of your brother ought to be in the case supposed, it must proceed upon as clear and explicit a recognition of your own standing as, in that case, there would be of his. If you are really to keep yourself, you must distinctly understand, and strongly realise, what it is about you that is to be kept; what is the character in which, and what the standard by which, and what the end for which, you are to keep yourself.

For instance, I may feel that I have to keep myself as a

good worldly man, or a good moral man, or a good man of business, or a good man of society, or a good neighbour and friend; a good husband, father, brother, son. I can only keep myself, in any of these characters, by first making it thoroughly, inwardly, intensely, my own, and then thoroughly acting it out. It will not do to assume it, or to imagine it; neither will it do to admit it in any doubtful or hesitating way. If I am to keep myself, I must know and apprehend myself actually to be what I mean, by keeping myself, to continue to be.

In keeping myself as born of God, this personal and realising faith is especially needful. The secret of my not keeping myself, with enough of watchfulness and prayer, is too often to be found in the want of it. I keep myself, perhaps, with tolerably decent consistency, as a professing member of the church; I keep myself as an upright, charitable, and correctly religious man. But do I take home to myself the obligation of keeping myself as more than that? Do I adequately apprehend the fact that I am more than that; that I am really and truly "born of God"? Do I sufficiently apprehend what that means? Nothing else will ensure my "keeping myself."

I do not speak now of assurance, in a doctrinal point of view. No question is raised here as to a believing man being assured, for his own comfort, of his present standing and of his final salvation. The whole strain of John's teaching is practical. Whether or not he that is born of God is to sit down and conclude reflexly that he is born of God, is not said. It is not even said that he is to raise the question. All that is said is, that he is to treat himself; he is to keep himself; as born of God. He is so to use and deal with himself, as he would use and deal with what is born of God. It is not to any reflex or subjective exercise of faith, ascertaining itself simply for its own con-

firmation and confidence, that he is called, but to the direct,
objective acting out of his faith. And that is all in the
line of his practically keeping himself, as he feels that what
is born of God ought to be and must be kept.

What sort of keeping of one's self should grow out of
such a vivid and realising sense as this implies of what
being born of God means, it is not necessary to describe
minutely or at large. The working out of the problem
may well be left to our own consciences and hearts. The
main thing is to secure here, as everywhere, singleness of
eye. Only let us settle it decidedly, firmly, unequivocally,
as the deep conviction of our souls, that it is as "born of
God" that we are to "keep ourselves."

Ah! if we did so, would there be so much careless
living among us ; so much unsteadfast walking ; so much
indifference to the way in which our customary manner of
spending our time and occupying our thoughts tells on our
spiritual state? Would there not be more of earnest
prayer, of secret fellowship with God, of diligent study of
his word, of anxious watchfulness ; more of an eager pressing on to higher attainments in divine insight and sympathy, in holiness and love?

For to keep ourselves as born of God, is to aim at
exhausting experimentally all that the privilege involves.
It is to keep ourselves, as sons and heirs, in the full enjoyment of our Father's love and in the full view of the many
mansions of our Father's house.

II. This keeping of ourselves, as born of God, will be
felt to be the more necessary, when we consider, secondly,
how liable that which is to be kept is to suffer damage and
be lost. If we are born of God, and if it is in that character that we are to keep ourselves; let us remember how
apt that character is to be marred and injured by the outer
world with which we are ever coming in contact; how apt

it is to lose its marked distinctiveness and fresh life in our own souls.

As born of God, we have to "keep ourselves unspotted from the world;" we have to keep ourselves also unspotted from the evil that is in us, as born in iniquity and conceived in sin. In both views, what is above all things needed is to cherish a deep, abiding, personal, practical persuasion that "all unrighteousness is sin, and that there is a sin unto death."

The risk of relaxed diligence in "keeping ourselves as born of God" lies mainly in our ceasing, more or less consciously, to regard sin as exceeding sinful, and the doom of sin as inevitably certain. Hence, in order to our keeping ourselves, it is of the utmost consequence, first of all, that we truly and fully apprehend that we are to keep ourselves as being born of God. And it is of equal consequence, secondly, that we truly and fully apprehend the absolute incompatibility of our sinning with our being born of God. Sin from without and from within is ever besetting us. And the temptation is very strong to begin to think that, in some form or degree, it may not be altogether damaging to our spiritual life, as born of God, or altogether fatal to our heavenly prospects, as having eternal life. The instant such a thought finds harbour in our bosom, all our faithfulness in keeping ourselves is gone. "Whosoever is born of God keepeth himself,"—only when he realises his own sacredness as "born of God;" and when moreover he realises,—and that too with special reference, not merely to the world with which he is ever in contact, but also to himself and his own tendencies and liabilities,—the solemn truth that "all unrighteousness is sin, and that there is a sin unto death."

There is no room for any question being raised here as to the certainty of his final salvation, or the security for his

preservation in grace to the end. That is not the point.
Be it that God keeps him, and will keep him, infallibly
safe : God does so, and can do so, only through his keeping
himself. And his keeping himself implies a constant sense
of his liability, after all, so far as he is himself concerned,
to be lost. So Paul kept himself: "I keep under my body,
and bring it into subjection : lest that by any means, when
I have preached to others, I myself should be a cast-away."
So will every one that is born of God keep himself;
remembering the exhortations, "Let him that thinketh he
standeth take heed lest he fall ;" "Thou standeth by faith ;
be not highminded, but fear."

And this fear, not slavish fear of an angry God, but filial
fear of a loving Father, the fear of filial love, will grow, and
will become more and more "fear and trembling." It will
do so in proportion as I apprehend, with growing vividness,
on the one hand, all the holy blessedness that there is in
being born of God, and on the other hand, all that there is
in sin; in any sin; in every sin; of deep and deadly
malignity, making it the very bane of that blessedness.
Thus, with increasing sensitiveness, will I be keeping
myself "as born of God, and not sinning." Thus will I be
" working out my own salvation with fear and trembling,
because it is God which worketh in me both to will and to
do of his good pleasure."

I do not now enter on the consideration of the promise
annexed to this self-keeping : "The wicked one toucheth
him not." I prefer to take that promise in connection
with what follows. I content myself with one observation
on its connection with what precedes.

"The wicked one" seeks to touch you ; to touch you at
the tenderest and most sensitive point, where alone lies
your security against sinning ; your being "born of God."

For it is only as born of God that you sin not. It is in your filial standing thoroughly realised, and in your filial spirit thoroughly cherished and exercised, that the secret of your not sinning lies. The wicked one knows that right well; he quite understands it. Full well he knows and understands that if he can get you, be it only for a brief hour or moment, to step off from the platform of your sonship;—or if he can insinuate into your breast at any time a single unchildlike thought of God;—he has you at his mercy. And you sin. You listen to his whispered suggestion that this or that commandment of God is grievous. You suffer his wily insinuation,—"Yea, hath God said that ye shall not?"—to poison your ear, to poison your soul. You let in the spirit of bondage again. The light and liberty of your loving cry, "Abba, Father," are gone. Shorn of your strength, you repine, you murmur, you sin.

Ah, friends! "keep yourselves." And see to it that you keep yourselves as "born of God." Keep yourselves in your conscious sonship, and in the spirit of it. Then "the wicked one toucheth you not." Be very sure that it is sonship believingly apprehended and realised, it is the spirit of sonship faithfully cherished and exercised, that is your only real shield and defence against the touch of the wicked one. For his touch, his stinging touch, is the suggestion of the poor servile thought that God's commandments are grievous. The filial, loving confidence of one keeping himself as a child of God instinctively and indignantly casts away the insinuation. The wicked one therefore cannot touch one living as a son of God. He could not touch, terribly as he tried to touch, the Son of God while he lived on earth; for never did he live otherwise than as the Son of God. He cannot touch any one to whom God gives "the Spirit of his Son, crying, Abba,

Father." For no one can be, at any moment, crying, in the Spirit, Abba, Father, and at the same moment counting any of God's commandments grievous. Therefore when "he that is begotten of God" keepeth himself as so begotten, "the wicked one toucheth him not."

44

OUR BEING OF GOD —THE WORLD LYING IN THE WICKED ONE

" And that [the] wicked one toucheth him not. We know that we are of
God, and the whole world lieth in wickedness " [the wicked one].—
1 John 5:18,19

INSTEAD of " wickedness," in the nineteenth verse, we may
rather read " the wicked one." There is now a general
agreement among critics and interpreters to that effect.
There is no good reason for any change in this verse from
the rendering in the verse before. There it must unavoid-
ably be personal, " the wicked one toucheth him not." It is
quite unnecessary and unwarrantable to make it impersonal
and abstract here, " the whole world lieth in wickedness."
It is the same expression and should be translated in the
same way, " the whole world lieth in the wicked one." For
the change mars the sense, and destroys the obvious contrast
that there is between the child of God, whom that wicked
one does not touch, and the world which, so far from being
safe from his touch, lies wholly in him.

We know this last fact, as knowing ourselves to be of
God ; and it is our thus knowing it that mainly contributes
to our security.

For that is the precise point and purpose of the statement, " the whole world lieth in the wicked one." It is a
statement introduced for a purely practical end ; an end or
purpose personal to us, as begotten of God, and, in that

character, "keeping ourselves." It has no reference to any other persons besides ourselves; it is strictly applicable, and meant to be applied, to ourselves alone. There is no contrast intended between us and the rest of mankind. There is no emphasis in the "we,"—"we are of God,"—as in contradistinction to those of our fellow-men who may be classed as "the world." In fact the "we" is not in the original at all. It is supplied, and of course necessarily supplied, in our translation. But its not being expressed in the original is plain proof, as all scholars know, that it is not intended to be emphatic, or to suggest any contrast between us and any other body of men. We have nothing here to do with any but ourselves; the text is written solely for our learning, for our warning. It bids us remember that we, being of God, are not of that world which lies wholly in the wicked one. It bids us do so, in order that, being begotten of God, we may so "keep ourselves," as being begotten of God, that the "wicked one shall not touch us."

Thus the world is here to be viewed rather as a system than as a society; with reference not so much to the question who constitute the world, as to the question what the world is; what is its character and constitution; what are its arrangements; its habits of thought, feeling, and action; its pursuits, occupations, and pleasures.

One common feature is brought out, helping us to identify and characterise it. The whole of it "lieth in the wicked one."

It is a strong expression; going beyond any of John's previous intimations on this subject. He makes early mention of "the wicked one" (ii. 13, 14). Believers are represented as, in the strength of their mature and vigorous spiritual youth, overcoming, or having overcome, "the wicked one." Thereafter, when "the wicked one" comes up again (iii. 12), he is plainly identified with the devil (iii. 8-10), in respect of his murderous hatred of God and of whatever is born of God; he kills or seeks to kill whatever and whoever is of God. Next, he appears as that "spirit of antichrist" which is in the world, as "the spirit that confesseth not that Jesus Christ is come in the flesh" (iv. 3). Here it is said, not that he is in the world, but that the world lies in him. It lies, and lies wholly in him. He has got the world into his arms; the whole world.

I. "The world lieth in the wicked one." The figure may suggest several different ideas. A stranded vessel lying embedded in the sand; a lost sheep lying engulphed in the treacherous swamp; a sow contented to lie wallowing in the mire; a Samson lying bewitched in Delilah's lap;— these are the images called forth; and they are all but too appropriate.

Considered in its origin, this lying of the world in the wicked one may be taken in a very literal and personal sense.

The fall is a fall out of the arms of God into the embrace of the wicked one. He is ready to receive the fallen; and, in a measure, to break their fall. He has a bed of his own prepared on which the fallen may lie in him. It is shrewdly and plausibly framed. It is like himself. It is the embodiment of his mind and spirit; the acting out of his very self. It is a couch composed of the very materials he had before woven into the subtle cord of that temptation which drew the unfallen out of God's hold into his. The same elements of unbelief which he turned to such cunning account in his work of seduction, he employs with equal skill in getting the seduced to lie, and to lie quiet, in him. For the most part, he finds this an easy task. The world listens willingly to its seducer, now become its comforter and guide; and frames its creed and constitution according to his teaching and under his inspiration. He is its doctor of divinity. Its faith, worship, discipline, and government are dictated by him. So "the world lies in him;" dependent on him and his theology for such assumed licence and imaginary peace as it affects to use and to enjoy.

For the essence of worldliness is at bottom the feeling that "God's commandments are grievous;" that his service is hard, and himself austere; but yet that somehow his indulgence may be largely reckoned upon in the end. It is as "lying in the wicked one," that the world so conceives of God, and acts upon that conception of him. It is as "lying in the wicked one," that it peevishly asks, "Who is the Almighty that we should serve him, and what profit shall we have if we bow down unto him?"—while at the same time it confidently presumes, "The Lord seeth not, the Lord regardeth not."

II. "The whole world thus lieth in the wicked one;" he has it all in his embrace. There is nothing in or about the world that is not thus lying in the wicked one; so lying in the wicked one as to be infected with the contagion of his hard thoughts of God, and his affected bravery in defying God's righteous judgment.

Take the world at its very best; all its grossness put away; no vile lust or passion polluting it; much pure virtue adorning it; many pious sentiments coming forth from it, not altogether insincerely. What trace is there here of the wicked one's poisonous touch? What necessity for your being warned to be on your guard against it or him?

Nay, but look deeper into the heart of what is so seeming fair. Do you not see, do you not instinctively feel, that there is throughout its sphere of influence a sad want of that entire surrender of self to God, that unreserved owning of his sovereignty, the sovereignty of his throne, his law, his grace, that full, loyal, loving trust, which alone can baffle Satan's wiles? Instead of that, is there not a hidden fear of coming to too close quarters and too confidential dealings with God; a disposition to stand aloof and make terms of compromise; a willingness to be persuaded that some questionable things may be tolerated and some slight liberties allowed? Is not all this what "lying in the wicked one" may best explain?

We are not safe unless we realise it as a fact that "the whole world lieth in the wicked one;" all of it; the best of it as well as the worst of it. Only thus can we "so keep ourselves that the wicked one shall not touch us." It is a sad fact, but we must realise it. And in the firm and full realisation of it, we must "keep ourselves."

For it is not with a view to our condemning or judging the world, but only in order to our "keeping ourselves," that we are to have this fact always before our eyes; it is in order to our so "keeping ourselves that the wicked one shall not touch us." For it is through the world which is lying in him that he seeks to touch us. We are coming constantly into contact with the world; we cannot help it; and yet we are to keep ourselves "unspotted from the world." How better may we hope, through grace, to do so, than by knowing, in the sense of always and everywhere acting upon the knowledge, that "we are of God, and the whole world lieth in the wicked one"?

Let us recognise our own standing in God, and the world's lying in the wicked one. We are of God, born of God; his sons in his Son Jesus Christ. That is our character and position. It is in that character, and with reference to that position, that we are to "keep ourselves." Let us be ever mindful of our high and holy calling. And that we may be ever mindful of it, let us be ever sensitively alive to the risk of the wicked one's contamination. True,

" the wicked one toucheth us not." But " the whole world lieth in him." And the world touches us, for we are in the world.

Ah! does not our danger spring from our practically forgetting that the world in which we are lieth wholly in the wicked one ? Have not we found it so ? We begin to think, or to live as if we thought, that after all the world does not lie absolutely and altogether in the wicked one ; that it is not so thoroughly evil as that would imply. We find, or fancy that we find, some of it at least, such as we would not choose to characterise so offensively. The world may be mostly, or for the most part, lying in the wicked one. But surely some exception may be made in favour of this or that about it that looks so harmless and so good.

O child of God, beware. The wicked one is touching you very closely, through the world that lieth in him, when he gets you thus to plead. The Spirit teaches you a safer and better lesson when he moves you to say : " We know that we are of God, and the whole world "—all of it— " lieth in the wicked one."

This teaching of John, concerning the world as lying in the wicked one, is in striking accordance with that of Paul in two remarkable passages of his Epistle to the Ephesians (ii. 1, vi. 12). One would almost think indeed that John had Paul's teaching in his view. At all events, it may be interesting and useful to notice the parallelism and harmony between the two apostles.

I. Consider the first of the two passages (Ephes. ii. 1) : " You hath he quickened, who were dead in trespasses and sins ; wherein in time past ye walked according to the course of this world, according to the prince of the power of the air, the spirit that now worketh in the children of disobedience." Writing to the Ephesians as now believers,

Paul reminds them of their former walk. It was " according to the course of this world." But "the world, the whole world, lieth in the wicked one." Therefore, walking according to the course of this world, they walked according to the wicked one in whom the world lies. How the world lies in him, so that walking according to the world's course is really walking according to him, is explained in two ways.

1. He is " the prince of the power of the air." He rules, as a powerful prince, the world's atmosphere ; its moral and spiritual atmosphere ; impregnating it with his own venom ; the poisonous vapour of his own dark and godless hell. The air which the world breathes is under his control ; he is the prince of the power of it ; its powerful prince. It is, as it were, compounded, concocted, and manufactured by him. Very wisely does he use his power ; very cunningly does he compose the air which he would have his subjects and victims to breathe. He mingles in it many good ingredients. For the worst of men he does so ; and indeed he must do so, if he is to make it palatable and seductive even to them. For the lowest company, he must needs prepare an atmosphere with something good in it ; good fellowship at the least, and a large measure of good humour and good feeling. Then, as he rises to higher circles, how does he contrive, in the exercise of his princely power, to make the air that is to intoxicate his votaries, or lull them to unsuspecting sleep, all redolent, as it might seem, of good ; good sense, good taste, good temper ; good breeding and behaviour ; good habits and good-heartedness ! Many noisome vapours also that might offend he carefully excludes ; so that the inhaling organ perceives nothing but what is pure and simple in what it imbibes and absorbs. But it is the wicked one's air or atmosphere after all ; he is the prince of the power of it. He contrives to have it all

pervaded with the latent influence of his own ungodliness ; his godless spirit is in it all through. The whole world is lying in that subtle atmosphere of his ; the air of which he is the powerful prince.

Have you not felt something of what it is to breathe the air of which the wicked one is thus the powerful prince, to breathe it at the time almost unconsciously, and afterwards to find the fruit of your having breathed it all but inexplicable ? You come home from a business engagement, or a party of pleasure. You feel an unwonted indisposition to serious thought ; you are less inclined than usual to prayer and meditation ; anxious calculations or frivolous fancies, and vain if not vicious imaginations, intrude into the sanctuary of your inner worship ; you are not so much at home as you were before in your closet-fellowship with your Father in heaven. You are at a loss to account for this. You have not been anywhere, or done anything, in known or conscious opposition to his will. But you have been living in an unwholesome atmosphere. You have been in scenes or societies ; all decent and proper no doubt ; but yet imbued with as thorough a spirit of indifference or alienation as the wicked one would care to inspire. You have forgotten that " the whole world lieth in the wicked one " as " the prince of the power of its air."

2. Nor is this all. He is " the spirit that now worketh in the children of disobedience." He is not content with exercising his power in concocting and compounding the world's atmosphere ; he is busily moving to and fro, and up and down, in the ranks of those who breathe it. He prepares for them the air he would like them to inhale, making it as soothing and seductive as he can. And then, while they are inhaling it, he deals with them personally ; going in and out among them ; whispering his suggestions ; speaking low into their ears ; insinuating into their hearts

such thoughts of God, and of his service, and of his gospel, as fit into the pervading godless spirit of the region into which he has got them to venture. In this view, he very specially works among them as "the children of dis-obedience." He takes advantage of every rising feeling of distrust and disaffection ; he watches for the first beginnings of discontent. Wherever there is any disposition to count any of God's appointments or commandments grievous, he is at hand ; to fan the flame ; to irritate the sore ; to widen the breach between the loving Father and his undutiful child, beginning to question and rebel.

So the whole world doubly, or in a double sense, lies in the wicked one ; inasmuch as he is the prince of the power of its air on the one hand, and inasmuch as, on the other hand, he is ever working in it among the children of disobedience. And in both views, it concerns you deeply, as "knowing yourselves to be of God," and called to keep yourselves accordingly, to know that "the whole world lieth in the wicked one." Know this, that you may beware of its seductive atmosphere, of which he is the powerful prince. Know it, that you may beware of the first rising in you of that insubordinate and impatient spirit of which he avails himself so skilfully in his "working among the children of disobedience." If you would keep yourselves, as being of God, so that in respect of your being begotten of God the wicked one may not touch you, you must be ever alive to this double risk ; the risk of your forgetting how thoroughly he controls the world's atmosphere ; and the risk also of your forgetting how busily and persuasively he works among the children of disobedience in it.

Keep yourselves, in both views, unspotted from the world. Keep yourselves, as born of God, in the atmosphere into which your new birth introduces you ; the atmosphere of pure light and love ; the Father's own light ; the Father's own love. And keep yourselves, as "obedient children, not fashioning yourselves according to the former lusts in your ignorance; but as he which hath called you is holy, so be ye holy in all manner of conversation; because it is written, Be ye holy, for I am holy."

II. Look now for a little at the second of the two passages in Ephesians (vi. 12.) : "We wrestle not against flesh and blood, but against principalities, against powers, against the rulers of the darkness of this world, against spiritual wickedness in high places." There is a double view here given of the influence which the wicked one, with his principalities and powers, exerts. On the one hand, he "rules the darkness of this world." On the other hand, he is "spiritual wickedness in high places."

1. He rules the dark world which lies wholly in him; rules it as the prince of the power of its air, and as the spirit now working in the children of disobedience. If he finds you there, he finds you within his own territory; at once breathing the worldly atmosphere he has mixed; and open at the same time to his influence as he is busy in his vocation, plying all his wiles among those whom he finds harbouring thoughts of insubordination. He has an advantage over you on his own ground; you cannot there cope with him; your only safety is in flight. "Come out and be separate." Flee to the stronghold; "the heavenly places." The wicked one's world is not your home. You are not to know it at all; or to know it only as lying wholly in the wicked one; to beware of it; to renounce it; to keep yourself unspotted from it. Your home is in "the heavenly places," in which "you sit with Christ." Abide there, and "the wicked one toucheth you not."*

---

* "The heavenly places," or "the heavenlies," is the right rendering of the phrase in all the four connections in which it occurs in the Epistle to the Ephesians, where alone it is found :—i. (ii. 9), as the home of bless-

2. Nay, but even into "the heavenly places" the wicked one may find access; and even in "the heavenly places" he may seek to touch you. But he does not, he cannot, really touch you there. He crept indeed into Paradise, which was "the heavenly places" before the fall; and touched fatally our first parents there. But in "the heavenly places" now, in your "heavenly places," you have a defence which they had not. You "sit with Christ in the heavenly places," being "begotten of God in his Son." You "know that you are of God," in a sense and to an effect that Adam and Eve, with all their innocence, could not realise. By redemption, by adoption, by regeneration; as bought and begotten; you are of God; his own very sons, as Jesus is. The wicked one may come to you in your heavenlies, as he came to them in theirs. He may come as "spiritual wickedness;" plying his old wicked spiritual arts of temptation; suggesting his old doubts of the love and equity and truth of God. But he "touches you not." He could touch you only by appealing to something in you of what he finds in the children of dis- obedience among whom he works in the world; something in you of their disobedience, some incipient leaning towards insubordination, some aptness to count the commandments of God grievous.

Is there at any time anything of that spirit in you? Is there any rising within you of the old feeling of impatience, of suspicion, in a word, of unbelief? Ah, then, even "in the heavenlies," you are not safe from the touch of the wicked one. Remember that you have to "wrestle against him even in the heavenlies;" to wrestle against him, not only as "rul- ing the world's darkness," but as "spiritual wickedness in the heavenlies."

---

ing; ii. (i. 20, ii. 6), as the seat of the risen life; iii. (iii. 10), as the theatre of the Divine drama; iv. (vi. 12), as the last retreat in the satanic struggle.

For he comes into the secret place where you dwell with God as his children ; transformed perhaps into an angel of light; insinuating his old doubts, surmises, questionings again ; putting in his old cavils between your Father's loving heart and your simple trust. Let him not, O my brother! let him not succeed in his attempt. Stand against him by faith. Bid him begone. He has no right to be in your heavenlies, whatever right he may have to "rule in the world's darkness." If you have faith you may cast him out. Keep yourself, as "born of God ;" keep yourself in the vivid realising sense of all that your "sitting with Christ in the heavenlies " involves. So keep yourself in the heavenlies, and that wicked one touches you not.

What shall I say, in closing, to you who are not of God, but of the world; of the world that is altogether lying in the wicked one ? Ah ! do you not know that the prince of the world is judged; that for this purpose the Son of God was manifested that he might destroy the works of the devil ? Are you still listening to the gospel of the wicked one : " Ye shall not surely die " ? Nay rather, hear another gospel : " God is love; in this was manifested the love of God towards us, because that God sent his Son into the world, that we might live through him."

45

KNOWING THE TRUE ONE AND BEING IN HIM

"And we know that the Son of God is come, and hath given us an understanding, that we may know him that is true ; and we are in him that is true, [*even*] in his Son Jesus Christ."*   1 John 5:20

THIS is the third and last "we know," in these closing verses of the epistle (18–20). John insists, in leaving us, upon our being Gnostics, or knowing ones, as the heretics of his day professed to be ; but in a better and safer sense. They affected to be knowing, in the lofty and transcendental region of abstract speculation about the divine nature ; whereas John would have us to be knowing, in the humbler yet really higher and holier experience of real, direct, personal acquaintance and fellowship with the Divine Being, as coming down to us, poor sinners, in his Son, and taking us up, by his Spirit, to be sons and saints in his holy child Jesus.

That whosoever is born of God sinneth not, because he keepeth himself so that the wicked one touches him not ; that we are thus of God, in contrast with the world which

---

* There is no occasion for the word "*even*" which our translators have inserted in the last clause of this verse ; it is not in the original, as the italics indicate ; and it is fitted to mislead. It is apt to suggest the idea that by "him that is true," or "the true one," we are to understand, not God the Father, but the Son of God. Some accordingly have so construed the clause ; but as it seems to me unwarrantably. For he who is called "the true one" is expressly distinguished from his Son. "We are in him that is true." How? Through our being "in his Son Jesus Christ."

lies wholly in the wicked one ; these are the two former " we know." And now the third " we know " has respect, neither to our standing as being of God, nor to the world's position as lying in the wicked one, but to him who causes or occasions the difference, " the Son of God."

It would almost seem as if there was a regular syllogism here; an argument built up in three propositions; two premises and a conclusion. First there is the major premiss, in the general assertion, abstract and impersonal ; " we know " that being born of God implies not sinning, inasmuch as " he that is begotten of God keepeth himself, and the wicked one touches him not." Then there is the minor premiss, in the assertion, particular and personal ; " we know " that we individually " are of God," and, therefore, separated from " the world that lieth wholly in the wicked one." The strict logical conclusion would be ; therefore " we know " that we do not sin. John, however, puts it somewhat differently, so as to place our not sinning on a surer footing ; more humbling to us ; more glorifying to God ;—" We know that the Son of God is come."

And yet this is a fair enough inference, and fits well enough into the argument when viewed in its full spiritual import. Nor is it inconsistent with the other. For if he that is born of God sinneth not; and if we consequently, being of God, sin not, it is all in virtue of " the Son of God being come ;" come, in the first place, to " give us a knowledge of the True One ; " come, secondly, to secure in that way our " being in the True One."

I. " The Son of God is come, and hath given us understanding, that we may know him that is true," or " the True One." It is God who is to be known; and he is to be known as " the True One."

The truth here ascribed to God is not truthfulness, as opposed to falsehood ; but reality, as opposed to fiction or imagination. That we may know God, as truly real, as a truly real being, "the Real One," strictly speaking, the only truly Real One, apart from whom all things and persons are shadowy and unreal; that is, in the first instance, the purpose for which his Son Jesus Christ is come, and "hath given us understanding" or insight "to know him that is true."

The inward working of the Holy Ghost is here assumed, or asserted; that is the "understanding" or insight that is meant. Jesus Christ coming as the Son of God has given us, not merely new outer light, but a new inner eye; otherwise even his coming could not make us know "the True One." His coming indeed may be said to be itself the outer light. His coming forth from the True One in whose bosom he dwells reveals the True One to us. But the discovery would be in vain if his coming did not secure to us, as his gift, "understanding to know" the True One when thus revealed. That is, we may say emphatically, his best gift; the best fruit of his " being come," and of all the travail of soul on our behalf which his " being come" includes in it. For the worst of our miserable state, from which he is come to save us, is that we have no understanding, no spiritual sense in us, by which we can discern and recognise, so as truly to know, him who alone is true. And the best part of his salvation is his giving us that knowledge, not only by revelation from without, but by enlightenment within.

It is a great thing to know God as he is here named— " the True One;" to know him as true and real; no imagination or mere idea, but true and real. That, I say, is a very great thing. It is indeed all in all; the one thing needful. What is God to me? Ah, momentous question! And as searching as it is momentous! Is he true? Is he real? Do I apprehend him to be so?

I know my friend when I see him and take him by the hand. I know him as true and real; no shadow, no myth, no visionary ghost, but verily real. There he is before me, not a wraith such as Highland seer beholds in the misty vapour, but invested with unmistakable, palpable reality. Is God thus ever before me? Whenever I think of my friend, even when he is out of my sight, I think of him as true and real; as having a real and actual existence; a real and actual personality. Do I always thus think of God? Do I always thus know him?

There are two conditions of this knowledge.

In the first place, if I am to know any one as true and real, I must have a distinct and well-defined conception of him in my mind. He must present himself to me as having a certain special individuality of his own, marking him out to me as separate from others. I thus identify him as true and real. But how confused and incoherent is my conception of God apt to be! A number of vague notions about him and his ways may be floating hazily, as it were, before me. But they lack unity, and are therefore unreal. A heap or bundle of attributes, such as I can name, enumerate, and define, may be all that I have for my God. If so, it is a heap or bundle of rags. It has no life, no living personality, no oneness, no reality, no truth. To know any person as real and true, I must know him as one; one living personality; living and true.

But, secondly, can I so know any one otherwise than by personal intercourse and personal acquaintanceship? It is in that way that I know an actual living friend as true. When our eyes meet and our hands join and our tongues exchange words, I know him as true and real. I know him better thus, than when he and I communicate by letter merely, or by message at second-hand. My knowledge of him has in it a truth and reality, a true and vivid realisation, that does not belong to the notion I have of any hero or martyr; however graphic may be the history, however lifelike the picture, by means of which I am to set him before my mind's eye.

Now "the Son of God has come, and given us understanding that we may know the True One;" that we may truly and really know, know as a living person, the Father whose Son he is. The very object of his "coming and giving us understanding," is to put truth and reality into our knowledge of God. He does so by bringing God and us personally together. His "coming" provides for that on the part of God; his "giving us understanding" provides for it on our part.

It is indeed, I repeat, a great thing thus to know "him that is true;" to have a true personal knowledge of him; such as you have of the friend you converse with every day about everything or anything that turns up, or of the father to whom you go every day and every hour for deeper counsel or for a passing embrace. The friend, the father, is a reality; a real and true friend, a real and true father. You feel him to be so. He is no dead, historical personage, exhibited on the stage of the historical drama. He is to you a real and living person: for there is life and reality in your present intercourse with him. And it is that there may be this present living intercourse with God as a living person, that "the Son of God is come," to make that possible on God's side; "and hath given us an understanding," to make it possible on ours. Only in that way, by his revelation of himself to us in the Son and by our fellowship with him in the Spirit, can we know "him that is true." Only thus can we know God personally; as "the True One;" a real person and not a mere abstraction or generalisation.

II. Knowing thus "him that is true," we are "in him."

But we are so, only as being "in his Son Jesus Christ."
The apostle's statement thus fits into the Lord's own saying,
in his farewell prayer, " I in them and thou in me" (John
xvii. 23). Both of them rest on that higher appeal which
the Lord makes to his Father :—" As thou, Father, art in
me, and I in thee, that they also may be one in us" (ver.
21). Thou in me, I in them, and so thou in them ;—they
in me, I in thee, and so they in thee ;—such is the wondrous
reciprocal line or chain between God and us. We are in
the True One, as being in his Son Jesus Christ, who is himself in him. We are therefore in the True One as his Son
Jesus Christ himself is in him.

Thus our being in the True One rests on very sure
ground, since it is in his Son Jesus Christ that we are in
him. And it implies a very high ideal of what being in the
True One means, and what it is.

1. It is in his Son Jesus Christ that we are in the True
One. We are in him, not directly or immediately, but by
mediation ; through and in a mediator. It is only thus
that we can be in God, as the one only living and true
God. It must be so. If the God whom our conscience indicates and owns is indeed true and real ; a real, true, living person ; we cannot dream of being in him, in any sense
implying rest and peace, or a refuge and home, otherwise
than through and in a mediator.

No doubt, if there are many gods, all alike true, or all
alike fabulous, though still imagined to be true ; I may find
among them one so congenial that I can conceive of his
drawing me into his embrace, so that I may be in him. Or
if the only true God is the universe, or universal being ; all
things and persons being but his parts ; and all actions and
events the unfoldings of his own self-consciousness : then
necessarily I am in him ; or rather I am he and he is I ;
there is no personal distinction between us. Or if God, ad-

mitted to be a real, true, and living person, is not known by me as such, I may amuse or soothe myself with some name or notion of my being in him, so far as to secure my safety, if I do but say a prayer occasionally, no matter though my saying it is really little better than speaking to vacancy, addressing idle words to the empty air.

But let me know God as true, as a reality. Let me be confronted face to face with God, as no far-off vision, but a real, present, living person. Let my inner sense be quickened ; and let there flash from heaven a light making clear as day the features of him in whose real presence I stand. Ah! what cry escapes me ?—" I have heard of thee by the hearing of the ear, but now mine eye seeth thee ; wherefore I abhor myself, and repent in dust and ashes ! "

Now I see clearly ; now I feel deeply ; the full difficulty of the case. If God is true and real, my sin is true and real ; and I, the sinner, am true and real. Guilt is real. Wrath is real. Judgment is real. Punishment is real.

Ah ! this knowing of the True One, as the True One, by the spiritual understanding which the Son of God is come to give ! It imparts to all things in heaven and earth and hell a terrible distinctness, an altogether new air of truth, an intense, vivid, burning reality, such as I cannot long stand without being maddened, if I am to stand alone ; a real sinner before a real God.

For me to be in him ! How utterly hopeless ! Nay, but let me consider. Who is he who has come to give me understanding thus to know the True One ? The Son of God ; his Son Jesus Christ. It is he who by his coming makes the True One known as he really is ; for he is himself "the image of the invisible God." It is he who by his Spirit gives me understanding that I may know the True One. And placing himself between the True One, whom now at last I truly know, and me, whom that knowledge must otherwise utterly appal, he, the very Son of this True One, his Son Jesus Christ, calls me to himself; to be one with him; to be "in him." It is not that he would again hide the True One from me, or hide me from the True One. No. But he makes it possible for me, if I will but consent to be in him, to be "in the True One," as he is himself in the True One.

For he says, I am a reality; the real Son of God, really come to you, in your real flesh. As his true and very Son, I give you understanding to know him who is true and very God. And in me you know him, not so as to be a castaway from him; but so as to be in him, as I am in him. For in me, whatever in you might seem to stand in the way, and did stand in the way, of your being in the True One, is met and obviated. In the Son of God, his Son Jesus Christ, you can be in God, known as the True One, and can have perfect peace.

Out of Christ, I can have peace only by not knowing truly the True One, not knowing him as he is, or by keeping away from him among the trees of the garden, and· under the veil of some apron of fig-leaves. Satan belies him to me, and I hide or cover myself from him. But there is no need now of guile, or concealment, or disguise; no room for evasion or compromise. The True One may be truly known, and I, the chief of sinners, may be in him, truly known as the True One, "in his Son Jesus Christ."

2. If it is thus that in his Son Jesus Christ we are in the True One, it is after a high ideal or model that we are so. For our being in the True One in his Son Jesus Christ, must be after the manner of his Son Jesus Christ's being himself in him. What a manner of being in the True One is that! What truth, what reality is there in it!

I would keep fast hold of the apostle's ground-thought or. leading idea in this passage; which is truth, reality, fact. There are other views that may be taken of the Son of God, his Son Jesus Christ, being in the True One, as the type and model, as well as the cause, of our being in the True One in him. But I fix on this one as chiefly relevant here ; " we are in the True One in his Son Jesus Christ ; " and therefore in him as truly as his Son Jesus Christ is in him. How truly then, how really, is his Son Jesus Christ in him !

His Son Jesus Christ ! For it is not his Son, as being in him from everlasting, that is here presented to us. It is with his Son as " being come," that we have to do. It is in his Son Jesus Christ as " being come," that we are in the True One. Let us look well and see how his Son Jesus Christ is in the True One ; how, in the days of his flesh, " he is in him that is true ! " How truly, really, thoroughly ! How naturally too ! He is in his native element when he is in the True One.

Who that ever followed Jesus in his earthly life could for a moment doubt that God was to him a reality, and that his being in God was a reality too ? It was a true God that he served ; and he himself was truly in him. My Father ! he is ever saying ; and so saying it as to show that it is a real and true Father he means ; and that he is really and truly in him, as a real and true Son. Yes ! his Son Jesus Christ is truly in the True One ; never out of him ; never away from him ; never at home but with him ; never thinking a thought, or feeling an emotion, that he did not think and feel in him ; never speaking a word or doing a work but as having his Father with him. Truly, all through his real and true humiliation, and obedience, and sacrifice, " he is in him that is true ; " in him, with a depth and intensity of real inness, if I may use the word, that the devout study of a lifetime will not suffice to fathom. Nay, the devout study of eternity will not suffice to exhaust the full truth of that ineffable complacency of the Everlasting Father of which his Son Jesus Christ, for his obedience unto the death in our stead even more than for his original relation to him, has become the object.

Yes ! " I in thee," says Jesus, as he leaves the world and goes to the Father Oh! that word " I in thee ! " What a word, as spoken then and there ! Who can understand its significancy, its intense reality, its living truth ? " I in thee ! "

Can it be that I, a sinner, of sinners the chief, am to be in the True One as his Son Jesus Christ is thus in him ? It must be so, at least in measure, if it is in his Son Jesus Christ that I am to be in the True One. My being in the True One must be after the model and manner of his being in the True One. It must at all events be as real and true as that. To me, as to him, God must be a reality ; and my being in God must be a reality too.

Is this too high an aim ? Does it seem to be beyond my reach ? Nay, let me look again at the way in which God comes down to me that I may rise to him. " Thou in me ; I in them," is the language of the Son. So " he that is true," the True One, first condescends to us. He is in the Son, in his Son Jesus Christ ; all his fulness dwells in him bodily ;—" Thou in me." And the Son is in us ;—" I in them." The Holy Spirit takes of what is his and shows it to us ; he forms Christ in us. So the Father, the True One, comes down to us ; he in Christ ; Christ in us. Let Christ then be in us. Let us open our hearts to him. Let us welcome, receive, embrace him ; and the Father in him. Then we are in the Son as the Son is in the Father. " We are in him that is true, in his Son Jesus Christ our Lord."

Let me make a twofold practical appeal, in two opposite directions.

1. If you will not know the True One now, by the understanding which the Son of God is come to give; know him so as to be in him, in his Son Jesus Christ; the day is coming when you must be compelled, by another sort of awakening, to know the True One; and to know him terribly as a reality, as a real God dealing with a real sinner about real sin!

Here, for a little longer, God may be to you as if he were not. You may live on as you would live if he were not; almost as if, like the fool, you said in your heart, There is no God. You may live as you would live if you believed God to be no real being at all, but a mere creature of the imagination; like a character in fiction; an airy nothing. Have you no apprehension that it may be far otherwise soon? It will not always be possible for you thus to ignore God. For he exists.

Yes! He does indeed exist. You may find that out to your cost sooner than you think; too soon for you. It is a great fact, however little you may make of it, or it may make of you. Were it not better for you to know it now; to take account of it now; to accommodate yourselves to it now? "It is hard for you to kick against the pricks." The Son of God is come to make God known to you now, in all his glorious reality, as "light" and "love." He gives you understanding now that you may thus "know God." Better surely that, than to go on darkly, as in a dream, until there comes a shock. And lo! there is God! No shadow, but too truly real! And there is the Son of God; real also; too truly real! "Behold he cometh with clouds; and every eye shall see him; and all kindreds of the earth shall wail because of him." Yes! God, and the Son of God, are realities then, when men "hide themselves in the dens and in the rocks of the mountains, and say to the mountains and rocks, Fall on us, and hide us from the face

of him that sitteth on the throne, and from the wrath of
the Lamb. For the great day of his wrath is come, and
who shall be able to stand ?" (Rev. vi. 15–17.)

2. Let me remind you who believe of the main end for
which John would have you to "know the True One, and
be in him, in his Son Jesus Christ." It is that "you may
not sin;" that you may "keep yourselves so that the
wicked one, in whom the whole world lieth, may not touch
you." Mark the contrast here. The world lieth wholly in
the wicked one; you are in the True One; in God truly
known, in his Son Jesus Christ. Let that contrast be ever
vividly realised by you. It is your great and only security.
Look well to it that your being in the True One, in his
Son Jesus Christ, is a reality. Let it be a true experience.
Be evermore "dwelling in the secret place of the Most
High, and abiding under the shadow of the Almighty."
"Let him cover thee with his feathers, for under his wings
you may trust." Is it not his Son Jesus Christ who thus
addresses you—"Because thou hast made the Lord, which
is my refuge, even the Most High thy habitation, there
shall no evil befall thee, neither shall any plague come nigh
thy dwelling"?

46

JESUS THE TRUE GOD AND ETERNAL LIFE
AGAINST ALL IDOLS

" This is the true God and [the] eternal life. Little children, keep
yourselves from idols." 1 John 5:20,21

THE Lord Jesus Christ is the person here meant. Such
seems to be the fair inference from the use of the pronoun
" this ; " which naturally and usually indicates the nearest
person spoken of in the context; and therefore, in this
instance, not " him that is true," but " his Son Jesus
Christ."

That inference indeed is so clear, in a merely grammatical and exegetical point of view, that there would not
probably have been any doubt about it, were it not for its
implying an assertion of our Lord's supreme divinity; an
assertion which no sophistry or special pleading can evade
or explain away. It is true that some who strongly hold
that doctrine have professed, on critical considerations, to
take the same view which the deniers of it take. But there
is room for suspecting that they have been half-unconsciously influenced by a sort of chivalrous desire to concede
debatable ground, rather than by a strict regard to the real
merits of the question. It is a forced construction only
that can get us past " his Son Jesus Christ," so as to send
us back to him whose Son he is. Certainly the simple and
natural reading of the words is, that " he who is come and
hath given us an understanding that we may know him

that is true,"—he in whom " we are in him that is true,"—
" his Son Jesus Christ,"—is " the true God, and eternal
life."

He is " the true God," and as such he is " eternal life,"
or rather the eternal life. It is our realisation of him in
that character, as " the true God and the eternal life," which
constitutes our best and only security against idolatry,
the idolatry which John exhorts us in his closing admoni-
tion to shun ;—" Little children, keep yourselves from
idols."

" This is the true God and the eternal life." First, he
is the true God. That may be said of each of the three
persons in the Godhead separately, as well as of the " three
in one " unitedly, " the Triune." The entire Godhead, in all
its reality and fulness, is in each one of the persons; each
therefore is in himself really and verily " the true God."
The mystery of the Holy Trinity involves this seeming
paradox. But there is a peculiar significance in the Son's
being thus designated here. He is " the Son of God " who
" is come ;" come in the flesh by water and blood ; attested
by the Spirit as come by water and blood ; giving us an
understanding that we may know the True One, and in
him and with him may be in the True One. In that
character and capacity, and with a view to these functions,
he is declared to be " the true God." Again, secondly, in
the same character and capacity, and with a view to the
same functions, he is declared to be " eternal life," or " the
eternal life."

Eternal life ! How much is there in this little phrase !
It suggests the ever awful idea of endless duration ; existence, if not from everlasting, yet to everlasting ; conscious
existence running on for ever. But that is the least part of
its meaning. The manner, rather than the term or duration, of the life is indicated ; not so much the continuance

of the life, as its kind, its character, its nature. It is life independent of time and its changes; of earth and its history; of the created universe itself. It is the life that God lives as the True One; in himself, from himself, for or to himself. His Son Jesus Christ is " this eternal life." As being " the true God," he is so. As the true God he is the eternally living one; in such sense the eternally living one that all who are in him are eternally living ones as he is himself. If I am one with him, then as he is "the eternal life," so also am I in him. My own life is not eternal. In a sense, indeed, it is so, as regards its duration, for it is to have no end. But it is not, as to its character, eternal life. On the contrary, it is eternal death. The life which I have naturally is the life of a doomed criminal, sentenced to perpetual servitude; bound over to penal suffering for the entire period of his existence. Such is the eternal death, of which the eternal life is the opposite. For that is the life which he who dooms the criminal to perpetual servitude has himself; the very life of him who binds the criminal over to penal suffering for ever. It must be, therefore, as being " the true God," that Jesus Christ is " the eternal life." He is so, and can only be so, as being one with that righteous Father whose judicial condemnation of us is our eternal death.

But if so, must not his being " the eternal life " be eternal death to us? Not so. For if, on the one hand, he is one with " him that is true," being his Son, and therefore, like his Father, " the eternal life,"—he is one, on the other hand, with us, as his Son Jesus Christ. He becomes, with us and for us, " the eternal death " which is our portion and characteristic; which indeed we are, for it is our very nature. As he shares always his father's eternal life, so he shares once for all our eternal death; takes it as his; makes it his own. Yes; he dies our eternal death, that we may live his eternal life. Not otherwise, even as "the true God," could he be, in any sense that could be available for us, "the eternal life;" not otherwise than by being "made sin" and "made a curse" for us; which means his taking upon himself as his our "eternal death."

And let it be well noted that not even his being thus made sin and made a curse for us; not even his becoming our partner and our substitute, in our eternal death; could have been of any benefit to us, or of any use, but for his being, in that very act and experience, "the true God," and as such "the eternal life." It is his being "the true God" that alone can make that eternal death terminable in his case, which it cannot be in ours. His becoming our eternal death for us must involve him in its terrible endlessness, but for his being still in himself "the true God," and as such "the eternal life." We cannot die the eternal death and yet live; but he can; because he is "the true God and the eternal life." Therefore he says, "I am he that liveth and was dead; and behold I am alive for evermore;" and again he says, "Because I live ye shall live also."

I have died your eternal death that I may share with you my eternal life. I can share with you this eternal life of mine, for it is as the true God that I have it;—"I am the true God and the eternal life." It is as the true God that I am the eternal life; as the true God; truly and verily the Son of "him that is true." For "this eternal life" is to know him and to be in him. I am the eternal life because I know him and am in him; being, as I am, myself "the true God." Were I not so, were I anything less than that; I might tell you about the eternal life; I might unfold it to you; I might show you the way to it. But I could not myself be that eternal life to you. I could not say to you, that having me you have the eternal life.

But I do say that. I give you the assurance that having me you have the eternal life; that being in me you are in the eternal life. All that you can imagine of peace, rest, joy; pure and holy love; perfect, endless, uninterrupted blessedness and glory;—and whatever else you may connect with that most pregnant phrase " the eternal life;"—you have it all when you have me; you are in it all when you are in me. For all that I am to the Father you are to the Father; all that I have from the Father you have from the Father; all that the Father is to me the Father is to you. Thus I am, for you and to you, "the true God and the eternal life."

This statement about Christ,—his being " the true God and the eternal life,"—has a very intimate connection with what is said of him as being come to give us knowledge of his Father, as the True One, and to secure our being in his Father, as the True One, in virtue of our being in him (ver. 20). And viewed in that light, it explains the earnest, emphatic, and affectionate appeal with which John closes his epistle :—"Little children, keep yourselves from idols " (ver. 21).

I. He "is come, and hath given us an understanding that we may know him that is true;" and, so coming, he is "the true God and the eternal life." In him the true God becomes really true to us. In his person God stands forth before our eyes as a reality, and is felt in our inmost hearts to be a reality. This is what we need and often crave for; that the true and living God should be to us, not a notion, but a reality. He is so to us, and is so known by us, in the person of his Son Jesus Christ, because his Son Jesus Christ is "the true God and eternal life." We need not seek elsewhere for what we want. We may " keep ourselves from idols."

For what is the use of an idol? What is the design and aim of those who frame or fancy visible images of the invisible God, grotesque figures, in wood, or stone, or metal; the heavenly orbs; deified heroes; personified divine attributes and influences? Is it not to bring God more within the range of their actual and sensible apprehension than otherwise he would be, and so to have him before them as a true and palpable reality?

The idols are real, and, in a sense, even living. The hideous, misshapen block before which yonder dark Hindoo bows and worships has for him a certain real life, akin to his own. The beasts so sacred in old Egypt's eyes were real and living emblems of divine powers and qualities of some sort. The suns and stars on which rapt Chaldæan gazed had a real and living significancy, as representative of deity. The men and women whom a more earthly superstition turned into gods and goddesses were real and living flesh and blood while on earth, and continued to be to their votaries much the same when they were gone. Even the strange, dreamy, mysterious spiritualities, with which the early heretics and Gnostic corrupters of Christianity peopled the divine fulness; the divine essences and emanations which they named as in some sense persons; had for their imaginative minds a living reality that they could grasp and feel. These last were the idols of John's day, within the church; from which, even more than from grosser idols outside, it concerned him to warn "his little children to keep themselves." They were the forerunners, as his prophetic eye partly saw, of idols still more seductive, with which Christendom was to be ere long tried; canonised martyrs and saints, with their images and pictures and relics; and high over all, alone in her glory, the blessed Virgin.

Now all these idolatries, however widely differing in

their nature, and in their effects upon their devotees, have this principle in common, that they are all attempts to give actual form and substance, true and living embodiment and realisation, as it were, to men's conceptions of deity ; those conceptions which otherwise are apt to be so indistinct, indefinite, misty, shadowy, as to be for the most part practically all but uninfluential. They bring what is divine within the range and grasp of humanity. The abstract becomes personal ; the ideal becomes real. The infinite takes the clear and sharp outline of a form or a face that can be pictured to the mind's eye at least, if not to that of the body. And what is apt to be little more than a great blank vacancy, becomes instinct with living personality.

Hence, even for refined natures, the more refined kinds of idol-worship have a strong fascination ; witness the hold which Mariolatry has over intellects the highest and hearts the tenderest and purest.

It is indeed the crown and masterpiece of idolatry, this worship of the Virgin. Fairer, holier, more lovely and lovable idol was never formed or fancied. Never idol like her, the ideal mother of our Lord.

I say the ideal mother of our Lord. For it is an idealised Mary that is idolised.

And yet we see and can understand how intensely real, even as thus idealised, she is and must be to her believing worshippers. In her they feel that they have a real mother, a real sister, a true and very woman ; with all of woman's warm love and none of woman's weakness. And she has to them divinity about her, being, as they put it, "the mother of God." That Mary, thus ideal and yet real, should be adored and loved, chivalrously and yet devoutly, with human passion rising into divine enthusiasm, is so far from seeming to me strange, that I doubt if any of us have not sometimes had some secret sympathy, if not with the superstitious homage, at least with the frame of mind that prompts it.

I take this highest instance of the charm that there is in idolatry, because it comes nearest to what John puts as a safeguard against it. The virgin-mother of our Lord is alone in the created universe of God. No other being ever has occupied, or ever can occupy, the same position with her. She stands in a relation to deity altogether peculiar; absolutely singular. It is a natural thought that she may be invoked as well as her Son; nay, that she may be invoked instead of her Son; as, in fact, a most persuasive pleader with her Son. And she grows to be so very true and real, as a genuine woman, kind and pitying and relenting; while her divine Son, as well as his heavenly Father, fades away in the dim distance of a sort of undefined and misty majesty; that knowing her, as it seems, so thoroughly and personally, one is fain to rest in her, and leave all to her, and be satisfied with her as virtually all in all. And it must be so, if we take her as our mediator. For she is not "the true God and eternal life." She is, when thus viewed, simply an idol. Now no idol brings us into communication with God as true and real. We accept the idol as real; but God, whose image he may profess to be, between whom and us he ought to mediate, is as unreal as ever, or more so. The virgin-mother I know; in her I can lie. But as for the Son and the Father, I look to her to deal with them for me. To me they are but names.

Nothing like that can happen when he through whom I am to know God truly, is himself, as his Son Jesus Christ, "the true God and the eternal life." He is as human as is his virgin-mother. He is, as much as she is, a real and living human person; as truly set before me as such. Nay, I have him, as a real and living person, more clearly and fully, with more of personal individuality, in my mind's eye, than ever I can have her.

The notices of Mary are few and far between; vague also and indefinite. We have nothing beyond the merest generalities to give us a notion of what sort of woman she was. But her divine Son, the Son of the Highest, the Son of the True One, his Son Jesus Christ, is as a living man amongst us, a real person. He is more truly, vividly, intensely real to us than even his mother Mary. And if more so than she, then more by far than any saints or martyrs that ever were canonised; any heroes that ever were deified; any representatives of deity, dead or alive, that ever were worshipped; any effluxes or emanations of deity that the highest imagination ever invested with the property of personality. Yes; here is Jesus Christ the Son of God, truly, vividly, intensely real; a real and living person; going in and out among us; one of whom we can really form a truer, fuller, more intimate conception, than we can form of our dearest and most familiar associate and intimate; whose hand we clasp in ours more really, because more inwardly, than we can clasp the hand of any friend; with whom we can talk more confidentially than we can with any brother. Here he is. And it is through and in him that I am to "know God as the True One." He is to represent God to me; it is with him that I have directly and immediately to do; in him I am to know "the True One."

But does not this arrangement really put aside "the True One," and substitute in his stead "his Son Jesus Christ"? Doubtless he is the best possible or conceivable substitute. But still, is it not a substitution? Does it not tend in the direction of making Jesus Christ, the Son of "the True One," the real and living "True One" to me; while God, his Father, the absolute and ultimate "True

One," becomes to me a dim and far-off vision? Is there no
danger of idolatry here? Am I not on the point of falling
into that sin, by setting him up instead of God? And is
not that equivalent to making him an idol?

It has been so often; and it would be so always; were
it not for the great and blessed fact that he is "the true
God and the eternal life." But I cannot make an idol of
him if I believe that. I cannot worship him in an idolatrous
manner, or after an idolatrous fashion, if I really own him
as being "the true God and the eternal life," and in that
view take in the full meaning of his own words: "Whosoever hath seen me hath seen the Father."

Is it not a blessed thing to know that there can be no
idolatry in your closest fellowship with Jesus, if only you
bear in mind that he is "the true God and the eternal life?"
Your warmest love to him, your most familiar intercourse
with him, your most affectionate clinging to him, your most
tender and trusting embrace of him, never can be idolatry;
for he is "the true God and the eternal life." You need
have no fear of your making too much of him, or making
an idol of him; as you must have in the case of any other
being, real or imaginary, whom you let in between God
and you; for "he is the true God and the eternal life."
You may admire others to excess, but you never can admire
him to excess; for "he is the true God and the eternal life."
You may be too devoted to others, but you can never be
too devoted to him; for "he is the true God and the eternal
life."

What ease and freedom may this thought impart to all
your dealings with him, as come especially to "give you an
understanding that you may know the True One;" that
you may know him as true and real.

The most perfect of God's creatures, the highest angel,
if he had come on such an errand, must have bid you look

away from him. You may listen to my voice, he might say; you may hear what I have to tell you about God. I will do my best to set him before you as a reality, in as lifelike a representation as I can give. But beware of fixing your eyes too much, or indeed at all, on me. You may imagine that I am so like him, as living so near him and seeing so much of him, that when you have formed a clear notion of me you really know him. But it is not so; it is far otherwise. Your very knowledge of me may mislead you as to him; tempting you to form inadequate, if not erroneous, conceptions of him; to enshrine him in my frame and clothe him in my vesture; the frame and vesture of a mere creature at the best.

But no such caution is needed on the part of Jesus; for he is the true God and the eternal life. Therefore let not Jesus, the Son of God, be a name or a notion to you; if he is so, much more will God his Father be so. Let him be a true, present, living reality. Be sitting at his feet as really as did Mary of Bethany. Be welcoming him to your house and table as really as did Zaccheus. Be leaning on his bosom as really as did John. Be grasping his hand, when you are sinking in the stormy sea, as really as did Peter when he cried, Lord, save me, I perish. You may do so with all safety, and with no risk of idolatry; for he is "the true God and the eternal life."

II. But not only are we "in his Son Jesus Christ so as to know him that is true," we are to be "in him so as to be in him that is true." In that view also it is all-important thoroughly to apprehend and feel that "he is the true God and the eternal life." For were he not so, we could not really be in the True One by being in him. Nay, our being in him, so far from a help, might be a hindrance. We might be in the True One through him, but scarcely in him, unless he were himself "the true God and the eternal life."

This word "in," be it observed, though small in size, is very great in significancy. It denotes a very close, real, and personal connection; and indeed almost, as it were, an identification; so much so that it may be said to be as impossible for me to be in the True One, and at the same time to be in any one else who is not "the true God and the eternal life," as it is for me to serve two masters, to serve God and Mammon. For what is this "inness," if I may so say, when it is spoken of a real and living person to whom I may sustain real and personal relations? Surely at the very least it implies that I give myself up entirely to him, and become wholly his. I consent to his taking me to be one with himself. It is a real unity, corresponding in its nature and character to the nature and character of him in whom I am; but still real; and intimate as real; so intimate as to be engrossing, absorbing, exclusive. He in whom I am is to me all in all. In a sense, I lose myself in him. I have no separate standing from him. I see, as it were, through his eyes; I judge with his understanding; I make his will my will; I make himself my supreme good, and my chiefest joy.

Now if, in any such sense, I am in one who is not "the true God and the eternal life;" can that be compatible with my being also "in him that is true"?

It is not needful here to suppose that it is an enemy of God in whom I thus am, and with whom I am thus identified. The case is better put when he is supposed to be a friend of God. For then I look to him to deal with God for me. I am in him as being his; so thoroughly his, that I have nothing of my own; I myself am not my own. He has made me part and parcel of his own very self. It belongs to him to make terms with God for himself; and for me as being in him. He has to do with God; not I. So it must be with me, if he in whom I am is not "the true God and the eternal life;" if he and the True One are separate and distinct; if he and the Father are not one. The higher he is, the nearer he·is to God, the more does my "being in him" supersede and supplant my "being in God."

But Jesus Christ is "the true God and the eternal life." I may be "in him," as much as ever I choose, as much as ever I can; his own good Spirit helping me; the more the better. For "in him I am in the True One." In the Son I am in the Father, even as he is in the Father. And all this is so, because "he is the True God and the eternal life."

It could not otherwise be so. I could not be in him as I long to be in him, without being not in, but out of, the True One, were he not himself "the true God and the eternal life." For how do I long to be in him, if I am at all awakened to a sense of what I am in myself? How do long to be in Christ? How thoroughly would I be hidden, and, as it were, swallowed up in him! A poor, naked, shelterless, child of sin and wrath, shrinking from the presence of "him that is true," shrinking from the glance of his true eye and the searching scrutiny of his true judgment,—ah! how fain would I be lost and merged altogether in that holy, righteous, loving Saviour, who has come to answer for me; to take my place; to fulfil my righteousness; to bear my guilt; to die for me, and yet live, so that I may live in him. Oh! to be in him; shut up into him; lost and merged altogether, I repeat, in him; and because lost and merged in him, therefore also safe in him.

Safe? From whom? From the True One? Am I to be in his Son Jesus Christ so as to be away from himself? No. For he in whom I am is "the true God and the eternal life." Therefore, being in him, I am in the True One, "in him that is true."

I would be in Christ incarnate. I would be in Christ crucified. I must be in Christ both incarnate and crucified. I must be in him as he becomes bone of my bone and flesh of my flesh. I must be in him as dying, yet not "given over to death," but rising again ; the living one ; who, having once died, dieth no more ; who living, though he was dead, liveth for ever. I would be, I must be, thus in Christ. Is it as against God ? Is it as if I were to be out of and away from God the True One ? No ! Emphatically no ! For he in whom I am is himself "the true God and the eternal life."

"Little children, keep yourselves from idols." And let this be the test or criterion of what an idol is. Whatever worship or fellowship or companionship, whatever system or society, whatever work or way, whatever habit or pursuit or occupation, is of such a sort in itself, or has such influence over you, that you cannot be in it and at the same time be in God, or that you may be in it and yet not be in God, as little children in a loving Father ; that to you is idolatry, be the object of your regard what it may. From all such idols keep yourselves. And that you may keep yourselves from them all, abide evermore in the Son of God, your Lord and Saviour Jesus Christ. To be in him is your only security, to be always "found in him." For to be in him is to be in the Father, even as he is in the Father. And there can be no idolatry in that.